DIGITAL HATE

DIGITAL HATE

*The Global Conjuncture of
Extreme Speech*

Edited by
Sahana Udupa
Iginio Gagliardone
Peter Hervik

INDIANA UNIVERSITY PRESS

This book is a publication of

Indiana University Press
Office of Scholarly Publishing
Herman B Wells Library 350
1320 East 10th Street
Bloomington, Indiana 47405 USA

iupress.org

Manufactured in the United States of America

First printing 2021

European Research Council
Established by the European Commission

Through the generous support of European Research Council (ERC) (funding under the
European Union's Horizon 2020 research and innovation program, grant agreement
No. 714285, Principal Investigator: Sahana Udupa), Indiana University Press is pleased
to make this monograph freely available as an Open Access monograph. To read
or download, visit https://publish.iupress.indiana.edu/projects/digital-hate/.

Library of Congress Cataloging-in-Publication Data

Names: Udupa, Sahana, editor. | Gagliardone, Iginio, editor. |
   Hervik, Peter, editor.
Title: Digital hate : the global conjuncture of extreme speech / edited by
   Sahana Udupa, Iginio Gagliardone, Peter Hervik.
Description: Bloomington, Indiana : Indiana University Press, [2021] |
   Includes bibliographical references and index.
Identifiers: LCCN 2021043281 (print) | LCCN 2021043282 (ebook) | ISBN
   9780253059253 (paperback) | ISBN 9780253059260 (ebook)
Subjects: LCSH: Online hate speech. | Internet—Moral and ethical aspects.
   | Internet—Social aspects. | Discrimination. | Other
   (Philosophy)—Social aspects. | Online identities. | Online social
   networks.
Classification: LCC HM851 .D533 2021 (print) | LCC HM851 (ebook) | DDC
   302.30285—dc23
LC record available at https://lccn.loc.gov/2021043281
LC ebook record available at https://lccn.loc.gov/2021043282

Cover illustration courtesy of Julia Molin.

CONTENTS

ACKNOWLEDGMENTS

IN THIS COLLECTIVE REFLECTION ON A PERTINENT AND sobering topic, we have received generous support from colleagues, institutions, media, and civil society collaborators. We wish to thank all our contributing authors for staying with us throughout this project, sending their input at every request, and never once missing a deadline. It is a feat any editors would dream of. Special thanks to the anonymous reviewers, whose insightful comments were helpful in strengthening this collection. Special thanks to Indiana University Press editor Jennika Baines for her tremendous support and for steering the project despite the COVID-19 crisis, and to Julia Molin, Humboldt University, Berlin, for the cover page illustration. We thank research assistants Laura Csuka and Miriam Homer and copyeditor Jatinder Padda for their excellent support. Sahana Udupa thanks the European Research Council, which generously funded her project on digital politics under the European Union's Horizon 2020 research and innovation program (grant agreement number 714285). The grant enabled the author to co-organize three international workshops with Iginio Gagliardone, Peter Hervik, and other colleagues that served as a backbone for this volume. Peter Hervik thanks the VELUX Foundations for a generous grant for the study of racialization in Denmark.

DIGITAL HATE

Introduction

HATE CULTURES IN THE DIGITAL AGE

The Global Conjuncture of Extreme Speech

Sahana Udupa, Iginio Gagliardone, and Peter Hervik

Taking the world by surprise, "nationalist" Buddhist monks in Myanmar turned into unapologetic perpetrators of violence against the Rohingya Muslim community, as they inflated their influence beyond the monasteries, amassing massive followings on social media. In Germany, street mobilizations of the far-right group Pegida gained strength through internet organizing and newfound confidence to publicly revive some of the nastiest expressions of the Nazi era, including accusations around "Lügenpresse" (the lying press). In Denmark, racialized speech against Muslims, immigrants, and left progressive groups is a provocative device for creating social cohesion among neonationalists. Trump's Twitter exploits are legendary, as are Brexiters' online spoils. In South Africa, social media and messaging apps have become tools to sustain, motivate, and organize xenophobic violence, mobilizing mobs against African migrants accused of selling "fake food" in their "spaza shops." In India, right-wing Hindu nationalist groups have successfully engaged online environments to seize political power, raising a troop of "internet Hindus" ready with abusive commentaries and insinuating derision of "pseudoliberals."

As these examples testify, the expansion of internet-enabled media around the world at the turn of the millennium saw the troubling rise of aggressive and hateful speech online. Right-wing nationalist and populist waves sought to reshape political cultures with a new lexicon of exclusionary discourse. In North America and Europe, the rise of the "far-right" and "neonationalist" movements triggered and relied on online belligerence of racialized joking, intimidation, and "fact-filled" untruths. In countries like Myanmar, India, Sri Lanka, Kenya, and South Africa, major social media tools such as Facebook and WhatsApp not only offered easy platforms to revive vitriol against religious minorities and ethnic "others" but also led to a "subterranean" flow of rumor and fear mongering that injected new velocity into lynching and targeted physical violence. Digital expressions pushed back liberal modulations of "civility," drawing strength from locally approved cultural idioms, globally shared formats of humor, and historically sanctioned structures of animosity. While huge numbers of dispersed, unorganized, "ordinary" online users participated in online extreme speech practices, regimes engaged in organized production of disinformation by using the very infrastructure of globalization around flexible, precarious, and outsourced labor.

We might call these related developments of inflamed rhetoric and its mediatic conditions a "global conjuncture" of exclusionary politics. How did digitally enabled exclusionary politics come about in the wake of the liberal euphoria around internet-enabled participatory equity? How did such a conjuncture emerge when optimistic predictions about internet media as harbingers of democratic freedom and global civic consciousness had buoyed a mood of change and progress? How did online speech become implicated in this conjuncture?

These questions compel reexamination of some assumptions about online vitriol and speech acts more broadly. A key concern in this conceptual reworking is the influential paradigm of "hate speech" and more recent articulations around "political extremism." Taking aim at these established traditions and political programs, we propose the framework of "extreme speech." We advance a critical inquiry into "wounding words" and "post-truth" realities by refusing to see hate speech as a self-evident category or political extremism as a natural response to a current crisis. In offering a critique of these long-established debates, we diverge from the casual interchangeability of the terms *hate speech* and *extreme speech* and instead insist on the ethnographic sensibility that marks extreme speech as a distinct concept. In particular, we depart from the dominant legal-normative definitions of hate speech and the discourse of securitization around terrorism and political extremism. In these definitions, hate speech is approached primarily as a "discourse of pathology" based on the need to diagnose, preempt, and mitigate its negative effects. Extreme speech signals and surpasses the normative bias toward recognizing, isolating, and combating vitriolic online speech practices and stresses the importance of comprehension over classification. Consequently, we argue that the production, circulation, and consumption of online vitriol should be approached critically as *cultural practice*, *social phenomenon*, and *technopolitical manifestation*, in addition to a legal-normative concept.

By emphasizing cultural practice, we foreground situated speech cultures of online use in relation to broader cultural struggles over meanings of civility and information. By examining the social phenomenon, we recognize that extreme speech cocreates relations of belonging and unbelonging, and as such, embedded in a broader set of social practices cohering around internet media. By considering technopolitical manifestation, we highlight the flow of political and market power through technology and the materialities of the internet in shaping and expressing political action.

Across these lines of analysis, extreme speech emphasizes the particularity of contexts—ranging from microcontexts of online-platform cultures to macrohistorical formations of empire and regional social hierarchies—as a necessary corrective to the seeming universality of the normative basis of hate speech.

Politics of Hate Speech and the Ambivalence of "Extremeness"

The affirmation of extreme speech as an analytical framework, rather than a regulatory instrument, opens new paths for bringing politics back in the analysis of hateful speech practices. It also allows for more clearly recognizing the complex ways in which a concept like hate speech, with its moral underpinnings, has been used politically in different national and cultural contexts. In international jurisprudence (e.g., International Covenant on Civic and Political Rights), hate speech has been confined to "national, racial, or religious hatred." The exclusion of politics—and thus, the recognition of the higher threshold allowed for the fierce competition of ideas—was meant to avoid the suppression of even radical conceptions of society. It was facilitated by the assumption that the horrors of the Second World War had created a shared enough moral ground from which to recognize the emergence of forms of discrimination that could lead to mass violence against groups that were unable to protect themselves.

Both past and contemporary uses (and abuses) of the concept of hate speech illustrate the many unintended consequences of that project. The pretense that an accusation of hate speech is not a political move but simply an attempt to protect society has not only allowed those in power to persecute their adversaries but also dented the legitimacy of the hate speech concept. As Robert Post poignantly recognized, "Hate speech regulation imagines itself as simply enforcing the given and natural norms of a decent society . . . but from a sociological or anthropological point of view we know that law is always actually enforcing the mores of the dominant group that controls the content of law" (2009, 130).

As a form of power, the discourse of hate speech is inextricably tied to the state and its political economies of violence. Historically, it emerged from projects of civility that coincided with (and partly constituted) the state's monopolization of violence (Giddens 1987; Thirangama, Kelly, and Forment 2018).[1] The moral claims of liberal thought have vested hate speech regulation with the responsibility of protecting substantive virtues such as sympathy and understanding (or at least in the procedural terms of decorum) that create the possibility of "a common good." Important as they are, liberal understandings premised on abstract principles of equality conceal the uneven political agendas that have grown around the regulatory discourse of hate speech.

Colonial and postcolonial contexts demonstrate the historical antecedents of the problem. In South Asia, restrictions on speech and expression date back to colonial times, when a substantive legal corpus was built around what is now understood as hate speech. Speech regulations in India are rooted in the colonial state's rationale of law and order and what it left behind in the postindependence period as the constitutional value of "ordered society" (Rajagopal 2001). Such regulations constituted the distinction between subject and citizen within colonies and a racialized order that hinged on the image of the "Oriental despot" as the "other" of European civilization (Said 1978). Similar examples could be found in apartheid South Africa and in the challenges that theorists of black consciousness have raised against norms of civility as a gloss for power. Steve Biko's (1978) famous column, "I Write What I Like," took aim precisely at the pretense of civility and benevolence of the apartheid regime toward those who accepted its domination.

The liberal moral principle of civility that partly informs the rationale of hate speech is "intimately tied up with class and race privilege" (Thirangama, Kelly, and Forment 2018, 155), which consolidated the colonial and postcolonial state. Furthermore, colonial histories have cemented the self-righteous schema of the liberal center and the extreme periphery, which is now manifest in diverse forms not only between (former) metropole and colony but also within the nation-states where similar structures of speech restriction based on moral self-understandings have taken root.

Under these conditions, the pressure to speak "polite" language has been an act of domination—a moral injunction linked to assertion of privilege.[2] Civility is thus an "effect of political recognition and of a responsive structure of authority" (Mitchell 2018, 217). In other words, incivility—or "extremeness" of speech more broadly—cannot be apprehended without analyzing particular forms of recognition and responsiveness to demands that exist in societies. Local and diverse speech forms including rumors and half-truths in the bazaar, argues Nayanika Mathur, are akin to "subaltern speech" (2015, 104), which should be mined not for its truth value but for how it provides people with social imaginaries and a means to articulate political anxieties "that remain unspeakable or unheard" (Fassin 2011, 41; see also Guha 1982).

The "thick" concept of hate speech comes with an evaluative load aimed at immediate action.[3] In this way, it raises the risk of glossing over historical trajectories, as well as the ambivalence toward extremeness within particular contexts of power. This issue is not merely conceptual but also, more gravely, political. Both historically and today, the ambivalence toward extreme speech is closed off when political actors under pressure to "do something about hate" invoke the label of "hate speech" (Pohjonen 2019), at times with brutal use of force targeting marginalized groups. Examples abound of regimes that have misused hate speech discourse to quash dissent or target minoritized groups. The politics of invoking blasphemy laws as hate speech and offence in Pakistan and Bangladesh is a case in point (Schaflechner 2019). As David Katiambo argues in chapter 3, "the polysemy of extreme speech is removed when incivility becomes known as hate speech, blocking us from ever knowing its alternative possibilities."

In social interactions, hate speech is a "charge" and "normative challenge" that signals where one stands politically. In chapter 1, David Boromisza-Habashi (see also Boromisza-Habashi 2013) shows how the social function of interpreting hate speech subsumes its referential function—that is, its "function as a description of a category of observable communication phenomena." As a normative challenge and position-taking, hate speech falls short of explaining how and why online actors engage in forms of speech that are disapproved of in other contexts of interaction.

Recognizing the limits of "hate speech" both as a regulatory value and as a concept for use in everyday interactions, the extreme-speech framework advocates for ethnographic sensibility and insists that the moral charge around vitriol and disinformation should come from lived concepts and situated contexts rather than frameworks imposed from outside. Such ethnographic sensibility requires a critical approach that is attentive to cultural variations in speech, including sanctioned forms of disrespect; political contexts in which "hate," as an order value of regulation, is assigned to speech acts; and historical conditions that implicate extreme speech with particular forms of power—subversive in some contexts and repressive in others.

Criss-crossing Concerns, Extreme Speech Framework, and New Directions

This book is part of a long-term exploration and shared ambition to develop concepts and tools that allow deeper understanding of today's conjuncture of exclusionary politics. Before developing this collection, each of the editors had distinctively experienced the limitations of hate speech as a concept and the need for an alternative framework that could more fully capture and critique vitriolic expressions. Peter Hervik repeatedly noted that appeals to report instances of online hateful speech concerned the tone of language and not the content and context of hateful claims. The normative, translocal focus on hatred was not useful for understanding the fuller ethnography behind the speech. The normative focus appeared much like appeals to tolerance, with its moral encouragements "to be nice" so that peacefulness could be reestablished.

Iginio Gagliardone recognized that most of the prevalent forms that had emerged in response to hate speech were geared toward identifying and neutralizing it. Frustration emerged from collaborations with often well-meaning organizations that sought to react to a perceived spike in online hate but eventually promoted a form of ventriloquism among groups with similar orientations. This approach was unable to make inroads into the spaces where online hate proliferates. In other cases, frustration originated from dissatisfaction with increasingly popular computational methods for the analysis of hate speech. These approaches have provided new insights into the magnitude and spread of wounding words but have contributed little to understanding the motivations behind them.

For Sahana Udupa, online vitriol was a lived reality and a vexing problem in ethnographic practice. Studying the online right in India entailed tense moments of meeting people with whom one did not necessarily agree. However, dismissing these actors in a polemical huff ran against the responsibility of serious critical inquiry and trust-based relationships as the epistemological cornerstone of ethnography—it amounted to evaluating actors before delving into their complex worlds. Ethnographic explorations of cantankerous exchanges in the Indian online sphere shaped the first ruminations around online extreme speech as a concept that could develop a critical vocabulary around online vitriol through lived practices and emic categories, that is, from the perspectives of users themselves (Udupa 2015b). This study also helped to emphasize how ethnographic attention to digital media practices and situated speech cultures should be inextricably linked to the analysis of grave colonial historical continuities within and beyond the national scenarios.

Our distinct trajectories converged in the two international workshops in Munich, Germany, in 2018 (the first with Matti Pohjonen), and we followed up on these exchanges in our subsequent meetings in Johannesburg, South Africa, and Copenhagen, Denmark. The special section on online extreme speech in the *International Journal of Communication* (Udupa and Pohjonen 2019) laid the ground for a comparative study of online vitriolic cultures, advancing our inquiry into extreme speech (Pohjonen and Udupa 2017) and raising critical questions about the relevance of extreme speech in broader debates on hate (Gagliardone 2019*b*) and patterns of racial formation (Hervik 2019). Our aim in these workshops and subsequent publications was to examine vitriolic exchange in different parts of the world and to account for particularities in discerning general trends.

Connecting public policy and theory, we discussed ways to further expand our inquiry. We were particularly keen on bringing the disciplinary perspectives of anthropology, communication studies, and critical cultural studies into close conversation in order to analyze vitriol as texts, media practices, and communicative structures. Together with the contributing authors, this volume represents our collective thinking through these events and discussions, as we struggled to take stock of the tumultuous times we inhabit. The resurgence of right-wing politics and violent speech in our "homelands" and "adopted lands" was a worrisome reality that confronted us as scholars and members of the world. Excited as we were about the extreme speech project, violent regimes provoked us to reimagine critical frameworks that are based on actual rather than abstract conditions of possibility. It compelled us to take a step back from heated debates on what to do about online hate speech and to examine, with all the nuance of ethnographic analysis, how and why this phenomenon has come about.

This collection reaffirms some common features that have emerged as part of the debate about the nature and usefulness of extreme speech, but it also breaks new ground. In particular, two key positions have been developed elsewhere (Udupa and Pohjonen 2019) and are important to return to here.

First, extreme speech foregrounds the radical situatedness of online speech acts in different cultural, social, and political milieus globally. It takes seriously the cultural variation of speech acts, the normative orders bundled around them, and the historical conditions that underpin them. This approach implies that there is no easy-to-define boundary between speech that is acceptable and speech that is not. The distinction is instead constantly reworked in public and political debates, and the boundaries are redrawn, used, and misused. Extreme speech analysis covers digital cultures that push the boundaries of legitimate speech along the twin axes of truth–falsity and civility–incivility, raising two critical questions for research: What are the processes that make hateful and aggressive language acceptable for its users and, indeed, make it appear normal and desirable? Conversely, how is the word *hate* assigned to speech acts online as a weapon of authority and control? In either case, there is no self-evident category of hate speech. Moving beyond the binary and normative divisions of acceptable and unacceptable speech forces us to pay attention to the everyday online practices that underlie contemporary digital cultures—that is, what people do with media in their everyday lived experiences and how the significance of their actions is mediated through discursive regimes across the world (Couldry 2010).

Second, extreme speech is inextricably linked to violence, but its implications are context specific. At a fundamental level, the concept builds on the premise that political action should be considered, among other things, as an aspect of situated speech acts and what Judith Butler (1997) considers the realm of linguistic performativity. Public ideals and their brutal decimation are morally laden and enacted through speech acts encompassing verbal and audiovisual expressions. Furthermore, the framework of extreme speech insists that the relations among vitriol, political hatred, and violent action must be ethnographically explicated. We draw on a strand of anthropological scholarlship studying political violence to advance this analysis (Verkaaik 2004). This scholarship suggests that collective aggression and transgressive behavior should not be seen as anomalies but rather as practices that are generative and constitutive of identity and political subjectivity. The generative capacity of extreme speech as a form of transgression from the mainstream norm signals deep ambiguity: extreme speech can be both progressive and destructive in relation to the situations in which it is implicated. Consequently, it helps to examine the specific contexts that instigate and shape online extreme speech as violence and its divergent and often unforeseen implications.

While reaffirming some distinctive characteristics of extreme speech and how they set this analysis apart from other concepts used in reference to online hate, this book expands aspects that have been touched on in previous debates through further research and reflection.

The first aspects of extreme speech that we develop in the book are digital materialities and technological situatedness (Suchman 1987; Law and Callon 1992). The call for better understanding of individuals and communities behind extreme speech practices and how they relate to specific cultural and political circumstances should not preclude analysis of how these practices rely on and interface with technology. Critically, although the variance of politics and culture is radically affirmed by a concept like extreme speech, technology should not be treated as a unitary canvas on which different practices emerge. Interrogations of what is special about online hate speech have become increasingly insistent, leading to the identification of features such as ease of access, anonymity, and instantaneousness as potentially distinctive of this form of communication (Brown 2018). Nevertheless, a list of affordances opened by new technological artifacts should not become a test against which to assess the presence or absence of a specific practice. If so, the skepticism toward universal definitions of hate speech as a form of expression would be erased when looking at its technological counterpart. Instead, recognizing the association of specific technological affordances with specific practices should be a starting point—a practical hunch—that suggests where and how to look.

The notion of "technopolitics" (Rodotà 1997; Hecht 1998; Gagliardone 2016; Treré and Carretero 2018) offers a conceptual and methodological framework for studying the emergence of technologically mediated practices by tracking shifts in technology in relation to actors, networks, and discourses that compose particular regimes. Technopolitics pays attention to technology's *longue durée*, seeking to uncover trajectories that lead to a specific phenomenon rather than "waking up" to realities deemed new or abruptly revolutionary (e.g., "fake news"). It accounts for how the "same" technology can be captured by competing actors and discourses to profoundly affect the way it is used and the shape it takes (Gagliardone 2019*a*). Methodologically, it encourages the researcher to "plunge" into a technical artifact or assemblage (Callon 2009) to uncover the internal functions—and the relationships they establish with surrounding elements—as an entry point to understanding the social formation that led to their creation or use.

The invitation to take technological situatedness seriously inevitably exists in tension with the need to acknowledge and account for the planetary reach of specific constellations of technologies and power. Inasmuch as these constellations are contingent, fluid, contested, and emerging, they also gain durability and momentum from the physical, financial, and institutional structures that support technology. As Faye Ginsburg, Lila Abu-Lughod, and Brian Larkin clarify, "While anthropologists are always firmly grounded in the local . . . certain sweeping technological and institutional changes have had irreversible consequences over the past decades" (2002, 2). We suggest a research program that encourages a relatively simple—at least from a methodological standpoint—escape from the normative and significantly more complex engagement concurrently with the cultural, social, and technological aspects without predetermining the greater or lesser weight each component should be given a priori. This approach allows for analysis of technology and actors as they unfold on the ground.

The second aspect of extreme speech that we develop in the book is how the concept connects with perspectives of decoloniality. We build on decoloniality as an epistemological agenda. Decentering the Western epistemic core entails paying attention to the cultural specificity of meaning making and categories of practice. Admittedly, this book is just a step toward—not a thoroughgoing excavation of—local histories, ideas, and practices of civility, as well as debates around what constitutes extremeness, politeness, and offense in complex political situations. Some of these contestations are highlighted in the chapters on India, Pakistan, Kenya, and Indonesia. These chapters delve into intricate political scenarios with internal rivalries and politicization of religious and ethnic identities that expanded during colonial rule. Gesturing toward the "decolonial option" (Mignolo and Escobar 2010), this book emphasizes the need for developing detailed genealogies around extremeness and civility and how these concepts have emerged in series of encounters with colonial modernity and rule. In this sense, the decolonial option is not an exploration of "pure" local concepts of civility or extremeness (as ethnohistorical essence) but rather calls for critical attention to a longer history of racialized colonialism that undergirds specific genealogies of vitriolic cultures—a point we will revisit in the concluding section. One implication of decentering Western epistemologies and paying attention to longer historical colonial formations is that they overturn the schema of the liberal center of calm rationality and irrational, impassionate publics of the periphery. Such moralizing schemas have had devastating effects in relations between nations and among different populations within individual nations. In an ironic twist, this logic has come back to haunt the previous colonial centers with ongoing toxification of social media in the heart of liberal democracies themselves (Udupa and Pohjonen 2019). Although there is greater acknowledgment that the Global North is as affectively charged as what was deemed as the "emotional periphery" (the Global South), the binary schema of the sane center (the standard) versus the deviant margin continues to animate racial extreme speech. This perception is amply illustrated, for instance, in the discourses that frame immigrants as prone to passion, irrationality, and crime.

Decoloniality is an essential component informing our comparative approach. The research agenda is to juxtapose different cases of online extreme speech around the world and to identify connections and shared tropes. In this way, we challenge implicit or explicit framing of the Global South as an aberration that needs explanation or a "lift up" in the measure of the West. Equally, we avoid romanticizing the South as an alternative that can salvage the world. We propose comparison as a way to push for epistemic parity through which both concepts and troubling questions around patterns of exclusion are considered in relation to the connected histories between the Global South and the Global North. Comparison reveals enduring hierarchies that are best analyzed by drawing connections rather than maintaining separations.

The decolonial move of extreme speech has important methodological implications. Again, we see convergences between the established methodological perspectives of anthropology and the decolonial emphasis on documenting plurality of practices and contexts without subsuming them in totalizing claims (e.g., hate speech). Anthropological studies of media have long advocated for a perspective that is "broadly comparative, holistic in its approach to complexity, ethnographically empirical, aware of historical contingency and relativistic" (Peterson 2009, 339). Furthermore, a decolonial methodological move involves an ethical stance that is rare—and might even seem outrageous—for debates around hateful expression. A key intervention is to understand worldviews, epistemological particularities, and lived environments, guided by an ethnographic commitment to learn and to see the insider views as a "working morality" (Boromisza-Habashi 2013; Hervik 2019). This approach offers a way to hone critical perspective rather than endorse the views expressed by extreme speech actors or claim moral equivalence between different ideological positions.

Recognizing some forms of expression as extreme speech means suppressing the urge to catalog and judge and to accept (with Chantal Mouffe [2005]) conflict as the site of democracy. Equally, a critical framework should account for broader structures of exploitative labor of vitriol that political regimes employ with market support. Attention to these structures of exploitation complicate easy narratives about online extreme speech actors as villainous perverts willingly breaching the norm (Ong and Cabanes 2018; Ong, chap. 2).

This recognition does not come without risks. Researchers adopting the lens of extreme speech may be accused of condoning practices that are considered abhorrent and potentially dangerous (Gagliardone 2019*b*). This potential criticism cannot be solved a priori. It is only the rigor and sensitivity of the researchers who accept the challenge of engaging in these types of inquiries and the balance achieved in each individual case that can offer an answer and practically illustrate the value of this approach.

Exclusionary Extreme Speech as a Global Conjuncture

In this introduction, we have so far discussed extreme speech as an ethnographically grounded concept that accounts for variation, meaning, and context and as a critical research framework that charts new analytical and methodological pathways. In particular, this discussion centers diverse geographies across the Global South and the North, upending frameworks that see regions beyond the transatlantic West as "conflicts" peripheral to the liberal metropole. Conceptually, this discussion has foregrounded the ambivalence toward extreme speech acts in terms of their political consequences. Vastly divergent experiences, struggles, and subjectivities surrounding extreme speech hold the potential of "backtalking" (Stewart 1990) while unleashing acts of repression with numbing violence where factors coalesce to accentuate dominant ideologies. These analytical advances draw attention to globally shared but locally translated digital media user cultures and to new geographies and material arrangements for vitriolic exchange.

Following these interventions, contributions in the first section, "Extreme Speech as a Critique," illustrate the limits of the hate speech discourse (Boromisza-Habashi, chap. 1), and how practices of extreme speech talk back to prevailing power, if not always successfully. Viral YouTube videos of a Muslim political party in India as a practice of "extreme speech from below" (Kramer, chap. 4) and technological counterfeits as a form of incivility in Kenya

(Katiambo, chap. 3) capture dislocations that occur when hegemonic boundaries are pushed through verbal or "technological" incivility. Backed with empirical evidence on a related yet different development, Jonathan Ong (chap. 2) advances the critique by complicating the depiction of extreme speech actors as indoctrinated ideologues or social misfits by revealing precarious labor arrangements that lie behind disinformation. These contributions show that online extreme speech is a culturally variant and politically fraught phenomenon.

Political indeterminacy of extreme speech should not however deflect our attention away from unfolding events and historical forces that have ramped up vitriol and disinformation in the past two decades. In documenting these developments, we conclude this introduction by thinking through the tenets of a theory of exclusionary digital extreme speech. This theory is based on the normative position that comes with the proposal that extreme speech might exhibit "reasonable hostility" (Tracy 2008) and creative uproar to challenge existing inequalities and injustices, as opposed to any kind of active attacks from positions of privilege.

The decades of the new millennium represent a tumultuous period in history when the political stunts of populist leaders and everyday content of millions of online users re-powered small and spectacular spaces of exclusion. We propose that this might be seen as a global conjuncture—beginning in the 1990s and precipitating at the turn of the millennium—that allowed the powerful to reject civility, deride inclusion, and attack dignity. The global resurgence of right-wing movements and antiminority and antimigrant politics in this period reveals a particular political formation with an expression and medium that is predominantly if not exclusively digital. Why and how did the values of "promoting restraint and respect in the face of difference" (Thirangama, Kelly, and Forment 2018, 156) come under such spectacular attack? How was this attack not seen as an attack but as an authentic grievance and remedy, applauded by cheering supporters and spurred on by the brutal use of speech (and more)?

Some of the most eloquent explanations for the phenomenon have come from Euro-American scholarship and the moral panics caused by Donald Trump's victory in the 2016 US presidential election and the slide to illiberal democracies in Europe (Udupa 2020). Influential works that have diagnosed this phenomenon have some common threads. Mouffe suggests that a "stifling consensus at the center" (2005, 66) has led to the moralizing of the political—a key driver of right-wing populist upsurge. According to Wendy Brown, it is "the aggrieved, reactive creature fashioned by neoliberal reason" that is fueling "anti-democratic and anti-social authoritarian freedom" (2019, 75). She traces this phenomenon to the formation of neoliberal reason in the West and its indictment of the political and the social as obstacles to freedom and knowledge. She draws on Nietzsche's *ressentiment* to define contemporary trolling "as grievous, resentful energies—just the opposite of self-overcoming, proud, world-making energies of the powerful" (69). Following Nietzsche, she understands this behavior as nihilistic pleasure. The defeating, envious energies of ressentiment are not only an affective outburst of aggrieved white masculine pride and suffering, she goes on to argue, but something that capital actively courts. Drawing on Herbert Marcuse (1964), Brown suggests that nonliberatory release of instinctual energies should be seen as "repressive desublimation" (2019, 72).

We build on this emphasis of pleasure's acquiescence to capital and aggrieved power as an undercutting theme of right-wing movements globally. Where Brown's explanation falls short is the emphasis she places on right-wing rancor as neoliberal subjectivity of nonfreedom and nihilism as an inevitable consequence of neoliberal reason. In this analysis, ressentiment as autovictimization and backbiting revenge is shaped by racial histories of the empire as well as the neoliberal turn in the economy—a real crisis that has driven large numbers of people out of jobs, welfare, and options for livelihood. Important as it is, this critique does not account for the variations wrought by uneven liberalization around the world. Some of the strongest right-wing votaries in India, for example, are beneficiaries of globalization. In China, online nationalism connects with cultural nationalism practiced by the state. In Chile, perpetrators of vituperative anti-immigrant speech are themselves marginalized within the nation-state. In Denmark, right-wing rancor is financed by mammoth donations of millionaires. Above all, affective intensities of ressentiment attach well to imaginary wounds—continuous braying about grievances that reaffirm privilege and entitlement rather than as a response to being victims of actual conditions of systemic economic inequalities. What, then, is the face of a global resurgence of exclusionary politics?

We argue that exclusionary politics targeting minoritized publics and domestic "liberal" rivals cannot be reduced to either the economic sphere or to the particular political economy of neoliberal reason in the transatlantic West. The turmoil, as Walsh and Mignolo (2018) convincingly argue, has erupted at different levels and along different axes of difference: "By the 1990s, decolonization's failure in most nations had become clear; with state in the hands of minority elites, the patterns of colonial power continued both internally (i.e., internal colonialism) and with relation to global structures. . . . The turmoil is now at once domestic, transnational, interstate, and global" (6).

Right-wing nationalism, religious majoritarianism, neoliberal globalism, ethnicized conflicts, and twenty-first-century capitalist extractivism are broad ranging factors that have precipitated this turmoil. However, we suggest that a cross-cutting influence of digital media is key to this formation.[4] Our argument follows recent studies showing that the global rise of right-wing movements and populist regimes has relied on digital disinformation campaigns and vitriolic attacks (Schroeder 2018; Hervik 2011; McGranahan 2017; Moffitt 2016; Udupa 2017). This formation ricocheting across different parts of the world is about not only a particular subjectivity (Brown 2019)—even less, a mere psychological disposition—but also, we suggest, a confluence of actors, affects, and affordances. We define this formation as a global conjuncture of exclusionary extreme speech.

The global conjuncture of exclusionary extreme speech gains force as much through the violence of racial and colonial histories as through economic transformation. Its force flows through social and technical domains. Digital media affordances shaped by data capitalism are thus not only a vehicle for right-wing ideologies—a discourse external to it—but also an important factor that enables and constitutes those ideologies. Similarly, "practice" is a crucial qualifier of the emphasis on social-technical factors. As opposed to Brown (2019), we argue that right-wing publics who spew hatred on online media are not malleable and manipulable masses but rather actors who bring their worldviews, meanings, affects, and tactics, buoyed by a sense of participatory autonomy that social media affordances proffer.

All the while, these actors are influenced by the culturally translated affordances that work in the background to delimit participation through interfaces, design decisions, advertisement models, content policy, and community standards. This complex amalgam of data capital, user practice, and political power lies behind online vitriol and disinformation. Such expressions and vehicles of right-wing reaction and exclusionary politics have swept polities, from liberal democracies of Europe and North America to new authoritarian regimes such as those in Turkey and the Philippines.

In particular, the mainstreaming of extreme speech and practices by "alt-right" movements in the United States can be interpreted as a shift from West Coast liberal imagery and actors heralding the emancipatory power of "liberation technologies" to an environment in which the everyday practices of far-right activists quietly but steadily nurtured alternative discourses on how the same technologies can be put to use. Continuous experimentation and transgressions progressively allowed tactics (i.e., courses of action that are short term, lack power, and may be sanctioned by a higher order) to turn into strategies (which aim for hegemony, depend on and reproduce power, and create their own norms). Liberals tended to dominate discourses about digital technologies, often failing to create enduring instantiations for claims of inclusivity and empowerment or progressively sliding toward forms of doublespeak, asserting visions of an open and connected world while opaquely monetizing on the interactions occurring in that world. In the same time period, the alt-right was able to inhabit the same technologies, amassing an expanding body of supporters. Even though the dominant discourses about technology were not challenged directly, they were affected by the emergence of increasingly vast, visible, and vocal networks of actors and the webs of innovations they introduced, coupled with the concrete results they produced.

This transformation adds a new perspective to long-term debates about the relevance and repercussions of online practices in offline contexts. As Miller and Slater (2000) illustrated at the onset of anthropological enquiries of the internet, some forms of speech that emerged online (including extreme speech) tended to be considered as lacking importance or consequence. These forms for speech remained segregated in virtual spaces, without being taken up in offline communications. As the growing political significance of the alt-right illustrates, prolonged experience and experimentation with extreme speech may indeed have consequences that are very real, including contributing to the election of a populist president. Determining direct causation between a vitriolic message and physical violence remains a significant challenge for researchers; however, the connections between cultural practices that emerged online and their larger consequences for society have become clearer over time.

With an aspiringly large repertoire of cases, this collection offers a rich (enough) body of evidence to understand the contours of a global conjuncture and the extent to which digital technology is acting, in specific rather than generic ways, as the connective tissue making it possible. The global conjuncture of digitally enabled exclusionary politics is, first and foremost, about new styles and resources for communicating the unsayable—of chest-thumping braggadocio and a bare-knuckles approach to speech. Some scholars see this style as "populist"—a "low" rather than "high" style favoring self-presentation and language that is "raw" and crude (but warm and unrestrained) over refined and cultivated (but cool and reserved) (Ostiguy 2009). Not limited to populist leaders, colloquial styles of online exchange shape the vast voluntary work and bottom-up enthusiasm for exclusionary ideologies. In the case of the United States and online white nationalism, this style is borne out by new media cultures of "lulz"—"the raw, jaded fun of knowingly cultivated outrage" (Coleman 2014; Mazzarella 2018), or what Deem (2019, 3183) defines as "larger affective economies of transgression." Angela Nagle (2017) attributes deliberate border crossing to online subcultural trends and traces the transition of online trolls and 4Chan from left-anarchic cultures to the alt-right movement.

Such affective intensities are not precognitive bursts that are channeled through digital media; they represent a mesh of media practices within situated speech cultures—the main focus of this book's second section, "Colloquialization of Exclusion." Hervik (2019) understands this as "ritualized opposition," leading to divisive use of language and naturalization of racialized difference. Such recurrent ritualistic communicative patterns include the use of a distinct indignant tone, sarcasm, racialized reasoning, the use of "high fives," and a general indifference to facts. Honing the focus further on media practice, Udupa (chap. 6) calls this phenomenon "fun as a metapractice of exclusionary extreme speech." "Fun" is not frivolity of action but a serious political activity that consolidates communities of supporters for exclusionary ideologies. In digital environments, fun instigates collective pleasures of identity that can mitigate risk and culpability for right-wing movements. It deepens the common-sense familiarity of exclusionary messages, thereby enabling political protection accorded to them. Through "fun as a metapractice," the logics of spreadable digital media infuse the performative effects of distance and deniability into the body politic of right-wing ideologies. Haynes (chap. 11) and Mack (chap. 9) see similar effects in the "formulaic language" of internet memes. These effects allow for the expression of ideas that may not be voiced under other circumstances. The genre of text and its "digitality," as Haynes argues, contribute to understanding of what discourse is acceptable or unacceptable. McGranahan (chap. 7) incisively excavates the Twitter feed of Trump as "an archive of lies" and shows the intersections of digital platform affordances with the cultural logic of organization and the concepts at play in the move from words to action. Trump's lies, she argues, are a form of extreme speech that generates not only political outrage but also "affiliative truths" that lead to specific forms of social community and action. Tuters and Hagen (chap. 5) locate this extreme speech within the situated speech cultures of 4Chan and define it as "memetic antagonism" in contemporary anonymous imageboard culture. Similarly, "muhei stickers" (de Seta, chap. 10) in China that circulate on online messaging apps target Muslim communities by reinforcing slanderous stereotypes through visual ethnic humor. We propose that a theory of global conjuncture of digital extreme speech foregrounds these processes of banalization of exclusion through the metapractice of fun, formulaic language, humor, and coded exchange within internet speech cultures. These practices provide the new enabling ground for right-wing movements and exclusionary politics to stabilize and complement conventional strategies of "serious" appeal and dissemination. Aside from community-building functions, these media practices enable "the rule of presupposition accommodation" (Langton 2018)—when bystanders become complicit in hate attacks—through the interlocking effects of fun and fear.

A related corollary is the way in which physical localities are evoked in intensely local right-wing mobilizations organized through networked features of digital social media. Attacks against refugee shelters in Germany, as Kaiser discusses in chapter 13, are coordinated on localized anti–refugee shelter pages on Facebook.

Beyond the effects of banalization and localized segues to offline action, the global conjuncture of digital extreme speech is characterized by complex contestations in local political contexts. This aspect is the key focus of the book's third section, "Organization and Disorganization." In some scenarios, the internet has provided new evidentiary grounds and networked resources to attack minorities and dissenting sectarian groups. Set in the context of "internal colonization" (Pandey 2013), in which minority religious groups are denied full citizenship or claims to history, internet organization has augmented the means of and grounds for majoritarian aggression. Schaflechner's analysis in chapter 12 of the chilling effects of the new laws enacted against online acts of blasphemy and Pratidina's study in chapter 14 of the partisan politics around "womanhood" reveal how internet channels have enabled religious actors and political groups to fabricate incidents of violation of religious laws and ethical norms and raise swarming armies against minorities. Encouraging a heckler's veto, these attacks have intensified brutalities of the law and vigilante justice. The illocutionary force of extreme speech—working with and through power structures—is multiplied not only because of new forms of visibility that digital media have provided for majoritized groups but also digital traces, evidencing, and resource sharing that solidify memory and community feelings in polymedia environments (Saka, chap. 15; see also, Deem 2019, Udupa 2015a).

Contributions in this collection demonstrate that media practices cohering around the global conjuncture of exclusionary extreme speech are powered by digital affordances of archiving, tracing, providing evidence and formats of memes and incentives for joking. Although these affordances cannot be isolated as technological entities, they constitute the condition of possibility for any digital mediation (see Manovich 2001). The resonance of digital features on a global scale is best seen as a shared set of practices enabled by the transnational circulation of tropes, formats, and discursive resources, rather than in terms of technological determinism or cultural imperialism—both models now amply challenged by critics of global culture.

Taken out of the larger context of political economy and historical delineations of privilege, media practices and affordances appear to be mere tactical resources for the global conjuncture of exclusionary extreme speech. They might mislead us into believing new sociotechnological formations as politically fungible in unpredictable ways. Moreover, they may encourage an erroneous diagnosis that the current precipitation is an abrupt deviation from established traditions of democracy. This collection of essays traces the historical lineages of the crisis, shaped by far-reaching consequences of the modern/colonial matrix of power (Walsh and Mignolo 2018). As we discussed in the first section of this introduction, histories of colonialism reveal that extremeness is racially marked—in the twin, and somewhat paradoxical sense, of moral injunctions against it and its explicit content targeting racialized groups. To follow De Genova, if colonial histories are not taken into account, right-wing rancor appears as "nothing more than populist reaction formations, provoked by the unseemly presence of the migrants themselves" (2010, 413). Brown's (2019) analysis has sharply captured the sense of dethronement that arises out of the longue durée of the empire. The targets of exclusionary extreme speech come marked by racialized prejudice, religious histories, and injustices of the past (Chakrabarty 2000). The nineteenth-century biological racism "where differences were fixed immutably in hierarchically organized bodies" (Thirangama, Kelly, and Forment 2018) is symptomatic of the enduring injustices. This perspective explains the seemingly surprising support of millionaires who throw their might and money into right-wing movements in countries like Denmark and the United States. They are not members of the disadvantaged white proletariat who have fallen on the wrong side of neoliberal economic transitions and immigration policies.

Structures of coercion, irreducible as they are to the economic sphere, are nonetheless enmeshed in complex shifts in political economy. The global conjuncture of digital extreme speech is, in significant ways, a reenactment of the logics of capitalist accumulation, now accelerated in terms of scale and organization through processes of digitalization. By foregrounding the digital labor behind disinformation, Ong (chap. 2) highlights this aspect of the modern-colonial matrix of power. Although vast numbers of dispersed, unorganized, "ordinary" online users are participating in exclusionary online extreme speech, regimes have also engaged organized production of disinformation, making use of the infrastructure of globalization—of flexible and outsourced labor—that extreme speech actors in the West deplore. As Ong elaborates further in chapter 2, "The chief architects of networked disinformation are themselves architects of precarious labor arrangements in the creative industries that make workers vulnerable to slipping into the digital underground." These developments are situated in broader processes of datafication that drive contemporary digital capitalism, which "should be understood in relation to, and measured against . . . the historical processes of dispossession, enslavement, appropriation and extraction . . . central to the emergence of the modern world" (Milan and Trere 2019, 324).

Finally, the global conjuncture of digital extreme speech is a result of interlocking systems of coercion and power. Closer attention to intersectionality and the matrix of domination brings to bear the tangle of race, class, gender, religion, and ethnicity that has precipitated the current conjuncture. Milan and Trere (2019) rightly argue that capitalism, white supremacy, and heteropatriarchy are interlocking systems.

Intersectionality also invites attention to structures of power that preexisted or remained quite independent of colonial occupation. Exclusionary extreme speech in India, Indonesia, Kenya, and Pakistan—explored in this collection—is influenced by deeply intermeshed structures of coercion that cannot be fully explained by histories of colonial encounter. As Thirangama, Kelly, and Forment argue, "There are multiple genealogies of distinction and prestige that underpin regional hierarchical structures, and which often come to mingle with colonial projects but are not invented by them" (2018, 165). The specificities of national and regional political contexts are highlighted in Saka's (chap. 15) extensive study of troll networks that support President Erdoğan in Turkey. Tactics include swarming, verbal abuse, rhetorical innovation, and cross-platform coordination, but the contexts that fuel these practices are equally complex. Describing the phenomenon as "trollification of ordinary users," Saka shows how intragroup factional conflicts have surfaced, even within "AKTrolls." It reveals intricate political rivalries that inform extreme speech practices on the ground.

The global conjuncture of exclusionary extreme speech is amplified by the uneven course that liberal-progressive projects have taken globally. In the West, analysis of this "crisis" points to the "rent-restoration project" of Trump and Tea Party supporters that has emerged as a "response to the liberal rent-destruction project that sought to overcome structural disadvantages based on race, gender and nativity" (Jackson and Grusky, cited in Brubaker 2017, 372). Others have argued that the progressive left project has been weakened by "hypermoralization" of public discourse that raises moral panics around the slightest of "mistakes" in speech and by the erosion of the core moral order of class solidarity. In contrast, the right is not apologetic about either factual errors or political incorrectness. At the same time, the right has solidified xenophobic moral order of otherness through rage, fun, and rancor. Left progressive projects in other national and regional contexts have hit similar blocks but for vastly different historical reasons. Left liberal projects in India, for instance, are crippled by vanguard elitism, on one hand, and the imaginary flattening of neoliberal aspiration, on the other. Documenting the failures of progressive movements in different scenarios is beyond the scope of this introduction. Suffice it to state here that the global conjuncture of exclusionary politics is as much about the failure of progressive movements as it is about right-wing extreme speech backed with the historical weight of power and coercion. By the same token, by calling this influence a conjuncture rather than a regime, we signal spaces for radical subversions and deviations that can arise through sustained struggles to regain the optimism around the internet's emancipatory possibilities, as exemplified by globally coordinated social justice movements of #MeToo and #BlackLivesMatter (Bonilla and Rosa 2015).

This book reaffirms the emphasis articulated in our long-term project—that the conjuncture of exclusionary politics that gained momentum at the turn of the millennium cannot be grasped with the "disembodied and disengaged abstractions" (Mignolo and Walsh 2018, 3) often seen around the use of hate speech. Our critique has emerged from keen eyes on the ground from various vantage points—from lived concepts, meanings, and situated cultures of online use to broader structures of precarious labor, religious histories, and racial formations of colonial injustices. By insidiously folding into the new normal of everyday speech and political action, extreme speech has been immensely productive of identity—of assertations, affects, and affinities—that tests the limits of civility while showing, on another axis, the limits of communities. This grounded understanding of online extreme speech is a critical step toward unpacking the troubling effects of digitally enabled exclusionary politics. A political rather than moralizing perspective adopted by extreme speech might also inspire us to imagine concepts, worldviews, and knowledge around what Mignolo and Walsh poignantly define as reexistence: "the redefining and re-signifying of life in conditions of dignity" (2018, 3). What such a reimagination might look like in internet speech is still a moot question.

Notes

1. By the same token, achieving peace has also proven to be hard without the support of state or similar structures of power (Thirangama, Kelly, and Forment 2018, 163).

2. Civility is also part of "self-making and community making practices in plural worlds" (Thirangama, Kelly, and Forment 2018, 168).

3. We refer to the distinction that Brubaker and Cooper (2000) draw between "thick" (heavily congested terms) and "thin" concepts (less congested terms).

4. This is not to suggest that offline activities or those unrelated to speech do not matter. In his ethnography of a "right-wing town" in France, Damien Stankiewicz (2019) reveals that "much less sensationalist discourse—indeed . . . non-discursive place-making is effective in disseminating far-right political ideologies." Far-right politician Rasmus Paludan in Denmark came to fame using street-level tactics, including demonstrations in front of schools.

References

Biko, Steve. 1978. *I Write What I Like*. Johannesburg: Picador Africa.

Bonilla, Yarimar, and Jonathan Rosa. 2015. "#Ferguson: Digital Protest, Hashtag Ethnography and the Racial Politics of Social Media in the United States." *American Ethnologist* 42(1): 4–17.

Boromisza-Habashi, David. 2013. *Speaking Hatefully: Culture, Communication, and Political Action in Hungary*. University Park: Pennsylvania State University.

Brown, Alexander. 2018. "What Is So Special about Online (as Compared to Offline) Hate Speech?" *Ethnicities* 18 (3): 297–326.

Brown, Wendy. 2019. "Neoliberalism's Frankenstein: Authoritarian Freedom in Twenty-First Century 'Democracies.'" *Critical Times* 1 (1): 60–79.

Brubaker, Rogers. 2017. "Why Populism?" *Theory Society* 46:357–385.

Brubaker, Rogers, and Frederick Cooper. 2000. "Beyond 'Identity.'" *Theory and Society* 29 (1): 1–47.

Butler, Judith. 1997. *Excitable Speech: A Politics of the Performative*. New York: Routledge.

Callon, Michel. 2009. "Foreword." In *The Radiance of France*. Cambridge, MA: MIT Press.

Chakrabarty, Dipesh. 2000. *Provincializing Europe: Postcolonial Thought and Historical Difference*. Princeton, NJ: Princeton University Press.

Coleman, Gabriella. 2014. *Hacker, Hoaxer, Whistleblower, Spy: The Many Faces of Anonymous*. London: Verso.

Couldry, Nick. 2010. "Theorizing Media as Practice." In *Theorizing Media and Practice*, edited by Birgit Brauchler and John Postill, 35–54. Oxford: Berghahn Books.

Deem, Alexandra. 2019. "The Digital Traces of #whitegenocide and Alt-Right Affective Economies of Transgression." *International Journal of Communication* 13:3183–3202.

De Genova, Nicholas. 2010. "Migration and Race in Europe: The Trans-Atlantic Metastases of a Post-colonial Cancer." *European Journal of Social Theory* 13 (3): 405–419.

Fassin, Didier. 2011. "The Politics of Conspiracy Theories: On AIDS in South Africa and Few Other Global Plots." *Brown Journal of World Affairs* 17 (2): 39–50.

Gagliardone, Iginio. 2016. *The Politics of Technology in Africa*. Cambridge: Cambridge University Press.

———. 2019a. *China, Africa, and the Future of the Internet*. London: Zed.

———. 2019b. "Defining Online Hate and Its 'Public Lives': What Is the Place for 'Extreme Speech'?" *International Journal of Communication* 13:3068–3087.

Giddens, Anthony. 1987. *The Nation State and Violence*. Cambridge: Polity.

Ginsburg, Faye, Lila Abu-Lughod, and Brian Larkin. 2002. "Introduction." In *Media Worlds: Anthropology on New Terrain*, edited by Faye Ginsburg, Lila Abu-Lughod, and Brian Larkin, 1–36. Berkeley: University of California Press.

Guha, Ranajit. 1982. "On Some Aspects of the Historiography of Colonial India." In *Subaltern Studies I: Writings on South Asian History and Society*, edited by Ranajit Guha, 1–8. New Delhi: Oxford University Press.

Haynes, Nell. 2019. "Writing on the Walls: Discourses on Bolivian Immigrants in Chilean Meme Humor." *International Journal of Communication* 13:3122–3142.

Hecht, Gabrielle. 1998. *The Radiance of France: Nuclear Power and National Identity after World War II*. Cambridge, MA: MIT Press.

Hervik, Peter. 2011. *The Annoying Difference: The Emergence of Danish Neonatinalism, Neoracism and Populism in the Post-1989 World*. New York: Berghahn Books.

———. 2019. "Ritualized Opposition in Danish Online Practices of Extremist Language and Thought." *International Journal of Communication* 13:3104–3121.

Langton, Rae. 2018. "The Authority of Hate Speech." In *Oxford Studies in Philosophy of Law.* Vol. 3, edited by John Gardner, Leslie Green, and Brian Leiter, 123–152. Oxford: Oxford University Press.

Law, John, and Michel Callon. 1992. "The Life and Death of an Aircraft: A Network Analysis of Technical Change." In *Shaping Technology/Building Society: Studies in Sociotechnical Change,* edited by Wiebe E. Bijker and John Law, 21–52. Cambridge, MA: MIT Press.

Manovich, Lev. 2001. *The Language of New Media.* Cambridge, MA: MIT Press.

Marcuse, Herbert. 1964. *One-Dimensional Man.* New York: Beacon.

Mathur, Nayanika. 2015. "'Its Conspiracy Theory and Climate Change': Of Beastly Encounters and Cervine Disappearances in Himalayan India." *HAU: Journal of Ethnographic Theory* 5 (1): 87–111.

Mazzarella, William. 2018. "Brand(ish)Ing the Name, or, Why Is Trump So Enjoyable?" In *Sovereignty, Inc.: Three Inquiries in Politics and Enjoyment,* edited by William Mazzarella, Eric L. Santner, and Aaron, Schuster, 113–160. Chicago: University of Chicago Press.

McGranahan, Carole. 2017. "An Anthropology of Lying: Trump and the Political Sociality of Moral Outrage." *American Ethnologist* 44 (2): 243–248.

———. 2019. "A Presidential Archive of Lies: Racism, Twitter, and a History of the Present." *International Journal of Communication* 13:3164–3182.

Mignolo, Walter D., and Arturo Escobar. 2010. *Globalization and the Decolonial Option.* London: Routledge.

Mignolo, Walter D., and Catherine E. Walsh. 2018. *On Decoloniality: Concepts, Analytics, Praxis.* Durham, NC: Duke University Press.

Milan, Stefania, and Emiliano Trere. 2019. "Big Data from the South(s): Beyond Data Universalism." *Television and New Media* 20 (4): 319–335.

Miller, Daniel, and Don Slater. 2000. *The Internet: An Ethnographic Approach.* London: Routledge.

Mitchell, Lisa. 2018. "Civility and Collective Action: Soft Speech, Loud Roars, and the Politics of Recognition." *Anthropological Theory* 18 (2–3): 217–247.

Moffitt, Benjamin. 2016. *The Global Rise of Populism: Performance, Political Style and Representation.* Stanford, CA: Stanford University Press.

Mouffe, Chantal. 2005. *On the Political.* London: Routledge.

Nagle, Angela. 2017. *Kill All Normies: Online Culture Wars from 4Chan and Tumblr to Trump and the Alt-Right.* Alresford: Zero.

Ong, Jonathan Corpus, and Jason V. Cabanes. 2018. *Architects of Networked Disinformation: Behind the Scenes of Troll Accounts and Fake News Production in the Philippines.* Newton Tech4Dev Network. https:// newtontechfordev.com/wp-content/uploads/2018/02/ARCHITECTS-OF-NETWORKED -DISINFORMATION-FULL-REPORT.pdf

Ostiguy, Pierre. 2009. "The High and the Low in Politics: A Two-Dimensional Political Space for Comparative Analysis and Electoral Studies." Working Paper 360. https://www.semanticscholar.org/paper/THE-HIGH -AND-THE-LOW-IN-POLITICS%3A-A-TWO-DIMENSIONAL-Ostiguy/a399dd77f16c07a5e39 fbbba4e917a0e48d17fc8

Pandey, Gyanendra. 2013. *A History of Prejudice: Race, Caste, and Difference in India and the United States.* New York: Cambridge University Press.

Peterson, Mark Allen. 2009. "What's the Point of Media Anthropology? Response to John Postill." *Social Anthropology* 17 (3): 337–339.

Pohjonen, Matti. 2019. "A Comparative Approach to Social Media Extreme Speech: Online Hate Speech as Media Commentary." *International Journal of Communication* 13:3088–3103.

Pohjonen, Matti, and Sahana Udupa. 2017. "Extreme Speech Online: An Anthropological Critique of Hate Speech Debates." *International Journal of Communication* 11:1173–1191.

Post, Robert. 2009. "Hate Speech." In *Extreme Speech and Democracy,* edited by Ivan Hare and Jeremy Weinstein, 123–138. Oxford: Oxford University Press.

Rajagopal, Arvind. 2001. *Politics after Television: Hindu Nationalism and the Reshaping of the Indian Public.* Cambridge: Cambridge University Press.

Rodotà, Stefano. 1997. *Tecnopolitica. La Democrazia e Le Nuove Tecnologie Della Comunicazione.* Bari: Laterza.

Said, Edward W. 1978. *Orientalism.* New York: Random House.

Schaflechner, Juergen. 2019."Blasphemy and the Appropriation of Vigilante Justice in 'Hagiographic' Writing in Pakistan." In *Outrage: The Rise of Religious Offence in South Asia*, edited by Kathinka Froystad, Paul Rollier, and Arild Engelsen Ruud, 207–234. London: UCL Press.

Schroeder, Ralph. 2018. *Social Theory after the Internet: Media, Technology and Globalization*. London: UCL Press.

Stankiewicz, Damien. 2019. "Placing Racialization: Public Space and Politics in a Far-Right Town in France." Paper presented at the workshop, "Critical Understanding of Racialization in the Era of Global Populism," Aalborg University, Copenhagen, June 3–4.

Stewart, Kathleen. 1990. "Backtalking the Wilderness: Appalachian En-Genderings." In *Uncertain Terms: Negotiating Gender in American Culture*, edited by Faye Ginsburg and Anna Lowenhaupt Tsing, 43–56. Boston: Beacon.

Suchman, Lucy. 1987. *Plans and Situated Actions: The Problem of Human-Machine Communication*. Cambridge: Cambridge University Press.

Thirangama, Sharika, Tobias Kelly, and Carlos Forment. 2018. "Introduction: Whose Civility?" *Anthropological Theory* 18 (2–3): 153–174.

Tracy, Karen. 2008. "'Reasonable Hostility': Situation-Appropriate Face-Attack." *Journal of Politeness Research* 4 (2): 169–191.

Treré, Emiliano, and Alejandro Barranquero Carretero. 2018. "Tracing the Roots of Technopolitics: Towards a North-South Dialogue." In *Networks, Movements and Technopolitics in Latin America: Critical Analysis and Current Challenges*, edited by Francisco Sierra Caballero and Tommaso Gravante, 43–63. Cham: Springer.

Udupa, Sahana. 2015a. *Making News in Global India: Media, Publics, Politics*. Cambridge: Cambridge University Press.

———. 2015b. Abusive Exchange on Social Media: The Politics of Online Gaali Cultures in India. Media Anthropology Network 52nd E-seminar, European Association of Social Anthropologists, July.

———. 2017. "Gaali Cultures: The Politics of Abusive Exchange on Social Media." *New Media and Society* 20 (4): 1506–1522.

———. 2020. "Decoloniality and Extreme Speech." Presented at European Association of Social Anthropologists Media Anthropology Network 65th e-Seminar, June 17–30.

Udupa, Sahana, and Matti Pohjonen. 2019. "Extreme Speech and Global Digital Cultures." *International Journal of Communication* 13:3049–3067.

United Nations. 1966. *International Covenant on Civil and Political Rights*. https://treaties.un.org/doc/publication/unts/volume%20999/volume-999-i-14668-english.pdf

Verkaaik, Oskar. 2004. *No Title Migrants and Militants: Fun and Urban Violence in Pakistan*. Princeton, NJ: Princeton University Press.

Walsh, Catherine E., and Walter D. Mignolo. 2018. "Introduction." In *On Decoloniality: Concepts, Analytics, Praxis*, edited by Walter D. Mignolo and Catherine E. Walsh, 1–12. Durham, NC: Duke University Press.

PART 1

EXTREME SPEECH AS CRITIQUE—POWER AND AGONISM

Part 1 deepens the understanding of extreme speech by offering concrete examples of how it operates in different cultural and political contexts. It connects cases from Eastern Europe, Southeast Asia, and Africa to provide a practical illustration of the limits of the "hate speech" framework. These connections show how this framework is unable to capture the ways in which extreme practices can provide means to talk back to prevailing power or, conversely, how the sanctioning of expressions labeled as "hate speech" can allow power to perpetrate its hegemonic control over political discourse.

In the first chapter, David Boromisza-Habashi describes how the trading of accusations of "hate speech" among Hungarian politicians invites a competition of moralities that can ultimately erode their own moral force. It also illustrates the power of ethnography to reveal diverse debates surrounding hate speech and free speech as value-laden metadiscourses vying to inform speech governance.

In chapter 2, Jonathan Corpus Ong develops the example of extreme speech as power. Through a unique set of interviews with digital organizers and influencers in the Philippines, Ong offers a snapshot that both captures the ordinariness of extreme speech and locates it in the broader context of digital capitalism and exploitation. Exploring the digital labor behind disinformation, the chapter recognizes disinformation producers as digital workers, composing a "digital sweatshop" of paid troll work.

In chapter 3, David Katiambo explains how institutional power in Kenya has been labeling extreme speech as hate speech to cement its authority. The regime covertly naturalizes its discourse through social media platforms and users in a way that exercises political power without calling attention to it, whereas platforms like Facebook and Twitter—by virtue of being near monopolies—control the definition of hate speech. The chapter also extends reflections on coloniality and decoloniality in Africa to the digital sphere and provides a conceptual toolbox that can be used to critically interrogate the endurance of old practices of domination in new communicative spaces.

In the last chapter of part 1, Max Kramer focuses on India and explains how democracy can be diminished by labeling the expressions of resentment by those living under discrimination and structural violence as "hate speech." Nietzsche's concept of "ressentiment" is used to analyze the reactions of the weak who cannot fight in any way other than to moralize and take what is suppressing them as amoral, which can lead to a cycle of autovictimization and revenge. Kramer explains that speech can be transgressive and legitimate at the same time, as the claims that minority citizens are permitted to make against the nation-state are part of a problematic moral-normative framework.

1

THERE'S NO SUCH THING AS HATE SPEECH AND IT'S A GOOD THING, TOO

David Boromisza-Habashi

THERE CAN BE NO QUESTION THAT DEROGATORY PUBLIC expression targeting historically disadvantaged ethnic and racial minorities is flourishing, especially as—at least in Europe and the United States—the moral and political agenda organized around human rights is under concerted attack by the radical right. Popular concern with hate speech is also very much alive throughout the Western world (Brown and Sinclair 2020). To use my current country of residence as an example, according to a recent survey by More in Common (Hawkins et al. 2018), 82 percent of US respondents across the political spectrum said hate speech was a problem in America today. Another survey conducted by the Cato Institute (Ekins 2017) reported that 79 percent of respondents said hate speech was a problem, but 82 percent said it was hard to ban hate speech because people cannot agree on what speech is hateful or offensive.

In light of widespread verbal aggression and the popular concern surrounding it, it may seem strange, or indeed preposterous, to suggest that hate speech does not exist. "Hate speech," interpreted as verbal aggression, certainly exists; however, other compelling interpretations of the term also circulate in public discourse. This, I argue, is a practical problem for antiracist advocacy. Unfortunately for anyone who wishes to alert others about acts of racist verbal aggression, the term "hate speech" is used by different types of speakers for various political purposes. One such purpose is to persuade others that, because hate speech does not clearly identify a finite set of morally objectionable speech acts, those who call out others for hate speech are making a thinly veiled attempt to sanction speech and speakers they do not agree with. The subversion of the antiracist meaning of hate speech in such a way is possible and, for some, desirable because "hate speech" is not just a term with a simple, direct referent but also a term for talk (Carbaugh 2017). It is a metadiscursive term used in particular contexts by particular categories of speakers for the purpose of labeling and evaluating speech and, in the process of its use, indicating those speakers' identification with (and against) other sociopolitical categories of speakers. Contested terms for talk such as hate speech are ripe for promoting moral and political agendas and undermining those of others.

The ethnographic approach to public discourse I showcase in this chapter reveals that, in a political landscape fraught with contestation and partisanship, discursively sustaining the status of hate speech as an observable entity with a "natural," autonomous existence through acts of accusation becomes impossible. The term's fractured meaning becomes an expression of, and a resource for, the fracturing of the political community into competing groups that regard one another as enemies. Contesting the original, antiracist meaning of "hate speech" as derogatory expression targeting historically disadvantaged minorities becomes a form of ritualized opposition (Hervik 2019), a form of expression that substitutes reasoned, fact-based argument with the signaling of one's belonging to a political tribe. I argue that, in light of these observations, antiracist political actors should reinvent their political vocabulary by seeking out new metadiscursive terms for the purpose of holding speakers of racist expression accountable. My arguments complement Udupa and Pohjonen's (2019) claims about the utility of "hate speech" as a metadiscursive term; whereas they argued that hate speech was too blunt an analytic concept, I argue that it is too blunt a rhetorical instrument.

As debates surrounding hate speech and campus speech codes were raging in the United States in the early 1990s, the literary critic Stanley Fish published a controversial essay titled, "There's No Such Thing as Free Speech and It's a Good Thing, Too" in the *Boston Review*, an expanded version of which was later included as a chapter in his book bearing the same title (Fish 1994). In the essay, Fish reflected on the ontology of free speech in the context of legal battles surrounding the question of what forms of expression are protected by the First Amendment. There was no such thing as free speech, Fish argued, because speech had no "natural" content that rendered it free. Rather, speech should be thought of as action and thus subject to evaluation based on its consequences. The category of free speech contains forms of expression deemed valuable by those who wield the necessary political power to restrict free speech. Acknowledging this was a "good thing," he concluded, because it awakened the political left to its moral responsibility (making clear evaluative distinctions between acceptable and unacceptable speech) and its political responsibility (doing everything in its power to be in control of the boundaries of free speech).

In my own ethnographic investigation of hate speech in Hungary during the first decade of this century, I reached many of the same conclusions as Fish about hate speech. Just as speech cannot be "naturally" free, it cannot be "naturally" hateful either. Debates surrounding hate speech and free speech are both value-laden metadiscourses vying to inform speech governance. The promotion of a definition of hate speech over others is most accurately seen as a political attempt to assign value to preferred forms of expression. Nevertheless, there is one significant difference between hate speech and free speech metadiscourse. Free speech tends to be used to assign positive value to public expression, despite its sometimes objectionable content. In the context of Hungarian public discourse, *gyűlöletbeszéd* (hate speech) was most frequently deployed as an element of normative challenges, that is, accusations or allegations. Such accusations were typically made by public speakers who were neither the targets of hate speech nor its speakers. The accused never avowed that they were speakers of hate—although on a few occasions they labeled their own speech as hate speech for comedic or ironic effect—and third-party judges never backed down from their accusations. This communication pattern reinforced sociopolitical divisions within the Hungarian political landscape and affirmed parallel moral systems informing opposing interpretations of hate speech. In the end, hate speech became so heavily contested and debates surrounding it so predictable that, apart from a few isolated exceptions, political actors have abandoned the use of the term.

Hungarian Hate Speech Metadiscourse: The Road to Failure

The findings and arguments I present in this chapter are based on ethnographic fieldwork I carried out in Budapest, Hungary, between 2004 and 2007, toward the end of a period during which hate speech was a hot-button political issue in national politics. The central goal of that project was not to catalogue acts or critique existing definitions of hate speech but rather to develop a comprehensive account of the various uses of the term in public discourse, the competing systems of meanings that informed those uses and understandings, and how contestation weakened antiracist uses of the term (Boromisza-Habashi 2013). During the time period studied, hardly a day went by without one public figure accusing another of hate speech. The political fervor surrounding hate speech is gone today. Occasional accusations of hate speech against the nationalist government's virulently racist and xenophobic rhetoric seldom prompt official responses.

My decision to use an ethnographic approach stemmed from the surprising and disorienting observation—what Agar (1994) would call a "rich point"—that by the mid-2000s, Hungarian political actors could reasonably apply the term hate speech to any type of public expression they found objectionable. A mere decade earlier, Hungarian legal scholars and social scientists were engaged in deep discussions regarding the possibility and wisdom of limiting free expression and were contemplating establishing "speech expressing hatred" as a legal category to protect ethnic and racial minorities from assault. By the time I was considering writing an ethnography of the chaotic social life of hate speech, these antiracist efforts were largely sidelined, and interpretations and uses of the term had proliferated. The indeterminacy of the term's meaning, however, did not seem to dampen either the fervor with which accusers lobbed allegations of hate speech against their political opponents or the outrage that the allegations caused among the accused.

Ethnography was the approach best suited to study the relationship between speech patterns and social upheaval. The ethnography of communication research tradition theorizes communication as a practice (patterned, context-bound, locally meaningful, accountable communicative action) and posits a mutually constitutive relationship between communication and the sociocultural lives of speakers (Boromisza-Habashi and Parks 2014; Carbaugh and Boromisza-Habashi 2015). Against this theoretical background, hate speech metadiscourse appears as a practice, and any use of the term is seen as meaningful communicative action in context. The meaning-in-use of the term is not only referential but also sociocultural, in the sense that it is informed by local beliefs about social organization, communicative action, and emotion, and that it facilitates social (dis)order.

Besides describing the meanings-in-use of hate speech, it is also necessary, from the perspective of practice, to evaluate those uses. Evaluation requires standards; the evaluation of action can be assessed, among other ways, according to criteria of success and failure.

How do accusations of hate speech succeed, and how do they fail? Accusations of racist hate speech have a number of social functions, including holding other participants of public discourse accountable, rallying citizens to the cause of antiracism, cultivating a set of norms for participation in public discourse, expressing support for those targeted by hate speech, and so on. In this discussion, I am particularly interested in the first one of these functions—the capacity of hate speech metadiscourse for holding others accountable. To charge another speaker, or group of speakers, with hate speech is a normative challenge (Hall 1988–1989), a communicative action performed to cast another action as being misaligned with a community's norms of communication and the speaker(s) who performed that action as running the risk of exclusion from the community. In the case of hate speech, such normative challenges tend to be issued by speakers in a third-party social position—that is, neither by those who performed the objectionable act nor its targets.

The normative challenge of hate speech can prompt counterchallenges or acquiescence. Counterchallenges take five forms (Hall 1991). The accused can find an excuse (e.g., "I did not say that, someone else in my group or another group did!"). They can minimize the degree of norm violation and invoke higher norms (e.g., "I am not hateful, I'm a patriot!"). They can call into question that the act had actually occurred (e.g., "I never said that!"). They can negotiate the interpretation of the act as a norm violation (e.g., "What I said was not hate speech—it was a joke! Lighten up!"). Finally, they can negotiate the legitimacy of the invoked norm—that is, the degree of consensus that exists about its force (e.g., "Is that what you think hate speech is? Well, that's your opinion."). Challenges and counterchallenges combine into what Hall calls "alignment episodes," bounded exchanges in the course of which participants display joint commitment to discussing and remedying breaches of local social order.

Normative challenges succeed when alignment episodes end with the accused participants' acquiescence. Accusations of hate speech as normative challenges succeed when they prompt one of three forms of acquiescence: the accused stops performing the type of expression the challenger labeled hate speech, they rephrase what they said in a way that does not contain the type of expression labeled hate speech, or they issue a verbal or nonverbal apology. These acts realign the accused and their speech with the social and communicative ecology of the community in the name of which the accuser acted. Acquiescence, however, was not the typical response to accusations of hate speech in the Hungarian context; in fact, I did not come across an alignment episode that concluded with acquiescence.

There are two reasons for Hungarian speakers' reluctance to acquiesce to public accusations of hate speech. On one hand, acquiescing to such an accusation places the accused in a position of moral and/or psychological inferiority. Accusers and the accused had two competing interpretations of hate speech at their disposal to label public expression as hate speech (Boromisza-Habashi 2013). According to the tone-oriented interpretation, public expression ought to be labeled hate speech if it is marked by a hateful tone that serves as a testament to a personal pathology of prejudice. Speakers of hate speech, in this view, cannot keep their prejudiced attitude toward minorities under control and let it bubble to the surface of public discourse. The content-oriented interpretation holds that the defining feature of hate speech is its (racist, discriminatory) content. This latter interpretation casts speakers of hate speech as morally inferior bigots. As a result of the coexistence of these interpretations, people who publicly accused others of hate speech could expect three outcomes: the accused either refused to accept the purported moral or psychological authority of the accuser, they defended themselves from accusations by opting for an interpretation of hate speech opposite to that held by the accusers, or both. Consider, for example, how the hosts of a televised far-right talk show, *Press Club* (*Sajtóklub*), collaborate on countering an anticipated challenge from the political left. Before the conversational excerpt below, the hosts expressed their support for a German politician who declared that one of his Jewish political opponents was contributing to growing antisemitism in Germany by (allegedly) trafficking drugs. Jewish public figures in Hungary, the hosts continued, should also "look in the mirror," mend their ways, and stop feeding antisemitic sentiment. To support his argument, one of the hosts read a salacious conversation from the transcript of a rival talk show that, he claimed, frequently featured leftist Jewish participants. In the excerpt below, he explains that, because of their unbridled political bias, the political or Jewish left will accuse him of hate speech just for reading the transcript (all translations of Hungarian data are mine):

> Host 1 They will call us fascists again because, why did I read this on the air? Obviously, because I am an antisemite. Or at least a latent antisemite. (*scattered audience laughter*)
>
> Host 2 And the saddest thing is that it is these gentlemen who lend their support to the law against hate speech. The very people who spout hatred and human debasement. They will introduce it in the parliament, and they will pass it and will use it against us, normal people, and they will continue these games of theirs in the media. (Bayer et al. [June 25, 2003], pt. 2, 7:49)

Host 1 objects to the political left's censorship of any view critical of Jews. In response, host 2 characterizes the talk of Jewish participants of the rival talk show as "spout[ing] hatred and human debasement" and accuses them of sponsoring "the law against hate speech" that "they" (Jews) will pass and use "against us, normal people" while continuing their own immoral public behavior. Host 1 anticipates a content-based moral challenge (i.e., they will be accused of voicing antisemitic sentiments), and host 2 formulates a counterchallenge by invoking a tone-oriented interpretation of hate speech (i.e., their political rivals are using a double standard by passing a law against hate speech while failing to admit that their own tone is hateful). Playing one interpretation of hate speech against another offers those expressing blatantly antisemitic views a way to deflect accusations of hate speech.

On the other hand, Hungarian public discourse surrounding hate speech did not result in any degree of normative consensus beyond a shared sense that hate speech was morally objectionable. Nevertheless, this minimal degree of moral agreement was not enough to keep accusers and the accused engaged in alignment episodes that might have led to the acquiescence of the accused and the attendant restoration of orderly public discourse. The accused quickly formed counterchallenges by negotiating the interpretation of the act or the legitimacy of the norm inherent in the accusation, both of which undermined the possibility of alignment.

The lack of normative consensus was on display not only in accusations of hate speech but also in political discourse aiming to institute speech governance. At the height of the Hungarian hate speech debates in 2003, for example, members of parliament engaged in an ultimately fruitless struggle to craft legislation that would establish limitations to "free speech" and thus create the legal foundations necessary for prosecuting hate speech (Boromisza-Habashi 2013). Their debates brought to the surface a fundamental dilemma immanent in the Hungarian Constitution in effect at the time and in the legal systems of numerous Western societies: curtailing free speech leads to the violation of one fundamental human right; not curtailing free speech leads to the violation of another—namely, the right to human dignity and security. Hungarian conservatives and liberals formed a rare alliance against the socialists who privileged the protection of human dignity over the protection of free speech. Based on an analysis of transcripts from various parliamentary committees, I glossed their interpretation of the relationship between the two fundamental rights in this way: "Hate speech (*gyűlöletbeszéd*) violates the human dignity (*emberi méltóság*) of others. Human dignity is protected by the Constitution. Freedom of expression (*véleménynyilvánítás szabadsága*) is also protected by the Constitution. Since the right to human dignity and the right to free expression are both within the Constitution, one cannot be compromised for the sake of the other. Therefore, hate speech is a mode of expression protected by the Constitution" (75). Socialists countered with the following interpretation: "Hate speech violates the human dignity of others. Human dignity is protected by the Constitution. Freedom of expression is also protected by the Constitution. Since the right to human dignity and the right to free expression are both within the Constitution, one can serve as the limit to the other. Therefore, hate speech is a mode of expression not protected by the Constitution" (75).

These conflicting readings of the Constitution were anchored in and affirmed two conflicting views of (legal) personhood. Socialists cast citizens as members of communities (*közösségek*) who, as such, deserved an equal degree of dignity and protection from verbal assault. In contrast, their political opponents called for the protection of the rights of the individual (*egyén*). Invocations of citizens-as-members-of-communities and citizens-as-individuals contributed—along with the two opposing interpretations of the law—to the entrenchment of the two sides' political positions on the law and two equally reasonable but incompatible political worldviews (Lakoff 2002).

In addition to derailing alignment episodes, the lack of crystallized norms relevant to the interpretation and prosecution of hate speech paved the way for the attacks on what Hungarian right-wing critics of antiracist advocacy saw as the hate speech agenda (Boromisza-Habashi 2011). This alleged agenda comprised three elements: antiracist allegations of hate speech, the promotion of antiracist interpretations of hate speech, and initiatives to create legal penalties against hate speech as a criminal or civic offense. The attacks took full advantage of the lack of consensus about the meaning and evaluation of hate speech. Anti-antiracist advocates rushed to point out the ideological inconsistency at the heart of the hate speech agenda—namely, that liberals who were otherwise deeply committed to protecting freedom of expression did not mind outlawing speech they did not like. (Never mind that Hungarian liberals were actually opposed to passing legislation criminalizing hate speech.) This line of argument built on the legal dilemma inherent in speech governance discussed earlier. Other critics argued that antiracist advocates of the hate speech agenda were themselves filled with hatred, a line of argument resting on the tension between tone- and content-oriented interpretations of the term. A particularly interesting (and somewhat bizarre) form of making such an argument was what I call "adversarial mirroring" (Boromisza-Habashi 2013). Adversarial mirroring can be explained loosely as, "You have just charged me or my group with hate speech. This implies that you are treating me or us as morally inferior to yourself. This is clear evidence that you hate me or us. Your accusation of hate speech reveals your hatred for me or us, and therefore counts as hate speech."

Other argumentative strategies attacked the hate speech agenda on the basis of its purportedly alien origins and suggested that the lack of the agenda's rootedness in the Hungarian language and history explained the lack of consensus surrounding the term's meaning and normative charge. The conservative historian Mária Schmidt published an article in 1996 in which she mounted an attack on the "Act Against Hatred" movement and sociologist György Csepeli for popularizing the term "hate speech." In the article, Schmidt cast the term as an Orwellian linguistic abomination:

> The slogan ["Act against hatred!"] is an attractive one. It makes one feel that hatred is shameful and that acting against it is commendable. Following the politicization and compromising of the word "hatred," György Csepeli also discredited the way words constitute speech in our language in an article in *Népszabadság*: "Words are also action. . . . The utterance of words by itself constitutes action. . . . Hence I don't have to shoot or slap someone, I can do the same with words." This is how we arrive at the new invention in the politics of language, "hate speech." The reason why hate speech must be penalized with severe laws is that hatred as such must be acted against, and speech, contrary to our existing conception of it, becomes action when combined with hatred. In a constitutional state, one must be held accountable for one's actions. Thus, the norms of the constitutional state remain unbroken if we extend criminal law to speech. "Hate speech" is an unintelligible and undefined compound whose meaning can perhaps only be compared with concepts like class enemy or enemy of the people, and its construction is downright Orwellian. (1996, 15)

Schmidt attempts to undermine the hate speech agenda by charging that the term at its core is an "invention" that violates "our existing conception" of what the words "hate" and "speech" mean in "our language." The term "hate speech" feels artificial and alien to any authentic Hungarian speaker, which should be reason enough to suspect that an insidious, politically motivated, Orwellian manipulation of language is taking place. Thus, the denial of the reality of hate speech—that is, its existence as a category of observable public expression—became a means of displaying an authentic national identity.

In a similar manner, denying the racist social reality that antiracists signal with the use of the term "hate speech" could also be made into a token of national belonging. Consider the following excerpt from a 1987 interview in which a young conservative explained one of the greatest dangers of the hate speech agenda to me—namely, that it conjures up an alien (global, American) reality that collides with and conceals actual Hungarian sociohistorical reality:

> The way I see it, the opium or dope is this idea of "let's recreate the world through the internet and globalization, and the really cool people work at globalized corporations, they are the ideal types, and those who don't really want this are spoiling this oh-so-diverse world that we are busy building here." [This] is a worldwide tendency. I mean that you have to, you are obliged to put a Chinese guy on the team, because you've got to have a Chinese guy in the series, you need the Chinese guy on *Star Trek*, and you need the black dude on *Star Trek* and you need the lesbian on *Star Trek* and you get these "[corporate] team" type collectives. . . . It's this American type of thing, and these are the cool people, and *Star Trek* forges ahead. . . . And people who say that

"this has nothing to do with the real situation, and Serbs are killing Hungarians and vice versa, and Bosnians and Croats kill Serbs, and these folks have really lived side-by-side for five hundred years, loving each other in peace is not exactly fashionable here," those people are considered jerks. Because they lift the veil. (interview, April 12, 2007)

The hate speech agenda, for this speaker, poses a moral threat. Accepting the American and globalist moral principles of this agenda—particularly, principles of ethnic and sexual diversity—robs Hungarians of a sense of local, regional reality and casts those who act as advocates of this reality as morally inferior "jerks." The media and corporate-driven "*Star Trek* reality" of diversity initiatives acts as "opium" and "dope," convincing onlookers that participants of such initiatives are "cool people" and "ideal types," whereas, in reality, it conceals the actual state of affairs under a veil that ought not to be lifted. The hate speech agenda interprets any attempt to lift the veil as hate speech.

Attacks on the hate speech agenda produced an effective argumentation playbook for its Hungarian critics, which I summarize as follows:

1. Achieve positive self-presentation by means of exposing the hidden political agenda and fallacies of the opponent.
2. Let the audience draw the conclusion that the opponent is morally inferior based on "factual" evidence. Leave implicit the claim to higher moral standing.
3. Treat antiracists as a united political faction with a unified "hate speech" agenda.
4. Display expertise on the antiracist position on "hate speech" without acknowledging the antiracist morality informing that position.
5. Avoid concession to the opponent's position even when displaying expertise on that position (e.g., by means of negative association, negative predication, irony, etc.). (Boromisza-Habashi 2011, 15).

A pattern running through failed alignment episodes, legal debates, and attacks on a purported hate speech agenda is that in all of these cases, competing interpretations of hate speech served as indexes of belonging. The social function of interpreting hate speech subsumed its referential function—that is, its function as a description of a category of observable communication phenomena. In the Hungarian context, invocations of hate speech and the implicit, oppositional interpretations of the term became enactments of social membership. On one hand, public speakers could take full advantage of the communal function (Philipsen 1989*b*) of the term's use. They could use the term to make claims to political group identities and could experience membership by using the term in ways that others in their political group did. On the other hand, they could not use hate speech metadiscourse in public without being positioned by others as a member of one political party or another—a conservative or a progressive, a patriot or an antiracist activist.

These observations reveal that, in the context of the Hungarian hate speech debates during the first decade of the twenty-first century, the term became an essentially contested political concept (Boromisza-Habashi 2010). The contestation of a concept is essential if contestation itself becomes the locus of its meaning and if the use of competing meanings of the concept are interpreted as norm violations. This was certainly the case in Hungary: labeling public expression as hate speech using one of the locally available meanings of hate speech inevitably brought into view other, competing meanings. This rendered the speaker a contestant for the authority to control the definition of hate speech and to attach negative sanctions not only to all forms of expression to which that definition applied but also to all competing interpretations of the term. The possession of such authority would have solidified the shifting moral landscape in Hungarian politics by instituting a clear, uncontested distinction between the righteous (those who can legitimately accuse others of hate speech) and the fallen (the accused). However, as in the case of the essential contestation of other political concepts like fascism, racism, or terrorism, the contestation of hate speech failed to produce clear winners and losers.

Essential contestation, however, had one clear outcome: the term gradually lost its significance as a means of social change. In the mid-1990s, hate speech metadiscourse was invariably interpreted with reference to antiracism; by the time of my fieldwork in Hungary, hate speech "could be a concept for speech intended to degrade a group of people based on their voting preferences, to intimidate a politician, a single person symbolizing a group, or to harshly criticize a party, a church, a medium, or even an idea" (Pál 2006, 19n38). The antiracist sentiments that the term originally captured were lost in the cacophony of all manner of politically motivated accusations of hatred.

Conclusion: A Cautionary Tale

The ethnographic study of the hate speech debates in Hungary indicates that decades of intense essential contestation have undermined the status of hate speech as a social fact. Contestation has also undermined our ability to simply point "it" out, calling it by its name and, by harnessing the power of shame, forcing it to disappear—what "it" is has become much too muddled. It appears that we need a new political vocabulary to call out discriminatory expression that targets historically disadvantaged racial and ethnic minorities and that, today, carries the rallying cries of violent nationalism and white supremacy to the farthest reaches of the globe.

In his classic book on ethnographic writing, John Van Maanen (2011) distinguished various "tales" that ethnographers told their audiences about what they had learned in the field. The tale I am telling in this chapter is perhaps closest to what he called the "advocacy tale." Such tales "put forth a strong, clear point of view in which no doubt is left in the reader as to what side the ethnographer is on. . . . [They] take on certain evils in the world, show what they have done (and are doing), and tell us what might be done about them" (171). As an ethnographer working in the institutional context of communication, a practical discipline (Craig 2018), I am equally compelled to suggest practical interventions into hate speech metadiscourse and to adhere to the axiom of particularity, according to which "the efficacious resources for creating shared meaning and motivating coordinated action vary across social groups" (Philipsen 1989a, 258). I hesitate to claim that the ethnographic study of Hungarian hate speech metadiscourse can produce findings that apply, directly and unproblematically, to public talk about hate speech in other geographic or virtual places at other times. The sociocultural life of Hungarian *gyűlöletbeszéd* will be different in some ways from the sociocultural lives of Polish *mowa nienawiści*, Serbian *govor mržnje*, US hate speech, Afrikaans *Haatspraak*, French *discours de haine*, German *Hassrede*, and Dutch *Haatzaaien*.

Some evidence suggests, for example, that the term's meaning is less contested in mediated public expression in the United States (Boromisza-Habashi 2012). The account of the term's Hungarian life that I share here can thus be best described as a cautionary tale to antiracist advocates who use the term "hate speech" to hold racists accountable.

Ethnography suggests that antiracist advocacy targeting racists with accusations of racism must maintain a precarious balance between accusation and identification. On their own, normative challenges of hate speech targeting racists are likely not only to produce and affirm entrenched political positions and to foster competing moralities but also to gradually corrode their own moral force. This corrosion is brought about by the ambiguity of the term and the essential contestation that such ambiguity makes possible. As a result, charges of hate speech are also unlikely to accomplish a key feature of rhetoric—identification (Burke 1969), without which a target's acquiescence to a moral challenge is impossible. Identification occurs when speakers use locally available symbolic resources to temporarily overcome social divisions between themselves and their audiences, engender a shared sense of consubstantiality, and enter into a negotiation of symbolic and material conditions. Hate speech, it appears, is not a symbolic resource with the necessary rhetorical force to produce the type of identification that prevents those who speak the language of racism from brushing off moral challenges. Antiracist advocates' failure to recognize this is a practical, tactical mistake (Boromisza-Habashi 2015).

But what is the "good thing" about the observation that hate speech seems to have lost its rhetorical "teeth" in the Hungarian context and likely in other contexts? Ethnographic insight into hate speech metadiscourse provides us with the warrant to free ourselves from a perceived moral and/or political obligation to salvage hate speech by redefining its referents. By acknowledging the limited rhetorical power of accusations of hate speech, we place ourselves in a position to produce better everyday metadiscourse and thereby sharpen antiracist advocacy. Such metadiscursive vocabularies can derive from scholarship—Hervik's (2019) "ritualized opposition" is a promising example—but also from indigenous vocabularies. Future ethnographies of the Hungarian context could study, for example, the use of metadiscursive terms generated by transforming nouns that signal targets of racist expression into verbs. Today, Hungarian progressives frequently accuse the nationalist government of *sorosozás* (attacks on George Soros with antisemitic overtones, literally "Soros-ing") and *migránsozás* (xenophobic attacks on asylum seekers, literally "migrant-ing"). Such terms successfully avoid the ambiguity of "hatred," tie racist expression to its particular targets, and allow antiracist advocates to call out more readily observable types of racist speech.

References

Agar, Michael. 1994. *Language Shock: Understanding the Culture of Conversation.* New York, NY: William Morrow.

Bayer, Zsolt. (Host), András Bencsik (Host), István Lovas (Host), Tamás Molnár (Host), and László Tóth Gy (Host). (June 25, 2003). *Sajtóklub* [Press Club] [Television talk show]. *Budapest TV.*

Boromisza-Habashi, David. 2010. "How Are Political Concepts 'Essentially' Contested?" *Language and Communication* 30 (4): 276–284. doi:10.1016/j.langcom.2010.04.002.

———. 2011. "Dismantling the Antiracist "Hate Speech" Agenda in Hungary: An Ethno-Rhetorical Analysis." *Text and Talk* 31 (1): 1–19. doi:10.1515/TEXT.2011.001.

———. 2012. "The Cultural Foundations of Denials of Hate Speech in Hungarian Broadcast Talk." *Discourse and Communication* 6 (1): 3–20. doi:10.1177/1750481311427793.

———. 2013. *Speaking Hatefully: Culture, Communication, and Political Action in Hungary.* University Park: Pennsylvania State University Press.

———. 2015. "Hate Speech." In *International Encyclopedia of Language and Social Interaction*, edited by Karen Tracy, 715–725. Hoboken, NJ: Wiley-Blackwell.

Boromisza-Habashi, David, and Russell Parks. 2014. "The Communal Function of Social Interaction on an Online Academic Newsgroup." *Western Journal of Communication* 78 (2): 194–212. doi:10.1080/10570314.2013.813061.

Brown, Alexander, and Adriana Sinclair. 2020. *The Politics of Hate Speech Laws.* London: Routledge.

Burke, Kenneth. 1969. *A Grammar of Motives.* Berkeley: University of California Press.

Carbaugh, Donal. 2017. "Terms for Talk, Take 2: Theorizing Communication through Its Cultural Terms and Practices." In *The Handbook of Communication in Cross-Cultural Perspective*, edited by Donal Carbaugh, 15–28. London: Routledge.

Carbaugh, Donal, and David Boromisza-Habashi. 2015. "Ethnography of Communication." In *International Encyclopedia of Language and Social Interaction*, edited by Karen Tracy, 537–552. Hoboken, NJ: Wiley-Blackwell.

Craig, Robert T. 2018. "For a Practical Discipline." *Journal of Communication* 68 (2): 289–297. doi:10.1093/joc/jqx013.

Ekins, Emily. 2017. *The State of Free Speech and Tolerance in America: Attitudes about Free Speech, Campus Speech, Religious Liberty, and Tolerance of Political Expression.* Washington, DC: Cato Institute.

Fish, Stanley. 1994. *There's No Such Thing as Free Speech . . . and It's a Good Thing Too.* New York, NY: Oxford University Press.

Hall, Bradford "J." 1988–1989. "Norms, Action, and Alignment: A Discursive Perspective." *Research on Language and Social Interaction* 22:23–44. doi:10.1080/08351818809389296.

———. 1991. "An Elaboration of the Structural Possibilities for Engaging in Alignment Episodes. *Communication Monographs* 58:79–100. doi:10.1080/03637759109376215.

Hawkins, Stephen, Daniel Yudkin, Miriam Juan-Torres, and Tim Dixon. 2018. *Hidden Tribes: A Study of America's Polarized Landscape.* New York, NY: More in Common.

Hervik, Peter. 2019. "Ritualized Opposition in Danish Online Practices of Extremist Language and Thought." *International Journal of Communication* 13:3104–3121. https://ijoc.org/index.php/ijoc/article/view/9106/2713.

Lakoff, George. 2002. *Moral Politics: How Liberals and Conservatives Think.* Chicago, IL: University of Chicago Press.

Pál, Gábor. 2006. "Hate Speech: The History of a Hungarian Controversy." In *On Politics: Rhetoric, Discourse, and Concepts*, edited by Márton Szabó, 18–21. Budapest: Institute for Political Science, Hungarian Academy of Sciences.

Philipsen, Gerry. 1989a. "An Ethnographic Approach to Communication Studies." In *Rethinking Communication.* Vol. 2, *Paradigm exemplars*, edited by Brenda Dervin, Lawrence Grossberg, Barbara J. O'Keefe, and Ellen Wartella, 258–268. Newbury Park, CA: SAGE.

———. 1989b. "Speech and the Communal Function in Four Cultures." *International and Intercultural Communication Annual* 13:79–92.

Schmidt, Mária. 1996. "Gyűlöletbeszéd, náci beszéd?" [Hate speech, Nazi speech?]. *Népszabadság*, April 25, 1996, 15.

Udupa, Sahana, and Matti Pohjonen. 2019. "Extreme Speech and Global Digital Cultures." *International Journal of Communication* 13:3049–3067.

Van Maanen, John. 2011. *Tales of the Field: On Writing Ethnography.* Chicago, IL: University of Chicago Press.

2

THE POLITICAL TROLLING INDUSTRY IN DUTERTE'S PHILIPPINES

Everyday Work Arrangements of Disinformation and Extreme Speech

Jonathan Corpus Ong

BEFORE THE TERMS *FAKE NEWS FACTORIES* AND *TROLL ARMIES* entered the global lexicon after the shocking revelations from the Brexit referendum and Donald Trump's election, the Philippines had already elected President Rodrigo Duterte based on a savvy campaign that ran largely on social media. While initially a cost-saving maneuver for an "outsider" candidate lacking national political machinery (BBC Trending 2016), this investment proved efficient as his angry anti-establishment narrative was amplified by the lurid posts of vociferous digital influencers and "clickbaity" headlines of imposter "fake news" websites. A Facebook executive later dubbed the Philippines as "patient zero" in the global misinformation epidemic (Harbath 2018), drawing attention to how social and historical convergences of deep populist sentiment, technological diffusion, and corruption within local creative industries gave rise to disinformation innovations and the proliferation of "extreme speech" in online environments (Pohjonen and Udupa 2017).

In this chapter, I discuss how and why the Philippines became this patient zero. Drawing from a larger project that involved myself and Jason Cabanes conducting interviews and participant observation with the actual authors of fake news and operators of fake accounts on Facebook (Ong and Cabanes 2018), I argue that the illness is much older and deeper than Duterte and his crass campaigners. Through an inquiry into the work arrangements behind the production of digital disinformation, this chapter sheds light onto the ways in which "fake news factories" and "troll armies" grew primarily out of the professional practice of political consultancies from within the Philippines's creative industries. Arguing against "moral panic" explanations of fake news that attribute this phenomenon to dark technological alchemy, foreign interference, or the exceptional evils of current political leaders (e.g., Ressa 2016), this chapter approaches the everyday aspects of deceptive political campaigning, which enlists many complicit strategists, influencers, and fake account operators for professional projects.

This approach is inspired by the literature of production studies in media and communications research that aims to explore, from the bottom-up, workers' "creativity within constraints" in media production processes (Mayer, Caldwell, and Banks 2009). By recording the intentions and experiences of disinformation producers in their own words, we can shed light on their opaque institutional procedures, the social conditions that led them to this kind of work, and the cultural scripts they use to justify this work to others and themselves. Bridging discussions in production studies and digital labor research (e.g., Casilli 2016; Roberts 2016) with the emerging area of disinformation studies, I argue that the chief architects of networked disinformation are themselves architects of precarious labor arrangements in the creative industries that make workers vulnerable to slipping into the digital underground. By exploring the Philippines as a non–Euro-American case of a phenomenon usually discussed in terms of the West, I also seek to contribute a global perspective to the issue of disinformation and digital publics and to provoke broader metatheoretical reflection on social transformations and digital innovations "from the South" (Arora 2019; Srinivasan, Diepeveen, and Karekwaivanane 2019).

Digital Disinformation as Everyday Digital Labor

This chapter contributes to the emerging area of disinformation studies in three significant ways.

The first aim is to reimagine disinformation producers and fake news authors not as exceptional villains but as ordinary digital workers. This approach requires a spirit of openness to understand why people take on political trolling projects in the first place. Considering them as precarious workers rather than evil masterminds helps us think about what safety nets we might set up to prevent them from slipping into the digital underground.

To achieve this perspective, this chapter engages with and is inspired by valuable ethnographic work on the sense-making processes of populist publics, such as Arlie Hochschild's (2016) work with white working-class voters in Louisiana and Hillary Pilkington's (2016) ethnography of members of the English Defence League in the United Kingdom. Their work invites us to dive into the "deep stories" behind populist publics' anger and resentment— that is, the careful construction of good-and-evil narratives that establish people's particular visions of the world. I build on their work in two ways. First, I unpack the ways in which disinformation strategists have strategically weaponized populist publics' anger and resentment with the liberal elite establishment by creating mistrust of establishment institutions and mainstream media while exploiting the vulnerabilities of social media's attention economy. Second, I advance a comparative perspective to the Euro-American literature on global populism through a specific inquiry into the Philippines case. I am inspired by the growing literature on populism in the Philippines, such as with Cleve Arguelles's (2016) and Nicole Curato's (2016) illuminating writings about Duterte's supporters in poor slums in the Philippines. Unlike the working-class Americans who feel left behind as "strangers in their own land" (Hochschild 2016), the Filipino populist public is one that, I argue, is feeling as if they are finally finding a voice through new opportunities for speech in social media. I build on Arguelles's and Curato's work by expanding on their focus on the rationalities of "working-class" or "lower-class" Duterte supporters and paying attention to the precarious middle class and professional elites who are complicit with an illiberal system as long as they gain or maintain power for themselves.

The second aim is to steer the narrative about technology in politics away from fetishizing new technologies toward seeing technologies as part of broader communication environments. Previous studies on digital disinformation devote exclusive attention to the impact of one medium, platform, or technology on political outcomes—for example, doing one whole study on Twitter bots (Woolley and Guilbeault 2017) and their impact on elections. Instead of panicked speculation about the powerful effects of a particular new technological platform on gullible masses, I zoomed out to consider digital weapons as part of a broader artillery for mass deception. This big-picture approach, which follows the spirit of frameworks for polymedia (Madianou and Miller 2013) and media-as-environment (Silverstone 2007), enables better understanding of how architects of disinformation design campaigns that travel across new and traditional media platforms. This approach is also consistent with disinformation studies research that emphasizes the ways in which techniques of trolling (Phillips 2015) and "attention hacking" (Marwick and Lewis 2017) fundamentally target the vulnerabilities of mainstream media using strategies of influence and manipulation coming from social media. It also connects with important research tracing historical precedents of digital disinformation and deceptive campaigning, such as how the phenomenon of "serial calling" in Kenyan and Ugandan radio talk shows predates contemporary political bloggers or social media influencers (Brisset-Foucault 2018; Gagliardone 2015).

The third aim is to shift the discussion from content regulation to process regulation. Intervention initiatives in the Philippines, such as those by *Rappler*—a key leader at the front lines of this worthy fight—involve lobbying Facebook and Google to flag fake or offensive content or to blacklist fake news sites. This alternative approach is to identify the systems and industries that normalize and incentivize fake news production. By shining a spotlight on the organizations and industries that are culpable and complicit in the production of fake news, we can then demand greater transparency and accountability from them with regard to their work arrangements and output. I am inspired by studies in digital labor that explore precarity in the work arrangements of global outsourcing (Casilli 2016; Roberts 2016). These studies highlight the interrelationship of the production contexts with the (problematic, racist, misogynistic) media content that persists on digital platforms.

A key inspiration is Pohjonen and Udupa's (2017) concept of "extreme speech." Their concept rejects tendencies in current disinformation debates to apply, from the top down, the legal frame of "hate speech" and its "assumptions around politeness, civility, or abuse as universal features of communication with little cultural variation" (Pohjonen and Udupa 2017, 1174). As an intervention to binary classifications between hate speech and acceptable speech, they propose that media and policy research draw from anthropological approaches that are sensitive to emic categories and the "complex politics involved in labeling certain kinds of speech as one thing or another" (1187). This insight is helpful in this study as I explore how deceptive political campaigning and professionalized online trolling exist within the same continuum as normalized corporate marketing practices of click-army mobilization and influencer management. But although this form of extreme speech has roots in corporate marketing, the key difference is the way in which angry narratives of mistrust of mainstream media and establishment institutions are systematically constructed and circulated for the benefit of particular political leaders (see Cabanes, Anderson, and Ong 2019).

Methods

The project from which this chapter draws consisted of one year of collaborative research with Jason Cabanes, consisting of in-depth interviews with twenty disinformation architects, at both managerial and staff levels, and participant observation of Facebook pages and communities and Twitter accounts used by our informants (see Ong and Cabanes 2018). Through our personal contacts in the advertising and public relations (PR) industry, we met the strategists behind corporate and political campaigns. We explained our research interest in digital labor, particularly in how digital political operations work in the Philippines. From our initial interviews with managers, we used snowball sampling to recruit lower-level workers to translate strategy to the language of the street.

Interviews

Table 2.1 presents the different categories of operators we interviewed and their roles in digital disinformation campaigns. A digital campaign team is often led by a senior professional with a background in advertising and the PR industry. Based on the campaign objective, the strategist then assembles digital influencers and fake account operators to carry out specific communication objectives.

The professional backgrounds of chief disinformation architects say a lot about the roots of digital political operations in the advertising and PR industry. These strategists maintain day jobs as account or creative directors for what is known in the industry as "boutique agencies," local (rather than multinational) advertising and PR firms. They apply their expertise in social media content management for consumer household brands to political clients.

Chief architects work closely with anonymous digital influencers, who each maintain multiple social media accounts with large numbers of followers (between fifty thousand and two million). These popular pages carry distinctive branding and have regular updates of humorous, inspirational, or pop culture or celebrity-oriented content. During campaign periods, these pages are "activated" and can be seen promoting hashtags and memes favorable to their clients, who are often corporate brands or celebrities but occasionally political clients. Page owners remain anonymous to their followers, and there is no disclosure of paid content to their followers. These anonymous digital influencers maintain day jobs as computer programmers, search engine optimization specialists, or marketing and finance staff.

Meanwhile, what we call "community-level fake-account operators" are usually new college graduates, members of politicians' administrative staff, and online freelance workers who juggle various clients commissioning piecemeal digital work. We learned that many of these operators also work from provinces outside Metro Manila.

Table 2.1 Respondent list (*N* = 20)

Category	*n*	Roles	Professional background
Elite advertising and PR strategists as chief disinformation architects	6	Authors communication plans, manages messaging schedules, hires influencers and fake account operators, operates several fake accounts themselves, manages campaign budget, reports to politician	Main job: advertising and PR account director or creative director, social media consultant Prior roles: broadcast or newspaper journalist
Aspirational middle-class digital workers as anonymous digital influencers	5	Operates one or more anonymous accounts that command >50,000 followers across Twitter and Facebook; subcontracted by advertising and PR strategist; often paid based on reach and engagement they produce for a campaign	Main job: computer programmer; search engine optimization specialist; online freelance worker Prior roles: broadcast or newspaper journalist, marketing or finance staff, call center employee
Precarious middle-class workers as community-level fake account operators	9	Subcontracted by advertising and PR strategist or politician's chief of staff; assigned to amplify influencers' messages by reposting and retweeting to create "illusions of engagement"	Main job: government staff, social media content producer, online freelance worker Prior jobs: call center employee, recent graduate

Before the interview, we briefed our informants that our approach was empathetic, as we did not intend to cast moral judgments on the participants' actions or write investigative journalism to "expose" troll account operations and name and shame the politicians involved in these activities. Conscious of the sensitive nature of labels such as "troll," especially in our initial recruitment of participants, we only used words such as *trolling* and *fake accounts* once we had established rapport during the course of the interviews or our respondents themselves opened up about trolling work.

One ethnographic surprise from our interviews was discovering that many fake-account operators and anonymous digital influencers are gay and transgender people. We learned from informal chats with them how they switch between "male" and "female" voices when operating their multiple fake accounts and use snarky Filipino gay humor to poke fun at their online rivals. Strategically using affordances for anonymity in social media while maximizing opportunities for monetizing different identities, they make use of skills at "gender code-switching" to effectively deploy the appropriate digital persona to suit the objectives of a campaign. Although some gay and transgender people we met refused to be formally interviewed—presumably, to avoid the risk of their identities being "exposed"—we gained some insight into the specific conditions of "purple collar labor" (David 2015), as it applies to the digital disinformation industry. Gay and transgender people are often assumed to have mastery of the latest pop culture references, exuberant image management skills (e.g., from their dating profiles to message board memberships), and fan mobilization discipline (e.g., from Miss Universe online voting techniques) that guarantee vivaciousness and "spirit" for the social media accounts and campaigns they handle.

Online Participant Observation

We supplemented our interviews with participant observation of online communities. We observed more than twenty publicly accessible Facebook groups and pages and Twitter accounts supporting various political players at both national and local levels. We made sure to include explicitly pro- and anti-Duterte groups and pages without explicit expression of candidates or political parties they support but that claim to curate "social media news."

Through participant observation, we examined the content and visual aesthetics of posts crafted by influencers and "followed the trail" of how those posts travel across Facebook groups and were retweeted across platforms. We observed the tone and speech styles of replies and comments to the original posts. This allowed us to better understand how digital disinformation campaigns were translated as specific posts or memes. During our fieldwork, some participants showed us fake accounts they operated and even shared their passwords to those accounts. This view provided us with an opportunity to compare and contrast what our participants said in the context of the interview with what they actually did in the online profiles they created, as we were able to check the digital traces they left in their Facebook histories.

Ethics

Following the protocols of university research ethics, we told our informants that we would disidentify information that could be traced to individuals. This is why some details about the digital disinformation campaigns that our participants wanted to keep confidential are occasionally discussed in more general terms.

Networked Disinformation Projects and Moral Justifications

The common image of people involved in doing so-called paid troll work—as is the case for most digital laborers in the Global South—is that of the exploited worker in a "digital sweatshop" or a "click farm." They are thought to spend their days executing monotonous and clerical tasks within highly regimented and exploitative arrangements. In the specific context of digital work for politics, for instance, Rongbin Han (2015) narrates the precarious labor arrangements that buttress China's "fifty-cent army," the state-sponsored workers who are paid to act like "spontaneous grassroots support[ers]" on online discussion boards. Following strict pay structures that emphasize quantity over quality of posts and often inflexible instructions in posting content, Han's insightful research demonstrates how rigid work arrangements lead to easy identification of posts authored by fifty-cent workers.

In contrast to the Chinese case, what I found in the Philippines is that digital political operations are more diversified, with operators working with clients across the political spectrum and occupying a hierarchy of roles. I define "networked disinformation" as the distributed labor of political deception to a set of loosely organized workers. This convenient structure provides a way for people to displace responsibility and project the stigma associated with the label of "paid troll" (*bayaran*) onto other people.

The first key feature of networked disinformation is its project-based nature, for which workers are employed on short-term contracts with their clients, who measure the delivery of output along specific industry criteria and metrics. These jobs are often taken on as added or sideline work, as people maintain day jobs in advertising, online marketing, or serving as politicians' administrative staff. As distributed labor, different workers are enlisted to achieve discrete objectives while having only loose and informal connections with their fellow workers. Often disinformation workers do not share the same office and are not always clear how certain campaigns relate to the overall objectives of political clients.

The second key feature of networked disinformation is how it is rooted in the general principles and strategies of advertising and PR. We discovered in our project that networked disinformation for Filipino politicians are hyperextensions of corporate marketing practices, in which techniques of "attention hacking" (Marwick and Lewis 2017) were first tested in advertising and PR campaigns for soft drinks or shampoo brands and then transposed to political marketing. Both campaign principles and work structures follow models developed in advertising and PR, and they are applied to campaigns for politicians across the political spectrum, beyond just Duterte's party, contrary to misleading reports such as in an Oxford Internet Institute study (Bradshaw and Howard 2017).

Because of the project-based and loosely organized nature of disinformation activity, workers within and across teams engaged in constant one-upmanship, which affected the quality of the disinformation work that they did. Although campaigns were designed at the top with a certain objective, distributing the execution of this objective among workers in competition with each other led to unpredictable consequences. Because disinformation producers are incentivized by strategists in a competitive matrix of reach and engagement, some end up producing racist or misogynist content that was not agreed upon at the beginning. For instance, one particularly misogynistic meme aiming to humiliate a journalist went viral even though the original intent was simply to discredit the news agency to which she belonged.

This aspect brings us to the third key feature of networked disinformation: its project-based and distributed labor arrangement enables moral displacement and denial. Among all the workers we met during the project, nobody self-identified as a "troll" or a producer of fake news; these labels were always projected to either imagined others of pure villainy and total power or "real" supporters or political fans. Real fans with enthusiastic zeal for their candidate are said to be more likely to be invested to make personalized attacks and hateful expressions in online arguments compared with professional, but casual, disinformation architects like them. Disinformation producers often engage in moral justifications that their work is not actually trolling or fake news. They mobilize various denial strategies that allow them to displace moral responsibility, often by citing that political consultancy is only one project or sideline that does not define their whole identity. The project-based nature of disinformation work makes moral displacement easier, given the casual, short-term nature of the arrangement, which downplays commitment and responsibility to the broader sphere of political practice.

Moral justifications differ across the three levels of disinformation architects. At the top level, strategists are more likely to express discourses of gamification and fictionalization to justify their work. They draw from cultural scripts based on Western entertainment ("It's like being Olivia Pope of *Scandal*") to video games ("It's game over when you're found out") to fictionalize the dangerous consequences of their actions and block feelings of real involvement. They even express a certain "thrill" to breaking the rules of the game, similar to experiences of "fun" in breaking taboos or generating humor in politics (Hervik 2019; Tuters and Hagen, chap. 5; Udupa, chap. 6).

During our fieldwork, for example, I met 29-year-old digital strategist Rachel, who shared, "I'd actually like to phase out our company practice of paying out journalists to seed or delete news because they can be entitled or unscrupulous. The reason why I'm more passionate and committed about online work is because I don't like the politics in journalism." In this quote, it is interesting how corruption in mainstream media is used as a moral justification to dispose of institutionalized practice by replacing it with another version—equally lacking in scruples and ultimately benefiting themselves. By expressing statements that normalize or even exaggerate evil or corruption in existing public institutions, these ambitious workers imagine themselves as self-styled agents of positive change.

At the middle level, influencers are more likely to express discourses of normalization to justify disinformation production. They cite how they do exactly the same work to promote corporate brands and entertainment products or even volunteer their digital expertise for free to support fandoms such as for celebrities or beauty pageant titlists. At the bottom level, community-level fake account operators have primarily financial or material reasons to justify their work; they take this on as added work and are often persuaded by others to take this on for extra cash. Unlike lead strategists and some digital influencers, who expressed "fun" and "thrill" in designing new forms of extreme speech for political clients, few lower-level workers cited ever experiencing fun while doing political troll projects. Many lower-level workers cited being pressured, intimidated, and harassed in their job, including by their demanding bosses and clients. To me, this unevenness in experiences of fun in transgressive digital production highlights the precarity of those workers in exploitative and emotionally draining race-to-the-bottom work arrangements (Cassili 2016; Roberts 2016).

My colleague and I were struck to learn how disinformation workers create implicit rules for themselves and their colleagues to help them manage the social pressures and moral burdens. Workers drew their own moral boundaries ("In a flame war, I only poke fun at people's bad grammar, but I will never slut shame") and created support systems ("If I don't really support the politician hiring me, then I pass on the account to someone I know who's a real fan") and even sabotaged the authenticity of their own avatar (see Ong and Cabanes 2018 for an ethnographic portrait of a politician's staff member who was "peer-pressured" to create a fake account in the name of "team spirit" during the election campaign season).

In the following sections, I discuss the three kinds of disinformation producers and identify their motivations and backgrounds, reflecting on how they become complicit in the work of political deception.

Advertising and PR Strategists as Chief Disinformation Architects

At the top level of networked disinformation campaigns are advertising and PR executives who take on the role of high-level political operators. Usually they occupy leadership roles in boutique agencies and handle portfolios of corporate brands while maintaining consultancies with political clients on the side. They transpose tried-and-tested industry techniques for reputation building and spin to networked disinformation campaigns. With a record of launching Facebook community pages and achieving worldwide trending status for digital campaigns for household brands, telecommunications companies, or celebrities, many executives saw political consultancy as a new challenge for them to apply their skills and leverage their networks.

The chief architects we met often complained that they are undervalued at times by politicians and their primary handlers. But again, they also saw tremendous opportunity in the reluctance of traditional political campaigners toward engaging digital media. This dynamic allows digital strategists to establish themselves as the de facto pioneers in a platform that they know will come to dominate the future of political propaganda. As one strategist told us, "The Philippines does not realize that it is sitting on a stockpile of digital weapons," as she recognizes that Filipino digital workers are highly entrepreneurial and resourceful, whether they be the computer hackers who infamously coded the Y2K virus or the platform freelance workers who diligently work with their global clientele.

Chief architects also see digital disinformation as an opportunity to disrupt existing social hierarchies and challenge established power players in political campaigning.

It is evident that some strategists also relish the thrill and adrenaline rush they get from their risky projects. The 40-year-old executive Dom told us, "Maybe if I had this power ten years ago, I would have abused it and I could toy with you guys (*kung ano-ano gagawin ko sa inyo*). But now I'm in my forties, it's a good thing I have a little maturity on how to use it. But what I'm really saying is we can fuck your digital life without you even knowing about it." In that moment, I shuddered to imagine the fates of powerless folks who had crossed this woman.

Anonymous Digital Influencers

At the middle level of the hierarchy of networked disinformation are digital influencers. It is important to distinguish between key opinion leaders, such as celebrities and political pundits who maintain public personas, and anonymous microinfluencers who work more clandestine political operations. In our research, we focused on the anonymous digital influencers, who usually operate one or more anonymous accounts (e.g., comedy or inspirational pages on Twitter or Facebook) that entertain their followers with their specific brand of hilarity or commentary while occasionally slipping paid content into their feed. These influencers harness their astute understanding of the public's pop culture tastes, political sentiments, and social media behaviors to become expert attention hackers.

These digital influencers expect between fifty thousand and two million followers to share and like their messages with the aim of gaming Twitter trending rankings and creating viral posts on Facebook so as to influence mainstream media coverage. Translating the campaign plans of the advertising and PR strategists, they use snark, humor, or inspirational messaging consistent with the social media personas they operate to author posts that are favorable or unfavorable to particular politicians and are often anchored by a hashtag agreed upon between them and the chief architects.

A few digital influencers take on the role of being second-level subcontractors. As sub-subcontractors, they work as intermediaries between chief architects and their fellow digital influencers to whom they redistribute disinformation work.

All the digital influencers we met perform this role on a part-time, per-project basis. Many of them have day jobs in IT, corporate marketing, and other sideline work such as online community management for celebrities' fan clubs. For the most part, this kind of work has the trappings of the "precarious middle-class" lifestyle common to most kinds of freelance digital work in the Philippines. Central to this role is the enjoyment of being in an aspirational work environment. They recall with pride how they do disinformation work while booked overnight in a five-star hotel suite or in a mansion in a gated village. They also get excited by the material and symbolic rewards that chief architects promise to the best performing digital worker in the team, which includes giving away the latest iPhone model or arranging a meet-and-greet with a top-level celebrity.

As part of the precarious middle class, anonymous digital influencers are driven by financial motivations in their disinformation work. They have previously endured less stable and financially and socially rewarding jobs in the creative and digital industries and see influencer work as giving them more freedom, including when choosing clients. Curiously, we found that there is usually alignment between digital influencers and the political clients they serve—not in terms of ideology or issues but in terms of fan admiration. Some influencers hired by political clients they do not like would subcontract work to a fellow influencer they know who is a "real fan" of that politician.

In our fieldwork, we met several digital influencers who are transgender women who operate approximately six anonymous accounts with diverse "brands" and different gender and sexual identities. We observed "gender code-switching" (David 2015) in how they chose to translate campaign objectives in various ways by using male, female, and gay "voices" in these different fake accounts. We observed how some male accounts often aimed for positive campaigns, given the inspirational nature of their content; female "bikini troll" accounts aim to use overt sexuality to gain followers and distribute deceptive content to them; and gay male accounts use snarky gay humor to poke fun at politicians' actions for negative campaigning. These influencers maximize monetization opportunities of the different identities they manage by creating gendered performances of political trolling for their clients.

Community-level Fake-Account Operators

At the lowest level of the networked disinformation hierarchy are community-level fake-account operators. These workers are tasked with following what I call "script-based disinformation work," which is often posting the strategists' previously designed written and/or visual content (memes) on a predetermined schedule and affirming and amplifying strategists' and influencers' key messages through likes and shares. Community-level fake-account operators are tasked with posting a prescribed number of posts or comments on Facebook community groups, news sites, or rival politicians' pages each day. By actively posting content from generic greetings to political messages within Facebook community groups, they are often responsible for maintaining activity and initiating bandwagon effects that would drive real grassroots supporters to actually come out and visualize their support for politicians.

The fact-account operators usually post positive messages of support for the politician and note their agreement with favorable news articles. At other times, they can initiate quarrels with supporters of rival politicians. They use ad hominem attacks, making fun of other people's bad grammar, often as a way of shutting down an opponent's argument. They mention that their ultimate failure as fake-account operators on Facebook is when they are called out as a fake account ("That's game over! That usually shuts us up.").

Labor arrangements differ for this kind of low-level troll work. Most respondents in our study were fake-account operators working within a politician's own administrative staff. These workers are usually junior-level employees tasked with "helping" a political campaign, and they usually begrudge the fact that there is no additional pay for this kind of publicly derided work that they did not originally sign up for. Other fake-account operators whom we have yet to formally interview face-to-face are freelancers who are paid on a per-day basis to achieve a set number of posts or comments or office-based fake-account operators who work in a "call center" type of arrangement—some operate in provinces that are the bailiwicks of politicians.

Community-level fake-account operators are driven primarily by financial motivations. We found out that some of their fake accounts on Facebook or Twitter had prior histories before their political trolling work. Some fake accounts had been used when they were once part of pyramid schemes. These "networking" schemes required them to visually display groups of friends; fake accounts were one way to artificially manufacture group support. Many fake account operators appear to be workers who have previously tried many other risky enterprises as a means to achieve financial stability.

From Content Regulation to Process Regulation

By discussing disinformation workers' social and financial motivations and moral justifications, this chapter ultimately aims for better understanding of the vulnerabilities in the political and media ecosystems that make political trolling a sideline job that is hard to refuse in the Philippine context. Digital disinformation is not an all-new Duterte novelty; it is the culmination of the most unscrupulous trends in the Philippines's media and political culture. Many of the disinformation techniques were tried and tested in marketing shampoos and soft drinks before hyperextending them to marketing politicians and their ideas. The difference is that seeded hashtags that aim for historical revisionism or drowning out dissent pose greater and unfathomable dangers to political futures. Within the broader context of Duterte's drug war and authoritarian populism, digital disinformation has volatile consequences in amplifying the culture of violence and impunity experienced in the streets. Although disinformation producers imagine themselves as ordinary entrepreneurs within an inherently corrupt media ecosystem, they neglect to say that they consistently circulate anti-establishment narratives that fuel not only mistrust in "elite" political leaders but also, crucially, in mainstream media. This narrative works to their advantage, as digital disinformation workers see themselves as "change-making" entrants competing with legal media to best represent the voice of "the people" (see also Chakravartty and Roy 2017).

While I emphasize the significant impact of the structural and institutional contexts in which disinformation workers are embedded, it is important not to absolve these workers of their moral responsibility. As my colleague and I discovered (Ong and Cabanes 2018), these individuals have capacities for agency in ways they translate, execute, or even resist in the production process. The moral failure is their complicity and collusion with evil infrastructures in the desire to gain political, social, and financial benefits. Although the ethnographically inspired approach of this study begins with an imperative for empathy to understand the conditions that push people to engage in precarious disinformation work, I assign great culpability to the chief architects, who are at the top level of influence and who benefit the most from the architecture they have built.

The production studies approach taken in this chapter also adds to current public debate about what the "right" interventions are for digital disinformation. In the Philippines, most responses from journalists and civil society have focused on fact-checking initiatives. Journalists have enlisted the support of the influential Catholic Bishops Council of the Philippines in circulating a blacklist of "fake news websites" (almost all associated with Duterte). Embattled journalists targeted by Duterte's administration have also received some support from Facebook in awarding them contracts as third-party fact-checkers who flag content to downvote (rather than completely censor) within the algorithm. Although these initiatives are well meaning, I am cautious because these approaches are not inclusive and comprehensive enough—they aim to catch content when it has already been produced and to "oxidize" this bad content through repetition (Phillips 2018), which might even contribute to further polarization (Wardle and Derakshan 2017).

A production studies approach demands spotlighting mechanisms that can prevent this kind of work from being produced in the first place. This approach means inviting open discussion about self-regulation in the media and creative industries, which have treated disinformation work as an open industry secret, and encouraging transparency in political marketing and advertising, particularly in the context of elections. The ethnographic material gathered in this chapter is meant to inform collaborations with civil society actors, election lobby groups, and lawyers to encourage greater transparency and accountability in digital campaigning. I argue that it is important for politicians in the Philippines to disclose their digital campaigns' content and strategy, which escape public visibility given platform affordances of microtargeting. This matter is of urgent concern because the May 2019 midterm elections witnessed a proliferation of disinformation innovations and further expansion of the Philippine political trolling industry (Ong, Tapsell, and Curato 2019). This issue has global repercussions, as other democracies such as India (Sharma 2019) similarly struggle to engage with innovations brought on by big tech and their historical antecedents in the unregulated practice of political consultancies.

References

Arguelles, Cleve. 2016. "Grounding Populism: Perspective from the Populist Publics." MA thesis, Central European University, Budapest.

Arora, Payal. 2019. "Politics of Algorithms, Indian Citizenship, and the Colonial Legacy." In *Global Digital Cultures: Perspectives from South Asia*, edited by Aswin Punathambekar and Sriram Mohan, 37–52. Ann Arbor: University of Michigan Press.

Banks, Miranda J., Vicki Mayer, and Bridget Conor. 2015. *Production Studies, The Sequel!: Cultural Studies of Media Industries*. New York: Routledge.

BBC Trending. 2016. "Trolls and Triumph: A Digital Battle in the Philippines." December 7. https://www.bbc.com/news/blogs-trending-38173842.

Bradshaw, Samantha, and Philip Howard. 2017. *Troops, Trolls, and Troublemakers: A Global Inventory of Organized Social Media Manipulation*. Computational Propaganda Research Project. Oxford: Oxford University. https://demtech.oii.ox.ac.uk/wp-content/uploads/sites/89/2017/07/Troops-Trolls-and-Troublemakers.pdf.

Brisset-Foucault, Florence. 2018. "Serial Callers: Communication Technologies and Political Personhood in Contemporary Uganda." *Ethnos* 83 (2): 255–273.

Cabanes, Jason, C. W. Anderson, and Jonathan Corpus Ong. 2019. "Fake News and Scandal." In *The Routledge Companion to Media and Scandal*, edited by Howard Tumber and Silvio Waisbord: 115–125. London: Routledge.

Casilli, Antonio. 2016. "Digital Labor Studies Go Global: Toward a Digital Decolonial Turn." *International Journal of Communication* 11:3934–3954.

Chakravartty, Paula, and Srirupa Roy. 2017. "Mediatized Populisms: Inter-Asian Lineages." *International Journal of Communication* 11:4073–4092.

Curato, Nicole. 2016. "Politics of Anxiety, Politics of Hope: Penal Populism and Duterte's Rise to Power." *Journal of Current Southeast Asian Affairs* 35 (3): 91–109.

David, Emmanuel. 2015. "Purple Collar Labor: Transgender Workers and Queer Value at Global Call Centers in the Philippines." *Gender and Society* 29 (2): 169–194.

Gagliardone, Iginio. 2015. "'Can You Hear Me?' Mobile-Radio Interactions and Governance in Africa." *New Media and Society* 18 (9): 2080–2095.

Han, Rongbin. 2015. "Manufacturing Consent in Cyberspace: China's 'Fifty-Cent Army.'" *Journal of Current Chinese Affairs* 44 (2): 105–134.

Harbarth, Katie. 2018. "Protecting Election Integrity on Facebook." Presented at 360/OS, Berlin, Germany. https://www.youtube.com/watch?time_continue=76&v=dJ1wcpsOtS4.

Hervik, Peter. 2019. "Ritualized Opposition in Danish Online Practices of Extremist Language and Thought." *International Journal of Communication* 13:3104–3121.

Hochschild, Arlie. 2016. *Strangers in Their Own Land*. New York: New Press.

Madianou, Mirca, and Daniel Miller. 2013. *Migration and Media: Transnational Families and Polymedia*. New York: Routledge.

Marwick, Alice, and Rebecca Lewis. 2017. *Media Manipulation and Disinformation Online*. New York: Data and Society Research Institute. https://datasociety.net/pubs/oh/DataAndSociety_MediaManipulationAndDisinformationOnline.pdf.

Ong, Jonathan Corpus, and Jason Cabanes. 2018. "Architects of Networked Disinformation: Behind the Scenes of Troll Accounts and Fake News Production in the Philippines." Newton Tech4Dev Network. https://newtontechfordev.com/wp-content/uploads/2018/02/ARCHITECTS-OF-NETWORKED-DISINFORMATION-FULL-REPORT.pdf.

Ong, Jonathan Corpus, Ross Tapsell, and Nicole Curato. 2019. "Social Media in the 2019 Philippine Midterm Election: A Public Report of the Digital Disinformation Tracker Project." New Mandala. https://www.newmandala.org/wp-content/uploads/2019/08/Digital-Disinformation-2019-Midterms.pdf.

Phillips, Whitney. 2015. *This Is Why We Can't Have Nice Things: Mapping the Relationship between Online Trolling and Mainstream Culture*. London: MIT Press.

———. 2018. "The Oxygen of Amplification: Better Practices for Reporting on Extremists, Antagonists, and Manipulators." Data and Society Research Institute. https://datasociety.net/output/oxygen-of-amplification/.

Pilkington, Hilary. 2016. *Loud and Proud: Passion and Politics in the English Defence League*. Manchester: Manchester University Press.

Pohjonen, Matti, and Sahana Udupa. 2017. "Extreme Speech Online: An Anthropological Critique of Hate Speech Debates." *International Journal of Communication* 11:1173–1191.

Ressa, Maria. 2016. "Propaganda War: Weaponizing the Internet." *Rappler*, October 3. https://www.rappler.com /nation/148007-propaganda-war-weaponizing-internet.

Roberts, Sarah. 2016. "Commercial Content Moderation: Digital Laborer's Dirty Work." In *The Intersectional Internet: Race, Sex, Class and Culture Online*, edited by Safiya Umoja Noble and Brendesha M. Tynes, 147–160. New York: Peter Lang.

Sharma, Amogh Dhar. 2019. "How Far Can Political Parties in India Be Made Accountable for Their Digital Propaganda." *Scroll.in*, May 10. https://scroll.in/article/921340/how-far-can-political-parties-in-india-be -made-accountable-for-their-digital-propaganda.

Silverstone, Roger. 2007. *Media and Morality: On the Rise of Mediapolis*. Cambridge: Polity.

Srinivasan, Sharath, Stephanie Diepeveen, and George Karekwaivanane. 2019. "Rethinking Publics in Africa in a Digital Age." *Journal of Eastern African Studies* 13 (1): 2–17.

Wardle, Claire, and Hossein Derakhshan. 2017. "Information Disorder: Toward an Interdisciplinary Framework for Research and Policy Making." Council of Europe Report DGI(2017)09. https://rm.coe.int/information -disorder-toward-an-interdisciplinary-framework-for-researc/168076277c.

Woolley, Samuel C. and Douglas R. Guilbeault. 2017. "Computational Propaganda in the United States of America: Manufacturing Consensus Online." Working Paper 2017.5, Project on Computational Propaganda. Oxford: Oxford University.

3

IT'S INCIVILITY, NOT HATE SPEECH

Application of Laclau and Mouffe's Discourse Theory to Analysis of Nonanthropocentric Agency

David Katiambo

ADOPTION OF DIGITAL COMMUNICATION WAS INITIALLY VIEWED AS an opportunity to cement democracy in Africa. However, this optimism of an internet-enriched democracy is contradicted by fear of it inspiring the spread of hate speech and other forms of exclusionary ideologies symptomatic of what Ogude (2002, 205) called the reemergence of the ethnocratic state, which undermines any real desire for nationhood. Violent online speech has reinvigorated calls for a return to control of freedom of expression through legal and political philosophies reminiscent of Cold War–era politics. The events surrounding two bloggers—one has been missing for more than six years and another humorously pleaded guilty for spreading hate on Facebook after he said the president's Kikuyu ethnic group should be confined to certain parts of the country illustrate the contradictions of this form of internet-enriched politics in Kenya.

In September 2013, a prominent Kenyan blogger was forced to disappear while in Nairobi or thereabouts (see Some 2015). It remains unconfirmed whether or not Dickson Bogonko Bosire, missing editor of the once-controversial blog *Jackal News*, is a victim of the government's extrajudicial killings; however, the blogger's disappearance can be attributed to the extreme content on his blog. The other blogger was a university student who attracted public attention after he pleaded guilty to abusing the head of state. Alan Wadi Okengo, alias Lieutenant Wadi, was jailed for two years after he pleaded guilty to insulting President Uhuru Kenyatta in a Facebook post (BBC News 2015; Karanja 2015; Munguti 2015). Okengo's conviction led to his appearing in both the local and international press, leading the blogger to trend online as #AlanWadiJailed (Alai 2015). The blogger was freed after he appealed the ruling, claiming he was of unsound mind when he pleaded (see *Alan Wadi Okengo v. Republic, Criminal Appeal No. 1 of 2015*, High Court of Kenya). Rather than fearing conviction, bloggers like Okengo perform publicity stunts from the court's dramaturgical spaces by engaging in "celebrification through humor"—that is, gaining of celebrity status through transgressive performances (Penfold-Mounce 2010, 1).

Bosire's disappearance and Okengo's self-conviction summarize the situation of "extreme speech" in Kenya: although the regime has come up with stringent ways of controlling "hate speech," from strict laws to extrajudicial responses, people have not relented. In addition, the two cases illustrate how regimes can broaden definitions of hate speech to include what Iginio Gagliardone and colleagues (2015, 10) warn is normal political practice, such as insults directed at those in power.

Nevertheless, the search for alternative definitions of extreme speech should not camouflage how hate speech, a category of extreme speech, can ignite violence. In Kenya, the current hate speech and violence discourses can be traced to the contested 2007 presidential election that was followed by a near civil war, leading to 1,300 deaths, internal displacement of more than 350,000 people, and massive property destruction (Republic of Kenya 2008, 290). The policy debates that followed the postelection violence underscore the risk of social media as a channel of hate speech. This risk can be seen in legislation aimed at controlling what the government claims is online hate (e.g., Kenya's National Cohesion and Integration Act, 2008; Information and Communications [Amendment] Act [KICA], 2013; and Computer Misuse and Cybercrimes Act, 2018).

Despite the concept of hate speech dominating regulatory debates, if viewed through the lens of "agonistic democracy" (Mouffe 2005), some forms of online vitriol are political practices by the "constitutive outsider" resisting existing subordination. Consequently, we can argue that incivility in social media is part of the struggle against hegemony—the regime's efforts to reinforce the dominant position of hate speech—through what Ernesto Laclau (2014, 56) would call, from an ontological perspective, metonymic relations of combination and metaphoric relations of substitution used to name the unnamable. That is to say, the regime is making incivility a metonym of hate speech, a process that can eventually metaphorize the relationship between the two and conceal its "metonymical origins." If the regime succeeds in this metaphorization, the hegemonic substitution of incivility with hate speech creates a catachresis as hate speech becomes a figural term without a literal meaning (see Laclau 2005, 71). This means the polysemy of extreme speech is removed when incivility becomes known as hate speech, blocking us from ever knowing its alternative possibilities.

This chapter avoids the binary division of speech into what is acceptable and what is not (see Pohjonen, and Udupa 2017, 1174). As an alternative to the regime's preference of *hate speech*, the term *incivility* is used to "avoid predetermining the effects of online volatile speech as vilifying, polarizing, or lethal" (1174). Through the concept of incivility, the common association of extreme speech with hatred is avoided. Instead, extreme speech is located in the carnivalesque tradition inspired by Mikhail Bakhtin (1981). Consequently, incivility is taken as part of "normal" political struggles, albeit "through play, ridicule, and seeming obscenity" (Bakhtin 1981, 273).

This chapter dissuades moralistic and antipolitical elimination of conflict from politics by viewing politics as permanently conflictual (see Mouffe 1992, 2005), with social media technologies expanding spaces for practice of the conflictual politics. In addition, it uses Ernesto Laclau and Chantal Mouffe's (1985) discourse theory to analyze how the agency of digital media permits incivility. The metaphor of ventriloquism (Cooren 2010, 131) is used to enrich Laclau and Mouffe's discourse theory, solving its methodological deficits. Through ventriloquism, we can discover how technological artifacts "engage in politics" by exercising force, coercing obedience, and suppressing deviance (see Cooren 2015; Pfaffenberger 1992). That is to say, through ventriloquism, technologies enable the regime to call extreme speech "hate speech" while supporting people spreading extreme speech—the government is the ventriloquist puppeteering the people and vice versa.

The following section draws parallels between Bakhtin's concept of the "carnivalesque" and *utani* (joking) relationships. The carnival extends back to the medieval period, whereas utani relationships are a recent phenomenon, but both can be seen as events that temporarily invert hierarchy through disorder.

From the Carnivalesque to Utani or "Mutual Zombification"?

Incivility in social media takes a socially sanctioned meaning, far from hate speech, when interpreted through appropriate cultural lenses—it can be equated to the practice of joking that allows tough criticism without labeling the jokes as hatred (Gueye 2011, 29). This category of speaking "truth to power" resembles Bakhtin's notion of the carnivalesque, the unrestricted ritual spectacles that create an "atmosphere of freedom, frankness and familiarity" (1984, 15–16). Despite being separated by place and the passage of time, the transgressive qualities of social media are reminiscent of Bakhtin's characterization of a disorderly but joyful reversal of hierarchy. However, to guard against the overutilization of utopian radicalism of the carnivalesque, it is noted that the carnival can also be coopted by dominant forces. As Terry Eagleton stated, a carnival is merely a licensed affair, "a permissible rupture of hegemony, a contained popular blow-off and disturbing and relatively ineffectual as a revolutionary work of art . . . there is no slander in an allowed fool" (1981, 148). This means that carnivals can have double meanings: on one hand, they can be a ritual equivalent to the folk culture of laughter, which plays a transformative role; on the other hand, they can be a snare to perpetuate and maintain dominance.

Africa has significant continuities with the premodern carnivalesque. In particular, joking relationships (*utani*) are part of the repertoire of subversive rituals in Africa. I use the Kiswahili term *utani* to describe the socially sanctioned meaning of incivility in social media because the language is the most widely spoken in eastern Africa, and the word has been used previously by anthropologists studying joking relationships (see Radcliffe-Brown 1940; Christensen 1963; Beidelman 1966). Although much has been published on utani as institutional joking, little if any work has been done to interpret extreme speech as a socially sanctioned joking relationship between the people and those in power.

Utani can resolve conflict by teaching people to take no offense at insults, by tolerating permitted or mutual disrespect (Radcliffe-Brown 1940, 198). Indeed, as Heald (1990, 382) argues, utani relationships originate from a prior state of hostility. Among the Gisu of eastern Uganda and their Bukusu cousins of western Kenya, for example, the utani practice (also known as *bukulo*) was marked by an exaggerated element of hostility between nonkin as a mechanism for ending feuds (see Heald 1990, 377). Through joking relationships, groups with previously weak kinship establish friendly antagonism, a fraternization that works through relaxation of verbal etiquette to allow affectionate use of indecent words. Although

Bakhtin (1984) lamented that the old rituals of fraternization in the carnival "have entirely lost their primitive connotation," this is not the case for utani in some Kenyan ethnic groups. With its carnival-like features, utani still plays a fraternization function in a primitive way.

Although utani is a social genre, online incivility—even with its political nature—clearly falls within this genre. If the incivility is viewed through the lens of utani, then verbal abuse online takes on meaning that is less controversial than what has become routine in regulatory narratives. Rather than hate speech, incivility as part of utani allows insults in a playful way, particularly when allowed to stay within the genre.

Despite its transgressive nature, joking relationships are not identical to utopian radicalism because regimes can use similar approaches. Furthermore, because utani is a regime-endorsed form of transgression, it validates regimes through permitted mockery and acts as a safety valve for accumulated anger. Put another way, permitted disorder is collusion between the people and the state to maintain harmony by allowing the periodic reversal of hierarchy—not as an alternative structure but as a distorted reflection of the dominant structure (Presdee and Carver 2000, 42).

To Achille Mbembe (2001, 103), the exercise of power in the postcolony is often "grotesque and obscene." This means that when elites use utani for hegemonic purposes, instead of the carnival inverting hierarchies, it guides, deceives, and toys with power. Through carnivals, the state can dramatize its own magnificence, make manifest its majesty, and create a spectacle for ordinary people to watch (Mbembe 2001, 104). The rulers and the ruled are entangled by intimate tyranny, and the politics of obscenity creates "mutual zombification"—the impotence or state of powerlessness of the ruler and the ruled, as "each has robbed the other of vitality and left both impotent" (104). Consequently, "The question of whether humor in the postcolony is an expression of 'resistance' or not, whether it is, a priori, opposition, or simply manifestation of hostility toward authority, is thus of secondary importance" (108).

Through digital media ventriloquism, the people act playfully with and make fun of the regime, enabling the people to achieve a status Mbembe (2001, 105) calls *homo ludens par excellence*, the split subjects who are neither in confrontation with the regime nor absolutely dominated—or in any other conventional binary oppositions against the state. The spaces for play and fun outside officialdom allow ordinary people to adhere to the "innumerable official rituals" (109) in the postcolony with amusement. Seriousness risks causing a confrontation.

Although Mbembe (2001) suggests conviviality through mutual zombification, the lack of hostility does not contradict the nature of politics, which, from an antagonistic perspective, is equivalent to the friend–enemy relationship. Instead, ordinary people use humor to conceal their grievances as they demystify the superhuman image that ruling elites inspire. Humor devalues domination and creates instability. According to Mbembe, "this explains why dictators can sleep at night lulled by roars of adulation and support only to wake up to find their golden calves smashed and their tablets of law overturned" (111).

The following section develops a method for locating joking relationships in digital media ventriloquism. These are the obscenities and grotesqueness in the material used by the regime to make itself felt and the neutralizing contradictions through the subjects' covert "underground" responses. Even though Mbembe (2001) did not discuss humor in material culture, technical things, as Winner (1980, 121) believes, "have political qualities" and should be judged by how "they can embody specific forms of power and authority." Without the current advances in "technopolitics" (Gagliardone 2016, 13), incivility would not be the way it is today. After all, how we communicate through social media is determined by the new media's affordances.

Social Media Affordances

Affordances are the cues triggered by "the particular ways in which an actor, or set of actors, perceives and uses [an] object" (Gibson 1986, 145). Social media technologies can be interpreted, for example, as affording different uses based on the interaction between a user's subjective perception and objective qualities of social media. Technologies alter communication practices by triggering cues; therefore, an affordance perspective of extreme speech highlights relationships between human beings and technologies in ways that are different from both medium specific and social constructivism communication theories. As explained by Gagliardone (2016, 13), digital media are part of the technopolitical regime. To Gabrielle Hecht (2001, 257), technopolitics is the strategic design or use of "technology to constitute, embody, or enact political goals." Indeed, the spontaneity logics of social media have inculcated in users new ways of evaluating acceptable and unacceptable speech.

From an actor-network theory perspective (Callon and Latour 1992; Brey 2005), technological artifacts should be analyzed as both real and constructed because artifacts are embedded in a network of human and nonhuman entities. Borrowing from Bruno Latour (1999, 303), I conceptualize agency in digital media as both human and nonhuman, moving away from the amateurish understanding of materiality—what Daniel Miller (2005, 7) termed a "vulgar" view of mere things as artifacts. This chapter transcends the subjects/objects dualism to discover how people speak through things (cf. McLuhan and Lapham 1994). The current technopolitical regime, as Gagliardone (2016, 14) stated, is not the result of a linear process but rather a network of actors competing to assert power and artifacts resisting or allowing this assertion.

This chapter extends Gagliardone's work on technopolitics by analyzing digital media affordances as ventriloquism tools. I am concerned more with affordances for regime instruments than linguistic texts. The study of the carnivalesque in extreme speech should not be restricted to linguistic texts; instead, it should be broadened to include study of the agency of "things" in social media. This material agency perspective can reveal the "force exercised by that which is not specifically human" (Bennett 2004, 351). As Miller asserts, "We need to engage with the issue of materiality as far more than a mere footnote or esoteric extra to the study of anthropology" (2005, 2). To study ventriloquism through digital media is to avoid the "tyranny of the subject" and to "critique approaches which view material culture as merely the semiotic representation of some bedrock of social relations" (Miller 2005, 3).

Considering that material-culture studies have been accused of remaining "methodologically unsophisticated" (Schiffer 2002, 6) by relying on statements gleaned from interviews instead of studying materials themselves, I propose a strategy of "interviewing" digital media technologies to find out how their affordances are being used by ventriloquists. In this regard, I follow Tilley's (2001, 258) suggestion to "identify a grammar of things, equivalent to a grammar of language," so that I can read and discover the affordances of digital media. I solve the methodological weakness in material-culture studies by developing a grammar of things, the rules used to identify "action possibilities" from what the technologies allow or forbid users to do (Akrich and Latour 1992, 259). The action possibilities can be seen in the perceived properties of an artifact that not only suggest how it should be used but also how it is susceptible to multiple interpretations (Norman 1988, 9; Pfaffenberger 1992, 284).

I will now turn to analysis of affordances to reveal how ventriloquism through social media technologies is affording metaphoric substitution of extreme speech with hate speech. The affordances noted are identification technologies, technologies of "efficiency," and technologies of "safety."

Forcing Functions

Forcing functions are affordances "that force the desired behavior" (Norman 2013, 141). In relation to the struggle about the meaning of extreme speech in social media, forcing functions are nonhuman gatekeepers that either forbid or require users to perform other indirect actions before allowing them to use social media. Through forcing functions, the regime attempts to name the unnamable by creating a preferred meaning of extreme speech. Consequently, forcing functions clandestinely make some myths about hate speech appear true. The forcing functions are explained in detail next.

Interlocks: Identification Technologies as Affordances

Interlocks are affordances designed to encourage performance of actions in a proper sequence (Norman 2013, 142). The interlocks metaphor refers to how artifacts inspire subjects to follow a predetermined sequence before accessing social media. Regarding identification technologies, interlocks demand that users identify themselves before using social media. Therefore, interlocks are action possibilities that repair dislocation caused by social media by removing anonymity and making users more responsible for their actions.

Among the most visible constraints designed to force regime-preferred behavior are the various social media identifications systems. The most obvious interlock is Subscriber Identity Module (SIM) registration. In 2010, the government of Kenya ordered telecommunications corporations to register SIM cards to reflect subscribers' official personal details (KICA, 2013). Although SIM card registration was supposed to remain "private," KICA states that telecommunication service providers should hand over this information if needed "in connection with the investigation of any criminal offence or for the purpose of any criminal proceedings; or . . . for the purpose of any civil proceedings." The act further states, "A subscriber shall be *prima facie* liable for activities or transactions carried out using a SIM-card registered under the subscriber's name."

Despite government claims that mandatory SIM card registration was aimed at curbing online fraud, registered SIM cards afford the regime the opportunity for misuse, for example, by tracking individuals who post antigovernment comments on social media.

Consequently, the aim of SIM card registration is not only to track criminals but also to create new affordances that can be used to redefine the meaning of hate speech.

Another category of identification technology is social media software. Users must create and authenticate personal accounts before using social media networks. Because user authentication systems make it easy for social media applications and the government to acquire user information, social media have affordances evocative of Foucault's (1977) concept of the panopticon.

In addition, digital media have self-disclosure affordances that induce users to identify themselves. The applications allow users to determine the type of information exposed, giving them the power to self-present. The network of real-life friendships limits anonymity and motivates users to create an "idealized projection of the real-life *'actual self'*" (Krasnova, et al. 2009, 42). The network of real-life friendships, combined with other self-disclosure features, prevents users from engaging in misrepresentation, unlike in purely anonymous online forums.

These identification technologies are the nonlinguistic affordances that enable regimes to metaphorize the meaning of extreme speech. The identification technologies name the unnamable by subtly changing incivility from a polysemic sign into hate speech—the regime's preferred meaning of extreme speech.

Lock-ins: Dominant Technologies as Affordances

Lock-ins are technologies designed to ensure continuous operation or to prevent users from prematurely terminating activities (Norman 2013, 143). These efficiency technologies might not be the best technology available on the market but can become the industry's most popular, thereby locking in users. Through lock-ins, users are restricted to the most popular applications, not the best ones; consequently, lock-ins support the regime's stand by encouraging use of popular, but not necessarily superior, social media applications.

The first lock-in affordances identified are technologies related to early adoption—advantages that make it possible for an innovation to hook users. Even if the technology is not the best on the market, the technology that penetrates the market first locks in users and makes them reluctant to switch because of the resources invested in the technology. Through technology lock-ins, users may prefer the social media application that has been on the market the longest, even if the application is perceived as less than optimal by its users. Using the examples of Twitter and Facebook, some messages can be flagged for hate speech or accounts may even be closed. Among Facebook's objectionable content categories is hate speech, which is defined as information that "creates an environment of intimidation and exclusion and in some cases may promote real-world violence" (Facebook 2019). Nevertheless, Facebook and Twitter are the most popular platforms in Kenya because they entered the market early.

The second category comprises incompatibility lock-ins for social media applications. The incompatibility lock-in hooks users on particular social media sites by restricting interoperability—the ability of a social media network to exchange and make use of information from other networks. Incompatible applications can substitute but not complement each other. This lack of complementarity limits users' freedom to get the best by combining the available affordances. Despite seven million users on Facebook and one million on Twitter (Boi 2018), for example, the two most popular social media networks in Kenya are currently incompatible. This implies that the affordances of Facebook and Twitter cannot be improved through their synthetization. Devoid of complete interoperability, each social media application retains the freedom of determining its definitions of extreme speech without fear of its affordances being appropriated by third-party applications. As explained by Inge Graef (2015, 502), after devoting time to building personal profiles, users may become locked in on one social networking site when the network makes it impossible to transfer the personal data or even post messages to another network. If networks were interoperable, social media users would push the boundaries of, for example, Facebook's extreme speech policy by posting from a different network or posting on networks other than Facebook. The freeing of social media through interoperability is similar to how newspapers have reduced gatekeeping by utilizing social media affordances to get readers' comments and encourage debate.

Lock-ins help the regime to name the unnamable when they deny people full control of social media features. Facebook's and Twitter's lock-in affordances have enabled them to have a final say regarding objections to information they believe falls into the category of hate speech. Consequently, lock-in affordances constrain the spectrum of extreme speech to what the dominant social media networks consider allowable. It also means the user guidelines for these two applications will continue to define "hate speech" a priori.

Lockouts: Safety Technologies as Affordances

The metaphor of lockouts is derived from features of artifacts that prevent users from using the artifacts "dangerously" or improperly. Safety technologies work through the force of material things to assist the regime in naming the unnamable. Social media features aimed at ensuring the safety of users also use tools of power as they compel users to behave in the regime's preferred ways.

The Device Management System (DMS) is one of the lockout technologies used in Kenya. The system enables telecommunications companies to monitor all gadgets used to access the internet. Although the government has denied installing a DMS on telecommunication networks in Kenya to monitor and access the private information of mobile phone users, it agrees that what was installed is a system for preventing use of counterfeit devices imported into the country illegally (Wangusi 2016). The Communication Authority of Kenya claims counterfeits should be blocked because they degrade the service quality and are a security threat because their owners cannot be traced.

What should be noted is that blacklisting fake phones through the DMS is in line with the binary of acceptable and unacceptable utilization of intellectual property. The acceptable intellectual property regime is one that supports the government's way of doing things—in this case, gadgets that can enable security agencies to track down users. Therefore, the antagonism in the reaction to restricting the use of counterfeit phones to access the internet is a form of incivility against global dominance in the telecommunications devices market that supports governmentality.

Counterfeits as physical incivility are part of an emerging economic and cultural phenomenon supported by development of duplication technology in the Global South. From a Marxist critique of the capitalistic mode of production, counterfeiting technology creates conditions that can make it possible to abolish capitalism (Benjamin 2008, 1). After all, some counterfeit technology has been "refined to the extent that virtually . . . products are indistinguishable from the official or authorized ones" (Chang 2004, 233). With improved "faking" technology, it has become difficult to distinguish the fake from the "original."

Another safety technology is content filtering. It is suspected that the government of Kenya, through the Communication Authority of Kenya or some state security agency, has installed content filtering technology. A study by Citizen Lab, a Canadian interdisciplinary laboratory hosted by the Munk School of Global Affairs at the University of Toronto, reported that Kenya is among sixteen countries that have installed Blue Coat devices to covertly filter and censor information (Marquis-Boire et al. 2013). The study found that by January 2013, there were three PacketShaper installations in Kenya.

A similar technical report by the Centre for Intellectual Property and Information Technology Law (CIPIT) of Kenya's Strathmore University indicated that there is "a middlebox on Safaricom's cellular network" (Safaricom is the largest telecommunications company in East Africa). According to CIPIT, this technology is "dual-use"—it can be used by the telecommunications company for legitimate functions like network optimization, but it can also be used for traffic manipulation, surveillance, and censorship.

Oppositional Reading of Technology Texts

The concept of oppositional reading developed by Stuart Hall can be extended to describe how users of social media contradict the government's preferred action possibilities. Just as the regime seeks to impose meaning and constrain action possibilities through social media artifacts, users counterhegemonically read the artifacts to resist the regime because "neither the writing nor the reading of technology-texts is determinate: both are open, negotiated processes" (Hutchby 2001, 445). In other words, discourses generated by technology design constituencies lend themselves to multiple interpretations that can challenge dominant discourses. To show oppositional reading of technology texts, I identified what Pfaffenberger calls "attempts to thwart a delegation strategy by disarming, muting, or otherwise suppressing the operation of a technical delegate" (1992, 302).

The Computer Misuse and Cybercrimes Act (2018) summarizes the majority of the oppositional "misuses." Although legislators claim that the law aimed to prevent unlawful computer use, to prosecute cybercrimes, and to protect the rights to privacy and freedom of expression, the law has several sections that attempt to fix the meaning of hate speech. Among the litany of hate crimes listed in this law are false news, forgery, online harassment, identity theft, and obscenity. However, because of the institutional void accompanying dislocation caused by social media, courts temporarily suspended twenty-six provisions of the act after the Bloggers Association of Kenya (BAKE) obtained a court order soon after the president's assent operationalized the law. BAKE had petitioned the court to find the act unconstitutional because it was aimed at reintroducing criminal defamation and other hate crimes that had been declared unconstitutional. As explained by Adrienne Shaw (2017, 6), a follower of Stuart Hall, "misuses" of technology should not all be viewed as erroneous. Shaw argues that what the regime claimed was misuse were some affordances "not accounted for by a designer" but that remained "plausible deployments" when identified by users of the technology.

Conclusion

The agency of artifacts, as illustrated in this chapter, shows how the regime is working through ventriloquism—speaking through nonhuman actors—to covertly patch up dislocation caused by incivility in social media. The regime tries to name the unnamable through metaphoric substitution of extreme speech with the catachresis of hate speech. While metaphors describe one thing as another, catachresis transfers "terms from one place to another . . . when no proper word exists" (Parker 1960, 60)—forms of misapplication of a word (Howarth and Griggs 2006, 32). Thus, it can be argued that, in addition to words, the regime is using artifacts to cement its catachrestical binary definition of hate speech. Artifacts conceal the regime's efforts to cement a singular meaning of extreme speech as to seem natural. Artifacts covertly naturalize the regime's discourses by moving incivility in social media out of politics by associating it with hate crimes. Through artifacts, the regime is able to covertly label incivility in social media as hate speech. This move takes incivility out of the sphere of normal politics and legitimizes the regime's use of extraordinary measures outside normal democratic principles. Consequently, it can be argued that social media artifacts are ideological tools that hide their traces of power, making us forget that the world is politically constructed (Laclau 1990, 60).

References

Akrich, Madeleine., and Bruno. Latour. 1992. "A Summary of a Convenient Vocabulary for the Semiotics of Human and Nonhuman Assemblies." In *Shaping Technology/Building Society: Studies in Sociotechnical Change*, edited by W. E. Bijker and J. Law, 259–264. Cambridge, MA: MIT Press.

Alai, Robert. (@RobertAlai). 2015, January 2. Visiting #AllanWadi in JAIL at 1pm. Join me if you can. He is at Industrial Area prison. Call 0708-677607 if lost. #AlanWadiJailed. Accessed July 17, 2017.

Bakhtin, Mikhail. 1981. *Discourse in the Novel. The Dialogic Imagination: Four Essays*, edited by M. Holquist. 269–422. Austin: University of Texas Press.

———. 1984. *Rabelais and His World*. Indianapolis: Indiana University Press.

BBC News. 2015. *Kenyan Jailed for Insulting President Uhuru Kenyatta*. January, 2, 2015. https://www.bbc.com/news/world-africa-30658461.

Beidelman, Thomas. O. 1966. "Utani—Some Kaguru Notions of Death, Sexuality, and Affinity." *Southwestern Journal of Anthropology* 22:354–381.

Benjamin, Walter. 2008. *The Work of Art in the Age of Mechanical Reproduction*. London: Penguin.

Bennett, Jane. 2004. "The Force of Things: Steps toward an Ecology of Matter." *Political Theory* 32 (3): 347–372.

Boi, Eva. 2018. "Digital Marketing: How Relevant Is It for Your Business in Kenya." https://www.kenyaweb.com/index.php/blog/77-digital-marketing-how-relevant-is-it-for-your-business-in-kenya-today.

Brey, Philip. 2005. "Artifacts as Social Agents." In *Inside the Politics of Technology: Agency and Normativity in the Co-production of Technology and Society*, edited by H. Harbers, 61–84. Amsterdam: Amsterdam University Press.

Callon, Michel, and Bruno Latour. 1992. "Don't Throw the Baby Out with the Bath School! A Reply to Collins and Yearley." In *Science as Practice and Culture*, edited by A. Pickering. Chicago: University of Chicago Press.

Chang, Hsiao-hung. (2004). "Fake Logos, Fake Theory, Fake Globalization." *Inter-Asia Cultural Studies*, 5 (2): 222–236.

Christensen, James Boyd. 1963. "Utani: Joking, Sexual License and Social Obligations among the Luguru." *American Anthropologist* 65 (6): 1314–1327.

Cooren, François. 2010. "Figures of Communication and Dialogue: Passion, Ventriloquism, and Incarnation." *Intercultural Pragmatics* 7 (1): 131–145.

———. 2015. "Studying Agency from a Ventriloqual Perspective." *Management Communication Quarterly* 29 (3): 475–480.

Eagleton, Benjamin, T. 1981. *Walter Benjamin or towards a Revolutionary Criticism*. London: Verso.

Facebook. 2019. "Objectionable Content." https://web.facebook.com/communitystandards/objectionable_content.

Foucault, Michel. 1977. *Discipline and Punish: The Birth of the Prison*. New York: Pantheon.

Gagliardone, Iginio.. 2016. *The Politics of Technology in Africa*. Cambridge: Cambridge University Press.

Gagliardone, Iginio., D. Gal, T. Alves, and G. Martinez. 2015. *Countering Online Hate Speech*. Paris: UNESCO.

Gibson, James Jerome, and James Gibson. 1986. *The Ecological Approach to Visual Perception*. Hillsdale, NJ: Lawrence Erlbaum Associates.

Graef, Inge. 2015. "Mandating Portability and Interoperability in Online Social Networks: Regulatory and Competition Law Issues in the European Union." *Telecommunications Policy* 39 (6): 502–514.

Gueye, Marame. 2011. "Modern Media and Culture in Senegal: Speaking Truth to Power." *African Studies Review* 54 (3): 27–43.

Heald, Suzette. 1990. "Joking and Avoidance, Hostility and Incest: An Essay on Gisu Moral Categories." *Man, New Series* 25 (3): 377–392.

Hecht, Gabrielle. 2001. "Technology, Politics, and National Identity in France." In *Technologies of Power: Essays in Honor of Thomas Parke Hughes and Agatha Chipley Hughes*, edited by M. T. Allen and G. Hecht, 253–293. Cambridge, MA: MIT Press.

Howarth, David. and Steven Griggs. 2006. "Metaphor, Catachresis and Equivalence: The Rhetoric of Freedom to Fly in the Struggle over Aviation Policy in the United Kingdom." *Policy and Society* 25 (2): 23–46. doi:10.1016/S1449-4035(06)70073-X.

Hutchby, Ian. 2001. "Technologies, Texts and Affordances." *Sociology* 35 (2): 441–456.

Karanja, Faith. 2015. "Hate Messages on President Uhuru Kenyatta Lands Student in Jail." *Standard*, January 3, 2015. https://www.standardmedia.co.ke/business/article/2000146557/hate-messages-on-president-uhuru -land-student-in-jail.

Krasnova, Hanna, Oliver Günther, Sarah Spiekermann, and Ksenia Koroleva. 2009. "Privacy Concerns and Identity in Online Social Networks." *Identity in the Information Society* 2 (1): 39–63.

Laclau, Ernesto. 1990. *New Reflections on the Revolution of Our Time*. London: Verso.

———. 2005. *On Populist Reason*. London: Verso.

———. 2014. *The Rhetorical Foundations of Society*. London: Verso.

Laclau, Ernesto, and Chantal Mouffe. 1985. *Hegemony and Socialist Strategy: Towards a Radical Democratic Politics*. London: Verso.

Latour, Bruno. 1999. *Pandora's Hope: Essays on the Reality of Science Studies*. Cambridge, MA: Harvard University Press.

Marquis-Boire, Morgan, Jakub Dalek, Sarah McKune, Matthew Carrieri, Masashi Crete-Nishihata, Ron Deibert, . . . Grege Wiseman. 2013. *Summary Analysis of Blue Coat "Countries of Interest."* https://citizenlab .ca/2013/01/appendix-a-summary-analysis-of-blue-coat-countries-of-interest/#90.

Mbembe, Achille 2001. *On the Postcolony*. Berkeley: University of California Press.

McLuhan, Marshall, and L. H. Lapham. 1994. *Understanding Media: The Extensions of Man*. Cambridge, MA: MIT Press.

Miller, Daniel. 2005. "Materiality: An Introduction." In *Materiality*, edited by Daniel Miller, 1–50. Durham, NC: Duke University Press.

Mouffe, Chantal. 1992. *Dimensions of Radical Democracy: Pluralism, Citizenship, Community*. London: Verso.

———. 2005. *On the Political*. London: Routledge.

Norman, Donald. 2013. *The Design of Everyday Things*, rev. and expanded ed. New York: Constellation.

Norman, Donald. 1988. *The Psychology of Everyday Things*. New York: Basic.

Ogude, James. 2002. "Ethnicity, Nationalism and the Making of Democracy in Kenya: An Introduction." *African Studies* 61 (2): 205–207. doi:10.1080/0002018022000032929.

Parker, Patricia. 1990. "Metaphor and Catachresis." In J. Bender and D. Wellbery (Eds), *The Ends of Rhetoric: History, Theory, Practice*. 60–73. Stanford, CA: Stanford University Press.

Penfold-Mounce, Ruth. 2010. *Celebrity Culture and Crime: The Joy of Transgression*. London: Springer.

Pfaffenberger, Bryan. 1992. "Technological Dramas." *Science, Technology, and Human Values* 17:282–312.

Pohjonen, Matti, and Sahana Udupa. 2017. "Extreme Speech Online: An Anthropological Critique of Hate Speech Debates." *International Journal of Communication* 11:1173–1191.

Presdee, Mike, and Gavin Carver. 2000. "From Carnival to the Carnival of Crime." In *Cultural Criminology and the Carnival of Crime*, edited by M. Presdee, 31–56. London: Routledge.

Radcliffe-Brown, Alfred. 1940. "On Joking Relationships." *Africa* 13 (3): 195–210.

Republic of Kenya. 2008. *Report of the Commission of Inquiry into Post-election Violence (CIPEV)*. Nairobi: Government Printer.

Schiffer, M. B. 2002. *The Material Life of Human Beings: Artefacts, Behaviour, and Communication*. London: Routledge.

Shaw, Adrienne. 2017. "Encoding and Decoding Affordances: Stuart Hall and Interactive Media Technologies." *Media, Culture, and Society* 39:592–602. doi:10.1177/0163443717692741.

Some, Kipchumba. 2015. "Two Years of Anguish Mark Family's Search for Missing Blogger Bogonko Bosire." *Standard*, December 20, 2015. https://www.standardmedia.co.ke/article/2000185799/two-years-of-anguish-mark-family-s-search-for-missing-blogger-bogonko-bosire.

Tilley, Christopher. 2001. "Ethnography and Material Culture." In *Handbook of Ethnography*, edited by P. Atkinson, A. Coffey, S. Delamont, J. Lofland, and L. Lofland, 258–272. London: Sage.

Wangusi, Francis. n.d. *Press Statement by Mr. Francis W. Wangusi, Director General, Communications Authority of Kenya (CA), on Misleading Media Reports Regarding the Regulatory Tool for Curbing Counterfeit Devices on Mobile Networks*. Nairobi: Communication Authority of Kenya.

Winner, Langdon. 1980. "Do Artifacts Have Politics?" *Daedalus* 109 (1): 121–136.

4

THE MORAL ECONOMY OF EXTREME SPEECH

Resentment and Anger in Indian Minority Politics

Max Kramer

A T A TIME WHEN A RIGHT-WING HINDU NATIONALIST party is in power and vigilante violence against Muslim minorities is a common occurrence in India, a Muslim-based dynastic party, All India Majlis-e-Ittehadul Muslimeen (All India Council of the Union of Muslims [AIMIM]), has made rapid inroads into national politics. The trajectory of AIMIM from a regional party that mediated minoritarian citizens' concerns in Hyderabad, in southern India, to the national voice of disenfranchised Muslims was advanced by a combination of social media activism by volunteers and mainstream media coverage of their leading figures, the brothers Asaduddin Owaisi and Akbaruddin Owaisi. Whereas Asaduddin's rhetorics are legalistic, polite, and guarded, Akbaruddin is known for viral videos of so-called hate speeches directed against the Hindu majority, with a number of legal cases pending against him and forty days already served in prison. This chapter explores minoritarian extreme speech within the moral economy of the Indian nation-state. It asks how Akbaruddin's most well-known speech "reacts" to the available moral frameworks and what such a reaction implies for the moral self-understanding of the Indian polity. I argue that alternative moral evaluations that go beyond the term *hate* are important in understanding this form of minority politics. In this context, "extreme speech" is a key concept that enables one to understand minority articulations from a non-normative perspective, highlighting the unequal distribution of the capacity to use extreme speech between minoritarian and majoritarian subject positions.

The chapter begins with an ethnographic discussion of Akbaruddin Owaisi's controversial speech that circulated widely on social media. Situating this incident within the broader climate of antiminority politics in contemporary India and its historical antecedents and legal precedents, I suggest that what is often called the "outrageousness" of Owaisi's speech should be understood within the trajectory of a reframed Muslim minority politics. This trajectory goes beyond the commonly invoked frame of "communalism" (interreligious conflicts) and its associated negative emotions in the Indian context. Drawing on the Nietzschean use of the French term *ressentiment* and its distinction from the English *resentment* in the liberal tradition, I argue in this chapter that the outrage of the Muslim minority is not the mirror image of majoritarian populism but rather should be understood in relation to the moral economy of the nation-state and its structures of social justice. If the resentment from those who are living under conditions of discrimination and structural violence cannot be legitimately expressed because that expression gets caught up in the term *hate*, this then reveals a serious limitation of a liberal democratic polity. The chapter concludes by returning to the term *extreme speech* to highlight its critical potential in delineating minority politics in the current digital media cultures.

An "Outrageous Speech" in the Nation's Moral Economy

"You haven't seen Akbaruddin's hate speech? It is outrageous!" My friend was laughing in disbelief and immediately reached out for his mobile phone to show me what he was referring to. The video contained a snippet of a speech in which the Indian politician Akbaruddin Owaisi rhetorically asks, "What could these twenty-five *crore* [250 million] Muslims do if you just take away the police for fifteen minutes?" The moral evaluation of the "outrageous" nature differed widely among mainstream news coverage, my conversations with Indian Muslims, and legal assessments. Akbaruddin seemed to invert the usual reverential attitude expected from minority leaders, who politely respect a polity that has delivered little in the name of development and representation to most Indian Muslims. His comment enables multiple readings depending on moral reasoning and political affiliation. One reading could be that of the myth of heroic Muslim warriors, a martial community that holds historical pride as former rulers of large stretches of what is today's India. His words imply martial pride, suggesting that "we would overcome the Hindu majority if the battle were fair."[1] His audience at a political rally in Nirmal—a small town in the southern Indian state of Telangana—would be aware of the police's role in past state-backed violence against the Muslim minority. In this reading, I assume a mixture of scandalous enjoyment, ire, indignation, and resentment also took hold of some of my Muslim conversation partners with whom I have discussed the clip. Although the speech is from 2012, it currently resonates strongly with a community going through some of its darkest times since the emergence of the modern Indian nation-state. Prime Minister Narendra Modi's Hindu nationalist government has been responsible for a climate of minority repression, intolerance, and mob violence (Palshikar 2017; Teltumbde 2018). Since 2012, the whole video of the speech and subsequent snippets have become among the most circulated online objects of Muslim minority politics in India—their popularity perhaps linked to the predicament of the community.

Muslim politics in India have been informed in recent years by the publication of a number of state-commissioned reports that have shown the abysmal socioeconomic conditions of most members of this community. The Sachar Committee Report (2006) indicates that Indian Muslims are disadvantaged in many respects, ranging from high poverty and low literacy levels to exclusion from government jobs and underrepresentation in business and media. This report and others (Ministry of Minority Affairs 2007) have stirred debate among journalists, academics, and the Muslim community in India. Some groups have pressed for affirmative action policies for all Indian Muslims. This follows a model already implemented among other groups classified by the state as "backward": scheduled caste (formerly "untouchables"), scheduled tribes, and other backward castes (OBCs). Nevertheless, commentators have stressed the internal diversity and inequalities within the category of "Indian Muslim" and the need for a more differentiated approach to affirmative action (Ansari [2016] discusses how Indian Muslims are part of caste society and, in many federal states, included in the OBC category). At the same time, strong arguments concerning their discrimination *as a minority* have been brought forward that focus on cultural aspects of discrimination (e.g., stereotyping) and underrepresentation (see Islam 2019 for a detailed discussion). These debates provide the backdrop to a new, more assertive phase of Muslim politics in India that coincides with the weakness of Indian National Congress, at the center, to claim representation of the religious minority through its own understanding of secular nationalism. I suggest that Akbaruddin Owaisi's persona and his "hate speech" have become such controversial topics because they open up various ways of questioning the moral order of the Indian nation-state in times of Hindu nationalist hegemony.

The growing importance of Akbaruddin can be judged by his substantial social media fan following and the mainstream media coverage of his scandals (Jha 2017).[2] However, his visibility as a star persona is aligned, augmented, and challenged by his even more famous brother, Asaduddin Owaisi, who was recently recognized by Facebook as India's second politician, in terms of interactions, just behind Narendra Modi (Tech Observer Desk 2018). While Asaduddin is a UK-educated "barrister" (a title that his followers rarely omit) who holds a seat in the Indian Lok Sabha and was recognized for good parliamentary practice, his brother Akbaruddin is a medical school dropout and has a reputation as a maverick. In his public image, he embodies a set of character types ranging from the tough politician to the comedian to the *dada* (local strongman). In his most famous online videos, he caters to comedy and scandal through extreme forms of speech.

Even though the term *hate* figures mostly in the press coverage of his Nirmal speech, this chapter is neither meant to confirm this term nor to dismiss it wholesale. Instead, I want to explore the politically more relevant question pertaining to the link among a speaking position (that of Muslim leader in India), an emotion (is it really hate?), its resonance among audiences, and its moral evaluation. When Akbaruddin says in his Nirmal speech that "every action calls for a reaction," I think it is important to ask, what conceptual stakes are in the claims of reaction and how are they aligned with the moral self-understanding of the Indian polity?

In the speech, Akbaruddin mostly addressed the importance of representation of Muslims by Muslims for the sake of community empowerment. However, his elaboration of current economic and cultural exclusions of the community were secondary to the media visibility that has evolved around this speech. Most commentators, be they his audience (a mostly male political rally), Muslim online users, the security forces, the prosecuting party, public intellectuals, or some segments of the English-language press, focused on the more scandalous moments and their professed emotional qualities. Akbaruddin was eventually imprisoned for forty days pending trial under suspicion of violating section 121 (waging or attempting to wage a war or abetting waging of war against the government of India) and section 153(A) (creating enmity between different communities) of the Indian Penal Code.

The latter claim is related to his mockery of Hindu gods.[3] In response, a number of public intellectuals, filmmakers, and social activists criticized his speech in a statement issued by the Hyderabad-based Confederation of Voluntary Associations (COVA), an organization founded in the aftermath of communal riots in the 1990s that strives to strengthen "communal harmony."[4] COVA called the speech obnoxious, divisive, and in violation of peace (echoing the principles largely associated with the Indian National Congress Party).[5] With film star Farhan Akhtar and veteran journalists like Karan Thapar and Swapan Dasgupta joining in after the speech via Twitter, Akbaruddin affirmed his reputation as a firebrand.[6] Among these highly visible secular-nationalist commentators, there is consensus concerning the problematic nature of this "hate speech," labeling it "outrageous" and "obnoxious."

Although often called "hate speech" in media coverage, the speech in Nirmal does not figure the radical othering that is typical of the politics of hate (which involves purification of one's own group against the hostile takeover of "rats" and "germs," etc.). That does not mean that its most extreme image of "twenty five *crore* unbound by the police" would not evoke the possibility of mass violence and thus may qualify as hateful if taken as a threat. Akbaruddin's speech, delivered at night to his *jalsa* public (an almost exclusively male political rally), includes a number of other chauvinistic assertions that add to the audience thrill in participating in these gatherings. Anthropologist Shefali Jha (2017, 341) describes how the speech was originally considered "private" by some members of his audience. For them, it was not proper to have Akbaruddin prosecuted for something "said in a jalsa." Jha argues that the unexpected online visibility of these speeches was part of a larger shift that enabled Akbaruddin's nationalization as an all-India Muslim star persona, as well as his media visibility as a "hate speaker."

I argue that this transition must now be analyzed in respect to the emotional resonance it can create among a national minority. There are aspects such as the implied understanding of fairness and the importance given to secularism that made me wonder how this widely professed "outrageousness" can be understood within the trajectory of a reframing of Muslim minority politics beyond the context of communalism and its associated negative emotions. In India, the term *communal* is used for popular leaders who assert their position with an emotional pitch through religious identities. They are often accused of "inciting communal passions," denoting two (post)colonial categories: one is the not yet rational colonial subject who is on the verge of group violence (Mazzarella 2013), and the other is seen through the British understanding of Indian society as being made up of internally coherent religious "communities" in an atavistic and perennial conflict. The different communalists are then often lifted into equivalence by those who consider themselves above "communal passions"—the harbingers of rational, unbiased justice. This balancing act is particularly disturbing considering the degree of Hindu dominance in various areas of the Indian polity, from the constitution, judiciary, and security services to the media (Singh 2015). The endeavor to question communalism is nothing new in itself (see Ahmed 2013; Islam 2019), but I argue that the link between moral evaluations of negative emotions and possible articulations of extreme speech has not yet been properly explored.

In Congress-aligned discourses of national secularism, Akbaruddin and his followers not only react but rather are reactionary—people led by hate and revenge turning the AIMIM into a "mirror image of the Hindu BJP [Bharatiya Janata Party]" (Shivshankar 2020). Some of the media's usages of the term *resentment* capture something about the way Akbaruddin "outrages" people by drawing on negative emotions.[7] This evaluation of Owaisi's position can also be found in some political science writing (Friedrichs 2018; Singh 2019). To address reaction and its position toward the political role of emotions in relation to minority politics, it is helpful to differentiate between the Nietzschean use of the French term *ressentiment* and *resentment*. Doing so allows me to speak about two politically relevant ways of subjectification (Fassin 2013, 250; Hunt 2013, 119), referring to the moral value of emotions such as indignation, anger, ire, bitterness, and a desire for revenge. From the perspective of conceptual history, the term *resentment* is misapplied in the journalistic and scholarly contexts mentioned. Instead, it is more of an accusation of Nietzschean ressentiment that lurks behind some of the media coverage—when, for example, it is suggested that because of a lack of real transformative power, the Owaisis are able to arouse only the "hate" of their constituencies when they use extreme speech (Alam 2018). For Nietzsche, ressentiment is a reaction of the weak in which they cannot fight in any other way than to moralize and take what is suppressing them as amoral. Ressentiment is caught in the self-affirming circularity of autovictimization and revenge—thus, it is reaction gone bad, where the active force was cut off by some sentimental or symbolic attachment to the master as a memory trace. In contrast, political philosopher Adam Smith considers "resentment" as a normal yet disagreeable passion that "can be disciplined as long as a sense of justice prevails" (Fassin 2013, 251). The point for Smith is that resentment can be legitimate when its reaction is aligned with the justice provided by the nation-state (liberal political philosophers such as John Rawls [1973] and Martha Nussbaum [2013] continue this tradition of nation-state–focused approaches to justice and political emotions).

How then does Akbaruddin himself interpret the emotional quality of his rhetoric? In the middle of the Nirmal speech, he says that he is the "voice of the *guṣṣa* [anger] of Indian Muslims." According to Platt's dictionary, غصّ guṣṣa[8] comes from the Arabic غص ("to be choked"). The semantic context is one of "choking, strangulation, suffocation"—thus "(choking) wrath, rage, anger, passion;—grief, disquietude of mind, anxiety"—and, as an adverb, *guṣṣe meṃ* ("in anger; from or through anger"). Even though guṣṣa is usually understood as a brief reaction—like a burst of anger—the historical dimensions of Akbaruddin's claim rather point to "resentment": a complex moral sentiment with a value that relates to a whole moral order. Consequently, instead of seeing Akbaruddin's guṣṣa as a mirror image of the Bharatiya Janata Party's (BJP's) majoritarian populism or the extreme speeches of Hindu nationalists, I argue that it is crucial to look at the exact wording, the rhetorical style, and the Indian polity to analyze which values are evoked and to what degree of legitimacy.

My questions are pursued in a media anthropology of "moral economy" (Fassin 2009) that discusses the way values are produced, circulated, regulated, and appropriated through media practices. These questions have immediate relevance when it comes to extreme speech (Udupa and Pohjonen 2019) in online vitriol and new digital media cultures. As a concept, extreme speech explores the boundaries of legitimate speech through context-sensitive studies. Udupa and Pohjonen question legalistic and universalizing moral assessments of "acceptable or non-acceptable speech" to engage with processes of mediation and performance within the larger context of different media-cultural environments where historically differ-ent notions of politeness, abuse, and comedy shape the way people practice extreme speech. Thus, what counts as "hate speech" depends on a multitude of factors including law, moral discourses, and historical experiences that have formed the basis of group and individual memory. In the case of India, the nation-state's moral order results partly from liberalism and from its (post)colonial history, including the partition of British India and the strug-gle of lower castes for democratic access. Colonial forms of governance and various group struggles led to citizenship that includes both collective and individual rights through which justice is demanded.

Crucial for the purpose of this chapter is Udupa and Pohjonen's (2019, 4–5) call to go beyond normative understandings of "hate speech" by looking at the ways control and au-thority are exerted in assigning the term "hate" to certain speeches and not to others. If the resentment from those who are living under conditions of discrimination and structural violence cannot be legitimately expressed because it gets caught up in the term "hate," then that situation reveals a serious limitation of a liberal democratic polity. Even if one does not propound a normative order oneself, it is still important to open up these questions of legitimacy by an immanent critique to those who identify with a national-secular and more liberal version of the Indian state. A closer historical contextualization of the AIMIM, elabo-rated in the next section, will help to explicate this critical intervention.

AIMIM: From Hyderabad to the Nation

Journalistic articles on the AIMIM usually begin with references to its former avatar, the Majlis-e-Ittehadul Muslimeen (MIM), and the historical role the party played in the de-fense of Muslim interests in the Nizam's state of Hyderabad. The MIM's private troops, the *razakars*, fought on the side of the Nizam's army against the Indian forces during Operation Polo, the war that led to the merger of the Hyderabad state with the Indian Union. In 1948, amid widespread violence against Muslims in the region, many Indian politicians identified the MIM as the main culprit in stirring "communal passions," and the party was banned. Confronted with evidence of the scale of violence directed against Muslims in the aftermath of Operation Polo, Indian politicians framed the incident in the classic colonial rhetoric of "equal violence on both sides," hurriedly dedicating the topic to history (Sherman 2015). The party reemerged only ten years later—now with an "All India" in front of the MIM—in 1958 with a new constitution and under the leadership of the Owaisi family. Since then, some landmark successes included a Lok Sabha seat won by Sultan Salahuddin Owaisi, the father of the brothers, and the defense of more than six seats in the state parliament (in 2019, they had seven) for several decades from constituencies located in and around the old town of Hyderabad.

The speech in Nirmal falls into a new expansive phase of the party since 2012. Some journalists I interviewed suggested that this timing cannot be coincidental but rather reveals a larger shift in the orientation of the party: from Hyderabad to the nation. The circulation of snippets of this speech furthered by the use of digital media is linked to the attempt to enter other Indian states with large Muslim populations. This approach has so far resulted in some victories in municipal corporations in a few cities and two seats in the legislative assembly of the federal state of Maharashtra. In September 2018, an official electoral alliance was forged with Prakash Ambedkar, grandson of famous Dalit leader Bhimrao Ambedkar. Arguably, this alliance helped in securing the second Lok Sabha seat for the party in the 2019 national elections in the Maharashtrian city of Aurangabad. Bajpai and Farooqui (2018, 293) noted the reliance of Asaduddin Owaisi's rhetoric on India's constitutional framework and the AIMIM's similarity to Dalit parties in terms of demands for state reservation (affirmative policy measures) and political self-representation as an articulation of mostly secular interests (they define this as "non-extremist outbidding"). But they confine their analysis to the formalities of Asaduddin's rhetoric, sidelining the ludic and transgressive aspects of the party's visibility mostly connected with his brother Akbaruddin (this perspective mirrors the overall trajectory in scholarship regarding the recent successes of AIMIM, concentrating on rhetorical style, ideological content, political patronage, and the mediation of citizenship; Moore 2016; Jha 2017; Bajpai and Farooqui 2018; Suneetha and Moid 2019). The astonishing visibility of the Owaisis cannot be explained by looking at organized media alone but rather should be read along with digital media practices of the party's new followers. The latter has played a critical role in the party's recent expansion and the popularity of the Owaisis, as "outrageous" speech continues to provide the fulcrum for digital popularity. Although the mediation of the speech would be a worthwhile subject on its own, in the next section, I will explore the link between the most "outrageous" content of the speech in Nirmal (ironically, the name of the town means "pure") and the nation-state's trope of secularism.

A Dirty Speech in Nirmal

The issue of the Bhagyalakshmi temple sets up the more immediate context of a series of eight speeches that became famous "hate speeches" in late 2012. The temple was constructed in the 1960s next to the iconic Charminar building in Hyderabad's old town. In November 2012, the roof was renovated, against the protests of AIMIM. Akbaruddin claimed that the police protected the illegal construction work, and he led a rally to the old town. There was some stone pelting and tear gassing by the police, which resulted in a few AIMIM supporters, including Akbaruddin, being taken into police custody. It is possible that this event and the confrontation with the police played a role in setting the tone for the speech. During the speech, Akbaruddin says that he is the "voice of gus̩s̩a of Indian Muslims." In the introduction, I pointed out that the Urdu term gus̩s̩a in the context of the Nirmal speech is more suggestive of the complex emotion of resentment rather than its preferred translation as "anger." Because many commentators understood his words as an expression of neither anger nor resentment but rather as hate, it is worth briefly exploring these differences.

Anger and hate are usually differentiated by their temporality and by their relation to an object. Anger is understood as a rather short outburst, whereas hate is marked by a long-term attachment. As noted earlier, resentment is linked to (community) memory and history of subjugation—thus acquiring a long-term dimension. Bursts of anger as part of a feeling of suffocation that derives from current situations and historical memory are not very different from the temporal attachment that hate requires—but different in the way they are directed toward an object. Resentment, as a politically theorized negative emotion, is directed at institutions that have so far failed to deliver justice. Its object is not just the resented other; it acquires a crucial third instance through which a "recognition" of the position from below may get justly acted upon (see the reconstruction of the concept of recognition by Axel Honneth [2018]). In contrast, the object-cause of hate, in the words of Sara Ahmed (2014), "presses against me," threatening the individual's very existence—it does not require institutions of recognition. Superficially, one could ask whether Akbaruddin talks about exactly this when he explains the reasons why AIMIM parted company with Congress on the issue of a temple construction next to Charminar that "used to be a mosque." The temple presses against the mosque as another wound in the history of Muslim subordination in India—a history he addresses in passing by speaking derogatorily about Hindu temples. He warned that "Muslims would take the Taj Mahal, Red Fort, and Qutb Minar [important monuments erected by Muslim rulers] with them," adding, "What will then remain here? Just a razed Ram temple in Ayodhya and the naked statues of Ellora and Ajanta." But his stressing that the mosque was a legal construction and that the encroachment was actually the illegal attack on the moral order makes one wonder if "hate" really captures it. Even in his most "outrageous" comments (e.g., the remark about the "police" referenced earlier), there is no demonization of the Hindu other. Rather, both instances suggest that they be understood along with the historical disappointments India's Muslims have experienced with Indian (national) secularism and Hindu nationalism. Akbaruddin thus aims at a comical inversion of the trope of communalism: "You who expect secularism [from us], rebuild the Babri masjid, and Akbar Owaisi will consider if he should be secular or not. (*Secularism kī tawaqqo rakh'ne wāloṃ, Babri masjid ko banā lo, Akbar Owaisi gaur karegā secular hone kā yā naī hone kā*). People will say Akbar Owaisi is communal. . . . I don't know about pro- this or pro- that; I am only pro-Muslim!" (*Log boleṃge Akbar Owaisi firqāparast hai . . . maiṃ naī jānta ye-parast, vah-parast, maiṃ sirf Muslim-parast hūṃ!*)" (Jha 2017, 292; changed transcription style by author).

Using the third person, Akbaruddin appears sly and assertive—playing among the *dada* (local strongman), the *ṭaporī* (a street-smart gangster with a popular film pedigree [Kramer 2014], indexed by the colloquial *hone kā*), and the floor leader of the party in the regional state assembly. The party brands him as *Habib-e-Millat* (beloved of the community), suggesting a popular sentiment that "Akbarbhai" (brother Akbar) may occasionally be "over the top" but only because he speaks from his heart (a notion that came across in many conversations I had with party workers). His words imply that Muslims might as well be communal since the polity is communal and that the Muslim community should accept citizenship mediated by group identities, which are a reality of the Indian polity. The attempts to gain authority over Akbaruddin's moral evaluation by calling it "hate" requires a critical investigation of the tropes of "harmony" and "secularism" that frame the type of emotional involvement (or noninvolvement) that is supposedly "good" for a nation-state polity under principles of justice—to which I turn next.

Polity and Emotions

In this section, I look at the way emotions are captured in the legal language and moral discourse of the Indian polity. Akbaruddin once said, "Our community (*qaum*) is emotional (*jazbātī*); therefore, we have to arouse their emotions."[9] His assumptions are connected to the already colonial debate on "Muslim rage" that is constantly reiterated in relation to different conflicts, be they Kashmir, blasphemy cases in Pakistan (Schaflechner, chap. 12), or discourse on the "Islamic hatred of the West" (Lewis 2001). Continuities between the above-mentioned "social activists" of COVA and older colonial discourses on "Muslim rage" can be traced to 1920s India. Julia Stephens (2014, 47) argues that "while colonial officials had long emphasized their religious neutrality, the term secularism, and its emphasis on removing religion from politics, first gained prominence in Indian politics in the 1920s. Such efforts to exclude 'fanaticism' from politics were in theory religiously neutral. In practice proponents of secularism singled out Islam as posing a particular threat, effectively marginalizing Muslims' political concerns."

Akbaruddin of 2012 seems to be an impolite, extreme intrusion into the official rhetoric of a party that tried to reinvent its public image. In recent years, Asaduddin has mostly made AIMIM look polite, constitutional, patriotic, and open in order to form a broad coalition with other discriminated groups (however, there are also extreme speeches by Asaduddin). Rhetorically, many of AIMIM's articulations are moderated by the fact that Asaduddin's legalist discourse tries to imagine the Indian nation as secular in a substantially Indian way: by opening avenues of affirmative action and representation for Muslims and Dalits. For the purposes of this chapter, the problem of a liberal public sphere does not rely primarily on its implicit assumptions of secularity as rational (somehow devoid of passions; see, e.g., Chaube 2018) but rather on the set of emotions that are deemed "problematic" when related to the assertion of cultural religious identities.

From a perspective of communal harmony, it is easy to frame Akbaruddin as a harbinger of hate speech and a staunch communalist. Ways of framing Akbaruddin as communal need to be addressed through the history of the Indian nation-state. The denial of being a constitutive and transformative element of Indian history forces most Muslims in India to become public through the nationalization of their articulation. Because hegemonic history writing is either secular-nationalist or Hindu nationalist in India, claims suggesting larger Muslim solidarity are often read against the partition of British India and thus firmly placed within the discursive framework of "secularism versus communalism." This can be seen as a result of what Gyanendra Pandey has called "internal colonization" (2006, 1781), "wherein they [Muslims] are not only perceived as second-class citizens, but are also unable to assert any independent claims to history or to seek an identity outside of and without assimilating into the dominant culture" (Khan 2015, 62). The denial of history also cuts many Indian Muslims off from possible arguments concerning historical injustice that have become the legal basis for affirmative action and reservation policies in the case of Dalit politics (Hasan 2011). Muslims' otherness, as Barbara Metcalf (1995) argues, should therefore not be misconstrued as primarily "cultural or religious difference" but placed firmly, in Khan's paraphrasing, as "a product of political expediencies aimed at preserving the hegemony and cohesiveness of the dominant Hindu community and of deflecting attention from the inequalities and lack of redistributive justice within the world's largest democracy" (2015, 113). Consequently, discourse on communalism frames the moral economy that Muslim minority agents find themselves within when using extreme forms of speech, and it is often used to delimit their space of self-assertion.

The legal context pertains to restrictions on free speech (given that *hate speech* is not a legal term). Legislation includes Indian Penal Code sections 153A, 295, and 295A (nonbailable, noncompoundable offenses), which focus on attacks on religion, race, place of birth, language, a particular group or class, or the founders and prophets of a religion; damaging places of worship; and insults to religion and religious beliefs. In addition, section 123(3A) of the election law, the Representation of People Act, prohibits attempts to promote enmity on grounds of religion. Key to a discussion of moral economies is the stress on "outraging the religious feelings of any class" (sec. 295A) and linking "public order" with the value of "harmony" (sec. 153A) and "national unity." In relation to minority politics, communities are "religious" and constitutive of the "diversity of India," in which state secularism is meant to enable "unity in diversity" against the background of the partition of British India along religious lines.

According to Jose Casanova (2010), secularism as an ideology explains why "we"—a group identity—need secularism while constructing time and again what the secular and the religious are and can do. *We* need it because *we* need to deal with diversity within the nation. In a judgment under the Representation of People Act, the judiciary has been shown to have given considerable leeway to Hindu nationalist articulations, going so far as conflating a reformist definition of Hinduism with some core understandings of Hindu nationalism (Sen 2019, 23). Thus, one needs to measure the above-mentioned laws and an ideology of secularism against their legal practice and enforcement. In 2017, a nongovernmental organization, the Association of Democratic Reforms, pointed out that while the majority of the fifty-eight members of the legislative assembly who have been booked as hate speech offenders belong to the Hindu-nationalist BJP (27), none of these lawmakers have been arrested by the police, whereas politicians like Akbaruddin Owaisi, academics, and journalists have been targeted.[10] The same is true for former Shiv Sena leader Bal Thackeray, leader of one of Maharashtra's most powerful political parties, who had several cases pending but has never spent more than brief stints in prison for his offenses (e.g., calling Muslims "rats"). This claim also pertains to the current chief minister of the politically significant state of Uttar Pradesh, Yogi Adityanath, who said, "You kill one of us [Hindus], we kill one hundred of you [Muslims]."[11] There have been riots in relation to Adityanath's speech and Thakeray's offenses—something that did not happen after Akbaruddin's Nirmal speech. Questions of effectiveness have been regarded by the Supreme Court in the case of *Ramesh v. Union of India* to have some bearing on restricting free speech. The Law Commission of India states that when it comes to section 19(2), "the relation between restriction and public order has to be proximate and direct as opposed to [having] a remote or fanciful connection" (2017, 11). Nevertheless, Adityanath and Thackeray were let off the hook by procedural arguments ("time barred," etc.) for extreme speeches of hateful content that had proximate connections to public order (Sahi 2017; Punwani 2017).

Conclusion—The Differences Made by Extreme Speech in Moral Economies

In 2019, the Hindu nationalist BJP returned to power with an overwhelming majority after running a campaign that involved warmongering and anti-Muslim propaganda. In a news article published right after the election results, well-known author and intellectual Pankaj Mishra argued that ressentiment linked to the inequalities of Indian society was a driving force behind the BJP and its leader Narendra Modi's triumph.[12] In a similar vein, Max Scheler (2004) has considered the imagination of equality as established in capitalist modernity and liberal democracy as the driving force of ressentiment. He argues that the formal equality given by modern constitutions establishes an abstract difference based on normative principles and public value ascribed to certain groups that may contrast with their actual social standing (Scheler 2004, 9). Mishra's concern is timely because the digitalized acceleration of the clickbait economy's moral outrage may reach a dead end where negative emotions can no longer be redressed effectively in existing institutions. At this very impasse hinges the term *resentment* as a way to approach the legitimacy of extreme speech.

The word *extreme* (instead of *transgressive*) signals an in-depth understanding of emotional intensities and their stakes for moral orders, which are part of an inquiry into how these speeches become politically relevant. Extreme speech is always extreme in relation to some moral interpretation—what is hate for some may be anger for others. This evaluation seriously affects how we can engage with highly emotional claims of minorities: Are they just the reactionary clamor of the weak without transformative force, or are these emotions legitimate and politically relevant to some extent? These stakes for moral orders are measured in an economy with its own rules within which a nation-state polity may or may not dispense justice. Seen from this perspective, Akbaruddin's references to secularism and jokes about the Hindu religion point to the lack of a language that navigates a path out of the minoritarian discontent. The constant affirmation of nationalism by politically engaged Muslims in India—the AIMIM being no exception—is thus ambiguously bound to expressions of extreme speech as objects in circulation, both valorized and scandalous. It is extreme because both the liberal and postcolonial frameworks of the polity render self-assertive forms of Muslim politics in India as fundamentally problematic while accepting strong forms of self-representation by other historically disadvantaged groups whom the state classifies as Hindu (even though the self-perception of many members of these groups, particularly the Dalits, may strongly go against this identification).

To conclude, I suggest that the following interpretative option based on a liberal self-understanding of the Indian polity may be available: Akbaruddin's so-called hate speeches often voiced the legitimate resentment of a victimized minority. Naming Akbaruddin's speech as "hate speech" contrasts with the failures of the Indian polity in regulating majoritarian forms of extreme speech with clearly hateful content. The snippets of the Nirmal speech that became viral are tied to notions of secularism and religion, especially as the Hindu nationalization of the Indian polity has centered the project to position Indian Muslims as second-class citizens.

What I argue, by extending the scope of the concept of extreme speech to the moral economy, is that the emotional value of speeches also requires fine-grained analysis within particular nation-state polities and their possibilities for claims on the nation from minority subject positions. For this endeavor, the term *extreme speech* is helpful precisely because the moral-normative framework is part of the analytic problem of extreme forms of speech and not of its solution (as liberal theorists may think). Consequently, the meaning of justice as it relates to resentment is always captured within the nation-state form—and this fact is the engine of what makes Akbaruddin's speech "transgressive" and "legitimate" at the same time. Even though, from a liberal perspective, Akbaruddin's extreme speech may fall into legitimate resentment, it is always at the brink of turning into ressentiment. Ressentiment is disempowered resentment—where not even some institutional safeguards can help a minority qua minority status—and this vulnerability is present in the form of the nation-state itself and bound up with its effectivity in delivering justice.

Notes

1. When I mentioned the comments of Akbaruddin to another Muslim friend in Delhi, he answered dryly and in a slightly teasing tone—probably because of the incorrectness of his comment—that Akbaruddin may be factually right: "Would those few OBCs [other backward castes] and Dalits [two low-caste groups] fight on behalf of the BJP's [Bharatiya Janata Party's] Brahmins and middle classes if the police wouldn't back them up?"

2. A large number of Akbaruddin's fan pages are available, some of which feature high numbers of subscribers. The accounts most subscribed to are Akbaruddin Owaisi The Great Leader (@AkbarUOwaisiTGL; subscribers in July 2019: 1,114,321) "Akbaruddin Owaisi (@ALHAJAKBARUDDINNOWAISI; subscribers: 729,220), and Akbaruddin Owaisi—Youth Icon (@AUOYI; subscribers: 647,164).

3. https://www.indiatoday.in/india/south/story/hate-speech-akbaruddin-owaisi-faces-additional-charges-of-sedition-and-waging-war-151152-2013-01-08 (Accessed March 28, 2019).

4. http://www.covanetwork.org/about-us/overview/ (Accessed December 17, 2018).

5. https://www.thehindu.com/news/cities/Hyderabad/bjp-breathes-fire-against-akbaruddin/article4259778.ece- 31 (Accessed March 14, 2019).

6. MIM leader Akbaruddin Owaisi's inflammatory speech triggers anger on Twitter. *India Today*, December 29, 2012.

7. https://timesofindia.indiatimes.com/city/hyderabad/Hate-speech-not-new-for-Owaisi-clan/articleshow/17963124.cms (Accessed December 17, 2018).

8. *A dictionary of Urdu, classical Hindi, and English.* London: W. H. Allen & Co., 1884.

9. https://thewire.in/politics/love-and-hate-in-hyderabad-the-fiery-political-life-of-akbaruddin-owaisi (Accessed March 31, 2019).

10. https://adrindia.org/content/let-india-be-melting-pot-ideas (Accessed November 7, 2018).

11. https://thewire.in/communalism/adityanath-anti-muslim-cover-up (Accessed December 17, 2018).

12. https://www.nytimes.com/2019/05/23/opinion/modi-india-election.html (Accessed May 28, 2019).

References

Ahmed, Hilal. 2013. *Muslim Political Discourse in Postcolonial India: Monuments, Memory and Contestation.* New Delhi: Routledge.

Ahmed, Sara. 2014. *The Cultural Politics of Emotion.* 2nd ed. Edinburgh: Edinburgh University Press.

Alam, Mahtab. 2018. "AIMIM's Akbaruddin Owaisi: Of Hyderabadi Salaams and Incendiary Speeches." Accessed March 7, 2019. https://www.business-standard.com/article/elections/aimim-s-akbaruddin-owaisi-of-hyderabadi-salaams-and-incendiary-speeches-118120700205_1.html.

Ansari, Khalid Anis. 2016. "The 'Muslim' Affirmative Action Debate: Post-Sachar Reflections." In *What Ails Indian Muslims*, edited by Murzban Jal, 147–166. Delhi: Aakar.

Bajpai, Rochana, and Adnan Farooqui. 2018. "Non-extremist Outbidding: Muslim Leadership in Majoritarian India." *Nationalism and Ethnic Politics* 24 (3): 276–298.

Casanova, José. 2010. "Säkularismus—Ideologie Oder Staatskunst." In *Den Säkularismus Neu Denken*, edited by Charles Taylor, 29–44. Frankfurt am Main: Neue Kritik.

Chaube, Sibani K. 2018. "Reflections on Secularism and Communalism in Constituent Assembly Debates and Beyond." In *Communalism in Postcolonial India: Changing Contours*, 2nd ed., edited by Mujibur Rehman, 11–27. New Delhi: Routledge.

Fassin, Didier. 2009. "Les économies morales revisitées." *Annales: Histoire, Sciences Sociales* 64 (6): 1237–66.

———. 2013. "On Resentment and Ressentiment: The Politics and Ethics of Moral Emotions." *Current Anthropology* 54 (3): 249–67.

Friedrichs, Jörg. 2018. *Hindu-Muslim Relations: What Europe Might Learn from India*. London: Routledge.

Hasan, Zoya. 2011. *Politics of Inclusion: Castes, Minorities, and Affirmative Action*. Oxford: Oxford University Press.

Honneth, Axel. 2018. *Anerkennung*. Frankfurt am Main: Suhrkamp.

Hunt, Grace. 2013. "Redeeming Resentment: Nietzsche's Affirmative Riposts." *American Dialectic* 2/3.

Islam, Maidul. 2019. *Indian Muslim(s) after Liberalization*. Oxford: Oxford University Press.

Jha, Shefali. 2017. "Democracy on a Minor Note: The All-India Majlis-e-Ittehadul Muslimin and Its Hyderabadi Muslim Publics." Chicago: University of Chicago.

Khan, Tabassum Ruhi. 2015. *Beyond Hybridity and Fundamentalism: Emerging Muslim Identity in Globalized India*. Oxford: Oxford University Press

Kramer, Max. 2014. *Sprachliche Imagination im Film—Tapori Hindi und die Verwendung sprachlicher Register im populären indischen Kino*. Working papers in modern South Asian languages and literatures, ARRAY(0x56251dc4e2f0). Master's thesis, Heidelberg University.

Lewis, Bernard. 2001. "The Roots of Muslim Rage [Article First Appeared in *The Atlantic Monthly*, September 1990.]." *Policy* 17 (4): 17–26.

Mazzarella, William. 2013. *Censorium*. Durham, NC: Duke University Press.

Metcalf, Barbara D. 1995. "Presidential Address: Too Little and Too Much: Reflections on Muslims in the History of India." *Journal of Asian Studies* 54 (4): 951–967.

Ministry of Minority Affairs. 2007. *Report of the National Commission for Religious and Linguistic Minorities*. Accessed July 17, 2017. http://www.minorityaffairs.gov.in/sites/upload_files/moma/files/pdfs/volume-1.pdf.

Moore, Nathan A. 2016. "Redefining Nationalism: Am Examination of the Rhetoric, Positions, and Postures of Asaduddin Owaisi." Thesis, University of Texas.

Nussbaum, Martha Craven. 2013. *Political Emotions: Why Love Matters for Justice*. Cambridge, MA: Belknap.

Pandey, Gyanendra. 2006. "The Time of the Dalit Conversion." *Economic and Political Weekly* 41 (18): 1779–1788.

Palshikar, Suhas. 2017. *Indian Democracy*. Oxford India Short Introductions Series. Oxford: Oxford University Press.

Punwani, Jyoti. 2017. "Hate Speech: Adityanath Isn't the First Powerful Offender to Be Shielded from Prosecution." *Scroll.in* (blog). Accessed July 24, 2019. https://scroll.in/article/837704/hate-speech-adityanath-isnt-the-first-powerful-offender-to-be-shielded-from-prosecution.

Rawls, John. 1973. *A Theory of Justice*. London: Oxford University Press.

Sachar Committee Report. 2006. *Prime Minister's High Level Committee, Social Economic and Educational Status of the Muslim Community of India*. Cabinet Secretariat Government of India. Accessed July 17, 2017. http://www.minorityaf-fairs.gov.in/sites/upload_files/moma/files/pdfs/sachar_comm.pdf.

Sahi, Ajit. 2017. "EXCLUSIVE: The UP Government's Colossal Cover-Up Attempt to Protect Adityanath." *The Wire* (blog). 2017. https://thewire.in/communalism/adityanath-anti-muslim-cover-up.

Scheler, Max. 2004. *Das Ressentiment im Aufbau der Moralen*. Frankfurt am Main: Vittorio Klostermann.

Sen, Ronojoy. 2019. *Articles of Faith: Religion, Secularism, and the Indian Supreme Court*. Law in India Series. New Delhi: Oxford University Press.

Sherman, Taylor C. 2015. *Muslim Belonging in Secular India: Negotiating Citizenship in Postcolonial Hyderabad*. Cambridge: Cambridge University Press.

Shivshankar, Rahul. 2020. 'Understanding AIMIM's Rise: Muslim Voters Have Rejected the Counterfeit Liberalism of "Secular" Parties'. *Times of India Blog* (blog). December 5, 2020. https://timesofindia.indiatimes.com/blogs/beyond-the-headline/understanding-aimims-rise-muslim-voters-have-rejected-the-counterfeit-liberalism-of-secular-parties/.

Singh, Pritam. 2015. "Institutional Communalism in India." *Economic and Political Weekly*.

———. 2019. *How to Win an Indian Election*. New Delhi: Penguin.

Stephens, Julia. 2014. "The Politics of Muslim Rage: Secular Law and Religious Sentiment in Late Colonial India." *History Workshop Journal 77* (1): 45–64.

Suneetha, A, and M. A Moid. 2019. "Mediating Muslim Citizenship? AIMIM and Its Letters." *Contemporary South Asia* 27 (1): 117–32.

Tech Observer Desk. 2018. "Modi, Yogi, Tendulkar and BJP Dominated Facebook in 2017." *Tech Observer* (blog), January 3, 2018. https://techobserver.in/2018/01/03/modi-yogi-tendulkar-bjp-dominated-facebook-platform-2017/.

Teltumbde, Anand. 2018. "The New Normal in Modi's 'New India.'" *Economic and Political Weekly* 53 (31): 7–8.

Udupa, Sahana, and Matti Pohjonen. 2019. "Extreme Speech and Global Digital Cultures." *International Journal of Communication* 13:3049–3067.

PART 2

COLLOQUIALIZATION OF EXCLUSION

PART 2 DEMONSTRATES THE ANALYTIC VALUE OF "EXTREME SPEECH" by exploring emerging connections among digital humor, fun, and extreme speech. These chapters illustrate how ethnographic nuance to situational features, user cultures, and formats of online expression can reveal new areas and forms of colloquial exchange through which exclusion is normalized. This approach opens up lines of inquiry that a regulatory-normative framework might overlook.

In chapter 5, on Internet memes and "alt-right" movements, Mark Tuters and Sal Hagen examine the controversial platform 4chan and how "politically incorrect" discussion in this platform builds antisemitic discourses online. They focus in particular on what they call "memetic antagonism"—that is, the use of internet memes to construct a sense of community through the creation of a common enemy. Through the "language games" of meme production, reactionary political projects such as the alt-right are allowed to build new "hegemonic articulations." Discussing the history of triple parentheses memes—for example, (((they)))—and its antisemitic origins, the authors observe that the situational features of 4chan push everything toward a game, the most basic "rule" of which has been the "juvenile axiom" of playful engagement that is used to excuse everything.

Sahana Udupa continues the emphasis on play and humor in chapter 6. She focuses on India and develops a theory of online fun as a "metapractice" that shapes the interlinked practices of fact-checking, abuse, assembly, and aggression among online volunteers for the right-wing movement. Being "funny" helps build prominence and can lead to validation through online virality and trending. It also celebrates aggression of group identity formation and expression. Udupa explains that digital manipulations (e.g., bots) have provoked cycles of rumor and street violence targeting minority communities and resulting in social media platforms restricting sharing. Digital and social media proponents of Hindu nationalism come from diverse backgrounds and levels of ideological commitment; Udupa notes that this strategy works with diffused logics and ties together fun and violence. What was once "fun" is used as a serious political activity that consolidates exclusionary ideologies.

In chapter 7, Carol McGranahan focuses on the United States and President Trump's Twitter feed to make the point that information today is not merely consumed—it is created and shared as a means of creating community. She proposes that Trump's archive should be seen as a form of extreme speech that generates not only political outrage but also specific forms of social community and action, including violent acts. McGranahan maintains that there is a scholarly responsibility to document and research the use of lies by political leaders to enable fear and "othering" and that result in hate-driven violence.

In chapter 8, Peter Hervik explores issues in Denmark through interviews and commentary on commercials and social media posts. He observes that populist pitches for power ("Elites betrayed the people") are built on networks owned by global media conglomerates and public service stations pressured by market forces. Hervik observes that the white hegemonic majority is driven by the cultural logic of a "nation in danger." In addition, commentators use strong language to stress negative things about the enemy to build community and comradeship ("You don't know who you are until you know who you hate").

Next, Amy C. Mack places the focus of chapter 9 on emerging movements of the "folk right" in the United States that use northern European culture, history, mythology, and spirituality. Identifying "Nordicism" as a prevalent theme in this phenomenon, Mack observes that the boundaries between the folk right and other right-wing groups are porous, and members and content move among groups and platforms. She notes that extreme speech can be generative, not merely destructive or simply bigoted—for example, the immigrant-as-problem meme rhetoric is grounded in "folk soul" (old gods and traditions tied to the blood and soil). By providing an ethnographic case study of Nordic-focused far-right communities on social media, the author reveals the role of memes and other online practices in constructing a collective identity rooted in Nordic exceptionalism, white supremacy, and race realism.

Gabriele de Seta turns to China in chapter 10. He recounts anecdotal experience with instant messaging apps, including the government calling the detention and indoctrination of Muslims a "vocational education and training program . . . to help eliminate the soil that breeds terrorism and extremism." De Seta examines the growing Islamophobic sentiment on Chinese social media platforms, primarily through ethnic humor and slanderous disinformation. Users add beards, turbans, and green-and-white striped shirts to existing memes, with these figures often depicted committing acts of violence. De Seta explains how incivility is articulated through "funny" stickers that quickly connect to narratives about extremism and socioeconomic grievances.

In the final chapter in part 2, Neil Haynes focuses on Chile. Haynes explores how humorous memes express distrust and dislike for Bolivian immigrants by northern Chileans (Nortinos) and how extreme language works "insidiously to reinforce racialized discrimination." The Nortinos build community on social media by reframing political issues and utilizing memes to gain power by denouncing others. They conflate being Bolivian with being racially inferior indigenous people while using humor in memes to mitigate the extremity of the ideas expressed. Memes are thus a central way that disenfranchised Chilean citizens reinforce a worldview in which they consider themselves deserving of greater access to resources than Bolivians, precisely because of their marginalized position in relation to the nation.

5

US AND (((THEM)))

Extreme Memes and Antisemitism on 4chan

Marc Tuters and Sal Hagen*

IN JULY 2017, AN ANGRY COMMENTER TO THE far-right Facebook page "This is Europa" fulminated that "(((Inbred psychopaths))) are trying to destroy Europe." While expressions of xenophobic vitriol in the course of political discussion have become increasingly normalized with the rise of the "populist radical right in Europe" (Mudde 2007), what stands out in this particular case is use of three parentheses—an internet meme with an antisemitic history. It began in 2014 as an audio "echo" effect used on an antisemitic podcast whenever a Jewish-sounding surname was mentioned. In 2016, the same concept was used by antisemitic and "alt-right trolls" on Twitter, who sought to draw attention to the apparently Jewish ancestry of journalists by placing their surnames within triple parentheses (Weisman 2018). Considered by historians of American conservatism as a "genuinely new" movement (Hawley 2017), the alt-right became notorious during the 2016 US presidential election period for its strategic promotion of slang expressions, such as "cuckservative," as a means to supposedly promote an antiliberal and "white nationalist" agenda (Heikkilä 2017). While many of the alt-right's ideas were not necessarily new, what was novel was the way in which their ideas became entangled with the abstract dynamics of internet memes and subcultural practices of internet "trolls," both of which arguably find their home in the notorious anonymous "imageboard" 4chan.

Although internet memes may have different meanings and uses in different online contexts, they frequently originate on subcultural or fringe corners of the web (Zannettou et al. 2018). Exemplary of the latter is the imageboard 4chan, a rather obscure website dedicated to the discussion of various topics. It is argued that 4chan's high volume of posts functions as a "powerful selection machine" for the production of attention-grabbing internet memes (Bernstein et al. 2011, 56). In the absence of the persistent markers of identity and reputation that are present on social media platforms like Facebook, participants in the anonymous and ephemeral conversations on 4chan must continually demonstrate their subcultural status and reformulate the boundaries of their community (Nissenbaum and Shifman 2017). Focusing specifically on how these dynamics play out on 4chan/pol/, a board or subforum explicitly dedicated to political discussion, we argue that this milieu produces innovations in forms of imitated expressions (in this case, bigoted ones) that may subsequently spread elsewhere—as the opening anecdote illustrates.

For the sake of focus, this chapter does not directly concern this diffusion of vernacular, nor does it directly tackle the important question of why it is that antisemitic speech is so ubiquitous in these online spaces at this particular historical juncture. Rather, in the chapter, we consider how internet memes can function as "floating signifiers," bringing together a cross-section of actors who may not necessarily share a common agenda but who are nevertheless united in their ritual opposition to a nebulous "other." In particular, we study 4chan as a site for what we refer to as *memetic antagonism*, whereby its anonymous users, or "anons," use internet memes to create a sense of community based around the construction of a common enemy. This animosity is salient considering internet memes' earlier framing in the field of new media as affording a means of progressive dissent for otherwise marginalized voices. In developing this concept, our objective is to offer a framework for assessing internet memes—an online visual cultural form usually characterized by a supposedly humorous tone (Knobel and Lankshear 2007; Shifman 2013)—as instances of "extreme speech" (Pohjonen and Udupa 2017). Acknowledging how such "humor operates as a cloak concealing racist nationalism" and in line with emerging scholarship on the topic, our approach may be described as a "critical tracing" of "politically incorrect participatory media" (Topinka 2018, 2052)—in this case, of the dynamics of the subcultural milieu of 4chan, from which new expressions of memetic antagonism frequently tend to emerge. We specifically consider the case of triple parentheses on 4chan/pol/, as it illustrates the process by which an antisemitic slur became reworked as a vehicle for expressing populist-style antagonism against a nebulous elite, most commonly referred to as *(((them)))*.

In the first section, we present a brief historical account of how political internet memes were initially received optimistically, as lowering the barrier for progressive dissent. We relate this optimism to the conceptual framework of "postpolitics" associated with Chantal Mouffe. In the second section, we introduce 4chan as the site of a new style of online political activism. Although studies of 4chan had earlier framed its activism as broadly consistent with the aforementioned postpolitics framework, with the increasing popularity of 4chan's /pol/ board, we observe that 4chan underwent a rightward shift alongside the emergence of the alt-right. However, rather than considering 4chan/pol/'s documented connections to extremist violence, our approach looks at instances of extreme speech that stop just short of overt expressions of hatred. Without minimizing the implicit potential danger in such speech, as recent events have made painfully clear, our aim in this chapter is to describe the contextual ambiguity of the different "situational features including technology, online agency, and political cultures" (Pohjonen and Udupa 2017, 1176) that may help to account for why its speakers might not consider their use of these expressions as hateful—at least not in the conventional legalistic sense.

Memes as Political Dissent

Derived from evolutionary biology, *memes* were initially hypothesized as "viruses of the mind," "informational parasite[s]," and "units of cultural transmission" subject to the competitive mechanisms of evolutionary biology (Dawkins 1976, 206). Following Richard Dawkins's infamous selfish gene hypothesis, the success of a given meme was to be measured based on its longevity, its widespread appeal, its copying fidelity, or its capacity to maintain a core meaning through the process of imitation. Having long been a form of vernacular expression within internet subcultures, it is argued that internet memes (hereafter "memes") started to go mainstream at around the same moment political events started to become "memetic" during the 2012 US election (Shifman 2013), as iconographies from the campaigns were avidly transformed, repurposed, and diffused online (Phillips and Milner 2017). The new category of the *political meme* arguably emerged at this point, although it would only go on to receive widespread international recognition in the news media with the notoriety of the Pepe the Frog meme during the subsequent 2016 election—to which we will return later. In the context of movements and events from Anonymous and Wikileaks to Occupy Wall Street and the 2011 Egyptian Revolution, political memes were initially interpreted in progressive terms as lowering the threshold for engaging in online activism. Following a framing established by media scholar Ethan Zuckerman's (2007) "Cute Cat Theory" of digital activism, which prophesied a new golden era for media activism in the era of visual social media, political memes were discussed in terms of a new kind of subaltern discourse. Within this dominant framing, political memes were theorized as expanding the broader spectrum of political debate to include otherwise marginalized viewpoints (Shifman 2013). Authors have championed memes, for instance, as an "enjoyable route for expressing political opinions" (Shifman 2013, 123) through which "democracy benefits" because "more people . . . engage in political discussion from more perspectives" (Milner 2013, 2361). While authors like Ryan Milner (2016) later also emphasized the exclusionary and antagonistic dynamics of "memetic logic," political memes were theorized in terms of offering democratizing and progressive "dissensus" against the dominant order.

In terms of political theory, the outlook on memes as vehicles for progressive dissent may be identified with Chantal Mouffe's concept of "agonistic pluralism." Mouffe developed her idea of agonistic pluralism as a remedy to a broader diagnosis concerning the relative absence of real political alternatives in the post–Cold War period of neoliberal hegemony, in what has been referred to as the postpolitics critique of liberalism (Dean 2009). In the postpolitical critique, "real" politics take place outside of the sphere of phony liberal consensus. From this perspective, it is on the ground and in the margins of activism that the important ideological struggles take place. Mouffe's particular contribution to this debate has been to advocate a foundational theory of political activism capable of challenging this dominant liberal hegemony, premised on the idea of grassroots collectives uniting in opposition to a clear adversary. Mouffe's theory of agonism is based on the simple idea that democratic politics are reducible to an existential struggle between the polis (us) and its adversaries (them), a concept whose essence she borrows from the political theorist and one-time Nazi jurist Carl Schmitt, whom she claims "highlights the fact that democracy always entails relations of inclusion/exclusion . . . a vital insight that democrats would be ill-advised to dismiss because they dislike its author" (Mouffe 1998, 164). While she follows Schmitt's antiliberalism to a point, Mouffe rejects what she correctly diagnoses as his essentially atavistic and essentialist view of "political and social identities as empirically given," arguing instead that they "must be seen as the result of the political process of hegemonic articulation," a process of homogeneity that paradoxically must remain open to "certain forms of pluralism" (171–172).

Citing Ludwig Wittgenstein's communitarian theory of language use, Mouffe (2018) argues it is through an "inscription in 'language games' . . . that social agents form specific beliefs and desires and acquire their subjectivity" (75). It is thus not always rational argumentation but rather the libidinal engagement in an "ensemble of language games that construct democratic forms of individuality" (75–76). Moreover, Mouffe emphasizes "the decisive role played by affective libidinal bonds in processes of collective identification" (73), a dimension that she argues is completely overlooked in the public sphere theory of communicative rationality. The corollary to Mouffe's hegemonic, discursive, and affective articulations of an "us" is the construction of a "them." For theorists of postpolitics, the problem becomes one of how to expand the scope of "the political" so as to include a much broader range of otherwise excluded and marginalized actors while avoiding a fatal descent into a state of unalloyed antagonism that Schmitt referred to as "the abyss of total devaluation" (2004, 67). Postpolitics theorists put forth the normative argument that symbolic dissent should exhibit a sense of propriety—what has been referred to as a "reasonable hostility" (Tracy 2008)—such that political memes, for example, should "remain sensitive to the socially rooted contextual standards of judgment" (Phillips and Milner 2017, 172), limiting their forms of symbolic dissent exclusively to responding to existing injustices as opposed to initiating any type of active attacks.

As a particularly influential voice in these debates, Mouffe developed her anti-essentialist political theory through an analysis of on-the-ground organization by social movements. Although Mouffe recently raised the alarm about right-wing populisms potentially leading to "nationalistic authoritarian forms of neoliberalism" (2018, 24), nowhere does she appear to seriously consider the problem of how political subjectivity is constructed in online environments—spaces with their own history of various idiosyncratic types of antagonisms, including "flame wars," bullying, "doxing," "trolling," and so forth (see Reagle 2015). In enabling dissent, political memes can also empower processes of "othering" based on the formulation of an organic and classless people bound together by existential antagonisms, considered as key elements in the overall "anatomy of fascism" (Paxton 2004). Dissent becomes othering when memetic antagonism falls into Schmitt's abyss of total devaluation. As we will see, due in part to its subculture and technical affordances, 4chan encourages a form of distancing and deniability in the exercise of what Sahana Udupa refers to in chapter 6 as "fun as a metapractice." Often expressed in a supposedly ironic manner, these instances of memetic antagonism function as affective "language games" for reactionary political projects, such as the alt-right, to build new "hegemonic articulations" often held together by vague floating signifiers. In light of this larger sociological problem, we look at how 4chan/pol/ may serve a kind of petri dish in which to concoct extreme and extremely virulent forms of right-wing populist antagonism.

4chan's Reactionary Turn

Over the past decade, the web has seen a trend toward "platformization," through which the infrastructures of a handful of social networking sites have become the dominant spaces for online social interaction (Helmond 2015). The prevalence of "profiles" and "friends" within these platforms is said to have eclipsed a culture of anonymity of an "older" internet of forums and message boards (Auerbach 2011). Arguably, the most notorious region of this anonymous "other" web is 4chan. With one million daily posts, 4chan is a so-called imageboard with subsections, or boards, dedicated to the discussion of specific topics, usually accompanied by the posting of images.[1] 4chan has two crucial affordances. First, it is anonymous: a lack of user accounts means everybody appears more or less the same. Second, it is ephemeral: posts are deleted after a few days or even minutes (Bernstein et al. 2011; Knuttila 2011). In the relatively limited academic literature on the topic, 4chan has been scrutinized in relation to its anonymous activism, unique subculture of memes, and trolling ethos (Coleman 2014; Phillips 2015; Nissenbaum and Shifman 2017). This literature mostly concerns the /b/ "Random" board, considered the birthplace of many of the web's most successful internet memes such as Rickrolling, Rage Faces, and LOLcats. This text, however, focuses on a different board, /pol/ "Politically Incorrect." The /pol/ board started in 2011 to siphon political extremist discussion from other areas of 4chan but has since become the most popular of all seventy boards.[2] Despite this popularity, /pol/ has received a limited amount of original academic research (see Hine et al. 2016; Zannettou et al. 2018; Hagen 2018*b*). It has, however, received a substantial amount of journalistic attention over the course of the past few years. It was identified as a far-right recruitment zone (Wendling 2018), it was connected to various acts of extreme violence (Hankes and Amend 2018), and it was claimed to have played a significant role in the 2016 US elections (Beran 2017; Shreckinger 2017)—although the latter claim is disputed (Phillips, Beyer, and Coleman 2017).

Given its subcultural status in relation to the mainstream web of platforms and apps, 4chan has a track record of innovating with vernacular web culture, whether those be memes, slang expressions, or some other subcultural ephemera. As such, chances are that edgy memes will have either started on 4chan or its users, "anons," are likely to be at the forefront of the most novel use. This avant garde status is particularly significant when considering that memes have no standardizing authority (e.g., unlike emojis). Their "meaning" can be understood as being constantly in flux. Indeed, when conceptualized as instances of multimodal speech acts, memes can be pragmatically theorized as "relevant to and also activated by the context of the utterance" (Grundlingh 2018, 153), such that memes can mean something different to different recipients in different contexts. This approach offers a frame through which to consider how anons may imagine themselves as participants in a kind of noninstitutional vernacular discourse standing in opposition to the mainstream (Howard 2008). Following Wittgenstein, if a meme's meaning may be understood as a function of its use, then we may observe different uses of memes in different regions of the web, with 4chan anons imagining their particular use as being the most up-to-date (see Miltner 2014; Milner 2016; Nissenbaum and Shifman 2017). When a meme like triple parentheses gets picked up by the "normies" of mainstream social media, as in the opening anecdote, anons will likely shift their own use of the vernacular expression or simply stop using it altogether.[3] Whereas such dynamics may be common in nonstandard dialects, they take on particular significance when it comes to the expression of seemingly hateful ideas.

Scholarship has identified 4chan as the preeminent venue for trolling as a subcultural practice. Although the term now more broadly refers to any number of "bad actors" online, historically, it refers specifically to an antagonistic rhetorical practice that aims at eliciting emotional responses from unwitting or unwilling targets (Phillips 2015). Although its subcultural origins predate the World Wide Web itself (see Donath 1999), Whitney Phillips (2015) argues that trolling experienced a proverbial "golden age" on 4chan in the late 2000s and early 2010s. In her account, trolling on 4chan sought to mock the sensationalism of American corporate media—for example, by baiting Fox News into labeling the imageboard as an "Internet Hate Machine" in 2007. In roughly this same period, 4chan was host to the Anonymous movement, described by the anthropologist Gabriella Coleman as "a wellspring of hackers and geeks who were taking political matters into their own hands and making their voices heard" (2014, 107)—a characterization arguably in line with the aforementioned Cute Cat Theory of digital activism. Among the many instances of coordinated online action from this period, anons would, for example, engage in trolling *Time*'s 2008 Most Influential Person poll so as to place 4chan's founder at the top of its list (see Deseriis 2015, 166). However, as meme culture went mainstream, post-2012 trolling seemed to turn darker. An example of this was the successful trolling of an online contest to name a new Mountain Dew soft drink flavor, a contest that anons won with the name "Hitler did nothing wrong."

Having moved past its golden age, it was not clear what 4chan had become or would be in the future. In its grotesquery, 4chan appeared like the babbling corpse of participatory culture, mocking the cyberutopian eschatology that had framed so much of the social media activism of the early 2010s. In the space of a few years, how could activists' activity on 4chan, which scholars had described in terms of an "ethical and political turn" (Deseriis 2015, 197), become so manifestly and self-evidently reactionary? One answer is that 4chan was always a reactionary site and that it had simply been misconstrued through the distorted lens of cyberutopian eschatology (Cramer 2017)—for example, in the case of playing with Nazi imagery, some incisive observers had indeed long viewed 4chan's subculture as fundamentally reactionary (Dibbell 2008). Another answer may simply lie in the emergence of /pol/, whose initially limited infamy might have drawn in various extremists. Indeed, in eclipsing other boards including /b/ in terms of overall popularity, /pol/ has broadly come to define 4chan in the public mind as a place of hate. What seems remarkable in retrospect is how, within the space of a few years, supposedly ironic 4chan in-jokes would provide an opening for a new style of white supremacist humor also appearing in the comment sections of websites like The Right Stuff with its podcast "The Daily Shoah"—where the triple-parentheses meme first emerged—and The Daily Stormer, whose founder memorably described this new philosophy as "non-ironic Nazism masquerading as ironic Nazism" (O'Brien 2017).

Memetic Antagonism

In addition to 4chan's aforementioned status as the native domain of the internet troll, anons have long cultivated a mythos of the site as the source of subcultural meme innovation. Given this track record, the particularly antagonistic manner in which in-group slang and memes are typically used on /pol/ seems to problematize the progressive agonistic theories outlined earlier. Whether expressed in the form of visual memes or textual expressions, the tendency toward antagonistic speech on 4chan may be understood as shaped by both its sub-cultural norms and its technical affordances. Since 4chan is effectively anonymous, it affords no persistent reputational capital, as opposed to social media. Instead of connected networks of user accounts, memes allow otherwise complete strangers to identify themselves as mem-bers of a community by employing them to demonstrate and negotiate in-group belong-ing. Accordingly, meme use on 4chan has been theorized through Pierre Bourdieu's lens of cultural capital (Nissenbaum and Shifman 2017). Extending this framework may also allow for consideration of 4chan as what Bourdieu referred to as a "linguistic market" (1991, 94) in which language use bestows a kind of wealth and authority on those who master the lan-guage, especially in the case of in-group slang, which Bourdieu considered as a quasi-aris-tocratic expression of distinction. Like all other forms of capital, Bourdieu conceptualized linguistic capital as being unevenly distributed, such that in licensing some to speak, it also has the effect of silencing others. In the struggle for this linguistic capital, actors on 4chan engage in "ritual opposition" (Tannen 1995, 140), in which language is used to negotiate rela-tionships of superiority. Within 4chan, this opposition exists as attempts at outsmarting op-ponents with provocations, wit, or insults (Phillips 2015), a gendered form of discourse with currency in the contemporary web culture of "toxic geek masculinity" (Salter and Blodgett 2017). Returning to Mouffe, one is led to question the extent to which a progressive theory of agonism can be usefully generalized to discuss forms of activism that emerge from these particularly antagonistic online spaces.

Apart from subcultural norms, the formal characteristics of "memetic logic" (Milner 2016) may also construct in- and out-group distinctions—not through political opposition but rather through the implicit formation of an "us" and "them" of, respectively, those aware and unaware of a meme's references. Independent of questions of their relative tastelessness, from a formal perspective, memes tend to engage in games of intertextuality (Knobel and Lankshear 2007; Shifman 2013). On 4chan especially, the use of memes operates according to a set of broader dynamics that tend toward abstraction and ironic subcultural style so that only those on the "inside" will "get" the latest innovation in the meme. This requires com-munity members to stay up to speed with its changing meaning—or multiple meanings—in terms of various proliferating subgenres and the intertextuality between them. Scholars of meme subcultures argue that these formal exercises can thus form "subcultural bat signals" (Phillips and Milner 2017, 112). Anons may identify the presence of these formal and stylistic qualities by deeming a given meme as "dank," which is to say that it engages with—or, bet-ter yet, innovates within—what scholars of 4chan have referred to as "the magical world of [4chan's] play frame" (Phillips and Milner 2017, 112). Given these dynamics of memetic in-novation, the use of memes on 4chan can become so arcane as to exceed the boundaries of comprehension, at least so far as the normies are concerned.[4]

In what may be referred to as a dynamic of abstraction, the minimal elements of a given memetic grammar can be isolated and reduced, often to the point that these memes become totally incomprehensible to outsiders. Since such exercises occur at the level of grammar, they are just as likely to occur in the case of "harmless" memes as with what we would call extreme memes. Figure 5.1, for example, shows memetic abstraction for both a harmless

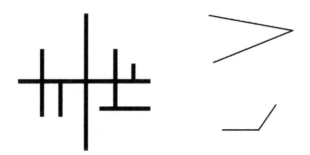

Figure 5.1 Minimalist versions of the Loss meme (left) and the Happy Merchant meme (right) derived from KnowYourMeme.com and 4plebs.org.

meme (left) and one with antisemitic connotations (right). These exercises of formal abstraction hinge on the reader's degree of meme literacy—indeed, an instance of the antisemitic meme posted to /pol/ was accompanied by the following post: "I'm actually impressed with how ingrained that image is in my head that I can identify it almost instantly even in this minimalist form."[5] This game of memetic abstraction may thus be seen as a demonstration of Mouffe's aforementioned emphasis: "the role played by affective libidinal bonds in processes of collective identification" (2018, 73).

To provide a tangible example of the interplay of these memes' formal characteristics with subcultural language games on 4chan/pol/, we briefly turn here to Pepe the Frog. Of all the memes used on/pol/, none is more popular than Pepe. Often used on /pol/ as a "reaction face" to accompany a textual post with a particular emotional state, the extreme adaptability of this meme—what we might refer to as *memetic versatility* (fig. 5.2)—makes it a nearly perfect example of what semioticians refer to as a *floating signifier*, which is to say a sign or symbol whose open-ended qualities render it broadly available to express practically anything. Given the fact that Pepe was embraced as a mascot by a variety of actors during the 2016 US election, including by the future US president himself (BBC 2017), it should be noted that this concept of the floating signifier was influentially developed by Mouffe's long-time collaborator Ernesto Laclau (2005) as a central concept in his influential analysis of populist politics. In Laclau's analysis, floating signifiers are indispensable to populism, as their very emptiness allows them to be invested with significance by a diverse variety of political constituencies. In this analysis, it is the very nebulousness of these signifiers that allows them to create what Laclau referred to as a "chain of equivalence" across various otherwise disparate publics. Like Mouffe, Laclau seems to have intended for this theory to benefit the left. In the case of the 2016 US election, however, it was actors on the right who managed to mobilize Pepe as floating signifier to temporarily hold together their loose alt-right network, which influential analysts described as including "conspiracy theorists, techno-libertarians, white nationalists, Men's Rights advocates, trolls, anti-feminists, anti-immigration activists, and bored young people" (Marwick and Lewis 2017, 3).

Although Pepe had been used in essentially apolitical contexts for many years on 4chan and other platforms like Tumblr, in summer 2016, the Anti-Defamation League, a US-based hate speech watchdog, put the frog into its database of hate symbols in recognition of the

Figure 5.2 Instances of the "Pepe" meme grammar posted to 4chan/pol/ on January 7, 2018 (Hagen 2018*a*).

new trend of combining him with Nazi imagery (BBC 2017). Despite categorizing Pepe as a hate symbol, the Anti-Defamation League recognized that the meme had other uses. But even in the case of Nazi Pepe, while there is evidence of instances of violent neo-Nazis frequenting /pol/ (Thompson 2018), many /pol/ anons likely had other explanations for how to interpret the meme's apparently hateful intent—for example, that it is a case of an incongruous juxtaposition of something innocent together with the worst thing ever; that it is a legitimate example of subcultural expression, akin to the use of swastika insignias by the mid-1970s UK punk subculture (Hebdige 1979); that it is an attempt to, in a sense, inoculate their style against the dynamics of commodification; or that it is an instance of the trolling tactic of "triggering normies." As it has been used on /pol/, Pepe exemplifies how extreme speech can unify a disparate and ephemeral community through disproval of others or, as we will discuss, through a shared object of antagonism.

(((Them))) as Nebulous Othering

This penultimate section returns to the triple-parentheses meme, introduced at the outset, to provide some empirical insights into a case of memetic antagonism on 4chan/pol/ and how the meme is used specifically as a vehicle for *nebulous othering*. In terms of methods, we use the 4plebs archive imported into 4CAT (Peeters and Hagen 2018), a tool to capture and analyze thread-based data, to visualize the posts per month of the triple parentheses on

4chan/pol/. From a semiotic perspective, what is unique about the triple parentheses is how, quite literally, the sign contains the signified. At the level of the corpus, this peculiar format offers a convenient marker to trace patterns in its dominant use. As such, we visualize the dominant contents within the three parentheses overall (using a word cloud) and per month (using RankFlow; Rieder 2016) from the start of its widespread use (June 2016) to the time of research (January 2019).

While the ultimate meaning of the triple-parentheses meme inevitably occurs in the local and multiple contexts of its reception, tracing thousands of instances of the triple-parentheses meme can arguably provide a macro overview of how the meme is commonly used. Moreover, when drawing from Wittgenstein's claim that the "meaning of words lies in their use" (1953, 80), it may also be argued that such tracing of the meme's dominant use will offer a perspective on its common meaning within 4chan/pol/. In response to the call to "critically trace politically incorrect participatory media" (Topinka 2018), we thus draw on this communitarian theory of language as the basis of an inductive method for determining the triple parentheses' dominant meaning and use in the service of ritual opposition (Tannen 1995).

As discussed at the outset of this chapter, triple parentheses began as an explicitly antisemitic meme on an alt-right podcast. Indeed, when the meme first appeared on 4chan/pol/, it was clearly antisemitic, accompanied by a version of the aforementioned "Happy Merchant" meme and posted in a discussion concerning Emma Lazarus's sonnet "The New Colossus," with the brackets encapsulating her surname (fig. 5.3). This first use is thus similar to the manner in which the triple parentheses were first used to "name" specific institutions and individuals. However, it was another year before that the meme became commonly used on /pol/, rapidly rising to roughly thirty-five thousand occurrences in almost 1 percent of all posts after June 2016 and remaining consistently popular thereafter (fig. 5.4). Compared with posts mentioning, for instance, Pepe, we see that the triple parentheses are remarkably consistently used (fig. 5.5).[6] Instead of a being meme appearing as part of incidental events or controversies, we can already say the triple parentheses form a consistent and common part of the vernacular of /pol/—implying a continued and fixed need for grammars with which to construct an outgroup within the ephemeral environment of 4chan.

Nevertheless, this "naming" seems to play a granular role only when looking at the dominant uses of the triple-parentheses meme on /pol/. Figure 5.4 shows a word cloud of the most-used words within three parentheses on 4chan/pol/ from May 2016 to March 2019, and figure 5.6 shows the same data but separated per month. We see specific names of individuals and institutions appearing—for instance, "cnn" is the second-most used word within the parentheses in September 2016 and "kushner" the fourth-most in April 2017, referring to Jared Kushner, who is the husband of Ivanka Trump and a senior advisor to Trump and who is also Jewish. However, what is most apparent is that the content of the parentheses is consistently dominated by a few words: "they" (used 84,303 times) and "them" (43,664), followed by "their" (16,516), "you" (14,065), and "media" (13,093).[7] What is noteworthy is how the dominant uses of triple parentheses mark an out-group, which, with the possible exception of "you," is figured in terms of a nebulous other.

Figure 5.7 offers a typical and mundane example of a post on /pol/ that employs this nebulous use. In this case, the poster uses "(((them)))" to refer to those responsible for

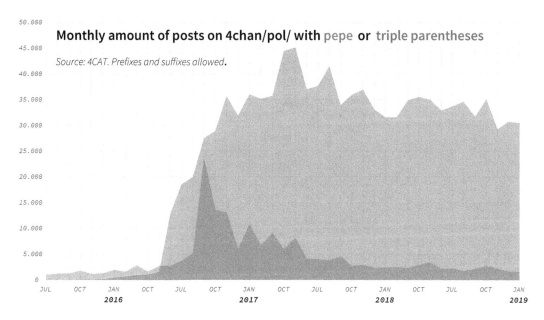

Monthly amount of posts on 4chan/pol/ with pepe **or** triple parentheses

Source: 4CAT. Prefixes and suffixes allowed.

Figure 5.3 The first appearance of the triple parentheses used around a name (September 2, 2015). Captured from 4plebs.org, November 20, 2018.

Figure 5.4 The 100 most used words within triple parentheses on 4chan/pol/ (June 2016-January 2019). Data derived from 4CAT (Peeters and Hagen 2018), word cloud made with Andreas Mueller's (2018) *word_cloud* library.

Figure 5.5 Posts containing "(((" and ")))" on 4chan/pol/, contrasted to posts containing "pepe" (July 2015 – January 2019). Pre- and suffixes allowed. Data derived with 4CAT (Peeters and Hagen 2018).

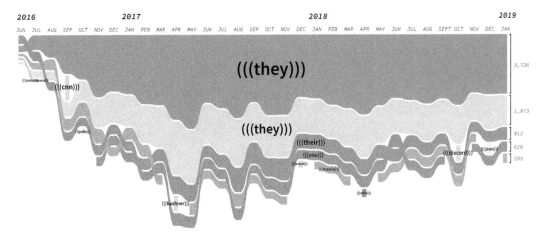

Figure 5.6 The five most used words within the triple parentheses per month on 4chan/pol/ (June 2016 to January 2019). Data derived from 4CAT (Peeters and Hagen 2018). Made with RankFlow (Rieder 2016).

Figure 5.7 A typical instance of a 4chan/pol/ post referencing "((((they)))" from November 20, 2018.

suppressing an esoteric "truth"—in this case, the archaic notion, once again popular in certain parts of the web, that the Earth is flat.[8] This use of triple parentheses resembles the vague and clichéd countercultural grievances against "the System." Although the meme is still occasionally used to target specific "jews" (appendix), its dominant function appears to be a means for anons to demonstrate their insider status by ferreting out an all-encompassing conspiracy theory. Similar to Pepe, on /pol/, the triple-parentheses meme seems to be used predominantly as a floating signifier whose nebulous significance offers a vehicle unifying multiple political constituencies in a common antagonism. Although the original use remains, what comes to the fore is a mode of use that, while consistent with antisemitic tropes, could also be interpreted as conspiratorial and vaguely populist.

While the subcultural practices and technical affordances underpinning this memetic antagonism are novel, as a form ritual opposition, it can be read as continuous with the "paranoid style of American politics" whose "spokesman sees the fate of conspiracy in apocalyptic terms" (Hofstadter 1964, 82). Typical of the "ironic" mode of speech on 4chan, the question of the intended meaning is left somewhat open, blurring distinctions between humor and seriousness, suspicion and hate. At the same time, the appeal of the meme derives from this nebulousness—that is, "real" anons will know who "((((they)))" really are.

By this means, the triple-parentheses meme comes to serve as a floating signifier; it "absorbs rather than emits meaning" and is "susceptible to multiple or even contradictory interpretations" (Buchanan 2010, 173). Through this process, it becomes transformed into a vernacular marker for the us/them antagonism that, as generally agreed, is the fundamental characteristic of the "thin ideology" of populism (Mudde and Kaltwasser 2017).

If we are to determine the meaning of a floating signifier by its use, can we then say that on 4chan/pol/, triple parentheses have transformed from an antisemitic slur into a technique of nebulous othering? While arguing that the term's meaning lies in its origins as opposed to its current use would be a genetic fallacy, one can still find instances in which the meme is used as an explicit antisemitic slur (appendix). Moreover, it can be argued that its current use as a marker for a nebulous other associated with the elite powers-that-be is also entirely in keeping with the long history of modern antisemitic canards extending back to the Protocols of the Elders of Zion (Renton and Gidley 2017). With its clearly antisemitic underpinnings, the memetic versatility of triple parentheses thus demonstrates how extreme antagonism can be obfuscated under the surface of a cartoonish version of populist rhetoric that appears to distance itself from its antisemitic origins by self-consciously and ironically aping the tropes of conspiracy theory.

In the face of what has been described as 4chan's "maze of irony" (Nagle 2017, 6), it is crucial to appreciate how contemporary forms of political ideology manage to persist even in the absence of self-conscious belief—an argument that philosophers of postmodernism have long asserted (Sloterdijk 1988; Žižek 1989). In contemporary speech, irony is often signaled through the use of "ironic quotation," which suggests that the full significance of the contents of the quotes is somehow suspect or even that the true meaning is contrary to what would otherwise be expected. Triple parentheses can, at least in part, be understood as a derivation of this particular language game. For those using triple parentheses—at least on /pol/—it beggars belief that they are unaware of the meme's antisemitic association. While they may not necessarily believe in antisemitic conspiracy theory, it is fair to say that in playing along with the meme, they assent to the broader narrative (see Rosenblum and Muirhead 2019).[9] But while this ironic and nihilistic type of extreme speech may seem quite new, antisemitism itself arguably has a long track record of using humor as a kind of rhetorical camouflage. As Jean-Paul Sartre noted, "Never believe that anti-Semites are completely unaware of the absurdity of their replies. They know that their remarks are frivolous, open to challenge. But they are amusing themselves, for it is their adversary who is obliged to use words responsibly, since he believes in words. The anti-Semites have the right to play. They even like to play with discourse for, by giving ridiculous reasons, they discredit the seriousness of their interlocutors. They delight in acting in bad faith, since they seek not to persuade by sound argument but to intimidate and disconcert" (1948, 13).

Conclusion

Political memes have been theorized as modes of postpolitical dissent in which a collective project arises through a "political process of hegemonic articulation" (Mouffe 1998,

172) that relies, above all, on the identification of a common opponent. This article has observed such a dynamic at work in the case of the triple-parentheses meme on 4chan/pol/, which, at least from a macroperspective, seems to have developed into a technique for nebulous othering resonant with the vague antagonisms of national populist xenophobic rhetoric. By juxtaposing an anecdotal instance of triple parentheses from Facebook as opposed to the meme's overt antisemitic origin, this chapter's initial intent was to speculate on the normalization of antisemitic discourse. In conclusion, we may thus ask how symptomatic this particular anecdote is of the mainstreaming of antisemitic rhetoric online in the current American context. Our analysis of the use of triple parentheses on 4chan/pol/ revealed its most common use as marker for a conspiratorial "them"—a discursively constructed enemy so vague it could have easily been misread, or rather, repurposed by the Facebook user.

In spite of its supposedly humorous valence in 4chan's discourse, the nebulous othering of triple parentheses marks an existential enemy opposed to a political adversary. This extreme form of memetic antagonism may be said to violate an implicit rule set that underpins the theory of agonistic pluralism—that there are particular lines that should not be crossed and rules that should not be broken in the expression of political dissent. Observing the dynamics of memetic antagonism may, however, bring us to legitimately question the extent to which Mouffe's nuanced distinctions remain useful in a digitized era in which national populist politicians like Donald Trump adopt a no-holds-barred style of antiliberalism that arguably flirts with antisemitic sentiment (Lipstadt 2019, 49) and whose campaign messaging has been observed to incorporate elements of memetic antagonism as developed on message boards (Lagorio-Chafkin 2018, 381–394).

What we hope to have made clear is that, although marginal, subcultural and vernacular web culture may nevertheless be considered as a site of innovation for new and extreme modes of political speech. These types of speech may resonate in the current antiliberal nationalist populist climate. It should be axiomatic in the study of internet memes that there is no transport without translation (Latour 2005); however, the greatest concern in this case involves the normalization of 4chan's memetic antagonism beyond its relatively circumscribed boundaries. Our argument has thus been that political memes as protest against the apparent hegemony of liberalism take on a different valence when used in this style of memetic antagonism—that is, the use of memes as vehicles for antagonistically articulating an out-group, unbound by civility. These articulations can explicitly name and shame, but we highlighted how memetic antagonism can collectivize online strangers through floating signifiers that allow formats for nebulous othering. An assessment of whether or not the collective identity of /pol/ is "dangerously" right-wing because of these dynamics has not been our objective. However, in the aftermath of the Christchurch shooting in March 2019, whose perpetrator was connected to 4chan's sibling forum 8chan (Knaus 2019), such an assessment would not appear to be in question. Concerning the pressing need to understand the relationship between these fringe internet communities and extremist ideologies, our contribution has sought to show the dynamics by which memes can be used to express forms of antagonism that are abstracted and thereby rendered nebulous.

Appendix. Most Used Words within Triple Parentheses

word	count	word	count	word	count	word	count	word	count
they	126,451	msm	5,210	democracy	3,075	bankers	2,131	elite	1,830
them	65,781	jews	5,134	alt-right	3,013	stein	2,101	capitalism	1,737
their	24,500	cnn	4,632	science	2,895	mods	2,000	scientists	1,737
you	20,002	polls	4,540	news	2,694	soros	1,993	banks	1,692
media	18,856	trump	4,322	elites	2568	journalists	1,982	op	1,667
who	11,489	someone	3,812	diversity	2,561	coincidences	1,975	wikipedia	1,663
white	6,776	we	3,785	they're	2,345	why	1,899	usa	1,637
people	6,622	globalists	3,241	jew	2,311	american	1,860	he	1,607
hollywood	6,139	google	3,187	us	2,238	christianity	1,851	communism	1,605
coincidence	5,366	eu	3,154	government	2,237	kushner	1,839	globalist	1,595

Notes

* This chapter is an adapted version of Marc Tuters and Sal Hagen, "(((They))) Rule: Memetic Antagonism and Nebulous Othering on 4chan," New Media and Society 22, no. 12 (2019): 2218–2237, doi:10.1177/1461444819888746. Thanks to Sahana Udupa, Iginio Gagliardone, Peter Hervik, and unnamed reviewers for their feedback on this work.

1. This number is as reported by 4chan itself at the time of writing (see 4chan.org/advertise).

2. See 4stats.io for live activity metrics. At the time of writing, /pol/ receives 115,560 posts per day, above /v/ (114,586), /vg/ (98,593), and /b/ (84,217).

3. As many scholars of internet memes have noted, meme subcultures have a history of acting with hostility to the recuperation of their artefacts by mainstream culture, especially when they are commodified by parties with monetary interests (Douglas 2014; Phillips 2015; Milner 2016).

4. "Normies" is a popular internet term to denote "regular" people, that is, those not up to speed with current internet culture.

5. See archive.4plebs.org/pol/thread/105649057/#105649189.

6. Although Pepe is usually communicated visually, making the comparison not entirely fair, the point still stands that Pepe seems more more event- and controversy-bound than the triple parentheses.

7. Specific names are less common, with "trump" (3,409), "stein" (3,409), and "soros" (1,841) being used considerably less. Note that as of late 2017, it was common to see posts professing Trump to be a "jewish puppet" (Hagen 2018b). See the appendix for a more expansive table.

8. Also note the reference here to the "red pill," another slang expression for esoteric awakening, which also developed on /pol/ before it trended in the mainstream (Wendling 2018).

9. Rosenblum and Muirhead (2019) argue that this distinction between "believe in" and "assent to" is a feature that differentiates the logic of the classical conspiracy theorist from that of what they call "the new conspiracism," the latter which seeks above all the delegitimation of established forms of institutional authority without necessarily proposing any coherent ideological project in its stead.

References

Auerbach, David. 2011. "Anonymity as Culture: Treatise." *Triple Canopy* 15. https://www.canopycanopycanopy.com/contents/anonymity_as_culture__treatise.

BBC. 2017. "'Hijacked' Pepe the Frog 'Killed off.'" May 8, 2017. https://www.bbc.com/news/world-us-canada-39843468.

Beran, Dale. 2017. "4chan: The Skeleton Key to the Rise of Trump." *Huffington Post*, February 20, 2017. https://www.huffingtonpost.com/entry/4chan-the-skeleton-key-to-the-rise-of-trump_us_58ab6156e4b0a855d1d8dfe4.

Bernstein, Michael S., Andrés Monroy-Hernández, Drew Harry, Paul André, Katrina Panovich, and Gregory G. Vargas. 2011. "4chan and/b: An Analysis of Anonymity and Ephemerality in a Large Online Community." In *Proceedings of the Fifth International AAAI Conference on Weblogs and Social Media*, Barcelona, 2011, 50–57.

Bourdieu, Pierre. 1991. *Language and Symbolic Power*. Cambridge: Harvard University Press.

Buchanan, Ian. 2010. *Dictionary of Critical Theory*. Oxford: Oxford University Press.

Coleman, Gabriella. 2014. *Hacker, Hoaxer, Whistleblower, Spy: The Many Faces of Anonymous*. London: Verso.

Cramer, Florian. 2017. *Meme Wars: Internet Culture and the "Alt Right."* Filmed March 2017, at FACTLiverpool. Video. https://www.youtube.com/watch?v=OiNYuhLKzi8.

Dawkins, Richard. 1976. *The Selfish Gene*. Oxford: Oxford University Press.

Dean, Jodi. 2009. *Democracy and Other Neoliberal Fantasies*. Durham, NC: Duke University Press.

Deseriis, Marco. 2015. *Improper Names: Collective Pseudonyms From the Luddites to Anonymous*. Minneapolis: University of Minnesota Press.

Dibbell, Julian. 2008. "Mutilated Furries, Flying Phalluses: Put the Blame on Griefers, the Sociopaths of the Virtual World." *Wired*, January 18, 2008. https://www.wired.com/2008/01/mf-goons/.

Donath, Judith S. 1999. "Identity and Deception in the Virtual Community." In *Communities in Cyberspace*, edited by Peter Kollock and Mark Smith. London: Routledge.

Douglas, Nick. 2014. "It's Supposed to Look Like Shit: The Internet Ugly Aesthetic." *Journal of Visual Culture* 13 (3): 314–339.

Grundlingh, Lezandra. 2018. "Memes as Speech Acts." *Social Semiotics* 28 (2): 147–168. https://doi.org/10.1080/10350330.2017.1303020.

Hagen, Sal. 2018a. "4chan/pol/ Image Walls: Memes." *OILab.eu*, March 1, 2018. https://oilab.eu/4chanpol-image-walls-memes/.

———. 2018b. "Here I Am, Praying to an Egyptian Frog: Exploring Political Fluidity on 4chan/pol/." Master's thesis, Universiteit van Amsterdam.

Hankes, Keegan, and Alex Amend. 2018. "The Alt-Right Is Killing People." *Southern Poverty Law Center*, February 5, 2018. https://www.splcenter.org/20180205/alt-right-killing-people.

Hawley, George. 2017. *Making Sense of the Alt-Right*. New York: Columbia University Press.

Hebdige, Dick. 1979. *Subculture: The Meaning of Style*. London: Routledge.

Heikkilä, Niko. 2017. "Online Antagonism of the Alt-Right in the 2016 Election." *European Journal of American Studies* 12 (2). https://doi.org/10.4000/ejas.12140.

Helmond, Anne. 2015. "The Platformization of the Web: Making Web Data Platform Ready." *Social Media + Society* 1 (2): 1–11. https://doi.org/10.1177/2056305115603080.

Hine, Gabriel Emile, Jeremiah Onaolapo, Emiliano De Cristofaro, Nicolas Kourtellis, Ilias Leontiadis, Riginos Samaras, Gianluca Stringhini, and Jeremy Blackburn. 2016. "Kek, Cucks, and God Emperor Trump: A Measurement Study of 4chan's Politically Incorrect Forum and Its Effects on the Web." *ArXiv:1610.03452*. https://arxiv.org/pdf/1610.03452.pdf.

Hofstadter, Richard. 1964. "The Paranoid Style in American Politics." *Harpers Magazine* (November): 77–86.

Howard, Robert G. 2008. "The Vernacular Web of Participatory Media." *Critical Studies in Media Communication* 25 (5): 490–513. https://doi:10.1080/15295030802468065.

Knaus, Christopher. 2019. "'A Perfect Platform': Internet's Abyss Becomes a Far-Right Breeding Ground." *The Guardian*, March 19, 2019. https://www.theguardian.com/world/2019/mar/19/a-perfect-platform-internets-abyss-becomes-a-far-right-breeding-ground.

Knobel, Michele, and Colin Lankshear. 2007. "Online Memes, Affinities and Cultural Production." In *A New Literacies Sampler*, edited by Knobel Michele and Colin Lankshear, 199–227. New York: Peter Lang.

Knuttila, Lee. 2011. "User Unknown: 4chan, Anonymity and Contingency." *First Monday* 16 (10). https://doi.org/10.5210/fm.v16i10.3665.

Laclau, Ernesto. 2005. *On Populist Reason*. New York: Verso.

Lagorio-Chafkin, Christine. 2018. *We Are the Nerds: The Birth and Tumultuous Life of Reddit, the Internet's Culture Laboratory*. London: Piatkus.

Latour, Bruno. 2005. *Reassembling the Social: an Introduction to Actor-Network-Theory*. Oxford: Oxford University Press.

Lipstadt, Deborah E. 2019. *Antisemitism: Here and Now*. New York: Schocken.

Marwick, Alice, and Rebecca Lewis. 2017. "Media Manipulation and Disinformation Online." *Data and Society*. https://datasociety.net/output/media-manipulation-and-disinfo-online/.

Milner, Ryan M. 2013. "Pop Polyvocality: Internet Memes, Public Participation, and the Occupy Wall Street Movement." *International Journal of Communication* 7:2357–2390.

———. 2016. *The World Made Meme: Discourse and Identity in Participatory Media*. Cambridge, MA: MIT Press.

Miltner, Kate. 2014. "'There's No Place for Lulz on LOLCats': The Role of Genre, Gender, and Group Identity in the Interpretation and Enjoyment of an Internet Meme." *First Monday* 18 (4). https://doi.org/10.5210/fm.v19i8.5391.

Mouffe, Chantal. 1998. "Carl Schmitt and the Paradox of Liberal Democracy." In *Law as Politics: Carl Schmitt's Critique of Liberalism*, edited by David Dyzenhaus. Durham, NC: Duke University Press.

———. 2013. *Agonistics: Thinking The World Politically*. New York: Verso.

———. 2018. *For a Left Populism*. London; New York: Verso.

Mudde, Cas. 2007. *Populist Radical Right Parties in Europe*. Cambridge: Cambridge University Press.

Mudde, Cas, and Cristobal Rovira Kaltwasser. 2017. *Populism: A Very Short Introduction*. Oxford: Oxford University Press.

Mueller, Andreas. 2018. *word_cloud* (version 1.5.0). Computer software. New York City. https://github.com/amueller/word_cloud.

Nagle, Angela. 2017. *Kill All Normies: The Online Culture Wars from Tumblr and 4chan to the Alt-Right and Trump*. Winchester: Zero.

Nissenbaum, Asaf, and Limor Shifman. 2017. "Internet Memes as Contested Cultural Capital: The Case of 4chan's /b/ Board." *New Media and Society* 19 (4): 483–501. https://doi.org/10.1177/1461444815609313.

O'Brien, Luke. 2017. "The Making of an American Nazi." *Atlantic*, December 2017. https://www.theatlantic.com/magazine/archive/2017/12/the-making-of-an-american-nazi/544119.

Paxton, Robert O. 2004. *The Anatomy of Fascism*. New York: Random House.

Peeters, Stijn, and Sal Hagen. 2018. *4CAT: Capturing and Analysis Toolkit* (version 1.0). Computer software. Amsterdam. https://github.com/digitalmethodsinitiative/4cat.

Phillips, Whitney. 2015. *This Is Why We Can't Have Nice Things: Mapping the Relationship between Online Trolling and Mainstream Culture*. Cambridge, MA: MIT Press.

Phillips, Whitney, Jessica Beyer, and Gabriella Coleman. 2017. "Trolling Scholars Debunk the Idea That the Alt-Right's Shitposters Have Magic Powers." *Motherboard*, March 22, 2017. https://motherboard.vice.com/en_us/article/z4k549/trolling-scholars-debunk-the-idea-that-the-alt-rights-trolls-have-magic-powers.

Phillips, Whitney, and Ryan M. Milner. 2017. *The Ambivalent Internet: Mischief, Oddity, and Antagonism Online*. Cambridge: Polity.

Pohjonen, Matti, and Sahana Udupa. 2017. "Extreme Speech Online: An Anthropological Critique of Hate Speech Debate." *International Journal of Communication* 11:1173–1191.

Rieder, Bernhard. 2016. *RankFlow* (version 1.0). Computer software. Amsterdam. http://labs.polsys.net/tools/rankflow/.

Reagle, Joseph M. 2015. *Reading the Comments: Likers, Haters, and Manipulators at the Bottom of the Web*. Cambridge, MA: MIT Press.

Renton, James, and Ben Gidley. 2017. "The Shared Story of Europe's Ideas of the Muslim and the Jew—A Diachronic Framework." In *Antisemitism and Islamophobia in Europe: A Shared Story?*, edited by James Renton and Ben Gidley, 1–21. London: Palgrave Macmillan. https://doi.org/10.1057/978-1-137-41302-4_1.

Rosenblum, Nancy L., and Russell Muirhead. 2019. *A Lot of People Are Saying: The New Conspiracism and the Assault on Democracy*. Princeton, NJ: Princeton University Press.

Salter, Anastasia, and Bridget Blodgett. 2017. *Toxic Geek Masculinity in Media: Sexism, Trolling, and Identity Policing*. London: Palgrave Macmillan.

Sartre, Jean-Paul. 1948. *Antisemite and Jew*, translated by George B. Becker. New York: Schocken.

Schmitt, Carl. 2004. *The Theory of the Partisan: A Commentary/Remark on the Concept of the Political*. East Lansing: Michigan State University Press.

Schreckinger, Ben. 2017. "World War Meme." *Politico*, March 2017. https://politi.co/2qK8kHH.

Shifman, Limor. 2013. *Memes in Digital Culture*. Cambridge, MA: MIT Press.

Sloterdijk, Peter. 1988. *Critique of Cynical Reason*. Minneapolis: University of Minnesota Press.

Tannen, Deborah. 1995. "The Power of Talk: Who Gets Heard and Why." *Harvard Business Review* 73 (5): 138–148.

Thompson, Andrew. 2018. "The Measure of Hate on 4chan." *Rolling Stone*, May 10, 2018. https://www.rollingstone.com/politics/politics-news/the-measure-of-hate-on-4chan-627922/.

Topinka, Robert J. 2018. "Politically Incorrect Participatory Media: Racist Nationalism on R/ImGoingTo HellForThis." *New Media and Society* 20 (5): 2050–2069. https://doi.org/10.1177/1461444817712516.

Tracy, Karen. 2008. ""Reasonable Hostility": Situation-Appropriate Face-Attack." *Journal of Politeness Research* 4 (2): 169–191. https://doi.org/10.1515/JPLR.2008.009.

Weisman, Jonathan. 2018. *(((Semitism))): Being Jewish in America in the Age of Trump*. New York: St. Martin's Press.

Wendling, Mike. 2018. *Alt-Right: From 4chan to the White House*. London: Pluto.

Wittgenstein, Ludwig. 1953. *Philosophical Investigations*. Oxford: Basil Blackwell.

Zannettou, Savvas, Tristan Caulfield, Jeremy Blackburn, Emiliano De Cristofaro, Michael Sirivianos, Gianluca Stringhini, and Guillermo Suarez-Tangil. 2018. "On the Origins of Memes by Means of Fringe Web Communities." *ArXiv:1805.12512*. http://arxiv.org/abs/1805.12512.

Zuckerman, Ethan. 2007. "The Connection between Cute Cats and Web Censorship." http://www.ethanzuckerman.com/blog/2007/07/16/the-connection-between-cute-cats-and-web-censorship/.

Žižek, Slavoj. 1989. *The Sublime Object of Ideology*. London: Verso.

6

NATIONALISM IN THE DIGITAL AGE

Fun as a Metapractice of Extreme Speech

Sahana Udupa*

"I AM THERE WITH ALL MY IDENTITY, I am original," declares Rakesh,[1] as he prepares to impress on us that his ideological battle cannot be compared with anonymous muckrakers online. As a top national media convener for the Akhil Bharatiya Vidyarti Parishad (ABVP; All India Student Association), the student wing of the right-wing Hindu nationalist organization in India,[2] Rakesh finds digital social media "sine qua non" of political life and a critical means to disseminate the right-wing ideology he has come to embrace. As a key figure in the youth mobilization of the Hindu nationalist ideology in contemporary India, Rakesh sees himself fighting a battle of ideological positions on online media against what he scathingly terms as "certain communists" and "pseudoliberals." His narration gains the tenor of a serious patriotic mission as we throw more questions on his online political activities, but he adds how he is "spiritual and traditional" but not "conservative in the Western sense of the term," and that he "enjoys life to the fullest," including dance and music. Enjoyment of life gains a purpose on online media, he indicates, since some of his online activities and advocacy have yielded tangible political results. "We [ABVP] have speeded up the passing of the Juvenile Justice Bill," he says, citing it as an example for the satisfaction of meeting a political goal with online mobilization that relies on no resources other than online networking and mobilization.

The short description of our conversation with a top Hindu nationalist youth leader brings out several points that this study seeks to sketch and analyze: the work of online social networking sites in drawing a large number of the digitally savvy generation toward Hindu nationalism; in familiarizing and reproducing the ideology of Hindu nationalism as a composite, yet distinct sensibility of Hindu-first India and majoritarian belligerence; and offering a force field where such an exclusivist ideology is rendered acceptable and enjoyable. The article will especially elaborate on the last point, since ideological enthusiasm on social media is still largely understood in the liberal frame of political action, with far less attention to the visceral aspects of fun and enjoyment that constitute right-wing mobilization.

In drawing out "fun" as an indelible feature of online right-wing affiliation, I delineate its four distinct, yet overlapping aspects:

- being "funny" as a tactical way to enter and rise to prominence within online debates and, by extension, the broader public domain;
- deriving fun from the sheer freshness of colloquialism in political debates, which stands in contrast to the serious tone of political deliberation and official centricity, and by mainstreaming the witty political campaign styles as an everyday form of political communication;
- fun as satisfaction of achieving a goal by working with one's own resources, and in finding tangible results such as hashtag trending, virality, and perceived "real world" changes; and
- as group identification and collective (if at times anonymous) celebration of aggression.

The key argument is that fun is a metapractice—practice of practices—that frames the distinct online activities of fact-checking, argumentative confrontations, assembly, and aggression, which are prominent among right-wing volunteers in digital India. Furthermore, fun as a metapractice remains crucial for an experience of absolute autonomy among online users in the ideological battles. Bringing to closer scrutiny the visceral aspects of fun, autonomy, and aggression in online political discourse, the article asks how these features enable ideological voluntary work as an everyday drip feed for exclusion, composing the online work for nationalist regimes.

The methodological approach draws from multisited internet related ethnography (Wittel 2000) to situate online discourses within a polymedia field (across different media forms; Madianou and Miller 2013) as well as material, political worlds of online-offline connections using anthropology's classic emphasis on long-term on-the-ground fieldwork. In studying digital networks and exchange, "the ethnographer actively and consciously participates in the construction of spaces. . . . In this respect, the framing of the network for the research not only pre-structures the findings and conclusions of any ethnographic inquiry, the framing also becomes a political practice" (Wittel 2000, 9).

Rooted in ongoing multisited ethnographic fieldwork that started in 2013 in the cities of Mumbai, Delhi, and Bangalore, comprising semistructured in-person interviews with politically active online users; social media campaign strategists for political parties; ethnographic observations of offline events; informal hanging out; and theoretically sampled content analysis of online exchange, this article foregrounds online activities of Hindu nationalist volunteers set in an intense climate of political patronage. The article will begin by examining this climate of organized ideological production mobilized by the social media savvy right-wing regime now in power in India. Reading it against the global rise of exclusionary nationalism, the next section reviews important approaches to online right-wing movements and highlights the value of the "media practice" framework (Couldry 2010; Postill and Brauchler 2010) to critically analyze key aspects of online work that comprise and sustain right-wing political cultures.

Fun as a metapractice should not be read in isolation, but in relation to a political milieu where online extreme speech acts concentrate among groups already dominant within particular historical and social conditions. The privileged position of Hindu nationalist volunteers as middle class, educated, intermediary, or upper caste groups provides the key context for domination within the online sphere, where fun perpetuates the commonsense beliefs about Hindu-first India. This underscores the need to launch a critique of "collective laughter," which takes as "its object common-sense assumptions about humor's desirability" (Billig 2005, 2; Haynes 2019; Hervik 2019). Equally, fun relates to the spread of the Hindu nationalist "common sense" and diverse contestations beyond the privileged middle-class groups, as humor and fun of sharing circulate on affordable mobile internet media accessed in recent years by a wider breadth of class groups.[3] The two sections on the practices of trending hashtags and creating internet memes will ethnographically chart this phenomenon. Based on the analysis, the concluding section develops preliminary arguments for a social critique of digital fun in times of nationalism on a rise.

Hindu Nationalism in Digital India

The 2014 electoral victory of the Bharatiya Janata Party (BJP), the right-wing Hindu nationalist political party, was a culmination of concerted political campaigning that infused electoral politics with a new scale of targeted appeal and spectacle enabled by digitalization. The campaign aimed foremost at transforming the public image of the party's controversial prime ministerial candidate Narendra Modi into a visionary leader for digital young India. The dramatic rebranding of a leader who faced the accusation of complicity in the mass murder of Muslim minorities in the state of Gujarat in 2002[4] into a messiah of "New India" owed its success largely to a sharply crafted campaign spearheaded by a small team of elite digital media marketers and tech entrepreneurs, and a top international advertising agency commissioned directly by a trusted group of Modi strategists after spending "unprecedented sums of money" (Jaffrelot 2015, 163; Pal, Chandra, and Vydiswaran 2016).[5] Modi's team of multimedia marketers "adapted high-tech tools to a variety of low-tech outlets" including massive holograms employed for Modi's "direct address" to people (Price 2015, 136). The team composed a structure that ran parallel to the party's media campaign, since Modi attempted to "short circuit the BJP apparatus," thereby sidelining several senior party leaders (Jaffrelot 2015, 151). Modi's active presence on Twitter helped to circumvent the party's senior leadership as well as organized media, which were still wary about his tainted tenure as the chief minister of the state of Gujarat. Some scholars have defined Modi's strategies to constitute a people beyond the collegial structure of the Hindu nationalist organizations and the party machinery as "populism" (Jaffrelot 2015; Schroeder 2018).

Although Modi's social media activities did circumvent the party's central leadership, the BJP, more than other political parties, was active in deploying social media resources for electoral gains and ideological recruitment. This built on the well-established transnational online networks of the RSS that had started cyber gatherings via dedicated websites and mailing lists as early as in the 1990s.[6] Well before a centralized Information Technology (IT) cell became functional at the party's national headquarters in New Delhi in 2010, different regional (subnational) units of the party had started to experiment with internet-enabled membership drives and mobilization. These experiments relied on the support of internet-savvy volunteers who were energized by their technological knowledge and the prospect

of challenging large-scale governmental corruption and state failures through social media use. The anticorruption support on social media developed a deep affinity for emerging icons of "clean leadership" such as Narendra Modi, although many of them were still
hesitant about Hindu majoritarian ideas. The seeming divide between the visions of development and Hindu nationalism was itself well managed by the Modi team, to appeal to a
people beyond the support base of Hindu nationalism while also safeguarding its majoritarian essence and reinforcing the association between them in the early years of economic
reforms in India (Rajagopal 2001).

In a triadic structure of influence comprising Modi's campaign strategy, the party's social media presence with regional trajectories, a Modi-centric campaign style (Jaffrelot 2015),
and an active middle class aspiring for a better India, right-wing Hindu nationalist mobilization gained momentum in new millennium India as a composite ideological space. In the
years after electoral victory and in preparation for the 2019 national elections, the campaign-
style management of online media by the Modi team accelerated on various social networking platforms including Facebook, Twitter, WhatsApp, Instagram, Telegram, and the short
video-sharing app TikTok, pushing the appeal beyond middle-class supporters. Twitter has
remained an important platform for the ideological work, but the party's social media presence is further diversified with the vast expansion of the messenger service WhatsApp after 2014, continued popularity of Facebook, and the emergence of TikTok.[7] Simultaneously,
ABVP, the student wing of the Hindu nationalist "parivar" (family or ideological coalition),
has started accumulating strength on online media, straddling the three layers of influence.[8]

BJP's social media presence was tinged by allegations of employing bots, when several
media reports revealed that Modi's online followers had a large number of fake handles.
Moreover, bots and rumors spreading on social media networks such as WhatsApp have
become the new feature of (interreligious) communal tensions and riots in India. In major
incidents of pre-election violence, digital manipulations have provoked cycles of rumor and
street violence targeting minority communities, forcing social media companies to respond
with restrictions on sharing activities.[9]

In an atmosphere of "permanent campaign" (Neyazi, Kumar, and Semetko 2016), the
central IT cell of the party keeps the momentum alive on social media, with war-like spikes
in provocation but also routine everyday exchanges that repeat and reproduce the "party
line." The IT cell has thus evolved into a significant wing of the party with a small team
of fully paid workers stationed in New Delhi but drawing support from a large number of
(unpaid) volunteers. Perceptive of the volatile nature of online communities, the party has
adopted the strategy of close distance nurturing rather than aiming for a tight-fist control
of the educated online support base, alongside a heavily funded campaign employing digital
marketers to reach out to a broader mass of supporters. Although the party organizes regular offline events for online supporters, the technique has been to regulate by staying with
the flow, allowing voluntary work to augment party campaigning (A. Malviya, head of BJP
IT cell, personal interview, July 24, 2017).

A crucial node in the triadic structure of online Hindu nationalism is the vast number
of volunteers whose everyday work feeds the top-down campaign with continuous engagement. In 2017, the BJP had more than 100,000 volunteers spread across the country and

the diaspora locations. The central IT cell could rely on their online support anytime. This group was separate from the volunteer base that the party's regional and subregional units cobbled up in various numbers across the country, as well as fuzzy enthusiasts online. The very presence of a large number of volunteers testifies to online ideological work that is neither fully directed nor bound by party mentoring.

Online volunteers of Hindu nationalism are far from a homogeneous group of indoctrinated foot soldiers. With diverse occupational backgrounds and levels of ideological commitment, online volunteers of Hindutva (Hinduness, a key ideological principle of Hindu nationalism) discuss mighty points of the ideology, gliding around a set corpus of themes (Udupa 2018). These themes include rhetorical patriotism, emotional reference to the sacrifice of the Indian army; territorial attachment to the sacred land of India; minority Muslim community as threats to the security of the nation; the symbolism of the sacral cow; global conspiracy for Christian proselytization; the glory of ancient, undivided Hindu India; and the flawed history of India built by the left-liberal intelligentsia, who are derided through various labels of ridicule, from "pseudoseculars" to "urban naxals." Historically, these have been the key tropes of the Hindu nationalist movement in postcolonial India (van der Veer 1994). Contradictory as social media debates may be, the maneuvering within the ideological space testifies to the diffused logics of Hindutva online, which I have defined as "enterprise Hindutva" (Udupa 2018).

The discussion above does not suggest a complete ideological capture of India's social media by the Hindutva ideology. After a decade of the BJP's "first mover advantage," major political parties are more active on social media, and social movements challenging the Hindutva perspectives have emerged from the vibrant and multivalent voices of Dalit, feminist, student activist, and caste-based groups, as well as digital campaigns of opposition parties (Neyazi et al. 2016; Paul and Dowling 2018). However, this does not diminish the importance of online Hindutva because neither can the latter be reduced to political instrumentality nor to the ebbs and flows of online contestation. Online Hindutva is better assessed as a cultural and political sensibility that is capable of working with diffused logics, reproducing through generations by articulating the entrails of the old with emerging concerns, and altering the modality with changing circumstances. While certainly being challenged from diverse online expressions and opposing claims, Hindu nationalism remains a potent cultural and political force. This is evidenced by the continued growth of online followers for the party, the diversification of its social media presence with regional and subregional sites, and more recently by the thumping victory of the BJP in national elections (2019).[10] How then do we approach the unique mediation of online networks in the resurgent, if contested, mobilization of Hindutva? How is it connected to the global rise of online nationalism and right-wing movements? A brief overview of key theoretical studies of media and nationalism in the following section will suggest that the relationship between fun and violence—ignored in many studies of online right-wing movements—is key to grasp the current phenomenon.

Nationalism in Digital Times

Recent scholarship has drawn attention to rising nationalist feelings in Europe and North America under the global conditions of migration and neoliberal economic reforms (Fuchs

2016; Hervik 2019), as well as under different, yet interconnected, conditions in China (Schneider 2018), Nepal (Dennis 2017), Sri Lanka (Azeez and Aguilera-Carnerero 2018), and other countries in the Global South. Defining the "re-emergence of nationalism" in Europe as "neo-nationalism," Banks and Gingrich argue that it is an "essentialist and seclusive reaction against the current phase of globalization" that relies on the concept of "culture" rather than "blood-based homogeneity to define the boundaries of the national" (2006, 9). Fuchs notes that anti-immigration and anti-EU mobilization has precipitated "differentialist racism" (2016, 177) under strong leadership that uses cultural populism. In Denmark, Hervik observes that growing "Danish distrust of ethnic minorities" has led to "rigid dichotomization . . . between a neo-national 'we' and 'the others'" (2011, 8–9) in popular consciousness. Similar to Fuchs's analysis, Hervik connects neonationalism with neoracism and populism as "relational concepts" (9). Deem (2019) notes that a resurgent white racial consciousness defined by the colonial logics has entrenched violent discriminatory nationalism as the new populist face of extreme right-wing groups.

Mouffe recognizes the crippling "consensus at the center" (2005, 66) in the neoliberal era as a key factor for right-wing populism. This analysis, however, does not hold true for cases beyond the advanced Western economies. In a useful comparative study of populism in the United States, Sweden, China, and India, Schroeder notes that "it is not just economically disadvantaged groups that turn to populism, and populism has not just been a response to economic crisis" (2018, 62). The explanation, he suggests, lies in the field of politics: within domestic national politics, the refusal to extend full citizenship to those who are not part of the "people" and externally, the "enemies that are also supposedly threatening the nation, economically and geopolitically" (62). Thus, religion, ethnicity and immigration, he suggests, shape contemporary articulations of populism with nationalism.

Studies show that recent articulations of anti-elite populism with exclusivist nationalism have relied prominently on internet-enabled media. Schroeder notes that "digital media have been a necessary precondition for the success" of right-wing populist movements, as they allowed circumventing "traditional media gatekeepers" (2018, 60). Fuchs has shown that social networking sites such as Facebook played a key role in the "rhetorical strategies that emotionalize nationalism" and in identifying a "negative outside" (2016, 181) for constructing a nationalistic identity. He argues that online discourses that take networked forms work in tandem with the "celebrity culture and personalization of politics" (182) that have brought neonationalist leaders to the front stage of political appeal.

These studies have highlighted several important features that define the current phenomenon, but the analysis still builds on a specific conception of nationalism as violent and extraordinary, put to use by populist leaders for rhetorical appeal and strategic political mobilization. The emphasis on Modi in India, for instance, falls into the analytical bias for political charisma and iconoclasm, paying less attention to common digital cultures that constitute contemporary attachments of nationalism. This is not to say that Modi's celebrity status is unimportant. Modi had indeed filled the need for a strong leadership figure—a need that had stemmed from a host of factors, including the perceived weak leadership of the incumbent government and an ambient mediated culture to legitimate "celebrity icons" to take charge of corruption-free new India (Udupa 2015). However, I suggest that the analytical model should include a broader sweep of online dynamics that constitute and exceed the aura of celebrity icons.

Moving beyond a leader-centric analysis entails attention to the materialities of nation-building (Postill 2006)—of nation as the site where divergent views of the nation contest and negotiate with each other, moving in "heterogenous time-space" (Chatterjee 1993). In a useful formulation, Mihelj (2011) emphasizes a distinction between "hot nationalism" and "banal nationalism" (Billig 1995). Hot nationalism refers to the "transgression of the national ethic," often dramatic and severe, "whether in the form of hate speech or physical acts of violence against communities considered as outsiders to the national whole or even as threats to the nation" (Mihelj 2011, 188). Banal nationalism is the "reassuring normality" of the nation as a frame—"the collection of ideological habits" and "unimaginative repetition" (Billig 1995, 10) that reproduce nation-states. In either case, it is not just the nation-state machinery that produces the effects, but in times of digital media, I suggest, also increasingly by the everyday work of millions of internet users. Furthermore, hot nationalism as a psychology of extraordinary emotions and the banality of repetition, habit, staging, and signaling the nation, enter a co-constitutive relation on digital media.

I have elsewhere argued that everyday nationalism on digital media is best understood as "nation-talk" (Udupa 2018). Nation-talk, the culture of verbal confrontations prominent among young online users in India, fans hypervocality in debates on national belonging. The confrontations precipitate along a perceived divide between the self-proclaimed liberals and Hindu nationalist volunteers. Although the divide appears irreconcilable and is positioned as such in online debates, the common discourse of national pride that runs between them reveals the blurred boundaries of ideology that constitute middle-class politics of online deliberation in urban India. Much of this confrontational dynamic online comes from the huge volunteer base of Hindutva. In many instances, Hindutva is not a preconstituted reality but emerges as a political subjectivity in online practice. As practice theory emphasizes, this prompts an examination of "the practices and discourses that people engage in and embody, and a focus on the actual ways people produce these practices and discourses within socio-cultural constraints which themselves are subject to reproduction and change through such human activities" (Holland and Skinner 1996, 193). Media practice scholars have adapted this usefully to ask what people do with media, what sense they make, and what uses they derive—and also to examine media texts in historicized, embodied, and contextualized ways (Couldry 2010; Hervik 2011; Postill and Brauchler 2010).

Online Hindutva volunteers, diffused and diverse as they are, engage in fact-checking to contest the mainstream media narratives; archive the confrontations for evidencing and future use; create memes, tweets, and Facebook texts to offer repetitive summaries of the Hindu first ideology and "Muslim menace"; boost the internet traffic for Hindutva reasoning through tags, retweets, mentions, and likes; complement the crafted bots of Hindutva with actual human labor; and confront opposing views with an arsenal of stinging ridicule, accusations, and abuse, riding on a wave of online vitriol, which is prevalent among diverse ideological groups. Fun, I suggest, is a metapractice that prominently shapes these practices. By metapractice, I mean a straightforward sense of practice of practices.

Fun is not frivolity of action. It is not pointless "timepass." Quite the contrary. It is laden with political purpose, but in a manner of gathering together on one's own will, chiding and clapping together, exchanging online "high fives" for "trending" or pushing back opposing narratives, and making merry with the colloquial use of online language and vibrant visuality, which are distinct from a serious style of political pontification or cadre-based disciplining. The metapractice of fun, to follow practice theory, does not refer to unchecked and autonomous individual agency. It is shaped by and shapes the ideological discourse that is increasingly organized through social media campaigning described in the previous section and emerging surveillance infrastructure (Anwer 2018). Quite often, online users are conscious of these structures. Most online users we interviewed shared a sharp awareness of paid trolls and political manipulations of social media, yet they articulated their online work with all seriousness of purpose, regardless of politics as usual, experiencing autonomous agency that came with the everyday resources of social media messaging. The next two sections will ethnographically chart two sets of online Hindutva practices—trending and memes-making—to delineate fun as a metapractice of violent nationalism. The section on trending will highlight fun in relation to satisfaction attached to online labor and palpable results of online visibility metrics, while the section on memes considers fun more specifically in terms of hilarity. The distinction is only an analytical one; in practice, achievement and hilarity intertwine and constitute one another.

Trending the Hashtag, Having Fun

"I follow almost 5000 handles on Twitter," says Amar, "most of them are politicians, bureaucrats, journalists—national and international. I have a range of interests from foreign policy to Indian politics to [the] Middle East." A student of international studies at the Jawaharlal Nehru University in New Delhi, Singh was known as a "staunch ABVP supporter" even before the campus started to see a sizeable number of right-wing activists. Amar pursues a PhD at the Jawaharlal Nehru University (JNU) and tweets regularly on Indian foreign policy, displaying a special interest in Modi's diplomacy. He aspires to become a politician or an academic. He tells us he is a "Hindu" and comes from "OBC-backward"—a category that refers to "other backward" groups in bureaucratic parlance. Although his mother tongue is Bajjika and Bhojpuri, and he is most comfortable speaking in Hindi, he tweets largely in English. "I think on an average I spend six hours on internet every day," he tells us after a quick calculation. Twitter, he believes, is "more intellectual." "You can interact with journalists, academics, or high profile bureaucrats and politicians . . . unless you are abusive, they will reply to your messages." When we ask him about his role model on Twitter, he names a prominent male, right-wing tweeter whom he thinks is "very intelligent" and witty. He also lists Eminent Intellectual (@padhalikha), a Twitter handle with a pseudonym. We notice that Amar's face lights up when he cites the handle. He says he does not know who runs Eminent Intellectual, but he addresses the tweeter as a male with unthinking certainty. "He tweets to the point and in a sarcastic language," he tells us enthusiastically. "After the ICJ [International Court of Justice] verdict on 18th of May, he tweeted: 'Third class *Bhakts* [literally devotees, a new media coinage for supporters of Modi] rejoicing a small victory in the International

Court of Justice. They will always lose in the International Court of Narrative.'" Perhaps sensing that we needed more explanation, he continues: "That is a very precise targeting of liberal intellectuals of India who think they create an international narrative about India on everything—politics and culture. He is attacking this understanding." He chuckles as he recounts the quote verbatim, admiring the wit and sarcasm.

Amar's fascination with witty, humorous tweets illustrates the appeal of hilarious tweets circulating on online media, aimed largely at discrediting mainstream, organized media; political parties seen as hostile to Hindutva; and the liberal intelligentsia. A large number of tweets—like this one—ridicule the left-liberal intelligentsia as hegemonic managers of the narrative about India for the rest of the world. During our ethnographic interviews, online right-wing users regularly referred to and defended the Twitter handles that infuse public discussions with "wit and humor" ranging from soft-touch sarcasm to aggressive ridicule of anti-Hindutva views. These included Facebook groups the Illogical Indian @illogicaldesi (64,207 followers),[11] the Frustrated Indian (1.1 million followers),[12] India Against Presstitutes (455,107 followers),[13] and Twitter handles such as Eminent Intellectual @padhalikha and @ UnSubtleDesi. As online users consume and create the content across these spaces, laughter trickles down and creates ripples across loops of tweeting followers, and fun turns politics into palpable pleasure.

Fun is not just funny. While hilarity is a key element of online fun—elaborated further in the next section—a great deal of fun is in trending the hashtag and making a mark, however momentary, in online discussions. Referring to the campaign "Letstalkabouttrolls" started by the English language newspaper *The Hindustan Times* in 2017, Pradip Jha, a prominent Hindutva activist, told us that the label of trolls for Hindutva tweeters is uncharitable and incorrect. These tweeters, according to him, were laudable because they not only exposed the hypocrisy of journalists; they also trended the tweets. "*Unhone kya kiya- in sab journalists ke filthy tweets ka screenshots le kar tweet kar diya aur ye sab ke tweets number 1 par trend kar rahe the* [What the tweeters (for Hindutva) were doing was that they took the screenshots of filthy tweets of all the journalists, tweeted them, and made these tweets the number one trend]."

A telling example for the fun of trending was the sudden death of the hashtag #ModiInsultsIndia, which was trending for a brief period in May 2015 when a section of online users criticized Prime Minister Modi for his statement on a foreign visit that Indians abroad need no longer feel ashamed about being born in India.[14] Online outcry about "insults to the nation" revealed that even Modi was an insufficient icon for digital nationalists. What followed was equally intriguing. The unexpected affront led Modi's team to brace up and undo the damage. On the morning of May 19, 2015, #ModiInsultsIndia started to trend. By that evening, it was overtaken by #ModiIndiasPride, which came in defense of the prime minister. #ModiIndiasPride is a more direct instance of hypernationalism converging on the figure of Modi, but the hashtag it superseded was no less nationalistic. In any case, #ModiIndiasPride tried to rid the nationalistic fervor with a possible challenge to Modi's leadership by raising a wave of tweets that hailed Modi as a committed, hard-working leader. The network graph (fig. 6.1) of tweets collected using the tool TAGS Hawksey between May 20, 2015, and May 27, 2015, for #ModiIndiasPride, suggests the significance of trending hashtags for online

Hindutva practices. The social network graph covering 14,468 tweets collected during this period reveals the top influencers of the network: @ShivshankarS, with 78,300 followers, was the strongest influencer in the network (Eigenvector centrality measure [ECM]: 1). The pinned tweet in Hindi on his Twitter page eulogizes the towering figure of Modi: "The entire universe is up in action to subdue the man, even God would be wondering which clay did it take for me to make Modi."[15] The other power users included @DheerajGbc (ECM: 0.42), SaundID (0.36), @Mahikainfra (0.34), @varanasilive (0.31), @tajinderbagga (0.3), and @KiranKS (0.29), several of whom are known among online political users as regular supporters of online Hindutva. Tajinder Bagga is also the spokesperson of the Delhi unit of the BJP. The network graph offers a snapshot of key actors with open support for the BJP as the drivers of online discussion. While hashtag tweetpools can be examined for various features, including the nature of retweet relations as a measure for polarization,[16] centrality scores of specific Twitter profiles combined with the ethnographic data used here is indicative of the enthusiasm of highly connected right-wing actors to drive discussions online. Ethnographic interviews revealed that trending the hashtags is experienced as absolute victory over opposing narratives within the gamified contexts of scoring on social media trendometers. Fun of trending nationalist hashtags is often seen as a collective endeavor buoyed by success, in ways that denial for the belligerent tone and abuses (Udupa 2017) is made possible by attributing the activity to a potentially expanding network of supporters of which they are a part.

Fun as satisfaction of achievement sometimes extends to "real world" changes. A prominent ABVP social media activist proudly told us how volunteers like him mobilized online posts to put pressure on the BJP to deny the election ticket to Pramod Muthalik, a controversial, local-level right-wing activist whose social conservative organization had barged into a pub and attacked women for consuming alcohol.[17] Amit Trivedi, another Hindu nationalist activist, was thrilled when his video from a television interview, explaining the constitutional provisions on freedom of expression, was retweeted by a BJP leader. This occurred in 2017 during the tense climate on the university campuses in Delhi, when right-wing student activists challenged free speech advocates by asserting that shouting slogans "against the nation" was unconstitutional.

Fun cultures—of hilarity and seemingly solid results of online labor—thus oscillate between real-world effects and those that are properly online. Internet memes, the imitable remediations of visual-textual expressions, belong to the latter category of "properly online" artifacts. Below, I discuss how memes-making illustrates the fun cultures of articulating political positions through the vibrant visuality of remixed images and provocative superimposed texts.

Memes-Making: Subversive Speech or Quotidian Infrastructure?

The polychromous landscape of memes in India straddles leisure and politics with a variety of cultural expressions, which are shared and archived on Facebook, Instagram, Twitter, Tumblr, WhatsApp, and YouTube and enabled by a growing number of instant "meme generators" in an upward global trend of mash-up cultures. Often untraceable to the points of origin or creators, meme circulations range from an explicitly pro-Hindutva position of Facebook pages, such as the Frustrated Indian, and "Internet Hindu" tweeters to those who

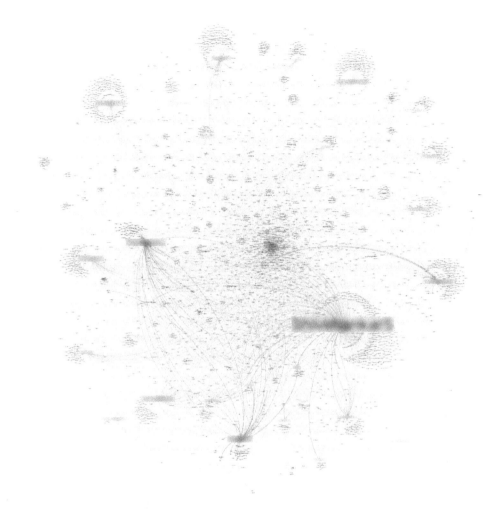

Figure 6.1 #ModiIndiasPride on Twitter in May 2015 by Eigenvector centrality measure. Visualization was done using Gephi to determine the retweet relationships using the Eigenvector centrality measure for the node size. The original file had 14,622 tweets of which 10,229 were retweets. The network graph consisted of 4,845 nodes and 10,229 edges. The layout used a modified version of the Force Atlas 2 algorithm.

directly challenge them (Facebook parody accounts of influential Hindutva leaders such as Unofficial: Subramanian Swamy and Adityanath[18]; Facebook pages such as Inedible India—49,920 followers,[19] @darshbalak—1.2 million followers[20]; Tumblr account Hindus of Hindutva; feminist groups the Spoilt Modern Indian Woman, the Empowered Indian Woman, and Feminist GIFs; and anticasteism groups such as Just Savarna Things—13,503 followers.[21] They also include meme groups that engage political themes with ambiguous stances (e.g., Hindu Nationalist Anime Girls) and a large number of leisure memes that feed political expressions with indirect references and popular cultural idioms (All India Meme, @sarcasmHubb; theindianindiot.com; Useless Talk; Sticky India; Bollywood existentialist memes). Such has been the growth of the memes scene that curators and creators came together to host the first Meme Fest in New Delhi in March 2018, promising "Memex (like Tedex) talks, comedy night, meme market, meme cosplay contest, meme photo-booths, meme awards, food trucks and what not."[22]

The central attribute of internet memes is to "spark . . . user-created derivatives articulated as parodies, remixes, or mashups" (Shifman 2013, 3) with no obligation to follow the formal communication styles. As Milner notes, "political, social, and playful purposes exist simultaneously in these images" (2016, 190). In an ongoing joint study, Krishanu Bhargav (2018) suggests that memes in India have emerged as an "important vernacular for the everyday communicative practices," which should be understood at the intersection of digital politics and creative digital leisure. Image macros, .gif animations, and audio/video files have proliferated on global media, but they also build on local media traditions of cartooning (Khanduri 2014) and the bazaar art (Jain 2007). In an insightful study on memes in India, Sangeet Kumar points to the "logic of repetition with difference" in text and medium that "allows the text to repeat at new sites creating new meanings" (2015, 232–233).

Internet memes complement the nondigital visual cultures that have been important for the Hindu nationalist movement (Rajagopal 2001), while giving access to "the shared production of affect on a transnational basis" (Brosius 2004, 139). The current meme scene is striking in its multimodality and the joy of irreverent and witty mash-ups that drive a political point through creative participatory labor. Fun lies in remediating memetic texts and infusing them with the splendor of pop cultural symbols—from Bollywood and regional cinema to folklore, local idioms, and wordplays.

A systematic content analysis of political memes in India is still an ongoing project, but several media events of confrontation testify to the vibrant creative labor that coalesces around Hindu nationalist claims online. A striking example is the "meme war" sparked by an online video that challenged nationalist jingoism of the Hindutva forces with an India–Pakistan peace message. Located within the sphere of online dissent politics (Kumar 2015), with a "healthy unwillingness to be taken in by stock explanations of complex phenomena" (Sengupta 2012, 309) and tied to the interests of digital marketing business, an independent collective called Voice of Ram[23] that is defined by its motto of "humanity comes first," crafted a video[24] with an India–Pakistan peace message. Such videos are encouraged by new media's "potentially global dimensions through simultaneity [and scale] of transmissions" (Sengupta 2012, 303). The video produced by Voice of Ram showed a female protagonist softly leafing through handwritten posters in front of a camera to narrate the story of her martyred father who had served in the Indian armed forces. The central message was delivered in an evocative expression: "Pakistan did not kill my dad; war killed him." Hindutva memes went on a rampage, ridiculing the video. The sharply worded message was turned and twisted in awkward angles to decimate the initiative, while hailing the sacrifice of the Indian army in protecting the borders. In a four-panel meme (fig. 6.2), the agency—or blame—for historic and contemporary events was shifted to objects (gas/Hitler, bombs/Obama, and bullets/Bollywood actor Salman Khan as "bhai")[25] to lampoon the original message. Several other memes dismissed the intention as an electoral stunt and a "drama" staged by political opponents.

"Hindutva memes," constructed as they are, regularly confront an active stream of critical memes that combine sarcasm, parody, allegory, and irony to caricaturize nationalist jingoism. In a multipanel meme (fig. 6.3), Inedible India drew a reference to the South Indian

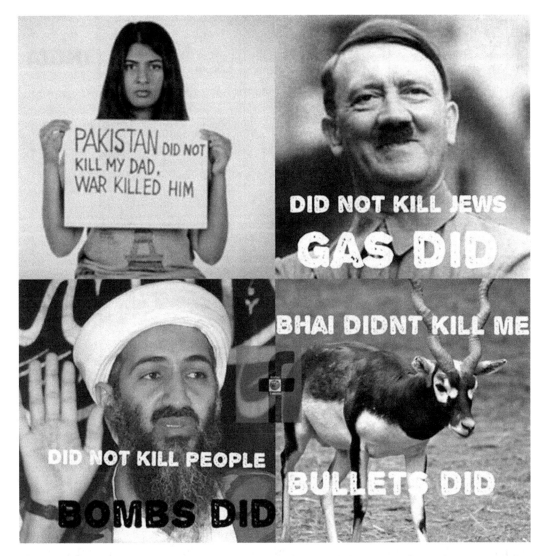

Figure 6.2 Meme shared by a popular sports star (accessed July 22, 2020). https://www.financialexpress.com/india-news/gurmehar-kaur-pakistan-row-yogeshwar-dutt-joins-virender-sehag-trolls-20-year-old-on-twitter/569786/.

Tamil movie *Mersal* and superimposed the short commentaries onto the famed nineteenth-century paintings of Raja Ravi Verma to satirize the key themes of Hindu nationalism and their aggressive defense of the right-wing regime, including accusatory labels of "antination-alism" and "anti-Hindu," the defensive justification of Digital India and Goods and Services Tax (GST), conspiracy theories around Christian missionaries. The meme also had a commentary on the regional politics of the southern Indian state of Tamil Nadu and a sarcastic comment on left, liberal "academics."

Meme repositories critical of Hindutva often feature watermarked memes, and several creators have come out in public to describe the motivation behind their meme creations. Vaibhav Vishal, who created parody accounts of Hindutva political leaders such as the Uttar

Figure 6.3 Meme shared by Inedible India. https://www.facebook.com/inedibleindia1/photos/a.867700539950464.1
073741827.867695293284322/1473008899419622/?type=3&theater.

Pradesh Chief Minister Yogi Adityanath, was worried by "the normalization of the Hindutva hardliner" and decided to challenge it with "humor and parody."[26] The "grammar of contention" (Kumar 2015), enunciated by his parody creations, speak to the intentions of subverting established power. "There is this simmering, ongoing grudge that we have against the people in power," he said in a media interview. "It is good to see them stripped of their power, so to say, with just some fun wordplay and random imagination. The smiles and the chuckles, therefore, are not just at the one-liners. The joy goes beyond that. It is the Davids having fun with the Goliaths." Similarly, the creator of Humans of Hindutva, a Facebook page directly challenging the Hindu nationalist claims, quipped: "My histrionic version of the truth is only slightly madder than what the nationalists actually believe."[27]

Competitive politics has added more dynamism to the relation between subversive memes and the political sphere, with many more political parties actively taking part in expressions of online hilarity in recent years.[28] Politicians from different parties and ideological persuasions have started to use social media to great effect, including through the use of regional languages (Pal and Bozarth 2018). On one level, this trend eats into the sacrality of visual symbolism, which was key to Hindutva mobilization in the 1990s. On another level, however, the fun of squabbling through improvised memes establishes a quotidian affective infrastructure for Hindu nationalism's just-in-time preparedness to frame unfolding events. It offers the daily means to express affiliations through playful outrage. This raises the question on whether fun, humor, and enjoyment are inextricable elements of contemporary right-wing movements. How does social media enable and modulate this relation?

Extreme Speech as Fun

Examining US President Donald Trump's popularity on Twitter, Mazzarella (2018) draws on Lacanian psychoanalysis to compare aesthetics with enjoyment and suggests they both enjoin "a kind of wild intimacy." Although his arguments on enjoyment as noneconomic and nonmoral need a more careful application for the case examined here, the point that collective energies of enjoyment should not be brushed away as irrational and destructive leads me to highlight the importance of online playfulness and enjoyment in co-constituting exclusionary social identities. In the case of the United States and online white nationalism, this is starkly borne out by the new media cultures of "lulz"—"the raw, jaded fun of knowingly cultivated outrage" (Coleman 2014; Mazzarella 2018), or what Deem (2019) defines as the collective "affective economies of transgression." Angela Nagle (2017) attributes deliberate border crossing to online subcultural trends and traces the transition of online trolls and 4chan from left-anarchic cultures to the alt-right movement (see also Philipps and Milner 2017).

Fun as a metapractice, I suggest, signals collective aggression as constitutive of identity that blends with and derives strength from the new media ecology of playfulness and outrage. By no means are hilarity, playfulness, and styles of expressions that are distinct from the official centricity of political discourse unique to internet media. In a study completely away from the internet world, Verkaaik (2004) shows how the ludic, absurd, and effervescent character of assembly were "attractive aspects" of the Muttehida Quami Movement (MQM) in Pakistan. What attracted the youth to the movement was its marked distinction from the "grave, solemn, hollow, ideological language" (Verkaaik 2004, 5). The fun of composing improvised memes and witty tweets in online political spheres is akin to the attraction of the ludic Verkaaik documents in the case of MQM. The foregoing discussion, however, illustrates that the trend of the ludic as a form of political discourse is mainstreamed and accelerated on online social media all while ensuring a sense of autonomy among online users through trending and other online results. Under the current global conjuncture of multidirectional "colonial matrix of power," which is at once "domestic, transnational, inter-state and global" (Mignolo and Walsh 2018, 5), fun as a metapractice has been crucial for right-wing mobilization online.

Furthermore, I suggest that online fun bears *formal* similarity to "objectivity" in the Western journalistic discourse (Tuchman 1972) and liberal communicative reason more broadly. They both embed distance and deniability. Here, deniability refers to a direct sense of protection from possible regulatory actions for online activities that are in favor of hegemonic nationalism (conversely, also through arrests of regime critical fun). As a political problem of skewed privilege for certain online political groups in India, such protection has drawn journalistic attention but requires further documentation in academic research.[29] Online right-wing fun in India highlights the proto-agentic privilege (Clark et al. 2015) and favorable political climate shaped by a longer history of religious majoritarian claims. However, distance and deniability should also be seen as performative and tactical features of right-wing practice more broadly. This means fun creates a transsubjective point of address and instigates collective pleasures of identity that can mitigate risk (see Hervik 2019). Distance and deniability implied in objectivity and liberal communicative reason based on idealized "impersonal norms of discourse" (Cody 2011, 40) are precisely the performative principles for online fun as a metapractice characterized by collective joking, networked vitriol, and trending. In a curious twist, fun and reason become substitutable in a formal sense.[30] This analysis thus questions the binary between rational action and fun, which has been the basis of political action in the self-performance of Western liberal democracy. It instead reveals the similarities between them, highlighting the historical formations of privilege that imbue fun with political power. Methodologically, this entails jettisoning the binaries to pay attention to what people actually do and what meanings they derive from their actions.[31]

As funny messaging, fun of satisfaction in achieving palpable political goals and as collective effervescence (Durkheim 1995), the metapractice of fun composes the daily work of online right-wing movements, transforming extreme speech to descend to the ordinary—to the new normal that is irrepressibly enjoyable.

Notes

* This chapter is the reprinted version of the article with the same title published in *International Journal of Communication* 13(2019), 3143–3163. This project received funding from the European Research Council under the European Union's Horizon 2020 research and innovation program (grant agreement number 714285). The author thanks Gazala Fareedi for her excellent fieldwork support in New Delhi.

1. All names are pseudonyms to protect anonymity.

2. ABVP had 3.2 million members in 2016. See https://indianexpress.com/article/india/india-news-india/jnu-protests-jnusu-behind-abvp-confidence-govt-and-growth-rohith-vemula/. A student organization that was started in 1949, ABVP declares its status as "above partisan politics" (https://www.abvp.org/history-2). However, it is widely known and recognized by its own members as the student wing of the Rashtriya Swayam Sevaka Sangha (RSS; Association of National Volunteers), a conservative right-wing political movement with several organizations working for the cause of Hindu nationalism through a variety of social voluntary work, political patronage, and vigilante activism.

3. National Digital Communications Policy-2018 (NDCP-2018), announced by the Government of India, aims to "provide broadband connectivity at 50 Mbps to every citizen." See http://pib.nic.in/newsite/PrintRelease.aspx?relid=183711. However, in global comparative terms, internet usage in India ranks among the lowest in the world: "Only one-in-four Indians . . . report using the internet or owning a smartphone." See http://www.pewglobal.org/2018/06/19/social-media-use-continues-to-rise-in-developing-countries-but-plateaus-across-developed-ones/.

4. Modi was not convicted by the courts for the Gujarat violence of 2002, but his justification of the riots as resulting from "justfied anger of people" sparked a resurgence of a polarized public discourse (Pal, Chandra and Vydiswaran 2016).

5. The BJP's victory in the national elections reflected a complex amalgam of factors, including a series of corruption scandals that raised a strong anti-incumbency wave against the ruling Indian National Congress Party. However, multimedia messaging remained at the center of Modi's electoral campaign.

6. The North American branch of the Hindu Students Council helped the RSS to launch the Global Hindu Electronic Network in 1996 (Therwath 2012).

7. At 241 million users in 2017, India had the largest user base for Facebook. Its messenger service, WhatsApp, had 200 million users. See https://www.livemint.com/Consumer/CyEKdaltF64YycZsU720EK/Indians-largest-audience-country-for-Facebook-Report.html.

8. In 2018, ABVP's official Facebook page had 274,313 followers, and the verified Twitter account @ABVP Voice had more than 73,000 followers. See https://www.facebook.com/ABVPVOICE/ and https://twitter.com /abvpvoice.

9. See https://timesofindia.indiatimes.com/india/whatsapp-limits-number-of-forwards-for-indian-users /articleshow/65330205.cms.

10. In 2018, the Facebook page for the national unit of BJP had 14 million likes https://www.facebook.com /BJP4India/ and the national unit of RSS had 5 million likes https://www.facebook.com/RSSOrg/.

11. https://www.facebook.com/illogicaldesi/.

12. https://www.facebook.com/TheFrustratedIndian/.

13. https://www.facebook.com/IndiaAgainstPresstitute/.

14. http://www.deccanchronicle.com/150519/nation-current-affairs/article/modiinsultsindia-trends-twitter -pm-gets-lashed-comments.

15. https://twitter.com/shivshankars?lang=en. The original tweet in Hindi was translated by the author.

16. For instance, in an analysis of 15 million tweets mentioning "Obama" and "Romney" during the 2012 US presidential election, Pablo Barberá (2015) found that "85% of retweet interactions take place among Twitter users with similar ideological positions," and political polarization is "particularly intense among right-leaning Twitter users" (87). Similarly, in a study on Pegida and Alternativ fur Deutschland (AfD), the far-right movements in Germany, Puschmann, Ausserhofer, and Slerka (2018) find that a large part of the commenting activity on the Facebook pages of these groups is carried out by a small number of highly active users.

17. It is a common practice among online volunteers of Hindutva to disown leaders such as Muthalik by defining them as "fringes," thereby constituting a fluid space of ideological belonging.

18. https://scroll.in/magazine/832707/the-alternate-universe-of-adityanath-where-he-tries-snapchat-filters -and-celebrates-bad-photoshop.

19. https://www.facebook.com/inedibleindia1/.

20. https://www.facebook.com/adarshbalak/.

21. https://www.facebook.com/justsavarnathings/.

22. http://theindianidiot.com/the-meme-fest-india/.

23. The group defines itself as "a collective of social commentators, innovators, political strategists, ad -filmmakers, marketing experts, movement creators and peace activists." See https://voiceofram.com/.

24. https://www.youtube.com/watch?v=97yJsfddi4w (accessed May 15, 2016). https://www.facebook.com/pg /VORdotcom/about/?ref=page_internal (accessed November 8, 2018).

25. Bollywood actor Salman Khan, referred to as "bhai," was convicted by the courts and granted bail in 2018 in a blackbuck poaching case 10 years after the reported incident. See https://economictimes.indiatimes.com /magazines/panache/1998-2016-a-timeline-of-the-blackbuck-killing-case/articleshow/53377957.cms.

26. https://scroll.in/magazine/832707/the-alternate-universe-of-adityanath-where-he-tries-snapchat-filters -and-celebrates-bad-photoshop.

27. https://scroll.in/magazine/837068/humans-of-hindutva-a-facebook-parody-touches-a-raw-nerve-for -some.

28. The Indian National Congress party leader Rahul Gandhi's tweets that became more regular and witty after 2017 were a result of meticulous social media campaigning. The party that had long neglected social media mobilization recruited a new team of digital strategists in 2017. In March 2018, the team had a core of forty paid social media workers creating gifs, memes, tweets, tags, and social media posts. Divya Spandana, the national social media head for the Indian National Congress Party, said 80% of the team were women, and they together aimed to challenge the BJP by matching the wit and humor of online exchange (personal interview, March 19, 2018). Other regional political parties also scrambled to recruit social media campaign strategists to augment influence online. These developments signal a certain deepening of the democratizing possibilities of humor, even if not necessarily their progressive outcomes.

29. https://timesofindia.indiatimes.com/india/how-a-whatsapp-message-can-get-you-arrested/articleshow /61718967.cms.

30. I am indebted to Andrew Graan, from the University of Helsinki, for pointing this out, although I am fully responsible for the way it is used here.

31. Recent studies on news adopt a similar methodological move to examine the historical conditions and actual practices that shape journalistic objectivity in postcolonial contexts (see Udupa 2015).

References

Anwer, Javed. 2018. "10 Govt Bodies Can Now Monitor Any Computer, but Calm Down India Is Not a Surveillance State Yet." *India Today*, December 21. https://www.indiatoday.in/technology/talking-points /story/10-govt-bodies-can-now-monitor-and-seize-any-computer-but-calm-down-india-is-not-a -surveillance-state-yet-1414420-2018-12-21.

Azeez, Abdul Halik, and Carmen Aguilera-Carnerero. 2018. "The Online Construction of National Identity in Post-war Sri Lanka." Paper presented at the international workshop on Global Digital Media Cultures and Extreme Speech, Munich, February 2018.

Banks, Marcus, and Andre Gingrich. 2006. "Introduction: Neo-Nationalism in Europe and Beyond." In *Neo-Nationalism in Europe and Beyond: Perspectives from Social Anthropology*, edited by A. Gingrich and M. Banks, 1–26. New York: Berghahn.

Barberá, Pablo. 2015. "Birds of the Same Feature Tweet Together: Bayesian Ideal Point Estimation Using Twitter Data." *Political Analysis* 23:76–91.

Bhargav, Krishanu. 2018. *Maymay wahi banaenge I: Ambiguous politics in globalized and localized online memetic cultures.* http://www.fordigitaldignity.com/maymay-wahi-banaenge-i-ambiguous-politics-in-globalized -and-localized-online-memetic-cultures/.

Billig, Michael. 1995. *Banal Nationalism.* Thousand Oaks, CA: Sage.

Billig, Michael. 2005. *Laughter and Ridicule: Towards a Social Critique of Humour.* London: Sage.

Brosius, Christiane. 2004. "'Of Nasty Pictures and 'Nice Guys': The Surreality of Online Hindutva." In *Sarai Reader 4: Crisis/Media*, edited by S. Sengupta and M. Narula, 139–151. New Delhi: Sarai.

Chatterjee, Partha. 1993. *The Nation and Its Fragments: Colonial and Postcolonial Histories.* Princeton, NJ: Princeton University Press.

Clark, Wilma, Nick Couldry, Richard MacDonald, and Hilde C. Stephansen. 2015. Digital Platforms and Narrative Exchange: Hidden Constraints, Emerging Agency. *New Media and Society* 17 (6): 919–938.

Cody, Francis. 2011. Publics and Politics. *Annual Review of Anthropology* 40:37–52.

Coleman, Gabriella. 2014. *Hacker, Hoaxer, Whistleblower, Spy: The Many Faces of Anonymous.* London: Verso.

Couldry, Nick. 2010. "Theorizing Media as Practice." In *Theorizing media and practice*, edited by B. Brauchler, and J. Postill, 35–54. Oxford: Berghahn.

Deem, Alexandra. 2019. "The Digital Traces of #whitegenocide and Alt-Right Affective Economies of Transgression." *International Journal of Communication* 13:3183–3202.

Dennis, Dannah. 2017. "Mediating Claims to Buddha's Birthplace and Nepali National Identity." In *Media as Politics in South Asia*, edited by S. Udupa and S. McDowell, 176–189. London: Routledge.

Durkheim, Emile. 1995. *The Elementary Forms of Religious Life*, translated by K. E. Fields. New York: Free.

Fuchs, Christian. 2016. "Racism, Nationalism, and Right-Wing Extremism Online: The Austrian Presidential Election 2016 on Facebook." *Momentum Quarterly* 5 (3): 172–196.

Haynes, Nell. 2019. "Writing on the Walls: Discourses on Bolivian Immigrants in Chilean Meme Humor." *International Journal of Communication* 13:3122–3142.

Hervik, Peter. 2011. *The Annoying Difference: The Emergence of Danish Neonatinalism, Neoracism, and Populism in the Post-1989 World.* New York: Berghahn.

———. 2019. "Ritualized Opposition in Danish Online Practices of Extremist Language and Thought." *International Journal of Communication* 13:3104–3121.

Holland, Dorothy C., and Debra G. Skinner. 1996. "The Co-development of Identity, Agency, and Lived Worlds." In *Comparisons in Human Development: Understanding Time and Context*, edited by J. Tudge, M. Shanahan, and J. Valsiner, 193–221. Cambridge: Cambridge University Press.

Jaffrelot, Christoph. 2015. "The Modi-Centric BJP 2014 Election Campaign: New Techniques and Old Tactics." *Contemporary South Asia* 23 (2): 151–166.

Jain, Kajri. 2007. *Gods in the Bazaar: The Economies of Indian Calendar Art.* Durham, NC: Duke University Press.

Khanduri, Ritu Gairola. 2014. *Caricaturing Culture in India: Cartoons and History in the Modern World.* Cambridge: Cambridge University Press.

Kumar, Sangeet. 2015. "Contagious Memes, Viral Videos and Subversive Parody: The Grammar of Contention." *International Communication Gazette* 77 (3): 232–247.

Madianou, Mirca, and Daniel Miller. 2013. "Polymedia: Towards a New Theory of Digital Media in Interpersonal Communication." *International Journal of Cultural Studies* 16 (2): 169–187.

Mazzarella, William. 2018. "Brand(ish)ing the Name, or, Why Is Trump So Enjoyable?" http://www.academia .edu/35333795/Brand_ish_ing_the_Name_or_Why_is_Trump_So_Enjoyable.

Mignolo, Walter D., and Catherine E. Walsh. 2018. *On Decoloniality: Concepts, Analytics, Praxis.* Durham, NC: Duke University Press.

Mihelj, Sabina. 2011. "Nationalism and the Media, East and West." In *Media, Nationalism, and European Identity*, edited by M. Suekoesd, and K. Jakubowicz, 203–226. Budapest: Central European University Press.

Milner, Ryan. M. 2016. *The World Made Meme: Public Conversations and Participatory Media.* Cambridge, MA: MIT Press.

Mouffe, Chantal. 2005. *The Return of the Political.* London: Verso.

Nagle, Angela. 2017. *Kill All Normies: Online Culture Wars from 4chan and Tumblr to Trump and the Alt-Right.* Alresford: Zero.

Neyazi, Taberez A., Anup Kumar, and Holli A. Semetko. 2016. "Campaigns, Digital Media and Mobilization in India." *International Journal of Press/Politics* 21 (3): 398–416.

Pal, Joyojeet, and Lia Bozarth. 2018. "Is Tweeting in Indian Languages Helping Politicians Widen Their Reach?" *Economic and Political Weekly* 53 (25). https://www.epw.in/engage/article/tweeting-indian-languages -helping-politicians-widen-reach.

Pal, Joyojeet, Priyank Chandra, and Vinod Vydiswaran. 2016. "Twitter and the Rebranding of Narendra Modi." *Economic and Political Weekly* 51 (8): 52–60.

Paul, Subin, and David O. Dowling. 2018. "Digital Archiving as Social Protest: Dalit Camera and the Mobilization of India's 'Untouchables.'" *Digital Journalism* 6 (9): 1239–1254.

Phillips, Whitney, and Ryan M. Milner. 2017. *The Ambivalent Internet: Mischief, Oddity, and Antagonism Online.* Cambridge: Polity.

Postill, John. 2006. *Media and Nation Building: How the Iban Became Malaysian.* New York: Berghahn.

Postill, John, and Birgit Brauchler. 2010. "Introduction: Theorizing Media and Practice." In *Theorizing Media and Practice*, edited by B. Brauchler and J. Postill, 1–32. New York: Berghahn.

Puschmann, Cornelius, Julian Ausserhofer, and Josef Slerka. 2018. "Converging on a Populist Core? Comparing Issues on the Facebook Pages of Pegida Movement and the Alternative for Germany." Paper presented at the international workshop on Global Digital Media Cultures and Extreme Speech, Munich, February.

Price, Lance. 2015. *The Modi Effect: Inside Narendra Modi's Campaign to Transform India.* London: Hodder & Stoughton.

Rajagopal, Arvind. 2001. *Politics after Television: Hindu Nationalism and the Reshaping of the Indian Public.* Cambridge: Cambridge University Press.

Schneider, Florian. 2018. *China's Digital Nationalism.* Oxford: Oxford University Press.

Schroeder, Ralph. 2018. *Social Theory after the Internet: Media, Technology, and Globalization.* London: UCL Press.

Sengupta, Shuddhabrata. 2012. "The 'Terrorist' and the Screen: Afterimages of the Batla House 'Encounter.'" In *No Limits: Media Studies from India*, edited by R. Sundaram, 300–326. New Delhi: Oxford University Press.

Shifman, Limor. 2013. *Memes in Digital Culture.* Cambridge, MA: MIT Press.

Therwath, Ingrid. 2012. "Cyber-Hindutva: Hindu Nationalism, the Diaspora, and the Web." *Social Science Information* 51 (4): 551–577.

Tuchman, Gaye. 1972. "Objectivity as Strategic Ritual: An Examination of Newsmen's Notions of Objectivity." *American Journal of Sociology* 77 (4): 660–679.

Udupa, Sahana. 2015. *Making News in Global India: Media, Publics, Politics.* Cambridge: Cambridge University Press.

———. 2017. "*Gaali* Cultures: The Politics of Abusive Exchange on Social Media." *New Media and Society* 20 (4): 1506–1522.

———. 2018. "Enterprise Hindutva and Social Media in Urban India." *Contemporary South Asia* 26 (4): 453–467.

van der Veer, Peter. 1994. *Religious Nationalism: Hindus and Muslims in India.* Berkeley: University of California Press.

Verkaaik, Oskar. 2004. *Migrants and Militants: Fun and Urban Violence in Pakistan.* Princeton, NJ: Princeton University Press.

Wittel, Andreas. 2000. "Ethnography on the Move: From Field to Net to Internet." *Forum: Qualitative Social Research* 1 (1): Art. 21. http://nbn-resolving.de/urn:nbn:de:0114-fqs0001213.

7

A PRESIDENTIAL ARCHIVE OF LIES

Racism, Twitter, and a History of the Present

Carole McGranahan*

CRISIS. CHAOS. TURNING POINT. DISASTER. ALL THESE TERMS have been used to describe the Trump presidency. But the story, and the criticisms, are broader and deeper than that of just one man. Instead, the saga opens to debates about Democrats and Republicans, class and race, democracy and authoritarianism, fear and trust, and history itself. As anthropologist Clifford Geertz (1973) might explain, it is a story about how the natives—in this case, US citizens—explain themselves to themselves. This is, of course, not a singular story but multiple, contradictory, and contested stories. For some Americans, it is a tale of triumph rather than tragedy. Vocabulary, affect, and comportment divide groups with different political views in seemingly new, stark, and even violent ways. And yet this is not just a story in or of the United States. Similar political divisions, including accompanying rhetoric and acts of hate and violence, are currently found in many democracies around the world—in India under Narendra Modi, in Brazil under Jair Bolsonaro, and in the United Kingdom under Boris Johnson. Writing from Oxford, sociologist Gina Neff argues that "the twentieth century ended in 2016" (2018, 127). The year of both the Brexit referendum and the US presidential election, did 2016 mark a new era? If so, how shall we know and name it? How shall we write a history of this present?

Technology is a primary driver of epochal change. When newspapers were first introduced, political scientist Benedict Anderson (1983) argued they connected people who had never met in person, enabling them to imagine themselves as part of a shared, national community. In the twentieth century, the introduction of radio and television extended Anderson's "print nationalism," furthering the project of connecting national "imagined communities" through new forms of technology. In the twenty-first century, new digital technologies—the internet, being online—connect friends, families, strangers, journalists, scholars, and politicians. Given the ubiquity of digital technology for people in many parts of the world, anthropologists Daniel Miller and Heather A. Horst argue that the digital is "becoming a constitutive part of what makes us human" (2012, 4). However, while digital technologies connect people in new ways, they are more of a rupture than a continuity with what came before. The rupture exists in the content and form of social media.

On social media, people no longer consume news and entertainment as they did with newspapers, radio, and television. Instead, they generate media, critically interacting with others online to share information, learn, and validate ideas—in other words, to build community. Coming to know others online involves building affiliative, positive community by recognizing kindred types by, for example, hobby or profession or politics. But something about social media also encourages the darkest elements of exclusion, such that the performance of community at times includes negative abuse and violence—flaming, trolling, lying, mobbing, doxing—often in registers deemed humorous or clever within the group and cruel or unethical outside it. Sometimes such online abuse is (just) political, and sometimes it is racist or misogynist or both, directed at those with whom one disagrees and also to whom one feels superior and thus justified in treating this way. Online social media exchanges have prompted fatal violence in real life in places around the world, including Myanmar, Sri Lanka, and the United States. From print nationalism and imagined communities, we now find ourselves in an era of digital nationalism and imagined enemies. This is not a neutral development. Instead, in scaling all the way up to world leaders such as Donald J. Trump, social media has an outsize importance as a political archive of contemporary racism, extreme speech, and lies as aspirational and actionable truths.

A history of the present is a story for the future. Understanding the current historical moment without the retrospective benefit of time can be difficult. As both an anthropologist and a historian, I draw on the theories and methods of each discipline. Ethnography is at the center of my inquiry. Ethnographic methodology combines immersion with analysis in order to understand cultural ways of organizing the world (McGranahan 2014, 2018). As lived systems of contradiction, cultures can be as contested within and across societies. Assessing what is considered normative and right, as well as the challenges to the status quo, requires attention to everyday life including as experienced on social media.

I conducted ethnographic participant-observation research on Twitter, including on the Twitter platform but also in the ethnographic ways that conversations on and about Twitter reach beyond the actual website. Twitter as a phenomenon extends beyond social media into domains such as journalism, political protests, and off-line, face-to-face conversations. I also turn to an interdisciplinary group of scholars and writers to help make sense of this conjuncture. This undertaking is, in some ways, to write a "public future of the past," as Jo Guldi and David Armitage (2014) call for in *The History Manifesto*. In another way, it is to be an ethnographer of the present, participating in and observing life as lived online and interpreted and acted on off-line. Writing the history of this present requires the skills and insights of those who crunch data, those who tell stories, and all those who work in the gray space between the quantitative and qualitative. Inside and outside the academy, two points are clear: (*a*) Trump's presidency may be both the culmination of a century of American "cultural anesthesia," in which the pain of others is dismissed and made publicly invisible (Feldman 1994), as well as the start of a new era of racism and disconnection; and (*b*) social media has ripped clear through existing rules of community and communication, disrupting some conventions long overdue for change and challenging others in dangerous, still unfolding ways. Combining these two issues, we have the "weaponization" of social media, the very technology that "now forms the foundation of commercial, political, and civic life"

(Singer and Brooking 2018, 262). At the center of US history in the Trump era is nothing other than a presidential archive of lies.

An Archive of Lies

What truths can be written from an archive of lies? History often presumes multiple truths or varied interpretations of a shared event. But plural possible truths are not the same as a collection of lies. Purposeful public lies unsettle the grounds of history (Arendt 1972). Over the twentieth and now twenty-first centuries, the idea that politicians lie is a common one, found across different countries and eras. And yet not all lies are of equivalent weight or consequence, nor are all liars of equivalent stature or competence. Americans witnessed an extreme example of the politician as liar in the form of the forty-fifth president of the United States, Donald J. Trump. Trump's lies exceed those told by any other contemporary US politician in terms of content, scope, and scale as well as in the normative status they possess among the public. Trump is expected to lie, to alter the facts, to present known falsehoods as truths, and to use extreme speech as a prelude to political policy. He does this in his public speaking and in his prolific public writing on the social media platform Twitter. Twitter is, in effect, an ongoing press conference for Trump (especially so given that his White House rarely holds press conferences). As such, Twitter has become a key site for the conversion of Trump's lies to social truths as well as to political action (McGranahan 2017; Ott 2017; Ott and Dickinson 2019). Twitter is thus an invaluable archive of this current moment, a history of the present that is as much ethnographic as it is historical.

As a social media platform, Twitter is distinct in its public, nonreciprocal nature. Founded in 2006, Twitter has more than 1.3 billion registered users, 336 million of whom are considered active monthly users, and these users post around 500 million tweets every day. Ninety-five percent of Twitter accounts are public and so are visible to anyone with internet access. Twitter is archived by the Library of Congress, and Trump's tweets are preserved in the online Trump Twitter Archive. As a "first draft of the present," Twitter is remarkably public, social, and egalitarian (Bruns and Weller 2016, 183, 187). Egalitarian in format, however, does not necessarily mean egalitarian in use or access (Bonilla and Rosa 2015). Regardless of whether or how one uses Twitter, the platform has become a ubiquitous part of the political world in the contemporary United States. Communication scholar Dhiraj Murthy goes even further, claiming, "For better or worse, one thing is clear: Twitter has shaped modern social communication" (2013, 153). Widely used by both public figures and ordinary people, Twitter is one of the few places where ordinary people can (attempt to) interact with and contact public figures such as politicians (Bruns and Weller 2016, 183). Of the many politicians on Twitter, Donald Trump is one of the most prolific: @realDonaldTrump has been an active user since March 2009 with more than 41,200 tweets; he follows forty-five accounts and has 59.6 million followers (as of April 10, 2019). Trump's writings on Twitter are unsurpassed in terms of public political statements ever made by a US president. Digital technology makes this possible, as does a May 23, 2018, federal court ruling that, due to First Amendment rights provided for in the US Constitution, Trump may not block users on Twitter. His tweets are thus open to all for reading and response.

Social media matters politically. This is as true for elections as it is for life in the real world, where extreme speech online can have serious, including violent, repercussions. Social media platforms have generated new and important types of political participation and action (Boczkowski and Papacharissi 2018; Bonilla and Rosa 2015; Kuntsman and Stein 2015; Mottahedeh 2015; Murthy 2013; Postill 2012; Tufekci 2017; Weller et al. 2014). However, social media's links to political projects might be more historical than many realize. As argued by communication scholar Fred Turner (2018), current social media are built on an earlier politically motivated post–World War II US project to combat authoritarianism by using media to shape democratic individuals. A democratic person was "a psychologically whole individual, able to freely choose what to believe, with whom to associate, and where to turn their attention" (Turner 2018, 145). This political character sketch was based, in part, on anthropological theories of culture and personality linked to Franz Boas, Margaret Mead, and Ruth Benedict. Ironically, argues Turner, when reconfigured as digital social media, this midcentury "democratic" media style suits an authoritarian such as Trump: "Trump has taken the logic of individual authenticity that animated the New Left in 1968 and American liberalism for thirty years before that and put it to work as a new mode of authoritarian charisma" (148). Charisma, as we know, has never relied on truth or kindness for its success.

In addition to providing new forms of communication and collaboration, social media serves as a platform for argument and antagonism, including hate speech (Jakubowicz 2017; Jane 2014; Murthy and Sharma 2019; Pohjonen and Udupa 2017; Udupa 2018). Trump's Twitter feed is one such an example. Hate speech is a legal and ethnographic category. Anthropologists Matti Pohjonen and Sahana Udupa (2017) suggest that hate is not a universal category and thus must be reckoned in particular ethnographic and historical contexts. As a model for doing so, they propose the term *extreme speech* as enabling anthropological investigation into online speech as social practice situated in specific "cultural and political milieus" in which it may or may not be considered "hateful" (Pohjonen and Udupa 2017, 1174). For Trump, anthropologists have done just this, considering the ways that his gestures and words are examples of the "mainstreaming of racist, xenophobic, Islamophobic and misogynist hate speech in the public sphere" (Bangstad 2017, par. 1; see also Bessire and Bond 2017; Lennon 2018; Roland 2017; Scheper-Hughes 2017). Taking Trump's Twitter feed as a form of extreme speech reveals the ethnographic work of lies in the dissemination of hate speech. In this context, what we are witnessing is not a history of extreme or hate speech but history *as* extreme or hate speech.

Twitter as Presidential Archive

On January 2, 2018, in a move many feared might launch a nuclear war, Donald Trump tweeted that his nuclear button was bigger than Kim Jong Un's (see fig. 7.1). A continuation of long-standing masculinist tropes and petulant defenses against emasculatory sentiment (e.g., the size of his hands; Hall, Goldstein, and Ingram 2016), this particular tweet of Trump's was read by many Twitter users as a violent threat and thus in violation of Twitter's policies. However, on reporting the tweet to Twitter, users received automatic rejections claiming that "there was no violation of the Twitter rules against abusive behavior" (Meyer 2017). This was not the first time Trump had threatened the supreme leader of North Korea on Twitter

Donald J. Trump @
@realDonaldTrump

(Follow)

North Korean Leader Kim Jong Un just
stated that the "Nuclear Button is on his
desk at all times." Will someone from his
depleted and food starved regime please
inform him that I too have a Nuclear Button,
but it is a much bigger & more powerful one
than his, and my Button works!

4:49 pm - 2 Jan 2018

Figure 7.1 Donald Trump tweet, January 2, 2018.

or insulted him through names such as "Little Rocket Man." Users have repeatedly reported Trump for such perceived violations of Twitter rules. In December 2017, in response to criticisms over the use of Twitter by hate groups, Twitter changed its rules—including those defining abusive behavior and hateful conduct—to be stricter and more enforceable. The new rules were applicable to all but had a notable exclusion: the rules exempted military or government figures or "newsworthy" behavior deemed by Twitter to be in "the legitimate public interest" (Meyer 2017). In their rules for threatening and hateful behavior, the executives at Twitter also created a Donald Trump exception. On Twitter, Trump's threats and hateful conduct are therefore not violations of the rules but are, instead, history.

Presidential libraries are important sites for the writing of US history. Such archives are formally opened after a president's term has ended, and they are staffed by professional archivists and are critical for scholarly understanding of "individual presidents and the presidency as an institution" (Stuckey 2006, 138). In the case of Donald Trump, however, one portion of his presidential archive—his Twitter feed—is visible to the public as he creates it. Never before has a president used with such regularity an unedited means of communicating with the public. In understanding the current political moment in the United States, therefore, ethnographic immersion in Trump's Twitter archive offers unprecedented access to both presidential speech and public reaction to it. Whether on Twitter or in a building housing documents, archives are documentary collections for assembling history or, as Michel-Rolph Trouillot (1995) contends, for producing both histories and silences. Yet if archives have long been treated as sources for history, they are also subjects themselves—a particular sort of "epistemological experiment" through which ideas of common sense are normalized (Stoler 2002, 87). In *Archaeology of Knowledge*, Foucault (1972) cautions that an archive shapes histories and regularities rather than neutrally preserves them for historians' retrieval at a future date. Given the particular structure of social media as distinct from a physical archive full of old documents, an attentiveness to the production of history alongside its storage must be paired with attention to the archiving technology (Derrida 1998). How, then, might we ethnographically assess documents found in archives, including tweets found on Twitter?

Taking Trump's Twitter archive as a history of the present is to consider the conditions of possibility for this moment (Foucault 1973). I do so via an "ethnography in the archives" approach of assessing the cultural logics that provide conceptual scaffolding for archival data, including systems of organizing and categorizing that data, and thus producing and legitimating it (Stoler 1992, 2002, 2009). Such cultural logics mark certain stories as important and others as not important, and they can appear to do so in neutral ways rather than in culturally specific ways responsive to particular historic and political concerns. Ethnography in the Twitter archives involves considering the social, political, and historic contexts of tweets.

Methodologically, this requires an ethnographic understanding of Twitter as a user immersed in this social media platform; that is, one needs to do participant observation rather than merely read online as a bystander. As with all ethnographic research, such participatory immersion is necessary to understand how the system works. For example, no two Twitter streams are alike, nor are Twitter streams possible to re-create. This has to do with algorithms of content display and the structure of the platform in that each user chooses via follows or content searches what he or she wants to see. My ethnography-in-the-archives approach for this project thus involved my regular participation on Twitter as an active registered user. My personally curated feed showed organically the way discussion of Trump's tweets appeared in my feed, which consisted mostly of academics, journalists, and activists, while targeted searches revealed how Twitter users in general reacted to Trump's tweets. Furthermore, research on Twitter as a pulse of the present moment cannot be limited to the Twitter platform alone. Twitter is part of a social and political ecology of communication and commentary. Journalists write about Trump's tweets; citizens discuss them; and world leaders turn to his Twitter feed to learn about his plans and policy decisions, including his firing of Secretary of State Rex Tillerson, his announcement that he was banning transgender individuals from the US military, and his withdrawal from the G7 joint statement in Quebec in June 2018. Trump, his critics, his fans, and the world, move back and forth from Twitter to other spaces of discussion and action. Twitter is thus an expansive, ethnographic space rather than a self-contained one.

An ethnographic space is inhabited, given form and meaning, and brought to life by humans. It is a space of connection and exchange, a place of sharing and policing, and a site where claims and demands may be made. Social media in particular—for example, Facebook, Twitter, WeChat, and Instagram—can be rich sites for the sort of daily rhythms and logics one might expect to find in face-to-face fieldwork. The new online world of fieldwork is not limited to the ethnography of digital communities but includes ethnography in and as part of them (Horst and Miller 2012; Pink et al. 2016; Postill 2011; Udupa 2018; Williams 2013, 2018). That is, we can do ethnography of specific topics in the digital, online world rather than research only about online communities. In this sense, online fieldwork can approximate some of the best parts of face-to-face fieldwork: the idea of being there, having a presence in a community, sharing space, and life beyond "the research"—all of which involve cultivating an ethnographic sensibility (McGranahan 2014, 2018). Much of the hanging out, living life, passing time, and coming to know one another that is part of classic ethnographic methods can also be part of fieldwork in social media.

Anthropologists never underestimate what it means to be part of community, to participate in something, to share. On Twitter, Trump's tweets engage the world. In my feed alone, people from numerous countries regularly responded to Trump's tweets, often addressing him directly; these were not world leaders but regular people, ordinary folks such as students, activists, and other engaged citizens publicly commenting on the tweets of the US president. In so doing, they produced and reproduced Twitter as a shared ethnographic space as well as a historical archive of the present.

If as ethnographic space, Twitter is a site of cultures in formation, then as public archive, Twitter is a site of history unfolding. As with all social formations, Twitter is not static. While being in motion is part of Twitter's very composition in that one's timeline is constantly additive and thus not stable, Twitter itself has also changed over the years. Digital media scholar Richard Rogers identifies three stages of Twitter: first "an ambient, friend-following medium," then a segue following several natural disasters and political elections to "a news medium for event-following," and finally the emergence of Twitter as an "(archived) data set and anticipatory medium" (2014, xii, xvi, xxi). For active Twitter users, regular use might include all three of these aspects simultaneously rather than as modes bound by platform evolution. On Twitter, as on other social media platforms, community is created around senses of connection. One connection might be shared beliefs, including ones about other people and a politics of legitimate or earned national belonging. Whether one is tweeting #MAGA ("Make America Great Again") in enthusiastic support or sarcastic criticism of Trump, this action is an index of present-day sentiments about race, racism, history, and truth in the United States.

Trump and Lies as Extreme Speech: Three Examples

Lies might often be extreme speech, but they are not always hate speech. As presidential candidate and president, Trump's lies fall into both categories as ethnographically determined in the contemporary United States. For example, his lies about the size of the crowd at his inauguration (largest ever!) and the viewership of his 2018 State of the Union address (largest ever!) are examples of extreme speech but not necessarily hate speech. If online practices of extreme speech "push the boundaries of acceptable norms of public culture toward what the mainstream considers a breach within historically constituted normative orders," hate speech is "vilifying, polarizing, or lethal" (Pohjonen and Udupa 2017, 1174; see also Boromisza-Habashi 2013; Waldron 2012). Although extreme speech and hate speech both may be inflammatory, they are not one and the same. However, when either extreme or hate speech comes in the form of a lie, there is an additional layer of volatility in terms of expected norms and the breach of them. And when the person articulating lies is the president of the United States, the cultural and political impact of such lies can be large (Alterman 2004; Hahl, Kim, and Zuckerman Sivan 2018).

As a presidential candidate, Trump's lies astounded some and energized others, politically mobilizing citizens around different interpretations of moral outrage. As president, Trump's lies have continued unabated. In his first year as president, he made over two thousand false claims, achieving this 11 days prior to the anniversary of his 2017 inauguration. As with gossip, the repetition of lies over time produces a sort of possible truth. Repeated lies produce affiliative truths, which people ascribe to for social and political reasons and which generate action as well as affiliation (McGranahan 2017). As a public figure, candidate, and president, Trump has repeated numerous lies: Obama was born in Kenya; "we are the highest taxed nation in the world"; denials of the official death toll from Hurricane Maria in Puerto Rico; and, among others, the false claim that three of four domestic terrorists in the United States are foreign born. All of these are false claims, and yet they have taken on the force of truth for many Trump supporters. For some people, then, these are not just possible or even probable truths; they are truth. Given this acceptance, any history of this political era in the United States must address anew the question of how falsehoods can generate actionable social truths.

Specific lies of Trump's provide examples of an ethnographic reading of extreme speech and hate speech. Responses to the following three lies from Trump's first year as president were prominent in my Twitter feed and on Twitter in general and were also widely discussed in other media domains.

Lie 1: Obama and Other Presidents Did Not Reach Out to the Families of Fallen Soldiers (October 16, 2017)

In a statement at a White House news conference, a reporter asked Trump why he had not spoken publicly about four US Special Forces soldiers who were killed in Niger almost two weeks earlier. Trump claimed he had written (unsent) letters to the families and would be calling them later that week, adding, "If you look at President Obama and other presidents, most of them didn't make calls. A lot of them didn't make calls. I like to call when it's appropriate" (Landler 2017, par. 3). Trump's statement was easily proven false by reporters of numerous publications, and Twitter was soon ablaze in indignant responses, including replies from members of Gold Star families (i.e., families of soldiers who died or were killed while serving in the armed forces). The response that generated the most attention was from Delilia O'Malley, the sister of a fallen soldier (see fig. 7.2). On her Twitter account, O'Malley claims she is a "Lifelong Republican who opposed Trump. Painfully disappointed in the weak, spineless leaders of my party. #DonTheCon Country over Party." Almost four months after her initial tweet on October 16, 2017, O'Malley's tweet had 7,928 replies, 183,951 retweets, and 499,951 likes. The replies ranged from insults to support, with insulters often accusing O'Malley of being a member of the "liberal left," an accusation she repeatedly and energetically challenged. Retweets also often included commentary in one political direction or the other, almost all in the service of building political truth with or against O'Malley's sentiment and not, as one might presume, in the direction of asserting the truth or falsity of Trump's statement. Instead, at issue among most Twitter users is asserting political affiliation through endorsement or critique. The content and context of such social activity is key to ethnographic investigation.

Confirming the public perception of Twitter as a domain for addressing Trump is a statement from Euvince Brooks, father of Sergeant Roshain E. Brooks, a US soldier who was killed in Iraq. As reported in *The Washington Post* on October 18, 2017, Brooks explained that

Figure 7.2 Delilia O'Malley's tweet to Donald Trump, October 16, 2017.

his response to Trump's claim was, "I said to my daughter, 'Can you teach me to tweet, so I can tweet at the president and tell him he's a liar?'" (Lamothe, Bever, and Rosenberg 2017, par. 41). Prominent in both of these examples, one an actual tweet and one a desire to tweet, is the public claim that Trump is a liar. Both of these individuals are ordinary citizens—one who is active on Twitter and one who is aware that Twitter is a place for active political participation, including for addressing the US president. Others, including politicians and military officials, joined in proclaiming Trump's statement a lie, while Trump's press secretary Sarah Huckabee Sanders claimed it was a "fact." Herein lies a core insight of the Twitter archive: amid the range of voices calling Trump a liar, he and his agents never concede that point. Instead, they shuffle the context of the original claim, or Trump deflects responsibility for it: "That's what I was told." Such language as this and the phrase "a lot of people are saying" serve to provide deniable cover if needed (Johnson 2016). The use of such qualifiers creates confusion, purposefully generating irrational fears that circulate accompanied by a possibility of violence.

Violence is not merely a possibility in Trump's United States. At a presidential campaign rally in Louisville, Kentucky, on March 1, 2016, Trump encouraged the crowd to eject protesters, proclaiming "Get 'em out of here." Crowd members then physically abused the protesters, who later sued Trump in federal court and won. On April 1, 2017, a federal judge ruled that Trump incited violence against the protesters at the rally. There are also correlations between Trump's tweets and public violence. Quantitative research by economists argues that Trump's anti-Muslim tweets correspond to rises in anti-Muslim hate crimes in the United States (Müller and Schwarz 2018). Pairing such quantitative findings with ethnographic and qualitative research enables scholars to gain a fuller understanding of the impact of Trump's public speech.

Lie 2: Trump's Retweeting of Anti-Muslim Videos Posted by Britain First Ultranationalist Activists (November 29, 2017)

Trump is often most active on Twitter early in the morning. While some journalists have correlated his tweets with the right-wing morning TV show *Fox and Friends*, the morning

.@Theresa_May, don't focus on me, focus on the destructive Radical Islamic Terrorism that is taking place within the United Kingdom. We are doing just fine!

8:02 PM · 29 Nov 2017

31,052 Retweets 89,529 Likes

○ 35K ⟲ 31K ♡ 90K ✉

Figure 7.3 Donald Trump tweet, November 29, 2017.

of November 29, 2017, was noteworthy for a different reason: Trump retweeted three videos posted by Jayda Fransen, a leader of Britain First, an ultranationalist, racist group in the United Kingdom. These were all anti-Muslim videos with sensationalist titles: "Islamist mob pushes teenage boy off roof and beats him to death!" "Muslim destroys a statue of Virgin Mary!" and "Muslim migrant beats up Dutch boy on crutches!" Twitter users immediately responded, either by retweeting the videos in support or commenting on the dubious, racist source and titling of the videos given that the "Muslim migrant" was actually a Dutch-born and -raised citizen, and the other two videos were filmed four years earlier rather than being of-the-moment news as the tweets implied.

The falsehoods and extreme Islamophobia of the videos were only part of the story. Another result was the diplomatic incident prompted by Trump's apparent support of a racist hate group. In a public statement, British prime minister Theresa May denounced Trump's action: "It was wrong for the president to have done this. Britain First seeks to divide communities by their use of hateful narratives that peddle lies and stoke tensions. They cause anxiety to law-abiding people" (Baker and Sullivan 2017, par. 9). In keeping with his regular use of Twitter to publicly communicate with world leaders, Trump replied to May on Twitter (see fig. 7.3). This deflection of attention from his retweeting of racist videos to "Radical Islamic Terrorism" was paralleled by Sarah Huckabee Sanders's official dismissal of the untruthful videos by stating that "the threat is real." The anti-Muslim messaging remained intact.

Several weeks after this incident, Twitter introduced new rules for hateful conduct, and Britain First leaders, including Jayda Fransen, were banned from the platform. In late January 2018, in an interview with British journalist Piers Morgan, Trump claimed he had not known who Britain First was at the time of his retweeting of the videos. He offered Morgan a highly qualified possible future apology: "If you are telling me they're horrible people—horrible, racist people—I would certainly apologize if you'd like me to do that." Despite this offer, Trump did not apologize.

*Lie 3: Trump's Claim That Certain Countries
Were "Shitholes" (January 11, 2018)*

In a meeting with several US senators about immigration, Trump referred to El Salvador, Haiti, and several African countries as "shitholes" when asked why we needed more immigrants from these countries. He suggested instead that Norwegians immigrate to the United States. Responses from the global community were immediate, including many responses on Twitter. Politicians around the world condemned the remarks, but most powerful were individual testimonies on Twitter. Individuals recounted their struggles and accomplishments—degrees held, languages spoken, awards granted, and professional titles—and ended their tweets with the phrase, "I'm from a #shithole country." These public statements—many of which were replied to, retweeted, and liked thousands of times—built antiracist community in response to Trump's immigration policies, from the Muslim ban to his negative comments on "chain migration" (i.e., family reunification policies) to his efforts to "build the wall." Counter to these responses, however, were ones supporting Trump's statement about "shithole" countries, including from individuals who claimed they escaped such places for life in the United States. Either way, the new availability of the term *shithole country* as an epithet is at best a form of extreme speech and at worst a form of hate speech. The online nature of the responses and their reproduction confirm Pohjonen and Udupa's (2017) observation that *hate speech* is as much a subjective and ethnographic term as it is a legal one.

Finally, despite many witnesses who claim Trump used the term *shithole*—and did so more than once—Trump later denied using the term. In other words, he lied to deny racist behavior. Across these three examples, and deeply embedded in the behavior on and off Twitter that preceded them, is an intertwining of lies, bluster, and discrimination or dismissal of some sort. This is not presidential politics or even renegade political language as we have known them before (Lempert and Silverstein 2012, 2017; Silverstein 2003, 2017). Instead, this marks a significant historical event, a "breach" as Foucault would have it, that has not merely captured the imagination of people around the world but also generated action and reaction (Foucault 1991, 76). A history of this present must capture both this generative/reactive sense as well as the form and tenor of Twitter as Trump's favorite media through which to speak. The opposite of a #shithole country, of course, would be a "great" one. For some, key to the nationalism that underlies the notion of making America great again are racist ideas of who constitutes a proper American. As Kevin Young writes in his book *Bunk*, the term *American* has become "the ultimate euphemism" (2017, 466); in the mouths of many, both on and off social media, American is shorthand for white.

The Right to Be Racist, or, Making America the 1950s Again

There are many ways to tell the story of Trump's ascendancy in US politics (Campbell 2018). Trump's Twitter feed narrates this story using language that speaks to his far-right base (Stolee and Caton 2018). It is a story of class and status. It is a story of resentment, frustration, outsider success, and a desire for change. Depending on the community in which the argument is situated, it may also be one of disenchantment or disengagement or disenfranchisement. There are many ways to vote no on the status quo. Trump's election was one of them.

But, as Trump himself often stated, his campaign was not only about rejecting something but also about building something (and not only a wall). What he promised to build was a return to an earlier era, a time when America was great and when one had the right to be racist and misogynist. As anthropologist L. Kaifa Roland explains, this is about claiming wealthy white masculinity as an expected and desired default of being American: "Wealthy white masculinity has always mattered in this country, while other bodies have required various forms of evaluation—extreme vetting, if you will—before their merits as fully American could be determined. Such ghosts from America's past have never left, and they are being reembodied in Trump's restored America" (2017, 441–442). This aspect of Trump's campaign message remains active in his Twitter archive. Nativist and masculinist claims to the country and to morality persist in this familiar but newly recharged version of America.

A romantic view of the 1950s Cold War era appears to be that to which Trump nostalgically wants to return the nation. This was the triumphant post–World War II period—a new era in terms of nuclear weapons, feel-good Americanism, and the shifting of global authority. It was also a new period of US empire, but in that anti-imperial, decolonial moment, it was not called empire (Collins and McGranahan 2018), just as US society was racist, but we did not necessarily call it racist. As such, the phrase "nostalgic racism" conjures a time when what is now pointedly and publicly called racism was not (Goldstein and Hall 2017; Maskovsky 2017). Nostalgia for a domestically celebrated version of mid-twentieth-century US power, with its unapologetic masculinity and whiteness, is the "again" of Donald Trump's "Make America Great Again." The 1950s were the era of *Leave It to Beaver, I Love Lucy, American Bandstand*, and *The Mickey Mouse Club*; of pretenses to good, clean fun and whitewashed presentations of race in the media. The civil rights movement was underway, but this was before its height in the 1960s. For some, the 1950s was a time of the consolidation of whiteness.

Who is white in the United States? The answer to this question changes over time, and the postwar era was a time of massive change (Brodkin 1998; Jacobson 1999; Omi and Winant 2014; Painter 2011; Roediger 2006). During World War II, service in the US military brought together individuals from different backgrounds in new ways. After the war, these shared experiences helped elevate some ethnic groups to new racial categories. Some Europeans, for example, came to be newly seen as white, or whiter than before. Not all soldiers, however, were afforded such new categorizations, and they returned from war to a United States that was just as racist as ever. Making America the 1950s again might thus be to deny some individuals full participation in US society and to be morally and legally okay with that. For example, full voting rights and protections for all citizens in the United States were not granted until 1965. Midcentury racism partnered with misogyny as normal and acceptable aspects of society. Civil rights victories in the 1960s and changes in the 1970s marked a radical shift. New policies of desegregation such as school busing and the new legality of interracial marriage with the 1967 *Loving v. Virginia* Supreme Court decision changed social practices and beliefs. Resistance to such changes was epitomized in the blatant racism of the all-too-real TV character Archie Bunker, who played a "lovable bigot." To whom is a bigot lovable? Only to other bigots. Only to those who need to find an excuse for racism.

Racism is an ideology of fear as much as of superiority, exclusion, and ignorance. Currently racism as white fear is manifest as white supremacist nationalism. Along with Trump's tweets, the presence of white nationalists in his administration—Stephen Bannon and Stephen Miller, for example—endorses and encourages this fear. So, too, did Trump's statement following a white supremacist rally in Charlottesville, Virginia, on August 12, 2017, in which many people protested against such racism: "We condemn in the strongest possible terms this egregious display of hatred, bigotry, and violence on many sides. On many sides." Trump's making of white supremacists' actions commensurate with those of antiracist activists is not a neutral statement. Instead, as with his tweets on presidents and fallen soldiers, anti-Muslim videos and "shithole" countries, this statement exists in a social ecology of others he has made or implied about race, nationality, and value.

Historical precision, and truth in general, were not key to Trump's presidential campaign, nor have they been a component of his administration. What Trump offered and the Trumpists bought was a feeling of disaffection with the status quo and a shared project of returning to a different status—that of a proud white past embodied in 1950s nostalgia. This is an America of the imagination, the era of Donald Trump's childhood, and a time when at least some Americans imagine their social or financial or racial status was better or more secure than it is now. Twitter has emerged as a key site for the dissemination of these ideas as well as for their normalization. Taken together as an archive, as an aggregate of the cultural pulse of some US (and global) citizens right now, the ideas reveal the extent to which extreme speech, including racist and even white supremacist speech, has newly surfaced as possible and defensible in the world. In thinking ethnographically of this project as a history of the present, it is important to remember this is not about documenting a revisionist history but identifying and analyzing contemporary efforts to shape a revisionist future.

Conclusion: History and Hate in an Archive of Lies

The normalization of extreme speech, hate speech, and racist speech is the history of the present in the United States. Trump is not the only purveyor of such speech, but given his public prominence first as a reality TV figure and businessman and second as US president, his role in articulating, spreading, and entrenching extreme and vitriolic speech and endorsing and enabling others' such speech and accompanying actions is, to quote Twitter executives, "newsworthy," and thus constitutes history. Trump's Twitter archive is essential to the crafting or, less neutrally, the manipulating of cultural dispositions toward certain ideas about belonging, race, and the nation. Some are repelled and repulsed by these ideas, and others are compelled and even relieved by them. Ethnography in the Twitter archives dispels easy notions that this is, in US political parlance, a "liberal versus conservative" fight. It is not. It is instead a cultural breach in the terms of what it means to be a good American. Posts on Twitter reproduce this breach every day, highlighting that transgressions in the current political moment are not merely of differing interpretations of the Constitution or nationalism, for example, but are also in the domain of codes of conduct.

On February 5, 2018, Trump claimed that members of Congress who did not stand to applaud him at various points during his State of the Union speech the week prior were committing treason: "They were like death and un-American. Un-American. Somebody said,

'Treasonous.' Yeah, I guess why not? Can we call that treason? Why not? I mean they certainly didn't seem to love our country that much." Responses on Twitter were fast and furious, including from politicians and veterans. One prominent reply was by US representative Tim Walz, whose Twitter bio reads as follows: "Teacher, Football Coach, Command Sergeant Major Proudly Representing Minnesota's 1st Congressional District; Ranking Member of House @VetAffairsDems." On the same day as Trump's statement, Representative Walz tweeted: "I didn't serve 24 years in the uniform of this country to be called treasonous for simply disagreeing with your disastrous policies, Mr. President." Their disagreement is not only about politics. History never is.

To write history from an archive of lies is not about only factual truths. It is not, for example, to end with the question of whether Trump really used the term *shithole countries*. Instead, writing history from such a source is to investigate the responses and actions that are generated by such lies, extreme speech, and hateful conduct. For example, regarding the anti-Muslim videos Trump retweeted, the point is not simply whether they were real or timely, or even that he retweeted them from a known racist, white supremacist organization, but rather that a cultivated fear of "Radical Islamic Terrorists" precedes and follows his action as justification for it. Recall Sarah Huckabee Sanders: the videos may not be real, but the threat is. Ethnographically, Trump's action consolidates several cultural logics in motion in the United States: anti-Muslim sentiment since 9/11; the mainstreaming of nativist, anti-immigrant sentiment in US public discourse; and support for both of these is a joint claim about who is American (white people) and who cannot ever truly be American in quite the same way (most others). This is a narrative of triumph over one of resentment. Making "America Great Again" is a nostalgic and racist narrative that, in emanating from the White House, legitimates these sentiments as desired and possible futures.

We must be historians of the future and ethnographers of the present. We must witness hate now so as to write its truths later. There is precedent for what a history written from lies and hate looks like: Holocaust denial. The scholar Deborah Lipstadt (1994, 2005) has devoted much of her career to writing about Holocaust deniers, even successfully defeating a libel case against her in the United Kingdom by leading Holocaust denier David Irving. As Lipstadt writes in her book *History on Trial*, to combat such denial is not only to insist on historical accuracy but also to fight against the derogatory and bigoted beliefs of white supremacy that underlie lies and denial: "I fought . . . to defeat a man who lied about history and expressed deeply contemptuous views of Jews and other minorities" (2005, 289). Those lies, she writes, were painful and enabled continuing acts of hate in the present. We are now in a similar moment. Lies of a political leader are enabling fear and the hate of an other as an imagined enemy, including the sorts of violent actions that often accompany such hate (Das 2001). As scholars, we need to use the tools available to us to make sense of this present now so that in the future we may make sense of it from other temporal perspectives. New digital technologies such as Twitter present an opportunity to do so. Twitter and other forms of social media are not just means of communication but also historical archives and ethnographic spaces laden with unconventionally transformative possibilities for research and action. Here, in this space, in this archive, is where new scholarly responsibilities lie.

Note

* This chapter is the reprinted version of the article with the same title published in *International Journal of Communication* 13(2019), 3164–3182, with some minor edits to reflect the latest developments.

References

Alterman, Eric. 2004. *When Presidents Lie: A History of Official Deception and Its Consequences*. London: Viking.

Anderson, Benedict. 1983. *Imagined Communities*. London: Verso.

Arendt, Hannah. 1972. *Crises of the Republic*. San Diego, CA: Harcourt.

Baker, Peter, and Eileen Sullivan. 2017. "Trump Shares Inflammatory Anti-Muslim Videos, and Britain's Leader Condemns Them." *New York Times*, November 29. https://nyti.ms/2kdekcs.

Bangstad, Sindre. 2017. "Can There Be an Anthropology of Hate Speech?" *Anthropology News*, May 11, 2017. https://anthrosource.onlinelibrary.wiley.com/doi/abs/10.1111/AN.439.

Bessire, Lucas, and David Bond, eds. 2017. "The Rise of Trumpism." *Fieldsights*, January 18. https://culanth.org/fieldsights/series/the-rise-of-trumpism.

Boczkowski, Pablo, and Zizi Papacharissi, eds. 2018. *Trump and the Media*. Cambridge, MA: MIT Press.

Bonilla, Yarimar, and Jonathan Rosa. 2015. "#Ferguson: Digital Protest, Hashtag Ethnography, and the Racial politics of social media in the United States." *American Ethnologist* 42 (1): 4–17. doi:10.1111/amet.12112.

Boromisza-Habashi, David. 2013. *Speaking hatefully: Culture, communication, and political action in Hungary*. University Park: Pennsylvania State University Press.

Brodkin, Karen. 1998. *How Jews became white folks and what that says about race in America*. New Brunswick, NJ: Rutgers University Press.

Bruns, Axel, and Katrin Weller. 2016. Twitter as a first draft of the present: And the challenges of preserving it for the future. In *Proceedings of the 8th ACM Conference on Web Science* (183–189. New York: Association for Computing Machinery. https://dl.acm.org/citation.cfm?id=2908174.

Campbell, Johhn L. 2018. *American discontent: The rise of Donald Trump and the decline of the golden age*. Oxford: Oxford University Press.

Collins, John Francis, and Carole McGranahan. 2018. Introduction: Ethnography and empire. In Carole McGranahan and John Francis Collins (Eds.), *Ethnographies of US empire* (1–24. Durham, NC: Duke University Press.

Das, Veena. 2001. Crisis and representation: Rumor and the circulation of hate. In M. S. Roth and C. G. Salas (Eds.), *Disturbing remains: Memory, history, and crisis in the 20th century* (37–62. Los Angeles: Getty Research Institute.

Derrida, Jacques. 1998. *Archive fever: A Freudian impression*. Chicago: University of Chicago Press.

Feldman, Allen. 1994. On cultural anesthesia: From Desert Storm to Rodney King. *American Ethnologist* 21 (2): 404–418.

Foucault, Michel. 1972. *Archaeology of knowledge* (A. M. Sheridan, Trans.). New York: Harper & Row.

———. 1973. *The order of things: An archaeology of the human sciences*. New York: Vintage.

———. 1991. Questions of method. In G. Burchell, C. Gordon, and P. Miller (Eds.), *The Foucault effect: Studies in governmentality with two lectures by and an interview with Michael Foucault* (73–86. Chicago: University of Chicago Press.

Geertz, Clifford. 1973. *The interpretation of cultures*. New York: Basic.

Goldstein, Donna M., and Kira Hall. 2017. Postelection surrealism and nostalgic racism in the hands of Donald Trump. *HAU: Journal of Ethnographic Theory* 7 (1): 397–406. doi:10.14318/hau7.1.026.

Guldi, Jo, and David Armitage. 2014. *The history manifesto*. Cambridge: Cambridge University Press.

Hahl, Oliver, Kim, Minjae, and Ezra W. Zuckerman Sivan. 2018. The authentic appeal of the lying demagogue: Proclaiming the deeper truth about political illegitimacy. *American Sociological Review* 83 (1): 1–33. doi:10.1177/0003122417749632.

Hall, Kira, Donna M. Goldstein, and Matthew B. Ingram. 2016. The hands of Donald Trump: Entertainment, gesture, spectacle. *HAU: Journal of Ethnographic Theory* 6 (2): 71–100. doi:10.14318/hau6.2.009.

Horst, Heather A., and Daniel Miller, eds. 2012. *Digital anthropology*. London, UK: Bloomsbury.

Jacobson, Matthew Frye. 1999. *Whiteness of a different color: European immigrants and the alchemy of race*. Cambridge, MA: Harvard University Press.

Jakubowicz, Andrew. 2017. Alt_right white lite: Trolling, hate speech, and cyber racism on social media. *Cosmopolitan Civil Societies* 9 (3): 2622–2640. doi:10.5130/ccs.v9i3.5655.

Jane, Emma A. 2014. "Your a ugly, whorish, slut": Understanding e-bile. *Feminist Media Studies*, 14(4), 531–546. doi:10.1080/14680777.2012.741073.

Johnson, Jenna. 2016. "A lot of people are saying . . .": How Trump spreads conspiracies and innuendos. *Washington Post*, June 13, 2016. https://www.washingtonpost.com/politics/a-lot-of-people-are-saying-how -trump-spreads-conspiracies-and-innuendo/2016/06/13/b21e59de-317e-11e6-8ff7-7b6c1998b7a0_story.html.

Kuntsman, Adi, and Rebecca L. Stein. 2015. *Digital militarism: Israel's occupation in the social media age*. Stanford, CA: Stanford University Press.

Lamothe, Dan, Lindsey Bever, and Eli Rosenberg. 2017. Trump offered a grieving military father $25,000 in a phone call. *Washington Post*, October 18. https://www.washingtonpost.com/world/national-security /trump-offered-a-grieving-military-father-25000-in-a-call-but-didnt-follow-through/2017/10/18/8d4cbc8c -b43a-11e7-be94-fabb0f1e9ffb_story.html.

Landler, Mark. 2017. Trump falsely claims Obama didn't contact families of fallen troops. *New York Times*, October 16. https://www.nytimes.com/2017/10/16/us/politics/trump-obama-killed-soldiers.html.

Lempert, Michael, and Michael Silverstein. 2012. *Creatures of politics: Media, message, and the American presidency*. Bloomington: Indiana University Press.

———. 2017. Unusual politics as usual? *Anthropology News*, February 2. https://anthrosource.onlinelibrary.wiley .com/doi/10.1111/AN.174.

Lennon, Myles. 2018. Revisiting "the repugnant other" in the era of Trump. *HAU: Journal of Ethnographic Theory* 8 (3): 439–454. doi:10.1086/700979.

Lipstadt, Deborah E. 1994. *Denying the Holocaust: The growing assault on truth and memory*. New York: Plume.

———. 2005. *History on trial: My day in court with David Irving*. New York: Ecco/HarperCollins.

Maskovsky, Jeff. 2017. Toward the anthropology of white nationalist postracism: Comments inspired by Hall, Goldstein, and Ingram's "The hands of Donald Trump." *HAU: Journal of Ethnographic Theory* 7 (1): 433–440. doi:10.14318/hau7.1.030.

McGranahan, Carole. 2014. What is ethnography? Teaching ethnographic sensibilities without fieldwork. *Teaching Anthropology* 4:22–36.

———. 2017. An anthropology of lying: Trump and the political sociality of moral outrage. *American Ethnologist* 44 (2): 243–248. doi:10.1111/amet.12475.

———. 2018. Ethnography beyond method: The importance of an ethnographic sensibility. *SITES* 15 (1): 1–10. doi:10.11157/sites-id373.

Meyer, Robinson. 2017. Does Twitter's new hate policy cover Trump's North Korea tweet? *The Atlantic*, December 18, 2017. https://www.theatlantic.com/technology/archive/2017/12/the-trump-exception/548648/.

Miller, Daniel, and Heather A. Horst. 2012. The digital and the human: A prospectus for digital anthropology. In H. A. Horst and D. Miller (Eds.), *Digital anthropology* (3–35. London: Bloomsbury.

Mottahedeh, Negar. 2015. *#iranelection: Hashtag solidarity and the transformation of online life*. Stanford, CA: Stanford University Press.

Müller, Karsten, and Carlo Schwarz. 2018, March 30. Making America hate again? Twitter and hate crime under Trump. *SSRN*. https://papers.ssrn.com/sol3/papers.cfm?abstract_id=3149103.

Murthy, Dhiraj. 2013. *Twitter: Social communication in the Twitter age*. Malden, MA: Polity.

Murthy, Dhiraj, and Sanjay Sharma. 2019. Visualizing YouTube's comment space: Online hostility as a networked phenomena. *New Media and Society* 21 (1): 191–213.

Neff, Gina. 2018. The potential of networked solidarity: Communication at the end of the long twentieth century. In P. J. Boczkowski and Z. Papacharissi (Eds.), *Trump and the media* (127–132. Cambridge, MA: MIT Press.

Omi, Michael, and Howard Winant. 2014. *Racial formations in the United States*. New York: Routledge.

Ott, Brian L. 2017. The age of Twitter: Donald J. Trump and the politics of debasement. *Critical Studies in Media Communication* 34 (1): 59–68. doi:10.1080/15295036.2016.1266686.

Ott, Brian L., and Greg Dickinson. 2019. *The Twitter presidency: Donald J. Trump and the politics of white rage*. New York: Routledge.

Painter, Nell I. 2011. *The history of white people*. New York: Norton.

Pink, Sarah, Heather Horst, John Postill, Larissa Hjorth, Tania Lewis, and Jo Tacchi. 2016. *Digital Ethnography*. London: Sage.

Pohjonen, Matti, and Sahana Udupa. 2017. Extreme speech online: An anthropological critique of hate speech debates. *International Journal of Communication* 11:1173–1191.

Postill, John. 2011. *Localizing the internet: An anthropological account*. New York: Berghahn.

———. 2012. Digital politics and political engagement. In H. A. Horst and D. Miller (Eds.), *Digital anthropology* (165–184. London: Bloomsbury.

Roediger, David R. 2006. *Working toward whiteness: How America's immigrants become white*. New York: Basic.

Rogers, Richard. 2014. Debanalising Twitter: The transformation of an object of study. In K. Weller, A. Bruns, J. Burgess, M. Mahrt, and C. Puschmann (Eds.), *Twitter and society* (ix–xxvi. New York: Peter Lang.

Roland, L. Kaifa. 2017. How bodies matter: Yesterday's America today. *HAU: Journal of Ethnographic Theory* 7 (1): 441–447. doi:10.14318/hau7.1.031.

Scheper-Hughes, Nancy. 2017. Another country? Racial hatred in the time of Trump. *HAU: Journal of Ethnographic Theory* 7 (1): 449–460. doi:10.14318/hau7.1.032.

Silverstein, Michael. 2003. *Talking politics: The substance of style from Abe to "W."* Chicago: Prickly Paradigm.

———. 2017. Message, myopia, dystopia. *HAU: Journal of Ethnographic Theory* 7 (1): 407–413. doi:10.14318 /hau7.1.027.

Singer, P. W., and Emerson T. Brooking. 2018. *LikeWar: The weaponization of social media*. Boston: Houghton Mifflin Harcourt.

Stolee, Galen, and Caton, Steve. 2018. Twitter, Trump, and the base: A shift to a new form of presidential talk. *Signs and Society* 6 (1): 147–165. doi:10.1086/694755.

Stoler, Ann L. 1992. "In cold blood": Hierarchies of credibility and the politics of colonial narratives. *Representations* 37:151–189.

———. 2002. Colonial archives and the arts of governance. *Archival Science*, 2, 87–109.

———. 2009. *Along the archival grain: Epistemic anxieties and colonial common sense*. Princeton, NJ: Princeton University Press.

Stuckey, Maray E. 2006. Presidential secrecy: Keeping archives open. *Rhetoric and Public Affairs* 9 (1): 138–144.

Trouillot, Michel-Rolph. 1995. *Silencing the past: Power and the production of history*. Boston: Beacon.

Tufekci, Zeynep. 2017. *Twitter and tear gas: The power and fragility of networked protest*. New Haven, CT: Yale University Press.

Turner, Fred. 2018. Trump on Twitter: How a medium designed for democracy became an authoritarian's mouthpiece. In P. J. Boczkowski and Z. Papacharissi (Eds.), *Trump and the media* (143–149. Cambridge, MA: MIT Press.

Udupa, Sahana. 2018. *Gaali* cultures: The politics of abusive exchange on social media. *New Media and Society*, 20(4), 1–17. doi:10.1177/1461444817698776.

Waldron, Jereemy. 2012. *The harm in hate speech*. Cambridge, MA: Harvard University Press.

Weller, Katrin, Axel Bruns, Jean Burgess, Merja Mahrt, and Cornelius Puschmann, eds. 2014. *Twitter and society*. New York: Peter Lang.

Williams, Bianca C. 2013. Virtual ethnography. In *Oxford bibliographies in anthropology*. Oxford: Oxford University Press. https://www.oxfordbibliographies.com/view/document/obo-9780199766567/obo -9780199766567-0107.xml?rskey=WTbvJWandresult=1andq=Virtual+ethnography#firstMatch.

———. 2018. *The pursuit of happiness: Black women, diasporic dreams, and the politics of emotional transnationalism*. Durham, NC: Duke University Press.

Young, Kevin. 2017. *Bunk: The rise of hoaxes, humbug, plagiarists, phonies, post-facts, and fake news*. Minneapolis, MN: Graywolf.

8

RACIALIZATION, RACISM, AND ANTIRACISM IN DANISH SOCIAL MEDIA PLATFORMS

Peter Hervik

Dumbed down politics and journalism, fake news, and planted news have emerged within a news media that is dominated by a small number of giant global media conglomerates and public service stations and pressured by the forces of the market. These large global processes lay a foundation on which powerful agents can exert their populist pitches for power (Boot 2016). In addition, tremendous efforts are being made by political and commercial interests to intensify their activities and seize upon social media and microtargeting. A large majority of people now get their information, opinions, and emotional engagement from social media (Gottfried 2017). It is against this background that populists make claims about "elites who have betrayed the people" and thereby tap into a broader anti-elitist and anti-intellectual trend in which the supply lines to research-based information are broken. Populists are also committed to "ordinary people," with an emphasis on "speaking the plain truth" about visible minorities, and most do so with nationalist overtones (Betz 1998; Schroeder 2018). With this background and the popularization of social media come verbal radicalism and bigotry, which deliver the kinds of drama, violence, and conflict on which the news media thrives.

In this chapter, the empirical object of interest is online extreme speech in Denmark that employs racialization as an exclusionary discourse directed at minorities with migrant, postmigrant, or refugee backgrounds and that, as such, belongs to the so-called far right. The far right embraces the idea that immigration threatens the nation's cultural homogeneity and national security. By establishing contact and rapport with outspoken far-right activists, this study combines the examination of online behavior with ethnographic interviews in the commentators' own homes. Before presenting interview data,* I will use a media event about blackface in Denmark, based on a discussion of a chocolate commercial, to illustrate features of the general debate.[1]

The analysis of the ethnographic material and the blackface event show that commentators disregard research into racialization or minority experiences of racism. In addition, these commentators reveal a lack of critical skills or insight into the use of sources; rather,

* All translations from Danish were done by author.

I will argue, they rely on a pseudoscientific scavenging for "documentation" that fits their view of how things are and should be—one of the effects of the informal, new digital culture. Instead of showing signs of decline, the extreme and divisive use of language and the naturalization of racialized difference continue to proliferate through efforts to recruit and consolidate communities of support. Meanwhile, the commentators do not see themselves as racists but rather as doing what they do to protect a nation in danger.

In Denmark, neoracism and neonationalism are closely connected and have been evolving since the early 1990s (Hervik 2011)[2]—and effectively challenging the image abroad of a fairy-tale country. Denmark has nearly 5.7 million inhabitants, of which 10 percent are statistically regarded as "immigrant" and another 3.2 percent as descendants of immigrants (Danmarks Statistik 2018). The country had its most homogeneous population in a 50-year period from 1920 (reunification of southern Denmark with Denmark following World War I) until the mid-1960s. Before the reunification, the region comprised six languages, and thus the idea of Denmark as a single-language, white-only country was simply not the reality. After the late 1960s, guest workers invited by industry and, in the 2000s, refugee arrivals brought more heterogeneity to the Danish population (Hervik 2014).

Set within a context of anti-elitist nationalist populism, extreme speech and thought has grown prodigiously since the mid-1990s; it was widespread during the Muhammad cartoon affair (2012) that took place before social media burst into popular use in the mid-2000s. Rather than the more norm-based term *hate speech*, the term *extreme speech* allows for a more grounded focus that encompasses the words and tone used, the messages conveyed, and the social relations involved (Udupa and Pohjonen 2019; Hervik 2019*b*). Extreme speech and thought have intensified with use by new political parties, at major critical media events, and with professionalization of political communication. Anti-immigrant, anti-Muslim, anti–non-Westerner, antileftist, antimulticulturalist, and antifeminist sentiment helps construct Danish national identity, which can best be seen as the consolidation of a hegemonic white majority. The neonational, neoracist, anti-elitist nexus is epitomized by the Facebook image posted by Minister of Integration Inger Støjberg, who recently celebrated fifty restrictive policies separating "native" Danes from minorities with refugee or migrant backgrounds with a smile and a big cake (fig. 8.1) (Bilefsky 2017). In addition, the official website of the Ministry of Immigration and Integration (2019) continues to count restrictions made by the government as an accomplishment: 114 in May 2019 (fig. 8.2). Additional restrictions can be found in other ministries, including the Ministry of Justice.

Neonationalism refers to nationalism under new conditions and set within well-established nation-states. Nationalism favors and generates an in-group and is inseparable from the production of an out-group. This is where the two *isms*, nationalism and racism, are two sides of the same coin (Hervik 2011; Miles 1993). The emotional language of anti-elitism, nationalist celebration, and racialization of visual others, real or imagined, becomes a formidable mobilizer of anger, anxiety, and moral outrage, which is the backdrop of extreme speech examined in this article.

In the rhetoric of anti-elitism, celebrations of "common sense," and promotion of nationalist values, it is not only research-based information that is bypassed. Facts, more generally, do not seem to matter unless they are in sync with the ideology, "common sense," and

Figure 8.1 Minister of Immigration Inger Støjberg's Facebook photo celebrating fifty restrictive policies of the Danish government. Source: https://politiken.dk/indland/art5870543/Støjberg -forarger-Fejrer-udlændingeshystramning-nr.-50-med-lagkage (accessed July 23, 2020).

"gut feelings." In political communication, fact-based information is often to be avoided or spun into something else. Spin can be seen as "an angle on truth" that aims to place you, your party, your message, or your company in the most favorable light (Press 2002). Spin is closely tied to efforts setting the agenda, priming, and using positive words for oneself and negative ones for adversaries, simple metaphors, catchy phrases, and so on (Hervik 2011).

By 2019, the white hegemonic majority was driven by a strong emotional attachment to the cultural logic of a nation in danger that must be defended against both external and domestic adversaries (Hervik 2018b, 2019a). As a hegemonic force, it repeats itself constantly, and sentiments beyond explicit awareness become commonplace and "so habituated, so deeply inscribed in everyday routine, that they may no longer be seen as forms of control—or seen at all" (Comaroff and Comaroff 1991). Members of this "white majority" end up feeling offended by any talk of racism, to the extent that they deny the experiences of racialization as expressed by Muslims, people of color, and certain white groups (particularly people from former Eastern European countries).[3] Researchers and activists in the emerging antiracism movement are using concepts like "everyday racism," "structural racism," and, to a lesser

Figure 8.2 The image posted on the official website of the ministry with
the count of restrictive policies of the Danish government
(since removed).

extent, "banal nationalism" to capture these muted and rejected experiences of racial and racializing discrimination (Essed 2002; Hervik 2019a; Billig 1995).

Racism is an ideology and a discriminatory social practice that is based on racializing certain other people. It refers to the process of assigning meaning to biological characteristics and naturalizing the culture of "others" and may be backed up by institutionalized power and hegemonic social groups. In an analytical sense, racism must first include an interpretive frame of reference that creates a division between a positively represented national "us" and a negatively represented nationalist "them."[4] Second, a hierarchy of the us–them division is established along the lines of racialization, which involves "endowing the characteristics, appearance, traditions, and lifestyles attributed to groups of different 'others' with negative signifiers that are deemed to be natural and insurmountable" (Lentin 2008, xv). Third, the aspect of power must be present and accounted for (see Hervik 2011).

One hideout for these online cultures of political aggression lies within the very concepts of the far right, the "extreme right," and the "radical right." They are spatial metaphors telling us that the problem is "out there," away from the center and the mainstream. However, several scholars have shown, on the basis of careful and meticulous analysis, what they see as the mainstreaming of the far right (Feischmidt and Hervik 2015; Hervik and Berg 2007; Mondon 2013). But if we maintain spatial images of "out there," then the concepts seem to lose their meaning and influence as they become mainstreamed imaginaries and practices, including policies. Perhaps we need to invent a new analytic category, mainstream extremism, to capture this seeming contradiction that otherwise seems to vanish. When extreme speech and thought enter the mainstream, extremism is naturalized—and/or the extreme is relegated to the politically motivated use of actual, physical violence. In the process, we brush aside the vital role of psychological violence, indirect violence, cultural violence, and the tacit acceptance of the everyday violence of extreme language.

When *extreme* is applied to speech, it refers to a combination of the words used, the (racialized) message conveyed, the tone of the language, the communicator, and the sources evoked. In my view, researchers make a huge mistake if they reduce extremism and extreme speech to the discourse and actions of members of toxic ideologies. Extreme online speech may arrive from a deontology, where the sense of ethical duty overrides the comprehension and knowledge of ideologies and propels people into extremist expression while seeing themselves as patriots or as people who fight the most obvious problems in the world, often saying, "Someone has to do it."

In the next section, I turn to a heated debate over a media event about a chocolate commercial that used blackface. The treatment of this event, chosen from a large pool of similar events, illustrates some shared features of Danish extreme speech, including denial of racialization, lack of interest in research-based facts, ridicule of the messenger, and reliance on pseudoscientific media searches for support for the "real truth" about the arrival and lives of migrants and postmigrants in Denmark (Caglar 2016). Then, I turn to interviews and encounters with online actors to capture more profoundly the lifeworld and reference world that lies underneath some of these extreme speech postings, repostings, shares, and comments during public events. The material is organized by roughly divided and interrelated themes that were clearly identifiable across the interviews. The large pool of interviews includes a set of eight interviews with confrontational, far-right, online writers.

KiMs Chocolate Commercial or Blackface?

Chosen from our pool of media events about issues of migrants, adoptees, refugees, and Danish minorities with ethnic origins outside Nordic countries, this case is particularly useful to convey broader features of web exchanges. It includes diverse points of view, styles, and strategies within the same thread.

One of the longest running series of commercials in Denmark, going back to 1997, is for the chips and snacks company KiMs. The company is part of the global Norwegian business Orkla, which has more than thirty thousand employees across the world. The figure of "Jørgen" is known to most Danes, and over the years, he has retained the same metanarrative as he introduces new products. In the commercial, Jørgen's face is covered by dark chocolate, and he says, "I am brown because I am going to tell you about my new chocolate buttons." At the end of the product promotion, we hear the sound of bongo drums, and then the commercial ends (TV2 2017).

Emore's Experience of Racialization

According to Danish news coverage, the turmoil surrounding a commercial for the company's new chocolate product began with a 2017 Facebook post by Nicole Jacqueline Obovo Emore.[5] On March 9, 2017, she explained, "I was outraged after I saw the commercial yesterday. Not only because it was a bad effort to make him look like somebody who had stuffed himself with chocolate and therefore, incidentally, had ended up with chocolate all over his face. I was also outraged because I, as an Afro-Dane, cannot avoid emphasizing the univocal exhibition. I cannot neglect the sound of Bongo drums as background noise. I cannot neglect the fact that he says, 'I am brown because . . .'"

The post triggered immediate comments from people who shared her outrage and called for the company to apologize and withdraw the commercial. The explosion of comments was noted by KiMs; however, the company did not respond directly. Instead, KiMs Company used Jørgen, the main character in the commercial, to respond in a cordial fashion that kept the theme within an aura of fun, amusement, and lightheartedness that characterizes the commercial series and the brand of chips "for the good times." Jørgen said, "Hi, the purpose of the commercial was to exhibit my new chocolate. That is the reason why I have painted my face brown just like chocolate. *It is an old sales trick, I have learned—although I cannot remember where.* It was not the intention to be perceived otherwise. I just wanted to state that it is alright to get it all over one's face when one regales oneself with chocolate. Kind regards, Jørgen" (emphasis added).

Nevertheless, comments continued to build up. A few hours later, "Jørgen" was backpedaling but not apologizing: "Many of you write to me that I have to re-do it and guess what? I recognize what you say. I edited myself out of the film! That is all there is to it. Now, the full focus will be on my new chocolate, which is still as good as it looks. I hope this will make up for the misunderstanding. I do not like to offend anyone. Kind regards, Jørgen."

Although these crisis communications on the part of KiMs Company acknowledge the company's concern, they do not stop the intense posts and spread on social media, news coverage, and blogs. By speaking through the comic figure Jørgen, the company uses a nonserious strategy to respond and does not apologize.

The intense exchange of comments continues and spreads to traditional media. In the comments on Emore's Facebook post and on newspaper commentaries, the language is extreme in content and form and threatens to grow out of control. Danes have come to know this tendency over the past few decades.

Facebook Commentaries: Dialogue, Bickering, or
Double Monologue?

The following sequence[6] of actual exchanges on Emore's 2017 Facebook post is slightly edited:

MARTIN WOLHARDT: Mia Wolhardt Søndergaard did you know that it is racist to have chocolate on one's face? It is as a matter of fact. Chocolate all over your face is no joke. It is, on the contrary, equal to genuine hate of brown people.

MICHAEL HANSEN: Martin: What part do you think the Bongo drums play? Are they also part of the chocolate?

MARTIN WOLHARDT: To sum up, it is the Bongo drums that are racists. Alright.

LYNNE RIE HANSSON: Martin, is it a little lame to speak about something that you, obviously, are neither able to understand nor aim to understand.

MARTIN WOLHARDT: You don't really know me, in case you don't think I either am able to or wish to understand the problems of racism.

MARTIN WOLHARDT: I just realised that my cinnamon buns [*kanel-snegle* in Danish, often referred to as simply *snegle* (snails), which is a popular Danish pastry for the morning] are racist. They are covered by chocolate icing. I am going to post a complaint to the baker saying that it is not alright.

Despite being one of the few exchanges that are direct, with several well-represented viewpoints, there is little will to enter into genuine dialogue. Instead, comments quickly become personal, agonistic, and baiting for additional applications of the argument.

Argument 1: This Is "Blackface"

Emore was far from alone in expressing her outrage. Eva Afewerki wrote, "Racism does not hurt you but US, so don't preach to us on how we should act against racism. Think it over and Google before you write factless bullshit like this. It is repulsive to be as uninformed and ignorant (as you). 'Know your nasty story.' Realize that your elders were nasty and racist toward Black people."

Others kept a more sanitized tone and tried to respond to "Jørgen's" claim that he is using an old sales trick to sell his chocolate product and, at the same time, explain what blackface is:

ANNE BETTINA PEDERSEN: I can explain to you, Jørgen, where you have picked it up (sales trick). You have picked it up through stereotypical and evil portrayals that go back to, for instance, the pre-civil war period in the US. Such stereotypes were also basic to the so-called "minstrel shows" exposing white people dressed up as Blacks ridiculing them. You can also take a look at D. W. Griffith's *The Birth of a Nation* from 1915. He portrays the Ku Klux Klan as heroes (you must see yourself as part of the proud "White Pride"!) racist hooligans in Aarhus, second largest city in Denmark. You can pick up more by reading Donald Bogles fabulous best-seller *Toms, Coons, Mulattoes, Mammies, and Bucks*. You can also find a good explanation of why Blackface is racist in Spike Lee's film *Bamboozled*. . . . The commercial builds on a dehumanization of brown people that goes back to the time of slavery. Yet, it presents a fruitful opportunity to acquire more knowledge about this topic and attempt to view the circumstances from the view of the offended one.

The next commentator is supportive of this view, which comes through his self-identifying as a white male. This makes him humble to the point of making himself invisible in the service of civility and decent manners:

GERT HANSEN: You cannot find any racist allusions because you have not felt them on your own body. You do not know what it means to be marginalized and prejudiced due to your skin color, and that is the reason why you cannot understand why anyone may be offended to see a white man perform a Blackface and exhibit your background as primitive and backwards. Well, you see, I am myself a white man and privileged and do not know from personal experience what these matters mean, but I have good manners, making me quiet when people speak about something I do not know anything about.

Argument 2: Reactions—This Is Not Racism, It Is a Chocolate Commercial

The first argument, "this is blackface," evolved from Emore's original post and derives from her experience and insight, which she shares with a number of other people. The second argument can be seen as a reaction to the first argument, but it can also be seen as the externalization of the strong denial concerning conversations about race that has been dominant for the majority of white Danes:

> HENRIK HANSEN FREDERIKSEN: People who find this commercial racist form part of a destruction of our country. What about joining forces and aim at maintaining funny words like nigger-bun, zuluhead, etc. Curiously nobody reacts to the word garlic [the Danish word, *hvidløg*, literally "white onion"]. Only idiots can see racism in this ad.

> ANDERS NIELSEN: Eva! Alone the fact that you say that I am an "aversive racist" [*hygge-racist*, literally "cozy racism"] is ridiculous, braindead, and underscores my point. . . . If you have such big problems with Danish humor and white people in general, what are you doing here? Because you cannot be born here if you have to explain yourself in English.

> JAN HØJVANG MATTHIESEN: By all means! Do you not have anything else and more important things to do than, I dare say, simulate offendedness in relation to something as marginal as a chocolate ad.

> TEDDI KLIT CHRISTENSEN: Jin, seek help. Taking a brief glance at your profile one sees that you are straight out looking for something that, if it was meant like that, might be termed xenophobic. If you do not like the heat, then get lost!

> JIM NIELSEN: You perceive even the most meaningless things as serious and racist. Why do you get so offended because somebody paints himself black in the face and applies Bongo drums as background sound? Are you ashamed of your origin?

The commentators who argue the commercial is an incident of blackface base their views on personal experience and literature, whereas people arguing against this interpretation tend to shift the focus away from the argument and instead to the people arguing. People who invoke the blackface argument are approached with warlike words such as "destruction of the country" and "joining forces" and with (nationalist) attempts to represent these commentators as "foreigners" and not belonging. Eva becomes foreign through her use of English words, whereas Jin is regarded as foreign based on a look at her Facebook profile.

Emore's Analysis

Following several hours of heated interventions and extreme language, the author of the original post, Emore, posted a new comment in which she reflected on what she sees happening in the commentaries. She said, "In the case of KiMs the Blackface is not intended. They do not know what Blackface is. They do not know at all, what I speak about. KiMs cannot or does not care to read about what Blackface means."

In the beginning, Emore told the story about the TV commercial that offended and outraged her and her friend. This story made others join in and share their similar experiences and generated further sympathies and alignments. However, comments about emotional reactions and outrage were not recognized or heard by opposing commentators, who continued to pitch in and support the KiMs Company and its commercial. After hours of comments appearing, Emore realized that after sharing her experience of seeing the black-face commercial, she had to shift the register to literature and facts about the history of blackface. However, again, the response to Emore was one of overall negation. More generally, we find these two features again and again in social media debates: denial of experiences of racialization and negation of the emotions involved.

Racism as the Topic of Social Media Commentaries

The analysis of the language and thought in the pool of eight interviews could be divided into five interrelated themes that progress from talk about separate spaces, the characters of different people, the dangers of mixing, solutions, and self-understanding of racism. In this chapter, I have chosen one particular, long, illustrative interview to convey how the racialized content unfolds.

Lissy (pseudonym) is a retired millionaire, a well-educated woman with a degree from a prominent university. Lissy is an active part of a closed Facebook group of approximately one thousand members. Through her online network activities and attendance at public meetings about migrants and their religions, she posts, reposts, and receives stories from a platform of several thousand members, although she holds common core ideas and narratives with far more Danes. In these activities, commentators again and again use strong language and affective statements about the same set of powerful political leaders and ex-leaders. They use a friend–enemy scheme that stresses negative things about the enemy in order to build community and comradeship (Wodak and Reisigl 1999), following the principle forwarded by Samuel Huntington and used by Carl Schmitt, that you do not know who you are until you know who you hate (Hervik 2011). Examples from the interview with Lissy and from her postings included an enemy approach to Angela Merkel, George Soros, Barack Obama, Hillary Clinton, and Oluf Palme.

Throughout the interviews, interviewees made use of anonymous depersonalizing pronouns: "Man," "De," "det," to refer to a whole group, people, or category. Nevertheless, the term is funneled again and again into "Muslims" and/or domestic adversaries (certain political parties, the "goodness industry"). The term *moral judgment* is used here in the empirical sense pointed out by Goodenough (1997) as an emotional judgment of what other people do, not what we do ourselves (see also Hervik 2018a). Obviously, moralizing is a reflexive process that bends back to the moralizer, since it is impossible to moralize about others without moralizing oneself.

Separate Spaces: Our Space, Their Space

The first pattern identified in the interviews is the separation of people into different geographic spaces. Such separation follows the logic of "naturally" belonging to certain spaces and the idea that you derive your identity from those spaces (Malkki 1992). In terms of neo-racism, everyone is regarded (rhetorically) as of equal morality and intelligence, but if you are in the wrong place, it is only "natural" that xenophobic reactions will occur (Hervik 2011) from members of the sovereign nation. Lissy observed, "They have to stay where they belong, where they are at home, and they shall not care to expand without permission. Nobody has ever allowed them to expand. I have nothing against Muslims. If I travel to their countries, they can do whatever they like."

Talking about refugees and migrants crossing the Mediterranean, Lissy explained: "Had they said clearly back then: 'You keep away from Europe!' And had they stopped those people on the highway who came to Denmark: 'You will be shot to pieces by our warships and those who come further than this zone will go back to Libya. North Africa. We don't want you in Europe. You cannot do anything productive, you don't want anything good. What you want is only rape, crime, and enriching yourself.' Then that party of immigrants would have been stopped."

The logic of these spaces is that of "nation-making," where "culture" is at the heart of organizing. It is the nation-state that is sovereign, with the legitimate use of power and deciding who is to be a member. But it is also necessary to emphasize that this nationalism has an inherent militaristic potential.

Moral Judgments: Civility and Intelligence

The second theme from the analysis of interviews consists of portraying the characteristics and making demands on people who are already living within "our" space:

> Everyone can see that the Muslims cannot manage by themselves. How would our society turn out if our culture becomes more and more Islamic, toward becoming "good-for-nothings" (*dønigte*). They do not have the same work ethic as we do, and the same goes for their view of women and humanity. Neither do they have the same idea about loyalty and welfare, and they don't even respect waste bins. They just throw their rubbish where they please.
>
> They pee in the water. And I am sorry to say, they defecate in the water. The indoor public swimming pool. I don't go there. I read in our local newspaper . . . that they relieve themselves in the water. That is obvious harassment. Peeing in the changing rooms. That makes you furious.
>
> Slowly, a minority [could begin to] to transform our culture. We [would have] to put up with politicians turning our food into halal food. We [would have] to put up with . . . more and more scarves. I dare to say that we are more civilized. (Lissy, interview)

The ascribed attributes of Muslims do not come from scientific analysis or readings of research-based literature. Lissy is correct that a story in the local paper told the story about people peeing and defecating in the pool (Warming 2014). However, the story does not relate to Arab boys or Muslims or who the perpetrators are. The only sources that connect them are the extreme-right ideological sites "Den Korte Avis" and "Uriasposten," which engage in speculation and rumors about who it could be. This is an illustration of a common trend of social media news exchanges in which accuracy of information goes unchecked and stories are not criticized but reposted endlessly. Lissy's use of the local newspaper and the two sites becomes a pseudoscientific type of search to verify an already established "fact."

Mixing Is the Problem

The third theme is mixing. In the dominant view of the interviewees, mixing is seen as a problem, whereas alternative but weaker views approach mixing as a necessary battle to overcome postcolonial biases in language and thought.

Interviewees often singled out one or two Muslims that they knew or worked with and were keen to allow exceptions to their general statements. These views are on par with Fredrik Barth's (1969) seminal work on ethnic boundaries, in which he found individuals could cross ethnic boundaries, but the group as a whole was organized in opposition to an explicitly identified ethnic other. Later research has shown that this other could be the state, the nation, modernization, globalization, and more:

> I do not believe we should mix up different people . . . Not a mass invasion that comes in and takes over our culture. That is what I am beginning to realize. That slowly, there is a minority that slowly begins a cultural upheaval. . . . The genuinely noble and, I think, also from a scientific point of view—apart from a few highly educated—we see it as an animal world. There is a selection, of course we have to be selective. We shall not mix with anyone. Neighbors can hardly get along. Neither can white people—if they come from different cultural backgrounds. . . . The plots of land are getting smaller. To put it bluntly: the proletariat are soon coming right into your living room, they mow the lawn all day, and do-it-yourself types, and everything that is noisy. . . . There will be a civil war if more and more of them get elected to the municipal councils. I do not think they should be allowed to vote, at all. . . . We are a homogeneous Norden in Europe, and, basically, I think it is beautiful. We, in Scandinavia, we form a distinct race (*folke-færd*). We are pale, light in our skin. We reason alike and we . . . we may ask when do people become genetically civilized. It is indeed a long process. (Lissy, interview)

For Lissy and the seven other far-right interviewees, mixing is regarded as outright dangerous and should be avoided. In our larger sample, Malou, a young mother who arrived as a child from Africa, represents a minority view that is concerned with this racialized view of mixing as a problem. She is particularly concerned with the conditions for bringing up children in a society with widespread structural discrimination and denial of it:

> I am constantly seen as different. Or spoken to as somebody who is different. Basically, I am fed up with it. I may say I am a refugee, but what about my children? As they grow up, they will not have the opportunity to pull out the race card. Would they be named second generation immigrants? When does it stop?
> There is not much of an African in me, regarding culture. Nothing at all in my children. If one keeps saying that I am an African just because I am dark, then I will never get the opportunity to be myself and Danish on equal footing with everybody else.
> We are Danes, we are brown. We are brown Danes. (Malou, interview)

These statements on mixing as a problem build on the nationalist ideology that people belong, by history and destiny, to certain spaces. "Our space" versus "their space" relies on this idea and that those within these spaces share not only the same history and "civility" but also a physical sameness. Such a view racializes people like Malou. For her part, she stands up and insists on not being "mixed." While Lissy divides people according to belonging, civility, and intelligence and sees such mixing as a threat to Nordic homogeneity, Malou refuses to let her children be regarded as mixed.

Solutions: What Should Be Done?

The fourth theme that appears in the interviews derives from normative statements about what should be done, as the host population, to solve the issue of mixing with people regarded as less civilized and deserving. Lissy told us that she had found herself at home and active within a new political party. Promoting the party and attending events is a form of activism that she sees as a helpful contribution to the defense of the Danish nation and to solving the problem of mixing:

> [The party leader] wants a full stop for asylum. They shall be repatriated. Parallel communities have to go. They should declare a state of emergency and kick in the doors and scrutinize their computers. And if there is the smallest discrepancy in relation to our democracy and society . . . then they are out. Now, they talk about prisoner camps in Africa. I don't care where they are sent, the door must be hermetically closed. And not like Merkel with an open Schengen door.
>
> They want to provoke a civil war. That's what I fear. That would be with the moderate people, which is us Danes in three to five generations, who speak Danish, read Danish, and think Danish and understand our culture and the Nordic world. (Lissy, interview)

Lissy's talk about a civil war is not a new idea in social media but can be traced back to the late 1990s, when a tabloid newspaper, *Ekstra Bladet*, ran a unique antimigrant, neonationalist campaign (Hervik 2011). Part of the campaign included visiting people who had written concerned letters to the editor and using their stories as separate news stories.

Racism in Self-Understanding of Racism

The fifth theme identified in the interviews comes from racist statements and from addressing racism directly. The underlying racist thought is present in all five themes.

When Lissy talks about her son being married, and later divorced, to a woman from the Middle East and about having her son's future partner in mind, she states:

> I prefer to have a European without the African man. Indeed, I would prefer to be free from Africans. . . . This has nothing to do with racism. . . . I would not like if my son brought home an African girl. Even though she might be well educated. She might be nice, cultivated, and loving. But I would feel unpleasant . . . that he would marry, and I should get mullato grandchildren. It would not please me, since he carries with him another cultural background from home. . . . More relentlessness, giving tit for tat. Close the Qur'an, cleansing, throwing people out of the country if they show the least sympathy for radicalized types. Protect our country and civilization. It is treason.

As far as self-understanding, Lissy does not see herself as racist. She said, "It is not my nature to be a racist. I get furious if anybody calls me a racist, Nazi, fascist, or whatever they can come up with. Regrettably, I often hear such terms. I am a patriot, I love my mother country. . . . We are neither racists, fascists, or Nazis because we like to have the good, old order in our mother country and we like to have a homogeneous population." Another interviewee, Linda, noted, "I have observed that the concept of racism is used as soon as you present a critical argument—without using vitriolic language. . . . Many people from the other political wing think I am a racist because I have a negative view on Islam. I am in no sense a racist." Lissy added, "You ought to realize that if the level of intelligence drops in Europe because we marry members of a group who are far less gifted and have more disabilities."

The statements presented in the first four themes are at odds with the self-understanding of interviewees, who do not perceive themselves to be racists. On one hand, racism conceptualized as "cultural racism," "cultural fundamentalism," and "neoracism" has aptly captured the notion of racism without racists. This is clear in the case of Lissy, who makes racist statements about the cultures of people who are more civilized, more intelligent, or more primitive than others and unreflectively uses the case of defecation in public pools as part of her dehumanizing, extreme vocabulary. Again, this view is similar to Lissy's perspective on herself and her group and is similar to the views of other interviewees. They emphasized that they are simply telling the truth about the numbers and characters of migrants coming and those already here. This truth is, they argue, not understood by their opponents, who instead rely on fake accusations of racism.

Conclusion

The pattern found in the chocolate commercial controversy and the themes identified in the interviews for this chapter echo public debate on social media and debate programs on television more generally in Denmark. With some variation, Danish social media platforms as well as national politics operate with a strong, spatially divided nationalist we-the-Danes and a racialized other; a classic us-them division, where the "we" form an ethnocentric as well as Eurocentric norm against which all others are evaluated. Whether these *others* are people approaching Denmark in search of a better life, fleeing from experiences of paralyzing economic and other inequalities, escaping from regimes with draconian surveillance routines, running from the horrors of war and other disasters, or Danish citizens with an ethnic family background, they are talked about in an extreme language that sees them as belonging to a different, non-Danish space. The nationalist idea of belonging "naturally" to certain spaces, and that one should stay in those spaces, is an important neoracism philosophy. According to this idea, people from the non-European world seem to be regarded as of equal moral and intellectual worth, but if they are in the "wrong" (unnatural) space, xenophobic reactions and extreme language will occur as a "natural" reaction. However, when people in "our space" and "their space" are portrayed, they are still represented as being less civilized in a variety of ways, including where they pee and defecate. This is obviously particularly strong in Lissy's reasoning.

Few people in Denmark have studied racism historically or in the contemporary society in which they live. Everyday perceptions of racism evoke dark forces that should be avoided and for good reasons. The understanding is that racism should be relegated to the historical past in Central Europe, the American South, and South Africa. Racism is denied, explained away in different ways, while facts are ignored. The statements about mixing bear witness to a practice of scavenging and evoking gut-level feelings and extreme speech with reference to anger in order to counter anyone who brings up expressions claimed to be racist. The implication is that online extreme speech appears as viable and resistant to the most important criticism of being factless, affectively driven, and ignoring minority experiences that do not fit the ideology.

Notes

1. These events are some of the most talked about events on Danish social media, capturing the attention of thousands of people who were commenting, posting, or reposting through their networks or having informal conversations with friends, family, coworkers, and others. Usually, the events were debated for 2–3 days, with 150–200 commentaries, and then died out (Hervik 2019a).

2. In this work, I build this finding on team research projects that took place precisely when three historic media events happened that are well documented in Danish language books: the birth and explosive growth of the far-right Danish People's Party along with an antimigrant campaign by a nationally circulated tabloid paper in 1997 (Hervik 1999); moral panic created in summer 2001 around the framing of young Danish Muslims with Pakistani heritage as "infiltrating" Danish politics and representing people consubstantial with the "Taliban" (Hervik 2002); and the Muhammad cartoon story of 2005–2006.

3. The term "white" is used because the research project "Structuring Diversity" documented how the Danish became "racially" aware of themselves as white in the late 1990s (Hervik 2011).

4. In a European context, the enforcement of the nation-state's borders and internal boundaries has been indicative of the reoccurrence of racism, or rather neoracism, reflecting the rhetorical shift of emphasis from "race" to "culture," among other features (see Hervik 2011).

5. The following commentary is from Emore's Facebook post, which we printed when it came out in March 2017 and was part of the public debate. At the time, there were 378 likes, 91 shares, and 189 comments, and it was broadly covered by the Danish news media outlets.

6. The editing is for clarity and includes some second commentators repeating the previous commentator's message.

References

Barth, Fredrik, ed. 1969. *Ethnic Groups and Boundaries: The Social Organization of Culture Difference*. Oslo: Universitetsforlaget.

Betz, Hans-Georg. 1998. "Introduction." In *The New Politics of the Right: Neopopulist Parties and Movements in Established Democracies*, edited by H-G. Betz and S. Immerfall, 1–10. New York: St. Martin's Press.

Bilefsky, D. 2017. "In Denmark, Passage of Rules on Immigraiton Called for Cake." *New York Times*, March 15.

Billig, Michael. 1995. *Banal Nationalism*. London: Sage.

Boot, Max. 2016. "How the 'Stupid Party' Created Donald Trump." *New York Times*, July 31, 2016. https://www.nytimes.com/2016/08/01/opinion/how-the-stupid-party-created-donald-trump.html.

Caglar, Ayse. 2016. "Still 'Migrants' after All Those Years: Foundational Mobilities, Temporal Frames, and Emplacement of Migrants." *Journal of Ethnic and Migration Studies* 42 (6): 952–969.

Comaroff, Jean, and John Comaroff. 1991. *Of Revelation and Revolution: Christianity, Colonialism, and Consciousness in South Africa*. Chicago: University of Chicago Press.

Danmarks Statistik. 2018. *Indvandrere i Danmark 2018*. https://www.dst.dk/Site/Dst/Udgivelser/GetPubFile.aspx?id=29445&sid=indv2018.

Essed, Philomena. 2002. "Everyday Racism." In *Encyclopedia of Race and Racism*, edited by John Hartwell Moore. Vol. 1, 447–449. Detroit: Macmillan.

Feischmidt, Margit, and Peter Hervik. 2015. "Mainstreaming the Extreme: Intersecting Challenges from the Far Right in Europe." *Intersections* 1:3–17.

Goodenough, Ward H. 1997. "Moral Outrage: Territoriality in Human Guise." *Zygon*, 32:5–27.

Gottfried, Jeffrey. 2017. "Most Americans Get Their Science News from General Outlets, but Many Doubt Their Accuracy." Pew Research Center, September 21, 2017. https://www.pewresearch.org/fact-tank/2017/09/21/most-americans-get-their-science-news-from-general-outlets-but-many-doubt-their-accuracy.

Hervik, Peter, ed. 1999. *Den generende forskellighed. Danske svar på den stigende multikulturalisme*. Copenhagen: Hans Reitzels Forlag.

———. 2002. *Mediernes muslimer. En antropologisk undersøgelse af mediernes dækning af religioner i Danmark*. Copenhagen: Board for Ethnic Equality.

———. 2011. *The Annoying Difference: The Emergence of Danish Neonationalism, Neoracism, and Populism in the Post-1989 World*. New York: Berghahn.

———. 2112. *The Danish Muhammad Cartoon Conflict*. Current Themes in IMER Research 13, Malmö Institute for Studies of Migration, Diversity and Welfare (MIM), Malmö University.

———. 2014. "Cultural War of Values: The Proliferation of Moral Identities in the Danish Public Sphere." In *Becoming Minority: How Discourses and Policies Produce Minorities in Europe and India*, edited by Jyotirmaya Tripathy and Sudarsan Padmanabhan, 154–173. New Delhi: Sage.

———. 2018a. "Afterword." *Conflict and Society* 4 (1): 85–93.

———. 2018b. "Refiguring the Public, Political and Personal in Current Danish Exclusionary Reasoning." In *"Political Sentiments and Social Movements: The Person in Politics and Culture*, edited by Claudia Strauss and Jack Friedman, 91–117. New York: Palgrave Macmillan.

———. 2019a. "Denmark's Blond Vision and the Fractal Logic of the Nation in danger." *Identities: Global Studies in Culture and Power.* (electronic version, ahead of print). DOI: 10.1080/1070289X.2019.1587905

———. 2019b. "Ritualized Opposition in Danish Online Practices of Extremist Language and thought." *International Journal of Communication* 13: 3104–3121.

Hervik, Peter, and Clarissa Berg. 2007. "Denmark: A Political Struggle in Danish Journalism." In *Reading the Mohammed Cartoons Controversy: An International Analysis of Press Discourses on Free Speech and Political Spin*, edited by Risto Kunelius, Elisabeth Eide, Oliver Hahn, and Roland Schroeder, 25–39. Working Papers in International Journalism. Bochum/Freiberg: Projekt Verlag.

Lentin, Alana. 2008. *Racism: A Beginner's Guide.* Oxford: Oneworld.

Malkki, Liisa. 1992. "National Geographic: The Rooting of Peoples and the Territorialization of National Identity among Scholars and Refugees." *Cultural Anthropology* 7 (1): 24–44.

Miles, R. 1993. *Racism after "Race Relations."* London: Routledge.

Ministry of Immigration and Integration. 2019. "Regeringen har gennemført [114] stramninger på udlændingeområdet." http://uim.dk.

Mondon, Aurélien. 2013. *The Mainstreaming of the Extreme Right in France and Australia: A Populist Hegemony?* Farnham: Ashgate.

Press, Bill. 2002. *Spin This! All the Ways We Don't Tell the Truth.* New York: Pocket.

Schroeder, Ralph. 2018. *Social Theory after the Internet.* London: University College Press.

TV2. 2017. "Kims beskyldes for racisme: Nu fjerner de 'brunt ansigt' fra reklame." http://nyheder.tv2.dk /samfund/2017-03-17-kims-beskyldes-for-racisme-nu-fjerner-de-brunt-ansigt-fra-reklame.

Udupa, Sahana, and Matti Pohjonen. 2019. "Introduction: Extreme Speech and Global Digital Cultures." *International Journal of Communication* 13:3049–3067.

Warming, Martin. 2014. "Svømmehal plages af bæ-terror: Hvem gør det i vandet?" http://www.lokalavisen .dk/112/2014-02-08/Svømmehal-plages-af-bæ-terror-Hvem-gør-det-i-vandet-1337674.html.

Wodak, Ruth, and M. Reisigl. 1999. "Discourse and Racism: European Perspectives." *Annual Review of Anthropology* 28:175–200.

9

FOLLOW THE MEMES

On the Construction of Far-Right Identities Online

Amy C. Mack

IN AUGUST 2017, THOUSANDS OF FAR-RIGHT PROTESTORS ARRIVED in Charlottesville, Virginia, for the violent Unite the Right rally, where protestors chanted that they would not be replaced nor permit the oppression of the white race (McLaren 2018). Much of the discourse and advertising for the rally, and indeed for the far right in general, occurred online and incorporated memes that circulated widely across social media (Sonnad 2018). Such meme-driven right-wing phenomena are not unique to the United States; Europe has also seen an increase in right-wing politicians (Bremmer 2018) and far-right, anti-immigration militant movements. In Canada, a similar rise in right-wing politics is exemplified by direct political engagement by conservative parties with anti-immigrant groups (Bellefontaine and Trynacity 2018). These groups use social media to organize events, build communities, and construct identities.

In this chapter, I present an ethnographic case study on the meme making and sharing practices of the "folk right movement" and advance the argument that these practices are fundamental to their identity construction. The data presented were collected between May and November 2018 during digital ethnographic fieldwork in the folk-right community. My analysis of their meme practices is supplemented with off-line ethnographic work conducted in early 2019.

The memes described in this chapter are not meant to represent the totality of folk-right meme sharing practices; rather, they reflect dominant cultural values and attitudes within the community and are a primary mode for transmitting these ideologies. The genre of memes included allude to the perceived racial purity and mythological strength of northern Europe (see Andersen 2018), and use extreme speech (Udupa and Pohjonen 2019) to promote anti-immigration, anti-Abrahamic, and nativist-oriented sentiments, culminating in what I refer to as a "white pagan nation fantasy." This is marked by not only anti-immigration and anti-Islam rhetoric but also an intense anti-Christian stance. This complex, and at times contradictory, process of identity construction makes the folk right a challenging and fascinating culture for anthropological inquiry.

Why the North? National Socialists, White Supremacists, and the Folk Right

Early on in my study of the folk right, I identified "Nordicism" (Bergmann 2017)—and "Northern-ness" more broadly—as prevalent themes when studying far-right communities. These refer to the use of northern European culture, history, mythology, and spirituality as a means of constructing a collective identity. Such themes are vital to consider as the far right moves from national identities to cultural and ethnic ones (Pasieka 2017).

This shift is not without precedent. The far right sees the world as one in crisis, and as Volquardsen (2014) argues, the North becomes attractive in precarious times. It is still conceptualized as a space of enduring whiteness, which is difficult to contest, even in today's globalized society (Nielsen 2019), and thus appealing to the folk right. Moreover, this attraction to Nordicism and Northern-ness has been documented in far right groups in North America since the late twentieth century (Gardell 2003; Ridgeway 1995) and can be traced back to Germany in the late nineteenth century. As anthropologist Karla Poewe (2006) notes, the National Socialist movement in pre–World War II Germany also sought an authentic German (Nordic) identity in which they could take pride. They looked to Germanic and Nordic culture and ancestry for an identity that fused race and religion, which culminated in the *völkisch* movement. However, as Zernack (2011) notes, much of the Germanic identity had already been borrowed from the Icelandic and reimagined as a Germanic history. This points to a long history of white nationalist movements looking to the North for new identities, and the folk right continues this process.

The folk right is a small subculture that has emerged from within the far right. Given the networked nature of the far right and its technological practices, the boundaries between right-wing groups are porous, and both members and content move back and forth between groups and platforms (e.g., Twitter, Gab, Minds, and Voat). These movements are contested, and animosity between the folk right and Christian-based alt-right members is not uncommon; this creates friction within the broader movement.

The movement has a geographically diverse membership. Although members are often unwilling to reveal their off-line identities, their social media bios, usernames, and post content reveal a clear American focus, with a smaller number of Canadians and Europeans. This might seem strange at first for a nationalist movement, but what binds these individuals together is a shared interest in and commitment to European cultural heritage and the folkways of their ancestors. The users may be from different regions today, but their ancestors shared a common place: northern Europe. They express this connection through music, imagery, literature, and memes, and there is repeated contact between the members and a high level of participation on the forums. It is this process of sharing and connecting that contributes to the identity construction of the folk right.

Methods: Virtual Ethnography

While the use of Nordicism has been well documented off-line, little anthropological attention has been turned to online manifestations of this phenomena. Given that the folk right emphasizes online connections, I use virtual ethnographic methods to experience and understand the everyday life of this community (cf. Boellstorff et al. 2012; Pink et al. 2016). To achieve this, I focused on participant observation, which meant posting, commenting, voting, and sharing alongside the folk-right users (Tikka and Sumiala 2014).

As Postill and Pink (2012) note, this approach results in a constant cycle of catching up on content; participating in the community; exploring other parts of their network; and archiving, downloading, and saving the experiences. My day would often begin on Gab and include brief visits to YouTube, Twitter, or Minds, where I would collect and catalog dozens of memes and the corresponding comments as screenshots and engage in asynchronous chats. This activity diverges from but complements social media analysis and quantitative analyses of large data sets. Ethnographic methods, like participant observation, "allow us to refigure social media as a fieldwork environment that is social, experiential and mobile" (Postill and Pink 2012, 3). While this approach limits my ability to make generalizations about the far right, it did allow me to explore why the folk right held particular values and how they were communicated.

Ethnographic Field Sites

Following Bowman-Grieve (2009) and Castle and Parsons (2017), I chose to focus on social media platforms because these sites allow for a more participatory approach to fieldwork. While selecting a single platform was appealing for an in-depth study, the nomadic nature of the users rendered such an approach problematic (Postill and Pink 2012). This was due in part to the volatile and unpredictable nature of censorship, bans, and de- or no-platforming, which necessitated a multisited approach (Falzon 2016; Marcus 1995). Consequently, my data include content shared by the folk right on Twitter, Gab, Instagram, Voat, Minds, and Facebook.

From Twitter to Gab and Beyond

Although this work began on Twitter, where I followed Nordicism-inspired hashtags and accounts, the folk right became increasingly vocal in criticisms of the platform's censorship practices. These, the group argued, were discriminatory and favored leftist accounts. As a result, users created new or backup accounts as a precaution, dedicated their time to new platforms, or endured periods of inactivity. All of this was disruptive to participant observation, as I spent much of my time remapping the movement.

Many users relocated to Gab, which promised to be a free speech alternative, and it quickly became the central focus of this project. The platform's interface is reminiscent of other sites: it is aesthetically similar to Reddit, and users can post content to subforums, but users can also follow other users and post to their own timeline, as on Twitter. This allows individuals to create a network of communities and users that share similar interests. I subscribed to a variety of Nordicism-related forums and several content producers on other platforms, and their interactions alerted me to new places for exploration.

While diverse in terms of content and users, Gab is known for attracting the far right (Grey Ellis 2016). The site received heavy criticism in the aftermath of the Pittsburgh Synagogue shooting (October 27, 2018) because the shooter used the site to broadcast his intended actions. The site was subsequently no-platformed, which meant all necessary infrastructure was restricted, and the site was rendered inaccessible for a time (Thompson 2018). As a result, many of the users I followed migrated to other far-right sites like Minds and Voat. In the days leading up to the shutdown, many users shared their alternative platform accounts accompanied with pleas to find one another in the new spaces. Comments such as, "I've set up a back up on Minds.com, if they pull the plug, come and find me," were frequent. Others highlighted that this was not the first time they had to move their community: "I haven't posted anything on [Minds] yet. If Gab goes the way of the Dodo, or worse, the way of the corporate cuck, I will be posting there. I hate starting over, but one needs clear land to build a solid home. One cannot build anything of note when it gets burned down every half year."

They also expressed frustration with the perceived Jewish control of the platform. In response to one user asking how many times the Jewish community would "demand we get wiped off here," another noted that "there seem to be a lot of our kind of people already [on Minds]. It's decentralized, so (((controlling)))[1] it is naturally a little more difficult." This confirmed that because the folk right was nomadic, dispersed, and continually making contingency plans, a multisited approach was necessary. This volatility makes for interesting ethnographic explorations and encourages a deep level of participation to quickly identify and map out new sites of engagement. These migration patterns have continued since my fieldwork in 2018, with users circulating among Gab, Twitter, and Telegram, and many identitarian groups have been banned from Facebook and Instagram following the Christchurch terrorist attacks.

On Memes

Despite their centrality to contemporary internet cultures, memes are difficult to define. First coined by Richard Dawkins in 1976, the term was used to describe cultural replicators that reproduced, imitated, and transmitted a cultural phenomenon (McGrath 2004). More recently, Shifman described memes as "pieces of cultural information that pass along from person to person, but gradually scale into a shared social phenomenon" (2014, 18). Davison provides an even simpler definition: "An Internet meme is a piece of culture, typically a joke, which gains influence through online transmission" (2012, 122). Although this points to the importance of transmission as well as growth, a meme does not need to go viral to be effective; indeed, many folk-right memes are shared less than a hundred times.

To understand folk-right memes, I use a multimodal analysis that attends to the imagery, text, content, and context of the memes and to the commentary by users (Doerr 2017). Such an approach allows me to explore the content, form, and stance of the folk-right memes (Shifman 2014). These three aspects are replicated, remixed, and adapted through the meme-making and sharing processes, and identifying why specific aspects are retained or remade provides insight into the values of the folk right.

In this chapter, *content* refers to the ideas or ideologies represented in the meme. The memes I have selected, for example, reflect far-right sentiments such as anti-Abrahamic and anti-immigration discourse. *Form* is the representation of these ideas, which are experienced by the user through aural and visual components. Given the sharing practices of the folk right, I have chosen memes with static, northern European–inspired images such as

Figure 9.1 "Looking to the Past for a Greater Future" meme created by Gab user and circulated in a folkish group dedicated to folkish paganism. Meme collected November 9, 2018, on gab.com.

heathen symbols or Viking motifs rather than video- or audio-based memes. *Stance* refers to the positioning of the creator in relation to the reader and may refer to style and tone of communication (e.g., ironic, mocking, sincere), which can be unique to the community or group of users. As a result, stance can produce ambiguities and inconsistencies in meaning when memes move between groups or when new users enter folk-right spaces. A seemingly pro-Christianity meme, for example, may be shared ironically, and it is up to the audience to know the stance and intended tone of the meme.

The importance of understanding stance was highlighted during my fieldwork in Iceland (January 2019), where I showed a selection of Nordicism-inspired memes to practicing universalist Norse pagans.[2] They noted that although the content and form of the meme itself may be agreeable (figs. 9.1 and 9.2), such as those that highlighted the geographic representations of European paganism discussed below, it was the surrounding discourse, indicating the stance of the poster and the community more broadly, that changed how they viewed the meme. This example illustrates how significantly the comments, captions, and interactions with users contribute to an understanding of the meme's stance and my analysis of extreme speech.

Figure 9.2 "Make Europa Great Again!" meme circulated on Gab in folkish, identitarian, and National Socialist groups. The meme remixes MAGA with National Socialist imagery. Meme collected August 19, 2018, on gab.com.

Theorizing Memes

As Bangstad (2013) notes, telecommunications infrastructure such as the internet facilitates the growth and naturalization of nativist ideologies beyond national boundaries. Such infrastructures promote the global circulation of extremist ideologies and hate speech through various means, including humor and memes. The latter facilitate the normalization of hate as they blur the line between objectionable and acceptable (Haynes, chap. 11) and are easy to dismiss as frivolous, trivial, and simplistic (Conway Morris 2003). Consequently, when challenged, users can claim that memes are "just a joke" and signal their disinterest in debating the subject. Indeed, those who attempt to criticize the memes are scorned for not understanding the joke (Hervik 2019). This is amplified by the inherent anonymity of memes. As Davison (2012) notes, memes eschew attribution, and this helps users who wish to engage in discriminatory or offensive discourse to avoid punitive measures from peers or authority figures.

Beyond making far-right rhetoric more palatable, sharing bigoted or derogatory memes for the "lulz" helps establish a collective identity for the folk right. The community can incorporate parts of its culture that members feel are oppressed or marginalized in other, often off-line spaces (e.g., "illegal runes, illegal memes") and "get a good laugh" out of the process. Part of their sense of community and belonging is rooted in sharing and appreciating deviant or objectionable jokes.

To understand this normalization of hatred through humor and the corresponding construction of a folk-right identity, I use extreme speech as a framework. Extreme speech is appealing for a number of reasons. It moves the discussion beyond the legal connotations and normative assumptions bound up in "hate speech" and similar terms and moves my research away from the "categorize, contain, and combat" process often associated with hate speech research (Gagliardone 2019). Moreover, as Udupa and Pohjonen (2019) argue, extreme speech recognizes the constant negotiation of what counts as hate speech and attends to the cultural and digital contexts of online vitriol. Therefore, extreme speech opens up pathways for understanding why the folk right engages in these meme-making and sharing practices and what it means for that community, and this framework parallels my use of ethnographic methods because it also obligates me to privilege *why* and *how* in my inquiries. Finally, it allows me to explore how memes can be understood beyond destructive utterances or simple bigotry (Haynes, chap. 11); instead, they can be seen as generative.

"Nothing Could Be Healthier Than European Tribalism": On Nativism and Anti-Immigration

In early May 2018, I was introduced to the term *identitarian*. Although not as common as the #altright or #MAGA hashtags, the term appeared frequently enough to pique my interest in identity formation in far-right groups. The identitarian movement began in France in the late twentieth century and purports to focus on the reclamation of Europe for ethnic Europeans. It is active across Europe, with growing numbers in North America (Zúquete 2018), and has gained traction with tech-savvy millennials who collaborate on social media through retweets, memes, and off-line meet-ups. The movement is concerned with three overarching issues: (*a*) the "Islamization" of Europe, (*b*) globalization, and (*c*) the "Great Replacement" (Generation Identity, https://www.generation-identity.org.uk/). This movement has been associated with the March 15, 2019, terrorist attack in Christchurch, New Zealand, as the shooter released a manifesto that detailed his concerns with the Great Replacement (Besley and Peters 2020).

At its core, identitarianism demonstrates a growing anxiety over the changing demographics of Europe, and the folk right echo these concerns for Europe despite being a largely North American phenomenon. This is partly because the West looks to Scandinavia in times of crisis, and the folk right movement sees current migration trends as a crisis for white identity (Volquardsen 2014). The remixing of the MAGA meme into a

Figure 9.3 "This is Europa" map meme circulated by Gab users in folkish groups. Meme collected August 21, 2018, on gab.com.

MEGA—"Make Europe Great Again"—meme (fig. 9.3) demonstrates this international investment and anxiety.

Through this meme, the folk right advocates for what it calls "retribalization," which seeks to organize society by ethnic groups. This process goes beyond typical identitarian discourse in its assertion that Christianity cannot save Europe or North America, which harkens back to the frustration of the National Socialist movement (Poewe 2006). In advocating for retribalization, the folk right creates what I call the "white pagan nation fantasy," in which Europe should be divided into biologically based ethnic groups (e.g., Celts,

Germans, Norse) and governed by those of pagan spirituality. Whereas the MAGA memes refer to 1950s America, MEGA memes reach much further back in history to a more distant time and ancestry.

Several variations of the MEGA memes include the "This is Europa" meme (fig. 9.2), which circulated on Gab, Twitter, Facebook, and Minds. In this meme and its variations, pagan symbols were placed over a map of the European continent to indicate the branch of paganism that was historically present in each region. Some include text (e.g., "This is Europa" and "The old gods are not forgotten"), whereas others allow the symbols to speak for themselves. My participant observation revealed the meme's circulation; however, it is difficult to quantify how many times it was shared and liked across platforms. The meme aggregation site Meme indicates that when this image was added to its database on December 2, 2016, the image had amassed 959 likes on Facebook alone ("This is Europa," n.d.). The meme was shared on Gab in August 2018, which also demonstrates its longevity.

Although this meme is not the most severe example of extreme speech in this community, its mild—if not innocuous—aesthetic makes it such a powerful vehicle for the folk right's ideologies. It does not include antisemitic or Islamophobic language or imagery; however, the meme and its associated comments still evoke an anti-immigrant and nativist ideology through text and symbols. The posters sincerely declare that Europe is a collection of pagan cultures that one can ethnically and geographically locate. Moreover, the explicit invocation of the "old gods," referring to pagan gods, precludes immigration and globalization, as the folk right argues that spirituality and biology are intrinsically linked. One Gab user remarked that "the biggest lie is that spirituality transcends race. Spirituality is one with biology. The world has wide racial diversity. Thus, our spirituality and worldviews will be distinct. Universalism is the enemy of the #Ethnos. #BloodandSoil is the ONLY truth. #FolkRight." Thus, a nonwhite person is unable to practice a European pagan faith and thus is unwelcome in Europe. The user clearly invokes the language of the völkisch movement by fusing race and religion in their comment, and this discourse was common on memes and surrounding posts. These memes carry a serious and often aggressive tone; they are not ironic or meant to mock pagan religions.

The visual aesthetics, or form, of the meme reinforce anti-immigration and retribalization. The symbols denote what ideologies belong in each region: Scotland is defined by the triquetra, a Celtic pagan symbol, while the historically Norse countries of Norway and Sweden are represented by Odin's horns. In each case, a pagan religion is associated with a geographically defined ethnic or racial group, and an idea is mapped onto these somewhat fuzzy geographic boundaries. Similar sentiments are prevalent throughout my field sites as users discuss the future of these spaces: "Perhaps I am wrong, but we must clearly define and delineate what our current countries or future homelands are about. What is America? What is Germany? These definitions have been warped, and we see the outcomes. This was done on purpose."

It is important to remember the identitarian movement's concern with the Great Replacement, which refers to the demographic shift in Europe due to the influx of non-European immigrants and refugees in recent years. For the folk right, land and spirituality are intrinsically linked, and there is no room—geographically, biologically, spiritually, or culturally—for individuals who are not white European pagans. Indeed, the folk right has little time for immigrants and universalists who do not fit within their "blood and soil" paradigm.

The recurring emphasis on blood and soil dovetails nicely with the white pagan nation fantasy, in which I combine nativist pagan ideology with Hage's (2000) "white nation fantasy" (see also Nielsen 2019). Hage argues that the white nation fantasy is the belief in white control over government and nation and that immigrants are a source of governmental problems. Nativism, or the preference for one's own people, has been well documented for generations, as immigrants were deemed "too infected by *Catholicism*, monarchism, anarchism, *Islam*, criminal tendencies, *defective genes, mongrel bloodlines*, or some other alien virus to become free men and women in our democratic society" (Schrag 2010, 14; emphasis added). Nativist discourse deems immigrants unfit to become real Europeans or Americans. The term has, however, migrated from the academy, and it is now widely used by the pagan community to divide universalist (i.e., anyone can be a Norse pagan) and folkish (i.e., only one of Northern European heritage can be a Norse pagan) approaches to faith. Together, nativism and white nation fantasy construct an image of a Europe that rightfully belongs to white pagans and all others are deemed unworthy problems.

The "This is Europa" and other MEGA memes evince this nativist sentiment: Europe belongs to ethnic Europeans, and it is incompatible with immigrants given their race and biology. The MEGA memes, through their mimicry of MAGA, demonstrates this fantasy of control and problem. US President Donald Trump's "Make America Great Again" campaign was grounded in immigrant-as-problem rhetoric and included travel bans, promises of building a wall between America and Mexico, and increasingly isolationist policies. The MEGA version of white nation fantasy goes beyond Trump's brand of nativism to one rooted in what the folk right calls the "native European spirituality" or "folk soul" and the National Socialists called *volk*. It is no longer enough for those in control to be of white European heritage; rather, they must reacquaint themselves with their old gods and traditions.

Despite this nativist approach—and the rampant anti-immigrant ideology—the comments surrounding these memes often include subtle disclaimers that they are not "really racist." To many, the white pagan nation fantasy is about love for one's race. There is a denial of racism within the retribalizing discourse, as they believe all peoples should retribalize around the world, so long as it is within their own ethnostates: "I don't hate anyone no matter their race, ethnicity, religion, sexuality, etc. however, I do believe a right to their own culture/own country. I do NOT approve of the outright discrimination against European peoples! #EuropeanPride #ItsOkToBeWhite #folkish #loveyourfolk #heathen." This sentiment was discussed in depth during a YouTube livestream that featured Stephen McNallen, founder of the Asatru Folk Assembly, which advocates for nativist Norse paganism. Moreover, he and others in the chat and livestream noted that this belief was not racist; they simply prefer their own group. Furthermore, he argued that his mandate, "the existence of our people is not negotiable," can be used by all races, and therefore renders it a nonracist approach to social and religious organization. This #allpeople approach is an appeal to neutrality, which is a common tactic in the denial of racism (see Vertelytė and Hervik 2019). Thus, within the white pagan nation fantasy, it is possible for the folk right to deny their racism while upholding anti-immigration views.

"Blood Calls to the Gods": Anti-Abrahamism

One of the most striking differences between the general far right and the folk right is the latter's disdain for Christianity. As the "This is Europa" memes suggest, the folk right does not make space for Christianity in Europe. They refer to it derogatorily as a "sand" or "desert religion," which references antisemitic and Islamophobic sentiments. Beyond their contempt for the racialized roots of Abrahamic faiths, they also see Christianity as a globalist or universalist religion that is incompatible with their white pagan nation fantasy. Therefore, in contrast to the anti-immigrant and retribalizing memes, which make an argument about what Europe is, the anti-Abrahamic memes construct an identity through what it is not—namely, Abrahamic.

Although folk-right memes vary with regard to form, they often evoke a European warrior or Viking motif (figs. 9.4 and 9.5). These include helmet- and axe-clad Vikings, thunderbolt and hammer-wielding Thor, Odin on a throne, and even a contemporary bare-chested, bearded man with a Mjolnir necklace. These memes argue that a strong, powerful, and ultimately successful Europa requires a revival of pre-Abrahamic European paganism and culture.

Anti-Christian memes are part of a broader movement against Abrahamic faiths in the folk right. While "It's Okay to Be White" memes began circulating during Trump's presidential campaign, the folk right has remixed this message to include anti-Christian sentiment and deploys this through #ItsNotOKToBeChristian or #INOTBC hashtags that explicitly invoke a white pagan nation ideology. These memes maintain the ideology of whiteness as ideal while discrediting Christians. This approach is evident in figure 9.4 and similar memes that explicitly contrast the values and attitudes of pagan traditions with Christianity. These images include depictions of Abrahamic faiths fighting among one another on one side of the image while the pagan faiths work together on the other side. These comparisons indicate that Christianity is unproductive, divisive, and disorderly. In contrast, European paganism is neatly delineated based on ethnicity and geography, and thus groups can work together to create a strong and vibrant Europe. This reinforces the regenerative and restorative messages of the "This is Europa" and MEGA memes.

In these memes, Christians are understood as a threat or an enemy, and the tone is often aggressive or critical of Christianity. These memes imply that Christianity seeks to destroy Europa, which places them at odds. Comments on these memes often discussed how Christianity was "anti-ethnos" and how "the problem is #Christianity forever tying us to and enslaving us under Abrahamism." Moreover, Christianity is no longer seen as an attribute that can be "accumulated and converted into Whiteness" (Hage 2000, 232) in the white pagan nation fantasy. Rather, Christianity is placed on par with Islam as a threat to Europe, and Christians are often accused of being "Jews in disguise." This narrative creates new alterities through ethnospiritual conflict, humor, and extreme speech.

Nevertheless, this process of defining the folk-right identity in opposition to Christianity is at risk of creating a pan-European group that is at odds with their desire for spiritually

Figure 9.4 "This is Christianity; This is Europa" meme circulated by Gab users in a folkish group that emphasized anti-Abrahamic discourse. Meme collected September 11, 2018, on gab.com.

based ethnostates. This strategy has been criticized by Christian trolls in the comment sections of many posts, who often repost folk-right memes ironically or with sardonic captions. However, this contradiction is to be expected: American and Canadian folk-right members hold hybrid identities given generations of interethnic marriage, and the folk right subsequently expresses a sense of constitutive displacement in which connection between individual identity and geography is weak or disrupted (Bhabha 2018). Users are encouraged to take DNA tests to trace their roots and will often post the results online for discussion; subsequent conversations often result in "you're mostly XYZ" summations. This makes a declaration of belonging difficult for many and explains the attractiveness of defining oneself in opposition to a more firmly established identity (Ezz El Din 2019). Extending this opposition to Abrahamic religions in general, this process also legitimizes inconsistent inclusions in whiteness. Mediterranean populations are welcome in the folk right given their Greco-Roman pagan heritage, whereas Jewish peoples are excluded from whiteness due to their faith, despite the similar whitening process both groups experienced (Vertelytė and Hervik 2019).

The treatment of Islam in the folk right often diverges from that of Christianity. Whereas Christians are treated with an academic derision, Islam is frequently mocked and belittled.

Figure 9.5 "Allah? Never heard of her" meme circulated by Gab users in anti-Muslim and folkish groups. Meme collected August 26, 2018, on gab.com.

Figure 9.5 clearly evokes what Essed (2013) has termed "entitlement racism," which refers to how individuals increasingly invoke their right to speak their mind, even if what they are saying is derogatory. The freedom of speech, as well as (digital) assembly, is understood as a license to offend (Finnis 2009), and I contend this is amplified within the white pagan nation fantasy—they have the right to control Europe and, therefore, the right to humiliate.

Memes have become one avenue through which far-right and folk-right users explicitly enact this right. The "Allah? Never heard of her!" meme (fig. 9.5) is a clear example of this use. The meme typically includes the text "Allah?" and "never heard of her" over a Norse motif (e.g., Odin or a Viking). The intent, or stance, of the meme is to offend Muslims, first, by using a feminine pronoun for Allah and, second, by indicating that Allah is not worth knowing to the folk right. Allah is rendered irrelevant in the lands of pagan gods.

The captions and comments associated with the memes echoed this desire to offend. One such comment reads, "I figure it's been a while since we offended anyone. Thank you Anders for the pic submission—Bloodaxe." Comments on anti-Islam memes like figure 9.5

were more likely to express jarring extreme speech and would include racial slurs including desert-themed plays on the "n-word" and crude caricatures of Muslims. These examples of entitlement racism can be understood as a response to political correctness in which what is considered overly sensitive or racist is increasingly polarized (Hubinette 2014; Hervik 2019). However, despite this explicit racism, the folk right denies charges of racism—members simply do not want immigrants and "Abrahamists" in their white nation. If users are offended by the extreme speech of the folk right, they are dismissed for not understanding the joke or told to return to politically correct spaces like Twitter, just as Muslims are invited to return to the Middle East.

Discussion

In this chapter, I have introduced the folk right—an emergent fringe group within the tech-savvy far-right movement—and argued that the memes members produce and circulate constitute important sites of inquiry for scholars interested in the intersection of nativism, Nordicism, and the far right. While the folk right shares many of the concerns of the far-right and identitarian movements, folk-right meme-sharing practices evince a slightly different narrative.

These practices cause friction between the folk right and other far-right groups. The most notable point of conflict is the folk right's disdain for Christianity, which puts them at odds with many groups and individuals in North America. Indeed, much of their time and energy is directed toward criticizing the Christian influence in the far right and fending off attacks from Christian trolls. This element has exacerbated the conflict between the folk right and the alt-right. These conflicts pose a dilemma for the far right in general, as users denounce the infighting. However, the folk right's emphasis on anti-immigration and anti-Islam rhetoric maintains connections with broader groups within the identitarian movement.

Whether or not this small group can destabilize or undermine a resurgent white supremacist movement has yet to be determined. In the years since my fieldwork, the folk right remains on the fringes of the far right and is increasingly fragmented. What this work has identified is that a growing number of far-right activists are looking to their European history for guidance. This approach, Andersen (2018) argues, constitutes a return to an ancestral knowledge, although, as Gardell (2003) and Poewe (2006) remind us, this phenomenon is not new. However, as the Unite the Right rally, the völkisch movement, and the Christchurch attacks have made clear, a holistic understanding of cultural practices—particularly those evincing extreme speech—is pivotal in combatting the rise of populism and fascism across the globe. The growing folk right movement must be considered a part of the troubling phenomenon.

Notes

1. Three consecutive parentheses are used to denote the Jewish community and are another means of avoiding censorship—for example, users might say "(((they))) control the media" instead of the Jewish community controls the media.
2. *Universalist* refers to groups who do not exclude members on the basis of race or ethnicity.

References

Andersen, Joakim. 2018. *Rising from the Ruins: The Right of the 21st Century*, Kindle ed. London: Arktos Media.

Bangstad, Sindre. 2013. "On Xenophobia and Nativism." In *Recycling Hatred: Racism(s) in Europe Today: A Dialogue between Academics, Equality Experts, and Civil Society Activists*, edited by European Network Against Racism, 87–94. Brussels: European Network Against Racism.

Bellefontaine, Michelle, and Kim Trynacity. 2018. "Alberta Premier Calls on Jason Kenney to Take Stronger Stand against Hate Groups." CBC, October 9, 2018. https://www.cbc.ca/news/canada/edmonton/notley-wants -kenney-stand-hate-groups-soldiers-of-odin-1.4855795.

Bergmann, Eirikur. 2017. *Nordic Nationalism and Right-Wing Populist Politics*. London: Palgrave Macmillan.

Besley, Tina, and Michael A. Peters. 2020. "Terrorism, Trauma, Tolerance: Bearing Witness to White Supremacist Attack on Muslims in Christchurch, New Zealand." *Educational Philosophy and Theory* 52 (2): 109–119. doi:10.1080/00131857.2019.1602891.

Bhabha, Jacqueline. 2018. "In but Not of Europe?: The Precarious Rights of Roman in the European Union." In *Territories and Trajectories: Cultures in Circulation*, edited by Homi. K. Bhabha and Diana Sorensen, 185–200. Durham, NC: Duke University Press.

Boellstorff, Tom, Bonnie Nardi, Celia Pearce, and T. L. Taylor. 2012. *Ethnography and Virtual Worlds: A Handbook of Method*. Princeton, NJ: Princeton University Press.

Bowman-Grieve, Lorraine. 2009. "Exploring 'Stormfront': A Virtual Community of the Radical Right." *Studies in Conflict and Terrorism* 32:989–1007. doi:10.1080/10576100903259951.

Bremmer, Ian. 2018. "These 5 Countries Show How the European Far-Right Is Growing in Power." *TIME*. http://time.com/5395444/europe-far-right-italy-salvini-sweden-france-germany/.

Castle, Tammy, and Tara Parsons. 2017. "Vigilante or Viking? Contesting the Mediated Constructions of Soldiers of Odin Norge." *Crime, Media, Culture* 15 (1): 47-66. doi:10.1177/1741659017731479.

Conway Morris, Simon. 2003. *Life's Solution: Inevitable Humans in a Lonely Universe*. Cambridge: Cambridge University Press. doi:10.1017/CBO9780511535499.

Davison, Patrick. 2012. "The Language of Internet Memes." In *The Social Media Reader*, edited by Michael Mandiberg, 120–134. New York: New York University Press.

Doerr, Nicole. 2017. "Bridging Language Barriers, Bonding against Immigrants: A Visual Case Study of Transnational Network Publics Created by Far-Right Activists in Europe." *Discourse and Society* 28 (1): 3–23. doi:10.1177/0957926516676689.

Essed, Philomena. 2013. "Entitlement Racism: License to Humiliate." In *Recycling Hatred: Racism(s) in Europe Today: A Dialogue between Academics, Equality Experts, and Civil Society Activists*, edited by European Network Against Racism. 62–76. Brussels: European Network Against Racism.

Ezz El Din, Mahitab. 2019. "News Media Racialization of Muslims: The Case of Nerikes Allenhanda's Publishing of the Mohamed Caricature." In *Racialization, Racism, and Anti-racism in the Nordic Countries*, edited by Peter Hervik, 93–110. London: Palgrave Macmillan.

Falzon, Mark-Anthony. 2016. *Multi-sited Ethnography: Theory, Praxis, and Locality in Contemporary Research*. New York: Routledge.

Finnis, John. 2009. "Endorsing Discrimination between Faiths: A Case of Extreme Speech?" In *Extreme Speech and Democracy*, edited by Ivan Hare and James Weinstein, 430–441. Oxford: Oxford University Press.

Gagliardone, Iginio. 2019. "Defining Online Hate and Its 'Public Lives': What Is the Place for 'Extreme speech?'" *International Journal of Communication* 13:3068–3087.

Gardell, Mattias. 2003. *Gods of the Blood: The Pagan Revival and White Separatism*, Kindle ed. Durham, NC: Duke University Press.

Grey Ellis, Emma. 2016. "Gab, the Alt-Right's Very Own Twitter, Is the Ultimate Filter Bubble." *Wired*, September 14, 2016. https://www.wired.com/2016/09/gab-alt-rights-twitter-ultimate-filter-bubble/.

Hage, Ghassan. 2000. *White Nation: Fantasies of White Supremacy in a Multicultural Society*. New York: Routledge.

Hervik, Peter. 2019. "Ritualized Opposition in Danish Online Practices of Extremist Language and Thought." *International Journal of Communication* 13:3143–3163.

Hubinette, Tobias. 2014. "Racial Stereotypes and Swedish Antiracism: A Swedish Crisis of Multiculturalism?" In *Crisis in the Nordic Nations and Beyond: At the Intersection of Environment, Finance, and Multiculturalism*, edited by Kristin Loftsdottir and Lars Jensen, 69–86. Surrey: Ashgate.

Marcus, George. 1995. "Ethnography in/of the World System: The Emergence of Multi-sited Ethnography." *Annual Review of Anthropology* 24:95–117. http://www.jstor.org/stable/2155931.

McGrath, Alister. E. 2004. *Dawkins' God: Genes, Memes, and the Meaning of Life*. Malden, MA: Blackwell.

McLaren, Evan. 2018. "Ground Zero at Charlottesville." In *A Fair Hearing: The Alt-Right in the Words of its Members and Leaders*, Kindle ed., edited by George T. Shaw. London: Arktos Media.

Nielsen, Asta Smedegaard. 2019. "White Fear: Habitual Whiteness and Racialization of the Threat of Terror in Danish News Journalism." In *Racialization, Racism, and Anti-racism in the Nordic Countries*, edited by Peter Hervik, 111–134. London: Palgrave Macmillan.

Pasieka, Agnieszka. 2017. "Taking Far-Right Claims Seriously and Literally: Anthropology and the Study of Right-Wing Radicalism." *Slavic Review* 76 (S1): S19–S29. doi:10.1017/slr.2017.154.

Pink, Sarah, Heather A. Horst, John Postill, Larissa Hjorth, Tania Lewis, and Jo Tacchi. 2016. *Digital Ethnography: Principles and Practice*. Los Angeles: Sage.

Poewe, Karla. 2006. *New Religions and the Nazis*. London: Routledge.

Postill, John, and Sarah Pink. 2012. "Social Media Ethnography: The Digital Researcher in a Messy Web." *Media International Australia* 145 (1): 123–134.

Ridgeway, James. 1995. *Blood in the Face: The Ku Klux Klan, Aryan Nations, Nazi Skinheads, and the Rise of a New White Culture*, 2nd ed. New York: Thunder's Mouth Press.

Schrag, Peter. 2010. *Not Fit for Our Society: Nativism and Immigration*. Berkley: University of California Press.

Shifman, Limor. 2014. *Memes in Digital Culture*. Cambridge, MA: MIT Press.

Sonnad, Nikhil. 2018. "Finally, a Scientific List of the Most Popular Memes on the Internet." *Quartz*, June 4, 2018. https://qz.com/1296094/most-popular-memes-finally-a-scientific-list-of-the-most-popular-memes-on-the-internet/.

Thompson, Nicholas. 2018. "Goodbye Gab, a Haven for the Far Right." *Wired*, October 29, 2018. https://www.wired.com/story/gab-offline-free-speech-alt-right/.

Tikka, Minttu, and Johanna Sumiala. 2014. "Media Witnessing on YouTube—Rethinking Crisis in a Mediatized Condition." In *Crisis in the Nordic Nations and Beyond: At the Intersection of Environment, Finance and Multiculturalism*, edited by Kristin Loftsdottir and Lars Jensen, 9–30. Surrey: Ashgate.

Udupa, Sahana, and Matti Pohjonen. 2019. "Extreme Speech and Global Digital Media Cultures: Introduction." *International Journal of Communication* 13:3019–3067.

Vertelytė, Mantė, and Peter Hervik. 2019. "The Vices of Debating Racial Epithets in Danish News Media Discourse." In *Racialization, Racism, and Anti-racism in the Nordic Countries*, edited by Peter Hervik, 1463–182. London: Palgrave Macmillan.

Volquardsen, Ebbe. 2014. "Scandinavia and 'the Land of UnSwedish Freedom': Jonathan Franzen, Susanne Bier, and Self-Conceptions of Exceptionalism in Crisis." In *Crisis in the Nordic Nation and Beyond: At the Intersection of Environment, Finance, and Multiculturalism*, edited by Kristin Loftsdottir and Lars Jensen, 31–50. Surrey: Ashgate.

Zernack, Julia. 2011. "Old Norse–Icelandic Literature and German Culture." In *Iceland and Images of the North*, edited by S. R. Isleifsson and D. Chartier. Quebec, QC: Presses de l'Université du Québec.

Zúquete, Jose Pedro. 2018. "The Identitarians: The Movement against Globalism and Islam in Europe." Notre Dame: University of Notre Dame Press.

10

THE POLITICS OF *MUHEI*

Ethnic Humor and Islamophobia on Chinese Social Media

Gabriele de Seta

No organization or individual may produce, duplicate, announce or disseminate information having the following contents: being against the cardinal principles set forth in the Constitution; endangering state security, divulging state secrets, subverting state power and jeopardizing national unification; damaging state honor and interests; instigating ethnic hatred or discrimination and jeopardizing ethnic unity; jeopardizing state religious policy, propagating heretical or superstitious ideas; spreading rumors, disrupting social order and stability; disseminating obscenity, pornography, gambling, violence, brutality and terror or abetting crime; humiliating or slandering others, trespassing on the lawful rights and interests of others; and other contents forbidden by laws and administrative regulations.

(Information Office of the State Council of the People's Republic of China 2010)

China, Muslim Minorities, and Digital Media

In the wake of reports emerging in late 2017 about the unlawful detention of thousands of Muslim minority citizens, the Chinese governance of Xinjiang has been once again propelled under the spotlight of news reports, nongovernmental organization campaigns, and international advocacy organizations (Human Rights Watch 2017). In November 2018, the United Nations Committee on the Elimination of Racial Discrimination expressed concern regarding reports of Chinese authorities detaining up to one million Muslim citizens in newly built internment camps situated in the Xinjiang Uygur Autonomous Region. If these numbers are accurate, this would constitute roughly a tenth of China's Uyghur population, one of the fifty-five ethnic minorities officially recognized by the Chinese government. Multiple investigative reports have confirmed the ongoing construction of detention facilities throughout Xinjiang, clustering around the regional capital Ürümqi and along the borders with Afghanistan, Kazakhstan, Kyrgyzstan, and Pakistan (Wen and Auyezov 2018). Testimonies from Uyghur and Kazakh individuals who have been detained in the camps paint a troubling picture, including overcrowding, duress, torture, and regular subjection to political indoctrination. Pressured by these reports, Chinese officials eventually admitted the construction of these facilities but framed them as sites offering a "vocational education and training program" that should be viewed "as a constructive effort to help eliminate the soil that breeds terrorism and extremism" (Mu 2018).

This renewed attention to the plight of Uyghurs in Xinjiang is much overdue given the long history of ethnic tensions plaguing the region (Becquelin 2004; Mackerras 2012). The economic migration of ethnic majority Han citizens, combined with intensified state oversight of the Uyghur population after the 9/11 attacks in the United States, fueled resentment and flares of violent turmoil throughout the 2000s that have occasionally resulted in violent attacks allegedly carried out by extremist cells of Uyghur separatists. The "People's War on Terror" (Roberts 2018) waged by Chinese authorities on what they identify as "separatist extremism" in the region has taken the form of periodic crackdowns accompanied by increasing restrictions on cultural and religious practices (Clarke 2010) and the establishment of pervasive layers of surveillance infrastructure (Brophy 2019). Since 2014, the "Strike Hard Campaign against Violent Terrorism" (launched by former Communist Party Secretary of the Xinjiang Uyghur Autonomous Region Zhang Chunxian and escalated in 2016 by current Communist Party Secretary Chen Quanguo) has enforced restrictive policies aimed at dismantling religious identity—including a ban on beards, religious clothing, and pilgrimages to Mecca (Brophy 2018)—and reinforced oversight by imposing regular "home stays" of party cadres in Uyghur families (Human Rights Watch 2018). As Darren Byler details, between 2014 and 2018, three waves of campaigns funneled more than one million Han civilians into Uyghur villages in Xinjiang, conscripting them into the "state-directed oppression of Muslim minorities" without the possibility of choice (Byler 2018).

The history of ethnic tensions in Xinjiang is also deeply bound with regional technological development. Along with other hinterland provinces, western China was subjected to the state-endorsed relocation of information and communication technology manufacturing, in pursuit of an economic restructuring capable of supporting the region's industrial development. This move did not shift the economy away from the coastal regions but rather resulted in infrastructural disconnections and the "industrial hollowing-out" of western China (Hong 2017, 15–19). The informatization of Xinjiang has largely followed Han settlement, and while it has fared relatively better than other hinterland provinces (CNNIC 2015, 29), ethnic turmoil has profoundly shaped the role of networked communications in the region. Following a series of violent riots taking place in the regional capital Ürümqi during July 2009 that resulted in the deaths of almost two hundred Chinese citizens (the majority reportedly being Han), Chinese authorities resorted to cutting off the entire region from the internet (Shan and Chen 2011). Attributing the riots to separatist incitement disseminated through the internet by the World Uygur Congress led by Rebiya Kadeer, the regional government suspended access to the internet along with SMS services and international direct dialing, throwing Xinjiang into an "internet blackout" that lasted almost a year (Cao 2014). When the region was reconnected to global networks in mid-2010, things had already changed dramatically: the incidents prompted the Chinese government to blacklist services like Facebook and Twitter throughout the country—a ban that persists to this day—and Xinjiang became a testing ground for increasingly pervasive disciplinary technologies (Lam

2017), ranging from facial recognition camera systems to surveillance apps forcibly installed on Uyghur citizens' smartphones (Leibold 2019).

Cognizant of the urgent implications of the context described above, in this chapter, I approach the intermeshing of ethnic tensions and digital media in contemporary China by tracing anti-Muslim sentiments to the everyday interactions of Chinese social media users. While acknowledging that the current surveillance and repression of ethnic populations in Xinjiang and other regions of the People's Republic of China requires academic research and humanitarian advocacy, in this chapter, I aim to highlight how the generalized approval and occasional resignation voiced by Chinese citizens regarding the Chinese government's treatment of Muslim minorities relates to—and can be partly explained through—the circulation of Islamophobic sentiments on Chinese social media platforms. Woven through repertoires of online content ranging from heavy-handed ethnic humor to slanderous disinformation, Islamophobia is clearly present on Chinese social media and colors everyday interactions among local users. The argument advanced in this chapter is not based on fieldwork in Xinjiang or other ethnic minority areas but rather is grounded in observations, interviews, and data that I collected between 2014 and 2018 over multiple stays in Chinese cities and ongoing participation in Chinese social media platforms, largely among ethnically Han citizens. Applying a digital ethnographic approach to the circulation of anti-Muslim sentiments on Chinese social media, I situate localized ethnic tensions and widely supported authoritarian measures by relating them to contentious discussions and uncivil practices mediated by digital platforms. After introducing the central topic of my analysis—the uncivil practice of *muhei*, or "slandering Muslims"—I move on to describe the stereotypes reinforced by the circulation of visual ethnic humor in instant messaging apps and analyze the discursive domains invoked by internet users debating muhei on microblogging platforms.

An Uncivil Practice: Muhei, or Slandering Muslims

Civility has been a constant matter of debate in the history of computer-mediated communication, and the popularization of internet access and social media use have only made it a topic even more relevant to public life at large (Benson 1996; Coe, Kenski, and Rains 2014). Recent research on online incivility and uncivil digital media practices trace the global span of this concern and the situated articulations of this category of behavior, which often reflect sociopolitical tensions and local contention (Pohjonen and Udupa 2017). As in many other national contexts, incivility has been a component of Chinese online life since its early days. Since the mid-1990s, Chinese internet users have argued, flamed, spammed, and offended each other on homepage guestbooks and bulletin boards (de Seta 2013; Leibold 2011; G. Yang 2008); as the 2000s brought hundreds of millions of new users online, new forms of contention arose around the exploits of *fenqing* (angry youth) or the self-styled vigilantism of *renrou sousuo* (crowd-sourced doxing) actions (L. Yang and Zheng 2012). Today's Chinese digital media landscape is as plentiful with platforms and services as it is rich in examples of incivility: forum wars between fandoms, international incidents triggered by patriotic publics, and tensions among fragmented political identities give rise to what Hu Yong (2008) has insightfully termed a "rising cacophony" of digitally mediated voices. In this context, it is not surprising to see Chinese authorities stress the ideological keyword *wenming* (civility, civilized) to steer the use of new communication technologies away from the boiling tensions of a *bu wenming* (uncivil) society (de Seta 2018*b*; G. Yang 2018).

Over years of ethnographic engagement with multiple Chinese social media platforms—including the Baidu Tieba forum community, the instant messaging software QQ, the microblogging service Sina Weibo, and the messaging app WeChat—I have encountered several kinds of uncivil online practices. These forms of incivility ranged from various kinds of trolling (de Seta 2013) and fishing (de Seta 2018*b*) to specific varieties of insult and slander (de Seta 2018*c*) and were clearly shaped by the degree of privacy or publicness of the social media platform where they were practiced. Among the many forms of *bu wenming* (incivility) highlighted by discussants and interviewees—including spreading rumors, paid spamming, and conducting scams—the practice of *diyu hei* (local offense, regional discrimination) emerged as one of the examples of uncivil sociality most evident from the online content I was collecting. During extended fieldwork stays in Shanghai, local contacts would often callously joke about the uncouthness of "hard drives," the nickname given to rural migrants and other non-Shanghainese residents of the city (in Mandarin *waidiren*, the "WD" acronym of which is also a brand of hard drives). Interurban and interregional rivalries would result in Chongqing friends lambasting their neighbors from Chengdu, northerners demeaning southerners and vice versa, and Hong Kongers expressing distaste for mainlanders at large (and often being reciprocated in kind). Regional and urban–rural discrimination is a well-documented phenomenon in China (Jiang 2016). The creative ways to *hei* (literally, "to blacken," to slander) others by virtue of their local provenance easily crossed over into social media as ethnic humor (Boxman-Shabtai and Shifman 2015), where anonymous interactions with citizens from the entire nation (and Chinese abroad) would easily devolve into stereotyped name-calling.

As shown by user-generated content like the "humorous" map circulated across WeChat groups (fig. 10.1), the stereotypes most prevalent in diyu hei happen most often on a regional basis, with citizens from different Chinese provinces labeled as poor, uncultured, or effeminate. When assigned to regions in western China, the stereotype of poverty seems to give way to the accusation of its inhabitants being "terrorists," conflating a genre of humor often deployed in jest with the official narrative about minority populations in regions with a history of ethnic tensions and violent incidents attributed to separatist movements. Among the variety of diyu hei, I started observing a recurring insistence on making fun of Muslim minorities, a practice that soon turned out to be defined by a Mandarin neologism in itself: muhei, from *mu* (the first syllable of *musilin*, Muslim) and *hei*, "slandering." Muhei, or slandering Muslims, could take multiple forms, from offhand remarks about Uyghur people being "poor" or "lazy" and cautionary tales about being pickpocketed by bands of Xinjiang youths to outright discriminatory instances of extreme speech against "Muslim terrorists"— even just on a lexical level, muhei often conflated Uyghur ethnicity with Chinese Islam as a whole (Ma 2017). Although widespread, these judgments were by no means shared by everyone around me, and the practice of muhei was, in fact, a contentious topic in itself that was debated among my interlocutors in both online discussions and in private conversations. Emerging from a repertoire of uncivil practices widespread on digital media, muhei is a specific form of regional discrimination that resonates with the overtones of religious and ethnic tension that have characterized western China for decades.

Figure 10.1 "Compilation of negative impressions about Chinese people, come take a shot at every region!" Map of regional stereotypes ranging from the provinces of Heilongjiang ("mafia") and Shaanxi ("poor") to the Western regions of Xinjiang ("thieves + terrorists") and Tibet ("terrorists + ignorant").

China's Muslim population includes various minorities with different degrees of integration in Chinese society—some, like Uyghurs, are subjected to harsher regimes of control, and others, like the Hui, are historically more integrated and integrated with the Han majority (Ho 2013). To understand an uncivil practice like muhei and its reinforcing of existing stereotypes about Muslim minorities, it is useful to contextualize it in a history of Islamophobic sentiments bound with postcolonial and patriotic reactions running through Chinese society at large (Li 2018). As James Leibold (2010) explains, younger generations of Chinese, confronted with the perceived inequalities resulting from the multiethnic culturalism pursued by the government's religious and ethnic policies, resort to articulating a "Han supremacism" that mobilizes racialist self-identification. Combined with the patriotic reactions to perceived judgments from Western governments and media about the country's handling of its minority populations, this articulation leads to Islamophobic sentiments being increasingly visible, especially on social media platforms (Huang 2018). Panics about purported "pan-halal tendencies" and the impending "arabization" of China (Liu 2018) drive Islamophobic interpretations of family-planning regulations (from which ethnic minorities are partially exempted) as components of an ongoing "genocide policy" aimed at the Han majority (Han 2015, 1012). These sentiments—strikingly parallel to the "white genocide" conspiracy theories promoted by neonationalist and supremacist groups in the United States, Europe, and South Africa—result in growing numbers of attacks on Muslim businesses and fuel ethnic tensions on Chinese soil. Unsurprisingly, Islamophobia is also underpinned by the stereotyped coverage of Islam on Chinese news media (Luqiu and Yang 2018) and amplified as it circulates among the Chinese diaspora worldwide (Huang 2018), commingling with similar theories propagated by North American and European conservative and far-right outlets (Jung 2018; Zhang 2018). As Matt Schrader (2018) notes, the circulation of Islamphobic content among Chinese-speaking social media publics results in the popular identification of entire minority populations with "terrorists" and "time bombs," which in turn underpins everyday discussions of government policies, discriminatory practices, violent incidents, and international outcry.

Personalized Stereotypes: Ethnic Humor and Muhei Stickers

My first exposure to muhei came during fieldwork conducted in 2015, when I started noticing a loose series of images circulating on two instant messaging software apps, QQ and WeChat. These apps are extremely popular among Chinese internet users and function in a way similar to WhatsApp, Facebook messenger, or LINE for the exchange of textual messages, audiovisual content, and files. One peculiarity of both QQ and WeChat is the support they provide for the personalization of emoticons and stickers, the kinds of visual communicative resources that in Chinese are commonly known as *biaoqing* (de Seta 2018a). Among the hundreds of *biaoqing* I collected and cataloged over the years, some shared a common repertoire of visual signifiers: they often depicted a stereotyped Muslim individual (often identified as a Chinese Muslim through markers of Uyghur, or at times Hui, ethnic identity) and were clearly created by amateur users through limited image-editing tools. Most were reworked versions of existing stickers, whose stylized figures were overlaid with long black beards, green and white striped shirts, *taqiyah* and turbans, the Holy Quran, and halal signage (fig. 10.2). These predominantly male Muslim characters were also often portrayed as engaging in threatening or aggressive behavior—wielding automatic weapons, large knives, explosives—and framed by textual captions ranging from the humorous to the outright offensive: "Ethnic unity is larger than the sky"; "This is not *qingzhen* (halal)"; "This chat group is not qingzhen"; "I suspect you are not qingzhen"; "I really want to eat pork meat." The humorous devices employed in these *biaoqing* were clear markers of a generalized Chinese Muslim identity: ironically praising the *minzu tuanjie* (ethnic unity), a policy keyword promoted by the government; policing the "halal-ness" of chat groups and topics of discussion; and craving or being repelled by pork meat. Users combined these stereotypical ethnic markers with elements drawn from popular youth culture (light sabers, Japanese anime characters), and collected them in personalized *biaoqing bao* (sticker packs) ready to be exchanged across chats.

Most examples of diyu hei that I observed during my fieldwork were relatively innocuous topical jokes drawing on interurban rivalries or urban–rural prejudices; the popularity of personalized stickers stereotyping Chinese Muslim minorities seemed to indicate a particular tension bubbling across social media. The connection between muhei stickers and interethnic tensions in western China was corroborated by some of my social media contacts (all Han Chinese), who admitted having saved some of these *biaoqing* on their devices, mostly because they were "funny" and could be shared in chats for humorous purposes. My interlocutors were aware of the context from which these stickers emerged, but they also felt it necessary to clarify how they thought that the *fennu* (angst) of the Han population against Uyghur Muslims was somewhat understandable considering recent episodes of violence. As put by Shao, a university student from Hangzhou, "I also have some of these *biaoqing* in my WeChat, actually . . . I think they are hilarious. But they exist because of some incidents in Western China, and because of the privileges that the government grants to minorities. Han people are not happy about it, it's natural to be *fennu* [outraged]. But of course, this mostly happens online, because it's a public space, and people are more unrestrained, that's why I think that online spaces are really difficult to manage."

Figure 10.2 A selection of *muhei* stickers circulated on instant messaging applications QQ and WeChat. Collage by the author.

In another discussion, Cheng, a university student from Hubei province, suggested that this sort of sticker revealed a pressing issue in Chinese society: "Recently there have been all these debates about qingzhen [halal] on Sina Weibo, have you followed them? People are posting photos of all kinds of qingzhen food they can find around them, as a way to complain about how Chinese Muslims get treated with privileges just because of their religion." According to Cheng, the symbolic grievance about qingzhen food was a reaction to multiple incidents reported across Chinese news media involving extremist Muslim citizens that had "left the *minzhong* [masses] outraged." Examples of incidents included the dramatic 2014 Kunming Railway Station terrorist attack that resulted in thirty-one civilian casualties, but also less violent events such as the case of a radical imam who traveled to Beijing to oppose an interethnic marriage. In his view, humorous stereotypes of Muslim minorities circulating on social media reflected the perceived difficulty of finetuning China's religious and ethnic policies: "I think that, on the one hand, this is because of ethnic policy, because, as you know, China's *shaoshu minzu* [ethnic minorities] have some privileges: the government helps them economically over Han people, and Han people feel this disparity, especially when some incident happens. . . . On the other hand, it is also because of religious management because, for a period of time, the government helped build a lot of mosques in minority areas, but then Muslim people became more radical, and this created social problems."

The interpretations offered by both Shao and Cheng paint a coherent picture of the Han perspective transpiring from behind the muhei stickers I collected—a narrative of legitimate interethnic grievances and resentment aggravated by media narratives depicting violent episodes as terrorist attacks (Clarke 2010, 17; Shan and Chen 2011, 14). The dozens of replies I received when I raised the issue of muhei in a WeChat group of well-educated Chinese university students testify to more complex reactions to ethnic stereotyping. While some group members explained that Muslim minorities tended to isolate themselves at the fringes of "mainstream society," deadlocking themselves with self-righteous judgments, others warned that discussing this issue online would most likely result in a polarization of positions without any consensus being reached. Some participants shared stories of Muslim minority citizens trying to integrate into Chinese society and being ultimately reined in by traditional parents and families, whereas others noted that muhei discourse was no-ticeably more present on social media than the voices of Muslim citizens themselves, with muhei social media accounts and discussion groups organizing outrage campaigns: "There are many large muhei accounts, they have a lot of followers, they are all dog whistlers fol-lowed by crazy dogs . . . Whenever they see something about qingzhen food or events in the Middle East they *qu pen* [go trolling], that's why Muslim people don't dare to speak online, they are afraid of stirring up these muhei."

While some discussants agreed that "Chinese people suffer from Islamophobia," oth-ers noted that sending a humorous picture should not be enough to automatically consider someone a muhei, a label that was already becoming devoid of critical edge: "I think that today, if you dare saying something critical about Muslims, it doesn't matter if you are cor-rect or not, you will be called a muhei, just like if you say something positive about China, people will call you a 'Little Pink' patriot."

Debating Islamophobia on Social Media Platforms

Discussing muhei with friends and social media contacts pointed me to wider debates hap-pening on online platforms supporting the public interactions of larger user bases, includ-ing forum boards, social networking services, Q&A websites, and microblogging platforms. While stereotypical ethnic humor was circulated through the private channels of instant messaging and chat groups as part of a broader online vernacular, the practice of muhei was articulated more explicitly on the public fronts of social media platforms. To grasp how muhei was being discussed on social media, I collected and analyzed posts shared in late 2018 on two relatively comparable microblogging services: Twitter and Sina Weibo. Sina Weibo is, at the time of writing, the most popular Chinese microblogging platform; multiple interviewees pointed out that the existence of muhei-related accounts and debates on Weibo made it an obvious choice for further research. Twitter is an American microblogging plat-form and is notoriously inaccessible from inside China without the use of a VPN (virtual private network). Despite recent crackdowns on Chinese citizens using Twitter, which no-ticeably affected the "simplified Chinese" Twitter user base (Xiao 2018), the wealth of muhei search results and the liveliness of debates around the topic convinced me that this platform offered a worthy comparative case. The data collection on Twitter was conducted through a script compiling all new tweets posted to the platform that included the Chinese characters for muhei. Given the limitations of the Sina Weibo application programming interface and internal search, posts from this platform were collected manually on a daily basis, allowing me to skim through false positives and to correctly flag promoted content. After polishing the corpus (282 tweets, 229 Sina Weibo posts), I conducted basic word-frequency counts and co-occurrence analyses on the two subsets of data, complementing these with discourse analysis of individual posts.[1]

One of the most evident features of the muhei discussions happening on Twitter is the proximity to voices critical of the Chinese government and the Chinese Communist Party. Given the role that Twitter has historically played as a platform for Chinese abroad, citizen journalists, and activists to discuss issues in terms that would not be allowed on local social media, it is not surprising to find a large majority of tweets about muhei, criticizing the practice by retweeting questionable tweets and labeling their authors: "This Jingjing woman is a muhei"; "This is just a muhei idiot"; "Being a muhei and being a Little Pink are both a waste of IQ." The constellation of terms co-occurring in these sorts of tweets pitch muhei users alongside *xiaofenhong* (Little Pink patriots) and *chuanfen* (Trump fans), denoting political connections being articulated across countries and political systems.

Muhei criticisms on Twitter also flared up around specific instances of Islamophobia and discriminatory behavior reposted from other platforms. Around the end of October 2018, for example, multiple users retweeted and commented on an alleged Chinese muhei woman who urinated on a copy of the Holy Quran in a toilet and posted photos of her desecration on local social media platforms. These posts included both hashtags #*fan qingzhenyundong* (anti-Halal movement) and #XinjiangCamps, directly correlating muhei Islamophobia with recent developments regarding the crackdown on Uyghurs. Although the majority of muhei-related tweets were critical of Islamophobia and relatively international in their outlook (with a clear prevalence of references to the United States and Taiwan), some tweets were clearly posted by Chinese users with different political leanings. These latter tweets supported the government line and encouraged their interlocutors to love their motherland and "study the classics," at times invoking the "Islamization" of Europe through sharia law as an argument for their grievances (Qihuang Zhongbian 2017).

In a similar way, posts collected from Sina Weibo consisted largely of reblogs and comments labeling other users as muhei: "This guy is an older leader of those online muhei that keep showing up"; "I can't stand those idiot muhei"; "Don't be dazzled by those international muhei groups, the more you know Islam, the more you will love Islam." Nevertheless, in contrast to Twitter, muhei debaters on Sina Weibo appear to be less outraged about broader issues such as the detention of Uyghurs in camps and more concerned about specific events targeting Chinese Muslims such as harassment, misinformation, and slander—with the obvious provision that extensive censorship on the platform has likely skewed these attitudes. Discussions regarding muhei on Sina Weibo seem to include more voices from Chinese Muslims (at least as far as nicknames, avatars, and profile descriptions would suggest) and to adopt an outlook decidedly more focused on national-level issues—although occasional comments on international, Muslim-related news also widened the conversation. Also in contrast to Twitter is the organization of Sina Weibo users in contesting muhei on the platform. One example is the account @fanmuheijituan (antimuhei group), which is entirely dedicated to reblogging and flagging muhei content. As its profile description explains, "Muhei are the most terrifying extremists of contemporary times! Using the internet to destroy ethnic unity, harming the citizens' faith! Attacking enterprises and architectures in ethnic minority areas."

Accounts like @fanmuheijituan deploy governmental terminology like *minzu tuanjie* (ethnic unity) in a defensive way, labeling muhei themselves as terrorists and extremists stirring up violence against minority populations. Almost a quarter of the posts collected on Sina Weibo (47 of 229) were created by verified account holders, and another fifty were created by users with a paid membership, highlighting the heightened visibility that the platform's internal search engine grants to privileged accounts. Studies of contention and controversy on Sina Weibo advance the hypothesis that verified accounts might be less prone to express extreme viewpoints and hateful speech (Ng and Han 2018, 2005); however, given the opacity of the Sina Weibo search engine and the vagaries of platform-side censorship mechanisms, it is difficult to draw conclusions from the prominence that verified accounts and paying members seem to have in discussions of muhei. Despite the predominance of critical and antimuhei posts on Sina Weibo, keyword searches occasionally revealed instances of offensive ethnic slander, usually directed at a specific user. In one case, a young female Muslim user who was praising the platform for dealing with some of her harassers was attacked by other muhei users with offensive responses, such as "eat more pork, say less bullshit" or "I saw a picture of a pig in your profile . . . aren't you scared to go to hell?"

Conclusion: Articulating Incivility

My exploratory analysis of the practice of muhei and its critical labeling illustrates how different genres of online content and seemingly unrelated practices resonate with each other and with issues of national and international relevance such as religious policy and ethnic minority rights. Muhei stickers and humorous images shared privately among messaging app users are commonly described by Han Chinese citizens as a by-product of interethnic tensions and unmanageable digital media platforms. However, the more public discussions happening around the term on microblogging platforms reveal more complex negotiations of how civility and incivility are deployed by different actors and publics in the country. Ethnic humor slandering Muslim minorities might be perceived as a "funny" genre of visual content until it circulates in the semiprivate friend circles of QQ and WeChat, but its foregrounding as muhei material in the discursive arenas of Sina Weibo or Twitter frames it in broader debates around the boundaries of civility and extreme speech. In fact, even the most recent campaigns launched by the Xinjiang administration—which resulted in the reported incarceration of hundreds of thousands of Uyghurs in "reeducation through transformation" camps—are justified by authorities through appeals to the "civilizing" power of state institutions "healing" Muslim minorities from the social illness of "extremist" religious thought (Zenz 2019). When examined as a social media practice, muhei can be understood as an uncivil reaction by Han Chinese to the perceived privileges of ethnic minorities and to the violent incidents attributed to extremist groups. The sustained circulation of muhei content on social media platforms suggests a failure of Chinese authorities to contain precisely the kind of content "instigating ethnic hatred or discrimination and jeopardizing ethnic unity" that documents such as the 2010 *White Paper on the Internet in China* (quoted at the beginning of this chapter) set forth to regulate.

In conclusion, the example of muhei confirms that forms of incivility and extreme speech are not reducible to clear-cut categories that are applicable throughout societies around the globe. These practices and discursive resources are often segmented and articulated according to situated historical and sociopolitical contexts. Moreover, muhei highlights how uncivil practices channel and provoke different interpretations and reactions at various scales. When shared in private chat conversations as a subset of regional humor, stereotypical depictions of Muslim minorities are widely framed as an ironic response to news events and connected to a Han majority disappointment with religious policy and perceived minority privileges. When they are scaled up to the more public fronts of social media platforms, examples of muhei become the focus of a backlash against ethnic and religious discrimination, and their connections to Han supremacism and global Islamophobia are positioned in broader political discussions about governance and international relations. Muhei offers a clear example of how, on digital media, in-group "fun" is deployed as a metapractice through which incivility is articulated at an accelerated pace (Udupa 2019). Once it is foregrounded in more public discussions, the sharing of "funny" stickers of bearded figures in ethnic garb becomes quickly connected to socioeconomic grievances, official narratives about extremism, and global politics. As personal attacks and targeted harassment of ethnic and religious minorities reveal the widespread currency of Islamophobic sentiments among Chinese citizens, ironic reprisal and satirical responses to muhei accounts become a strategy of deploying the official government line of ethnic unity against uncivil practices.

Note

1. These data were collected from search queries for posts containing the term *muhei* (in Chinese characters) while logged in with my personal account on both platforms. Data collection on Twitter was automated through a script and run between October and December 2018, resulting in 282 posts. Data collection on Sina Weibo was conducted manually between November 2018 and January 2019, resulting in 229 posts.

References

Becquelin, Nicolas. 2004. "Criminalizing Ethnicity: Political Repression in Xinjiang." *China Rights Forum* 1:39–46.

Benson, Thomas W. 1996. "Rhetoric, Civility, and Community: Political Debate on Computer Bulletin Boards." *Communication Quarterly* 44 (3): 359–378. https://doi.org/10.1080/01463379609370023.

Boxman-Shabtai, Lillian, and Limor Shifman. 2015. "When Ethnic Humor Goes Digital." *New Media and Society* 17 (4): 520–539. https://doi.org/10.1177/1461444813506972.

Brophy, David. 2018. "China's Uyghur Repression." *Jacobin*, May 31, 2018. http://jacobinmag.com/2018/05/xinjiang-uyghur-china-repression-surveillance-islamophobia.

———. 2019. "Good and Bad Muslims in Xinjiang." *Made in China Journal* 4 (2): 44–53.

Byler, Darren. 2018. "China's Government Has Ordered a Million Citizens to Occupy Uighur Homes. Here's What They Think They're Doing." *ChinaFile*, October 24, 2018. http://www.chinafile.com/reporting-opinion/postcard/million-citizens-occupy-uighur-homes-xinjiang.

Cao, Bin. 2014. "Xinhua Insight: A Year without Internet in Xinjiang." *Xinhuawang*, April 20, 2014. http://news.xinhuanet.com/english/indepth/2014-04/20/c_133276600.htm.

Clarke, Michael. 2010. "China, Xinjiang and the Internationalisation of the Uyghur Issue." *Global Change, Peace, and Security* 22 (2): 213–229. https://doi.org/10.1080/14781151003770846.

CNNIC (China Internet Network Information Center). 2015. "The 35th Statistical Survey on Internet Development in China." http://www1.cnnic.cn/IDR/ReportDownloads/201507/P020150720486421654597.pdf.

Coe, Kevin, Kate Kenski, and Stephen A. Rains. 2014. "Online and Uncivil? Patterns and Determinants of Incivility in Newspaper Website Comments." *Journal of Communication* 64 (4): 658–679. https://doi.org/10.1111/jcom.12104.

de Seta, Gabriele. 2013. "Spraying, Fishing, Looking for Trouble: The Chinese Internet and a Critical Perspective on the Concept of Trolling." *Fibreculture Journal* 22:301–317.

———. 2018a. "Biaoqing: The Circulation of Emoticons, Emoji, Stickers, and Custom Images on Chinese Digital Media Platforms." *First Monday* 23 (9). https://doi.org/10.5210/fm.v23i9.9391.

———. 2018b. "Trolling, and Other Problematic Social Media Practices." In *The SAGE Handbook of Social Media*, edited by J. Burgess, A. Marwick, and T. Poell, 390–411. London, UK: Sage.

———. 2018c. "Wenming bu wenming: The Socialization of Incivility in Postdigital China." *International Journal of Communication* 12:2010–2030.

Han, Rongbin. 2015. "Defending the Authoritarian Regime Online: China's 'Voluntary Fifty-Cent Army'." *The China Quarterly*, 224:1006–1025.

Ho, Wai-Yip. 2013. "Mobilizing the Muslim Minority for China's Development: Hui Muslims, Ethnic Relations and Sino-Arab Connections." *Journal of Comparative Asian Development* 12 (1): 84–112. https://doi.org/10.10 80/15339114.2012.749119.

Hong, Yu. 2017. *Networking China: The Digital Transformation of the Chinese Economy.* Urbana: University of Illinois Press.

Hu, Yong. 2008. *Zhongsheng xuanhua: Wangluo shidai de geren biaoda yu gonggong taolun* [The rising cacophony: personal expression and public discussion in the internet age]. Guilin, China: Guangxi Shifan Daxue Chubanshe.

Huang, Frankie. 2018. "China's Most Popular App Is Full of Hate." *Foreign Policy*, November 27, 2018. https://foreignpolicy.com/2018/11/27/chinas-most-popular-app-is-full-of-hate/.

Human Rights Watch. 2017. "China: Free Xinjiang 'Political Education' Detainees." September 10, 2017. https://www.hrw.org/news/2017/09/10/china-free-xinjiang-political-education-detainees

———. 2018. "China: Visiting Officials Occupy Homes in Muslim Region." May 13, 2018. https://www.hrw.org/news/2018/05/13/china-visiting-officials-occupy-homes-muslim-region.

Information Office of the State Council of the People's Republic of China. 2010. "The internet in China." June 8, 2010. http://www.gov.cn/english/2010-06/08/content_1622956_7.htm.

Jiang, Suihan. 2016. Understanding the "Phoenix Man" on the Internet [master thesis], Lund University.

Jung, Chauncey. 2018. "Wo suojian de huayi yimin weihe choushi musilin?" [Why do I see Chinese immigrants look upon Muslims with hatred?]. *New York Times*, October 11, 2018. https://cn.nytimes.com/opinion/20181010/canada-immigrant-chinese-conservatives-islamophobia/.

Lam, Oiwan. 2017. "China's Xinjiang Residents Are Being Forced to Install Surveillance Apps on Mobile Phones." *Global Voices*, July 19, 2017. https://globalvoices.org/2017/07/19/chinas-xinjiang-residents-are-being-forced-to-install-surveillance-apps-on-mobile-phones/.

Leibold, James. 2010. "More Than a Category: Han Supremacism on the Chinese Internet." *China Quarterly* 203: 539–559. https://doi.org/10.1017/S0305741010000585.

———. 2011. "Blogging Alone: China, the Internet, and the Democratic Illusion?" *Journal of Asian Studies* 70 (4): 1023–1041. https://doi.org/10.1017/S0021911811001550.

———. 2019. "Surveillance in China's Xinjiang Region: Ethnic Sorting, Coercion, and Inducement." *Journal of Contemporary China* 29 (121): 46–60. https://doi.org/10.1080/10670564.2019.1621529.

Li, Haiyang. 2018. "Dui Zhongguo muhei fanyi xianxiang de sikao" [Reflections on China's muhei phenomenon]. *Huizu Xuewang*, August 19, 2018. http://www.zghzxw.com/content-169-2126-1.html.

Liu, Xin. 2018. "Ningxia Changes Halal Label amid Pan-Islam Backlash." *Global Times*, March 26, 2018. http://www.globaltimes.cn/content/1095291.shtml.

Luqiu, Luwei Rose, and Fan Yang. 2018. "Islamophobia in China: News Coverage, Stereotypes, and Chinese Muslims' Perceptions of Themselves and Islam." *Asian Journal of Communication* 28 (6): 598–619. https://doi.org/10.1080/01292986.2018.1457063.

Ma, Guibao. 2017. "Tingxialai ba, muheimen!" [Stop it, muhei!]. *Sohu*, July 21, 2017. www.sohu.com/a/159032302_336921.

Mackerras, Colin. 2012. "Causes and Ramifications of the Xinjiang July 2009 Disturbances." *Sociology Study* 2 (7): 496–510.

Mu, Xuequan. 2018. "Xinjiang's Vocational Education, Training Program Constructive for Anti-terrorism: Expert." *Xinhuawang*, October 30, 2018. http://www.xinhuanet.com/english/2018-10/30/c_137569858.htm.

Ng, Jason Q., and Eileen Le Han. 2018. "Slogans and Slurs, Misogyny and Nationalism: A Case Study of Anti-Japanese Sentiment by Chinese Netizens in Contentious Social Media Comments." *International Journal of Communication* 12:1988–2009.

Pohjonen, Matti, and Sahana Udupa. 2017. "Extreme Speech Online: An Anthropological Critique of Hate Speech Debates." *International Journal of Communication* 11:1173–1191.

Qihuang Zhongbian. 2017. *Lvlvmen de xidi taolu* [The greens' floor-scrubbing routines]. Sina Weibo, January 4, 2017. https://www.weibo.com/ttarticle/p/show?id=2309404060334536133084.

Roberts, Sean R. 2018. "The Biopolitics of China's 'War on Terror' and the Exclusion of the Uyghurs." *Critical Asian Studies* 50 (2): 232–258. https://doi.org/10.1080/14672715.2018.1454111.

Schrader, Matt. 2018. "Censorship, Geopolitical Time Bombs, and China's Islamophobia Problem." *ChinaBrief* 18 (13). https://jamestown.org/program/censorship-geopolitical-time-bombs-and-chinas-islamophobia -problem/.

Shan, Wei, and Gang Chen. 2011. "The Urumqi Riots and China's Ethnic Policy in Xinjiang." *East Asian Policy* 1 (3): 14–22.

Udupa, S. 2019. "Nationalism in the Digital Age: Fun as a Metapractice of Extreme Speech." *International Journal of Communication*, 13:3143–3163.

Wen, Philip, and O. Auyezovlzhas. 2018. *Tracking China's Muslim Gulag.* Reuters, November 29, 2018. https:// www.reuters.com/investigates/special-report/muslims-camps-china/.

Xiao, Eva. 2018. "Stealth Crackdown: Chinese Censorship Extends to Twitter as Activists' Accounts Disappear." *Hong Kong Free Press*, November 18, 2018. https://www.hongkongfp.com/2018/11/18/stealth-crackdown -chinese-censorship-extends-twitter-activists-accounts-disappear/.

Yang, Guobin. 2008. "Contention in Cyberspace." In *Popular Protest in China*, edited by Kevin J. O'Brien, 126–143. Cambridge, MA: Harvard University Press. https://doi.org/10.4159/9780674041585.

———. 2018. "Demobilizing the Emotions of Online Activism in China: A Civilizing Process." *International Journal of Communication* 11:1945–1965.

Yang, Lijun, and Yongnian Zheng. 2012. "Fen Qings (Angry Youth) in Contemporary China." *Journal of Contemporary China* 21 (76): 637–653. https://doi.org/10.1080/10670564.2012.666834.

Zenz, Adrian. 2019. "'Thoroughly Reforming Them towards a Healthy Heart Attitude': China's Political Re-Education Campaign in Xinjiang." *Central Asian Survey*, 38 (1): 102–128.

Zhang, Chi. 2018. *WeChatting American Politics: Misinformation, Polarization, and Immigrant Chinese Media* (TOW Reports). Tow Center for Digital Journalism. https://www.cjr.org/tow_center_reports/wechatting -american-politics-misinformation-polarization-and-immigrant-chinese-media.php/.

11

WRITING ON THE WALLS

Discourses on Bolivian Immigrants in Chilean Meme Humor

Nell Haynes*

In his influential essay, "The Work of Art in the Age of Mechanical Reproduction," Walter Benjamin argued that the ability to mass-produce and mass-circulate images would have a profoundly democratic impact. The internet meme has become iconic of mass circulation, traveling through social media unbound by platform, language, or internet-enabled device. Yet memes, in some instances, contravene movement toward greater democracy and social equality. This chapter explores how racializing anti-immigrant discourses become embedded in humorous memes in Chile's northern region of Tarapacá. As Bolivians migrate to this region in high numbers, some northern Chileans (*nortinos*) feel threatened by the increasing presence of immigrants. As a result, they express distrust and dislike for immigrants through discourses that circulate verbally, in analog written forms, and through digital texts such as memes. In doing so, they reproduce nationalistic understandings of race and modernity that contrast with perceptions of Bolivians as Indigenous and culturally backward. These discourses reinforce inequalities that immigrants experience, even as most nortinos are marginalized within the nation state as well.

Chile's Tarapacá region is geographically peripheral within the country, economically exploited, and politically disenfranchised. Despite Tarapacá's reputation as an inhospitable place, the area draws large numbers of migrants from nearby Bolivia and Peru. In this border region, locals have a long history of perpetuating animosity and structural injustices toward migrants. These practices are sustained by discourses that situate migrants as backward, unhygienic, uneducated, plunderers of limited resources, and contributors to cultural degradation. Sentiments toward Bolivian immigrants take on a racializing character, conflating Bolivianness with indigeneity, in order to differentiate between "Others," and "true Chileans," who are assumed to be non-Indigenous mestizos. These discourses have long circulated through official policy, news media, and everyday speech. More recently, social media platforms have become spaces for locals to reinstantiate anti-immigrant discourses, often through humorous genres, and specifically memes.

Considering anti-immigrant memes as "extreme speech" draws attention to discursive continuities between objectionable rhetoric and mundane genres that make anti-Bolivian sentiments more palatable to a general audience. This conceptual framework acknowledges acceptability and objectionability as a spectrum rather than binary (Hervik 2019; Udupa and Pohjonen 2017). In this article, I use critical discourse analysis to examine Facebook posts that draw humor from long-standing negative discourses on Bolivian immigrants. Nortinos view these posts as "weas chistosas, no más" [just funny stuff]. However, I argue that their relationships with more extreme language, in combination with their quotidian nature, work insidiously to reinforce racialized discrimination against Bolivian immigrants.

Throughout the world, memes have become an important mode of expression. They may support socially progressive causes, extreme fascist stances, the status quo, or even espouse ridiculous thoughts entirely divorced from reality. Messages are conveyed through a wide range of genres, including moralizing, inspirational, informative, and humorous texts. Here, I concentrate on funny memes to examine how humor mediates the division between acceptable and objectionable speech. These memes subtly support discrimination against immigrants by casting "real Chileans" as more deserving of social and economic resources. Yet understanding wider national and global systems that economically and politically marginalize almost all residents of the region forces us to consider the individuals who create and share these memes, not as simple bigots, but part of a broader struggle for resources and recognition. The examples in this article demonstrate not only how mundane humor and extreme speech are intimately connected, but also how nested forms of marginalization provide conditions conducive to discriminatory discourses.

Methods: Contextual and Comparative

This research draws from a lineage of "digital ethnography methods" dating back to Coleman's (2010) "Ethnographic Approaches to Digital Media," and Horst and Miller's (2012) volume, *Digital Anthropology*. Many scholars have subsequently developed methods using digital resources as a basis for conducting ethnography. This has allowed researchers to study digital phenomena during short stays (Pink et al. 2016) or from remote locations (Postill 2016). In contrast, my work more closely reflects the approach of "internet-related ethnography" (Postill and Pink 2012, 126) that follows discourses across multiple online and offline instantiations to understand how the digital and analog are mutually constitutive (Juris 2012). My work relies on the established anthropological practice of long term in situ fieldwork (Madison 2012; Spradley 1979, 1980) as a means of contextualizing digital practices. This article is based on fifteen months of integrated online and offline fieldwork in northern Chile spaced between September 2013 and June 2015, engaging with about two hundred interlocutors. My research included in-person interviews, surveying, and map-making, as well as participant-observation at events including lunches with neighbors, funerals of community members, and even sleeping on a mattress in a kind local family's kitchen after an 8.2 magnitude earthquake made my apartment uninhabitable. My work also employs digital methods, connecting with nortinos on social media, including Facebook (110 friends), Instagram (following seventy-five users), Tumblr (following forty users), Twitter (following thirty accounts), and WhatsApp (forty-seven individual contacts and fifteen groups). As with in-person ethnographic methods, social media sites allowed me to interact with nortinos, see how they interact with others, and gain valuable insights about their lives.

This research was enhanced through comparative work with the Global Social Media Impact Study (GSMIS). By using the same set of methods and thematic foci in nine cities across the world, the GSMIS was able to provide in-depth analyses of social media practices in particular locations, while working toward broader comprehension of the use and consequences of social media. Comparisons, along with quantitative work on surveys and Facebook post counting, allowed me to distinguish among near universal practices across distant geographic spaces, locally inflected particularities, and idiosyncratic individual examples.

Digital research methods range from computer analysis of Twitter data to the ethnographic practice of actually watching over people's shoulders as they post on Instagram. The ethnographic approach that I take here is important for understanding the ways digital media are embedded people's lives holistically (Pertierra 2018), but also in contemplating confluences of digital practices with issues of social inequalities and social justice. I argue that the ways that race, gender, sexuality, social class, and citizenship status inflect and are performatively created through online media must be understood, not only in local historical context, but also with attention to how they are sustained, shifted, or contested in quotidian practices.

Scholars have paid attention to expressions, organizing, and political engagement through internet media since the 1990s (Castells 1996). More recently, many have concentrated on politics and social media with attention to digital divides (Nayaran 2007; Norris 2001), building democratic spaces (Papacharissi 2010), and the activism–revolution spectrum (Coleman 2012; Fu and Chan 2015; Fuchs 2012; Gerbaudo 2012; Lim 2012; Morozov 2009; Postill 2012, 2018; Tufekci and Wilson 2012). In contrast to these studies that concentrate on the ways people participate in online groups with explicit political aims, most nortinos do not engage in what they would define as political action, seeing "politics" as that which metropolitan elites enact. Instead, they distance themselves from such pursuits and from elites they perceive as "political." Nortinos see social media as a place to build community around issues that affect their daily experiences. Even as these issues are sometimes related to national political debates and policy, nortinos frame them in ways that extract them from their overtly political context and reestablish them as mundane complaints.

Many northern Chileans reframe political issues through the use of humor and formulism associated with memes. Humor in memes is widely recognized as central to audience engagement (Milner 2013; Miltner 2014; Shifman 2013). Indeed, most nortinos I interviewed noted humor as the most important consideration in sharing social media posts. They were particularly fond of the "image macro," the most recognized type of internet meme, which is essentially a stylistic formula for combining text and image. In these memes, both text and image direct the viewer to interpret the other in a certain manner. Much of the meaning is connected to the memes' intertextuality—the ways in which images are reused in different contexts. This format is used to express a variety of sentiments, from greetings and celebratory messages to "indirects" and warnings. But most often we associate image macro memes with humor—cats desiring cheeseburgers or Willy Wonka's ironic request "Go on . . ." This humor, as Miltner (2018) notes, is an effective means for commenting on the mistakes and hypocrisy of the powerful, making memes a "weapon of the weak" (Weiping 2009, par. 24). Yet nortinos leverage memes against the weakest members of society, thereby carving out a space where they may symbolically gain power by denouncing those with less.

The popularity of particular memes often hinges on their "emotional resonance" with audiences (Miltner 2014). With this in mind, I analyze memes that appeared most often in the feeds of the nortinos I interacted with personally. They are not representative of the memes being shared daily, but rather are exceptional in that they were the most popular memes commenting on immigration, likely considered to be the most humorous, and corresponded to the kinds of formulism most prevalent in memes shared in northern Chile. This approach recognizes that individuals are not mechanistically induced to create or share memes, but do so because they are compelled by the meme's engaging qualities and the significance of its message.

Like other forms of social media, the content of a meme is made meaningful through relationships to cultural discourses that exist within and beyond social media (Faulkner, Farida, and D'Orazio 2018). The ideological positioning on racial categories and citizenship evident in the memes I analyzed was similar to that found in local and national politicians' speeches, news stories, conversations among friends and family, and, as I explore here, graffiti. Thus, I use critical discourse analysis to uncover the intertextual relationships of discourse in disparate genres. My interest lies, as with Milner, in the "interdiscursive, intertwining multiple texts and commentaries" that are embedded in these "complex collages" (2013, 67). These examples demonstrate the ways language acts as a mode of symbolic power (Bourdieu 1991), thus illuminating social and cultural processes (Bucholtz and Hall 2008) associated with immigration, citizenship, racial categories, and marginalization in northern Chile.

Marginalized Identities in Northern Chile

In my first few months in Tarapacá, I noticed a number of walls inscribed with graffiti about Bolivians. One read, "Cholos fuera! Bolis, pata raja! Monos culiao"[1] [Cholos (urban Indigenous Andeans) get out! Dirty-footed Bolivians! Fucking monkeys]. Another, more to the point, simply said, "Muerte a los bolivianos" [Death to Bolivians]. The most perplexing read, "Cuidado con los brujos bolivianos" [Be careful with Bolivian witches]. And though the particular vulgar language of these graffiti scribbles caught me off guard, the sentiments did not surprise me. Anti-Bolivian attitudes are common throughout Chile, particularly in the border region.

While a recent survey found that 68 percent of Chileans want to restrict immigration (INDH 2018; see also Meseguer and Kemmerling 2016; Noy and Voorend 2015) and that anti-immigrant sentiments take on a racializing and moralistic character, it notes that these characteristics are accentuated in the northern region. Nortinos often think of Bolivians as prototypical immigrants in the region who are criminals, stealing jobs, and exploiting resources that rightfully belong to "real Chileans." The focus on Bolivians stems from their high numbers. About half of all Bolivian immigrants in Chile live in the north, where they make up roughly 5 percent of the population, a far higher number than any other immigrant group.[2]

My research was primarily based in Alto Hospicio, a city of about 100,000 situated in the Atacama Desert. The city is about five hours from the border with Peru to the north, and two hours from the Bolivian border to the east. In contrast, it is more than thirty hours by bus from the national capital, Santiago. Many residents characterized the area as marginalized and disenfranchised, citing this distance, national politicians' disregard for the area, and economic conditions of the region. Nortinos often employ marginalization as a form of identification in which they reject a victimized status and instead highlight the ways in which they toil through hardships and struggle to improve living conditions (Haynes 2016). I use the term *marginalization*, as opposed to *marginality*, to distance it from notions of a static state and instead concentrate on processes that change with time as an effect of socioeconomic and geopolitical contexts (Tsing 1993).

Nortinos often voice complaints of being forgotten by national politicians. During the presidential election of 2013, many scoffed at candidates who came to Tarapacá and waved from their cars, but never engaged in conversations with local people. These feelings were reinforced in the aftermath of the 8.2 magnitude earthquake of April 2014, when many nortinos were left without water, electricity, and gas for several weeks. Many of the one thousand families whose homes were beyond repair lived in tents for more than a year while waiting for temporary trailers. Most nortinos perceived this government assistance as insufficient and slow to arrive—a clear indication of nortinos' political insignificance.

Nortinos equally note the region is exploited for economic benefit of Santiago elites and foreign companies. The region is home to vast mineral resources and, as a result, an extraction-based economy. Nitrate was first discovered in the area in the late 1800s, when the land was governed by Peru. This discovery shifted perceptions about this piece of the Atacama Desert from a useless tract of *terra nullius* to valuable property. Chile dispossessed the territory from Peru and the area to the south from Bolivia, launching the War of the Pacific (1879–1884). By the war's end, Chile had taken Bolivia's entire coastline and Peru's southernmost province of Tarapacá, thus moving Chile's northern border more than 700 km north. The nitrate of Tarapacá benefited a wealthy class of mining barons based in Santiago. These barons further profited from the exploitative conditions under which workers in the north labored, including low pay, shoddy facilities, and coercive employment strategies.

Though the nitrate boom was short lived, extraction of other Atacama resources has perpetuated regional and global inequalities. In the 1980s, copper became the major mining resource in Tarapacá. As of 2011, northern Chile supplied one third of the world's copper, making up 60 percent of the country's exports and 20 percent of its GDP. The Chilean government has averaged about $11.5 billion per year in mining profits (*The Economist* 2013). But more importantly, large multinational companies such as Phelps Dodge and Sumitomo have partnered with the state-owned copper company, CODELCO, sending profits abroad to Japan, the United States, and the United Kingdom. These multinational mining companies have not reinvested profits in the region, nor do they pay workers wages comparable with the national average.[3] It is not unusual for nortinos, even those with skilled labor jobs in mining, to live in houses with cement floors, no hot water, and unfinished ceilings. During my fieldwork, Chile was the most unequal highly developed country in the world (Organization for Economic Cooperation and Development 2015), with the National Index of Quality of Urban

Life ranking Alto Hospicio very last among cities in Chile. This designation took into consideration working conditions, business climate, sociocultural conditions, transportation connectivity, health, environment, and housing (Núcleo de Estudios Metropolitanos 2015).

Referencing these disparities, nortinos use Santiago as a foil for what they see as authentically Chilean. This is poignantly illustrated by a series of memes popular among nortinos in 2015 proclaiming "Santiago no es Chile" [Santiago is not Chile]. Beneath the text, these memes used images of regional industries such as mining in the north and logging in the south. Through these memes, Chileans outside Santiago illustrated the ways they perceive their own marginalized experiences to be more representative of true "Chileanness" than privileged experiences of the elite. Through such logic, nortinos express fierce nationalism, while distinguishing themselves from politically and economically powerful Chileans represented by "Santiago." As the meme series makes clear, nortinos consider natural resources and the jobs that depend on them as central to what it means to be Chilean, suggesting that only certain people have rights connected to these resources. This formulation differentiates nortinos from metropolitan elites, but also distinguishes them from immigrants.

Bolivian immigrants are particularly vulnerable to claims that they are unfairly using Chilean resources because of economic disparities between the two countries, and resulting conceptualizations of Bolivians as poverty stricken. Bolivians residing in northern Chile are usually employed in the worst paying jobs and live in the most impoverished neighborhoods. Rather than working directly in mining, they earn closer to the national minimum salary in the retail or service sectors as part of a secondary economy that relies on the strength of the copper industry. This compounds Chileans' views of Bolivia as an economically lagging nation. Though the Bolivian government has succeeded in cutting poverty drastically since 2000 (World Bank 2017), Bolivia is still considered one of the poorest and least developed countries in the hemisphere. The economic differential between the two nations leads many Chileans to conceptualize Bolivians as "atrasados" (behind or backward) and lacking in markers of cultural modernity. These views depoliticize Chile's historical role in Bolivia's lagging economy. After losing its coastline to Chile in 1879, Bolivia is now begrudgingly landlocked, which affects industries' ability to export, subjects imports to international taxes and regulations, and requires Bolivia to pay other countries for access to fiber optic cables, driving internet prices up and connection speeds down. As a result, Bolivians are less connected to world systems through which individuals might easily gain access to the kinds of consumer goods and even media that index cultural modernity.

These notions of Bolivians as atrasados also take on a racializing character, because many nortinos connect both poverty and judgments of cultural stagnation to indigeneity. This has historic antecedents extending back to the War of the Pacific. At the conclusion of the war, the Chilean government was satisfied with its new resource-rich territory, but less pleased with the residents of the area—primarily small groups of Indigenous peoples living rural lifestyles who spoke Aymara or Quechua. Chilean military troops were stationed in the area as deterrents to Peruvian and Bolivian forces, but also to remind the populace of their new nationality. The Chilean government launched projects aimed at incorporating the northern population into the nation-state through religion and education for both children and adults (Frazier 2007). These nationalization projects effectively silenced Indigenous languages, valorized racial homogeneity under ideals of mestizaje, and incorporated discourses of "modernity" into nationalistic exceptionalism, thereby ideologically linking indigeneity to foreignness.

Today, whereas more than 60 percent of Bolivia's population identifies as part of an Indigenous group, less than 10 percent of the Chilean population describes itself as Indigenous.[4] Chileans often point to Bolivians' language and phenotypic features as evidence of racial difference between the two countries' populations. So although Bolivians' skin color does not differ significantly from that of darker Chileans, Bolivians often have a shorter, broader stature, and what many refer to as "Indigenous facial features," including close-set eyes and a large nose. At times, Chileans suggest that Bolivians' typically slower speech is indicative of their indigeneity and signals inferior intellect. Chileans also question Bolivians' hygiene, evidenced by the common joke that Bolivians have a particular unpleasant odor. This itself is a racializing stereotype, in which indigeneity is associated with certain bodily characteristics. It turns attention to the body as the origin and location of racial difference (see Weismantel 2001). As Patricia Richards notes, "It may seem strange to use words like 'race' and 'racism' in describing Indigenous peoples who more often are conceptualized in terms of ethnicity" (2013, 15), but the ways in which social meanings become attached to phenotype require attention to processes of racialization (Omi and Winant 1994; Wade 1997). Indeed, "the cultural and the phenotypic are often mutually implicated in popular understandings of where purportedly racial and ethnic attributes come from" (Richards 2013, 15), and most racism stems from a combination of physical and cultural attributes (Hooker 2009). The social value, or lack thereof, attributed to phenotype and culture then becomes embedded in social institutions, ideologies, and discourses, institutionalizing racism's effects. Over time, social markers such as dress and language eventually supersede phenotype or biology in popular understandings of racial categories (Postero 2007).

Indigeneity is not just a racial classification, but is tied to a lack of modernity, poverty, and cultural deficiency. Indigenous peoples living in rural communities or otherwise excluded from industrialized urban publics are often not considered to be "Chilean" regardless of their citizenship or ancestry (Richards 2013). Assessments of Bolivians' backwardness contrast with discourses of Chilean progress, development, modernity, and mestizaje, all of which are connected to resource extraction in the north. This process of conflating national citizenship with racial and ethnic subjectivity (Vergara and Gundermann 2012) then leads to both anti-immigrant discourses and material instances of discrimination.

I conceptualize these discourses and discrimination not as a product of some inherent bigotry on the part of Chilean nationals, but as a product of nested marginalization that triangulates privilege and inequality among nortino citizens, Santiago elites, and immigrants to the region. I use the concept of nested marginalization to understand the ways in which power relations exist not only on the level of hegemon and subaltern, but also among different subaltern groups. The concept relies on approaches to intersectionality (Crenshaw 2003) in order to understand how race, socioeconomic class, gender, sexuality, citizenship status, and other social categories combine to impact the privileges and forms of marginalization individuals and groups experience. This is not an argument for ranking inequalities, but instead draws attention to the multiple motivations a group may feel within a situation of marginalization, compelling them to further marginalize others as a by-product of their own self-positioning; at times, this might involve strategic essentialism (Spivak 1988). The concept draws from Levi's (1989) "grey zone," which understands the marginalization of one group by another subaltern group as a strategy employed by hegemonic forces. It is also related to the notion of "symbolic violence" (Bourdieu and Wacquant 2004), in which people reinforce their own subordination through ideas of deservedness. This concept of nested marginalization thus concentrates on popular formations in which scapegoating and exclusion of another group benefit a marginalized group or are perceived by members of that marginalized group as beneficial to them.

I take the concept of nesting from the term *nested inequalities* (Hochschild 2003), which describes the ways students are impacted by disparities at the national, regional, local, and intra–school district levels. I look at the ways processes of marginalization work at the global, national, regional, local, and intergroup levels. Thus, the marginalization experienced by Bolivian immigrants is impacted by the ways that all nortinos are marginalized within the nation-state (in contrast to Chilean elites), and even the ways all Chilean residents are impacted by global capitalism through resource extraction industries, thus creating a nesting effect through which marginalization is enacted at multiple levels.

Walls: Physical and Virtual

The words scrawled on the walls of Tarapacá are clear examples of extreme speech. They use inflammatory naming practices, such as "brujos bolivianos" or "monos culiao," and even invoke death, as in "Muerte a los Bolivianos." But less extreme manifestations of these same anti-immigrant discourses appear on Facebook walls as well. Many nortinos create different genres of posts commenting on immigrants, framed as everyday complaints.

Using Facebook as a public forum for communications, including complaints, is a quotidian practice for nortinos. Chile has long been at the forefront of telecommunications technology in South America, and internet connections were first available in the north in the late 1990s. During my fieldwork, Chile ranked as the third most highly penetrated market for Facebook in the world, and one of the most engaged social media markets worldwide, averaging 9.5 hours per day per visitor. Smartphones are the most common way nortinos connect to social media, often paying less than $15 a month for 1 GB of data. This makes social media accessible to most nortinos, though recent migrants and rural people tend to be less well connected, or place less importance on their ability to access social media. As a result, social media is a space where nortinos expect that their interlocutors will primarily be working class, but not impoverished, mestizo Chileans. Their posts do little to hide or downplay anti-Indigenous or xenophobic feelings.

Fabian, in his early thirties, wrote in 2014, "These Bolivians, they come, and they take our resources. Indigenous people, they get help with school, a place to live, health care. And what do we get? Where are our bonuses? We the real Chileans who deserve them?" Fabian was born in Santiago but lived most of his life in the north, working in construction. Most of his colleagues were Chileans from various parts of the country, with the addition of a few Bolivians who had lived in northern Chile for several years. When I asked Fabian about his Bolivian coworkers, he spoke of them fondly, but described them as soft-spoken, keeping to themselves, and having "strange habits." Both his Facebook post and these statements reflect common discourses that conflate Bolivian nationality with being Indigenous. The Facebook post also draws on widely circulating (mis)conceptions that by virtue of being Indigenous, immigrants can take advantage of resources allocated to officially recognized "vulnerable populations" in Chile. Indigenous peoples with Chilean citizenship are eligible for housing on originary lands, funding for irrigation projects, seed money and subsidies for entrepreneurial projects, subsidized technical training, special credit funding, and educational benefits (Corporación Nacional de Desarrollo Indígena 2014). The Corporación Nacional de Desarrollo Indígena (CONADI) also coordinates with other government offices to ensure access to housing, education, and healthcare for Indigenous peoples. These resources are aimed at Indigenous peoples who are Chilean citizens, but many non-Indigenous Chileans misconstrue the existence of CONADI as an indication that noncitizen Indigenous people are "stealing" resources.

Other Facebook posts speak of immigrants more generally, such as a post by Jorge, a man in his midforties. He wrote, "How infantile, and unthinking, there still exist people that want to give things to another country, why don't they go back to that country and leave this large country to those of us who really have paid a ton of things with our work." Fabian and Jorge both make complaints about resources that "rightfully belong to real Chileans," whereas Bolivians are deemed unfit because of their status as Indigenous, backward, and not rightfully part of the Chilean labor force.

Whereas posts like Fabian's and Jorge's are original thoughts in response to their experiences, other Facebook posts express anti-immigrant stances through content that has been shared from user to user. Though Jenkins, Ford, and Green (2013) define memes as a key part of participatory culture, nortinos' social media use relies more heavily on curation (Taylor 2014) than participation. Rather than actively creating new memes, nortinos more often share, unchanged, those of others that show up on their feeds. Those that are most popular have the "emotional resonance," to which Miltner (2014) refers, often highlighting the ways in which locals are marginalized. Kermit the Frog memes lament, "Sometimes I have the urge to complain to the government, later I remember that I'm nortino and I get over it" (Haynes 2016, 80–82). Other memes parody popular soda advertisements to suggest that Santiago politicians "live in another world" (Haynes 2016, 156), in a similar sentiment to the "Santiago no es Chile" meme series.

While these memes frame being authentically Chilean as rooted in marginalized experience rather than citizenship, the memes I examine here define "real Chileanness" in contrast to racialized notions of foreignness. Certainly, Chileans share memes relating to Colombian, Peruvian, and Venezuelan immigrants, who are sometimes racialized in different ways than Bolivians. But in the northern region, the vast majority of anti-immigrant memes relate to Bolivians. I offer here three examples.

The first example (fig. 11.1) was shared by 40-year-old Catalina in early 2014. The photo depicts *The Big Bang Theory* character Sheldon, with his T-shirt pulled over his nose and mouth, spraying an aerosol can. The meme simply states, "Anti-Bolivian Repellent." This type of meme uses an image drawn from media with a popular following in the area, overlaid with language that is explicitly anti-Bolivian. The aerosol can could easily be interpreted

Figure 11.1 "Anti-Bolivian repellant" meme.

as air freshener, a reference to joking discourse about the propensity of Bolivians to have a foul odor. But this meme also works on a double entendre; the text suggests something more extreme than simply mitigating unpleasant smells. "Anti-Bolivian repellant" is associated with bug repellant, which either drives them away, as may be suggested by the graffiti "Cholos get out," or worse, "Death to Bolivians."

A second meme (fig. 11.2) was shared by at least ten different Facebook users from Alto Hospicio over several months in 2015. The underlying image depicts Giorgio A. Tsoukalos from the History Channel's program *Ancient Aliens*, another popular television show in the north. This "alien expert's" face is contorted in explanation, with text written above, "There is only one explanation for this." Below his face appears the answer: "Bolivians." This meme was posted almost exclusively as a "comment" on friends' Facebook posts. These posts usually concerned complaints, from the types that Fabian and Jorge wrote, to quotidian annoyances like neighbors playing music too loud, or too much traffic on the commute to work. Again, the image underlying the text plays an important role. Given the photo's origin, the expected finish to the sentence would be "Aliens," thus drawing a parallel between aliens and Bolivians. Indeed, though less directly used than in English, Chileans recognize a confluence of concepts between extraterrestrial beings and foreigners. So, this particular image is especially appropriate in referring to Bolivians and blaming them for social ills.

The final example (fig. 11.3) comes from Jorge. In July 2016, he shared a meme depicting an Altiplano Indigenous man at a social gathering. The man's brightly colored stocking cap (*lluchu* in Aymara, *chullu* in Quechua) is the visual focus of the image. It is overlaid with the text, "Meanwhile in Tarapolivia . . . more Chilean than ever, Jallalla." The humor here

Figure 11.2 "There is only one explanation" meme.

Figure 11.3 "More Chilean than ever" meme.

works on morphological and lexical levels as well as through incongruence between image and language.

Morphologically, our attention is drawn to Tarapolivia—an amalgamation of the words Tarapacá and Bolivia. This alludes to a sense that the two are becoming indistinguishable. As the latter encroaches on the former, it evokes the idea that Bolivia (or Bolivians) is intruding on the region of Tarapacá.

On the lexical level, the meme prominently uses "Jallalla," an Aymara and Quechua word that unites concepts of hope, festivity, and blessings. The word is commonly used by Bolivians in celebratory contexts. This contrasts sharply with a number of distinctly Chilean slang words such as *wea*—in Jorge's textual post (fig. 11.3), and *culiao*—as written on a physical wall in Alto Hospicio. Chilean Spanish is well known for distinct cadence, conjugational forms, and extensive slang lexicon. Slang in memes and other public texts acts as an indexical marker (Gumperz and Cook-Gumperz 1982) of the writer's or sharer's Chileanness. This meme uses *Jallalla* as a marker of Bolivianness, because Chileans would more likely use *conchatumadre* to capture a celebratory spirit. Although both locally inflected words evoke extreme emotion, the latter would be understood as distinctly Chilean, whereas the former is marked as Other.

Finally, considering the way the image frames the text, we see a direct contradiction between "More Chilean than ever" and the man with his eye-catching hat, which is distinctly "not Chilean" by local standards. This style of dress is usually accompanied by leather or rubber sandals and associated with rural areas and agrarian lifestyles. Individuals wearing sandals frequently walk through mud and dust in agricultural fields, leaving their feet dirty. This image, then, is precisely what one would associate with a "dirty-footed Bolivian." Indeed, the man's facial features, missing teeth, and garments; the appearance of other individuals in the background of the photo; and even the word *Jallalla* work to racialize Bolivians as Indigenous and by contrast reinforce the notion of Chile as a country of mestizos. Overall, this framing establishes Bolivian immigrants as, in the words of Yilmaz, an "incompatible ontological category predicated on culture" (2012, 368). Bolivians are distinctly the opposite of "more Chilean than ever."

Intertextuality

In each of these memes, humor mitigates the extremity of ideas, but critical discourse analysis reveals the ways this humorous genre relies on discourses present in more "extreme speech." Although the undeniably extreme text of the graffiti remains anonymous, plenty of people feel no shame in having their name emblazoned above memes drawing on the same ideas. Considering these two genres as intimately connected reminds us that seemingly mundane statements are always part of larger and sometimes more dangerous discursive circulations. Indeed, as Udupa (2019) comments, extreme and mundane forms of nationalism "enter a co-constitutive relation on digital media."

Without leaving the space of social media, we can relate these humorous memes to more explicit posts, which give graphic form to grievances for which Chileans blame immigrants. One prominently shared meme lists types of innocuous resource exploitation associated with immigrants such as school scholarships, social support, housing vouchers, and the creation of precarity in the labor market. These phrases are interspersed with dangerous characterizations, including drug traffic(king), delinquency, and sexual aggression, as well as loss of "our" identity and imposition of cultural customs. Only with the framing words of *¿Inmigrantes?* above and *¡No Gracias!* below in typical meme layout do these contrasting phrases take on local meaning.

Looking beyond the internet, these online texts reflect and comment on what people do in the material world. As Thurlough (2018) notes, boundaries between talk and technology are often blurred when considering the social meanings of communication. As a consequence, proper understanding of digital discourse requires that large-scale discourses related to systems of power and the linguistic specificities of quotidian communication be considered alongside each other. Herein lies the importance of internet-related ethnography and in situ fieldwork. Anti-immigrant discourses do not originate with these memes, but draw on already established media representations and political rhetoric (Ekman 2015). They are contextualized by politicians and news organizations that associate foreigners with crime, including Chile's President Sebastián Piñera, who has equated "bands of delinquents" in Chile with immigrants (Carreño 2016). These intertextual linkages provide the means for interpreting new instances of discourse in light of familiar textual categories. Social media users' interpretations of these memes are conditioned by the other ways that they see immigrants treated in a variety of media. In a cyclical manner, the familiar attitudes embedded in memes contribute to their popularity, while the memes as mundane texts naturalize the more extreme expressions of anti-Bolivian sentiments in graffiti, news reports, and political speeches.

The manifestation of these common sentiments on social media is central to their importance. As I have written elsewhere, the visibility associated with social media in northern Chile has made it a space in which normative notions of cultural acceptability are more often upheld and reproduced rather than challenged (Haynes 2016). While one may paint graffiti on a wall under the cover of night, the name of someone sharing a meme appears alongside the post on Facebook. Whereas a wall in a particular neighborhood is only likely to be seen by people who frequent that area, a social media post may be visible to the sharer's full range of friends, and those of past and future sharers.

As van Dijk notes, "dominance may be enacted and reproduced by subtle, routine, everyday forms of text and talk that appear natural and quite acceptable" (1993, 254). Although graffiti is more extreme, these memes exhibit language that naturalizes the social order and relations of inequality (Fairclough 1985). As Launay (2006) instructs, for a joke to work, it must be construed by its audience as appropriate. Indeed, Hervik (2019) notes that humorous texts may foreclose discussion, allowing those who invoke them to contend that adversaries simply do not understand the comedy. Although counterdiscourses appear in other memes, these generally take on a factual approach, rather than invoking humor. Because humor is key to the popularity of sharing, and thus visibility, these pro-immigrant memes, then, have far less visible presence on social media. Precisely because anti-immigrant memes use humor, they have greater impact, entering everyday discourse and thus desensitizing the issue so that the sight of extreme speech on any sort of wall is less noteworthy.

Further, considering memes as formulaic language draws our attention to the ways they allow for expression of that which may not be voiced under other circumstances. Genre of text contributes to understandings of what is acceptable or unacceptable discourse (Fairclough 2003). As Abu-Lughod points out, poetry among Bedouin women "renders content impersonal or nonindividual, allowing people to dissociate themselves from the sentiments they express, if revealed to the wrong audience" (1986/2016, 239). A Bedouin woman may claim "it was just a song," and social media users may claim "it was just a meme" (see Hervik 2019). In both cases, the formulaic aspects of the language protect those who invoke it, as they express messages that may contravene more widely accepted ideals (Abu-Lughod 1986/2016; Davison 2012), while reinforcing the notion of collectivity implicit in sharing.

What otherwise may be hidden to all but close social circles or subtly implied in face-to-face communication is teased out publicly on social media. More important, through social media, anti-immigrant discourses are socially reinstilled and taught to younger generations. The visibility of these ideological texts, rather than creating public space for discussion over their viability, reinforces their hegemony.

Meme language may appear as superficial, but certain instances of anti-immigrant violence remind us of the material consequences. For example, in July 2017, a group of fishermen in the northern port town of Tocopilla doused two Peruvian immigrants with gasoline and set them ablaze (Kozak 2017). The men survived, but this incident took place amid an "increasingly heated debate over the recent surge in migration to Chile . . . and growing racial tensions," as reported by *The Guardian* (Kozak 2017). And this violent incident stood amid far more numerous smaller attacks. According to the Annual Report on the Situation of Human Rights in Chile (INDH 2017), more than half of Chileans admit to having been present or knowledgeable of intimidation and verbal or physical attacks on immigrants. As verbal and physical attacks become more mundane, it is precisely the popular nature of social media as a form of entertainment that allows anti-immigrant discourse to be naturalized in insidious ways.

Conclusion: Humor, Extreme Speech, and Marginalization

The precise language of humorous memes in this article is quite obviously less "extreme" than the graffiti on Tarapacá's literal walls, but expresses the same sentiments. These mundane types of humorous online speech are linked to speech associated with fear, hate, and extremist positions. The kinds of discourse represented by these memes painting Bolivians as racially distinct and suggesting they take up resources provide, or at least reinforce, foundational assumptions on which the more extreme texts on physical walls rely. This confluence of discourse between public walls with anonymous writers and social media accounts with named sharers provides an example of how the digital is always connected to the material world. More precisely, it demonstrates the ways discourses in virtual spaces are always linked to those circulating outside social media.

The formulaic nature of memes, and the fact that they are most often shared rather than directly authored by nortinos, demonstrates the importance of formulaic language to a study of extreme speech. Formulaic texts both diminish the apparent impact of the message through depoliticizing platitudes and mitigate the culpability of the sharer. Humor furthers both of these goals, making memes an important mode through which unpopular or potentially offensive notions may be publicly expressed with limited liability. Thus, this case study points to important ways that memes, as both formulaic and humorous, are potential vehicles for discourses that contravene societal expectations.

This social function of the meme is equally implicated in the ways it may provide members of the public a space to express extreme opinions insidiously, even if the sharer does not recognize it as such. When asking nortinos about anti-immigrant sentiments in both memes and graffiti, many explained them as a way of alleviating frustration about immigrants and related it to stress about their own marginalized or precarious position. This example then further points to nested marginalization in creating conditions that support or naturalize exclusionary discourses. In the case of nortinos, their positioning outside economic and political power leads them to define "Chileanness" against elite subjectivity, but equally creates an urge to protect the resources of the area (including copper, jobs associated with mining, and social services provided by the government) from outsiders construed as less deserving. The nexus of memes such as "Santiago no es Chile" with the ironic "Más chileno que nunca" illustrates the connection between these two groups, who are framed by nortinos as outside true Chilean experience. For people who consider their marginalization to be closely connected to a lack of public forum to express their frustrations with both groups, social media becomes an important site for defining and further reinforcing their own definitions of who belongs as a "true Chilean."

Extreme speech may be embedded within complex notions of citizenship, belonging, authenticity, and marginality (Bloemraad, Korteweg, and Yurdakul 2008) in which those marginalized through race, class, or other social categories enact exclusionary practices against others to gain some hold on social or political power. The maintenance of power structures in northern Chile—ideals of mestizaje and Chile as a country of modernity, among them—requires legitimation. Discourses are employed to naturalize, justify, and make it appear necessary that certain people have access to valuable social resources and others do not (van Dijk 1993). In sharing these memes, nortinos reinforce a worldview in which they are considered to be deserving of greater access to resources than Bolivians, but still maintain their marginal position in relation to the nation. The extreme speech of the physical walls and the mundane humor of the virtual walls work doubly to paint "real Chileans" as more deserving, precisely because they are marginalized within the nation and global capitalism.

Looking beyond northern Chile, then, this example demonstrates how memes provide a public forum for grievances, yet temper them through humor, formulism, and the collectivity of sharing. These three aspects of memes further reinforce group identity through limiting full understanding of the text to those who are familiar with humorous genres relevant to the in-group, who recognize the kinds of formulism at play, and who participate in sharing and appreciation through likes and commenting. So although memes may often be a key way in which marginalized people are able to speak back to power, the same features that make this work possible may equally be employed for opposite effect. Memes give voice to those who consider themselves voiceless, but also may shield them from culpability for racist and xenophobic speech.

Notes

*   This chapter is the reprinted version of the article with the same tile published in *International Journal of Communication* 2019, 13: 3122–3142.

1. Though graffiti and Facebook posts are disparate forms of public expression, they often share lackadaisical attention to grammar. In this case, "monos culiaos" is grammatically correct, but as with many of the social media examples in this article, the text's author seems unconcerned with grammatical accuracy.

2. Bolivian immigrants make up about 9% of all immigrants in Chile, about half of whom (18,000) live in Tarapacá, making up 5.5% of the region's population. The number of visas solicited by Bolivian nationals in Tarapacá between 2011 and 2015 (21,488), for example, was almost 150% of the number solicited by Argentine (293), Colombian (3,435), Ecuadorian (1,094), and Peruvian (11,147) nationals combined (Biblioteca del Congreso Nacional de Chile 2015)

3. While those working in the mining industry make roughly twice the national minimum monthly wage (CLP 402,000 or US$670 a month vs. CLP 250,000 or US$371 a month), national averages are closer to CLP 1,020,000 or US$1700.

4. While the Calendela Project finds that Chilean genetics are approximately 44% Indigenous American, 52% European, and 4% African, the 2011 Latinobarómetro survey found that 66% of Chileans identify as white, 25% categorize themselves as mestizo, and 8% consider themselves Indigenous (Corporación Latinobarómetro 2011).

References

Abu-Lughod, Lila. (1986) 2016. *Veiled Sentiments: Honor and Poetry in a Bedouin Society*. Berkeley: University of California Press.

Biblioteca del Congreso Nacional de Chile. 2015. "Chile y la migración: Los extranjeros en Chile" [Chile and migration: the foreigners in Chile]. https://www.bcn.cl/siit/actualidad-territorial/chile-y-la-migracion-los -extranjeros-en-chile.

Bloemraad, Irene, Anna Korteweg, and Gökçe Yurdakul. 2008. "Citizenship and Immigration: Multiculturalism, Assimilation, and Challenges to the Nation-State." *Annual Review of Sociology* 34:153–179.

Bourdieu, Pierre. 1991. *Language and Symbolic Power*, edited by J. B. Thompson. Cambridge, MA: Harvard University Press.

Bourdieu, Pierre, and Loïc Wacquant. 2004. Symbolic Violence. In *Violence in War and Peace*, edited by N. Scheper-Hughes and P. Bourgouis, 272–274. Malden, MA: Blackwell.

Bucholtz, Mary, and Kira Hall. 2008. "All of the Above: New Coalitions in Sociocultural Linguistics." *Journal of Sociolinguistics* 12 (4): 401–431.

Carreño, Camilo. 2016. "Piñera: Muchas de las bandas de delincuentes en Chile son de extranjeros" [Piñera: Many of the bands of deliquents in Chile are foreigners]. *La Tercera*, November 29. http://www.latercera.com /noticia/pinera-muchas-las-bandas-delincuentes-chile-extranjeros/.

Castells, Manuel. 1996. *The Rise of the Network Society*. Vol. 1 of *The Information Age: Economy, Society, and Culture*. Oxford: Blackwell.

Coleman, E. Gabriella. 2010. "Ethnographic Approaches to Digital Media." *Annual Review of Anthropology* 39:487–505.

———. 2012. "Phreaks, Hackers, and Trolls: The Politics of Transgression and Spectacle." In *The Social Media Reader*, edited by M. Mandeberg, 99–119. New York: New York University Press.

Corporación Latinobarómetro. 2011. "Latinobarómetro" [Latino barometer]. http://www.latinobarometro.org /lat.jsp.

Corporación Nacional de Desarrollo Indígena. 2014. "Áreas de desarrollo indígena del norte de Chile" (Areas of Indigenous development of the north of Chile). http://siic.conadi.cl/.

Crenshaw, Kimberlé. 2003. "Demarginalizing the Intersection of Race and Sex: A Black Feminist Critique of Antidiscrimination Doctrine, Feminist Theory, and Antiracist Politics." In *Critical Race Feminism: A Reader*, edited by A. K. Wing, 23–33. New York: New York University Press.

Davison, Patrick. 2012. "The Language of Internet Memes." In *The Social Media Reader*, edited by M. Mandiberg, 120–136. New York: New York University Press.

The Economist. 2013. "Mining in Chile: Copper Solution." April 27, 2013. https://www.economist.com/business /2013/04/27/copper-solution.

Ekman, Mattias. 2015. "Online Islamophobia and the Politics of Fear: Manufacturing the Green Scare." *Ethnic and Racial Studies* 38:1986–2002.

Fairclough, Norman. 1985. "Critical and Descriptive Goals in Discourse Analysis." *Journal of Pragmatics* 9:739–763.

———. 2003. *Analysing Discourse: Textual Analysis for Social Research*. New York: Routledge.

Faulkner, Simon, Vis Farida, and Francesco D'Orazio. 2018. "Analyzing Social Media Images." In *The SAGE Handbook of Social Media*, edited by J. Burgess, A. Marwick, and T. Poell, 160–178. Thousand Oaks, CA: Sage.

Frazier, Lessie Jo. 2007. *Salt in the Sand: Memory, Violence, and the Nation-State in Chile, 1890 to the Present.* Durham, NC: Duke University Press.

Fu, King Wa, and Chung Hong Chan. 2015. "Networked Collective Action in the 2014 Hong Kong Occupy Movement: Analysing a Facebook Sharing Network." Presented at the 2nd International Conference on Public Policy, Milan.

Fuchs, Christian. 2012. "Social Media, Riots, and Revolutions." *Capital and Class* 36 (3): 383–391.

Gerbaudo, Paolo. 2012. *Tweets and the Streets: Social Media and Contemporary Activism*. London: Pluto.

Gumperz, John, and Jenny Cook-Gumperz. 1982. *Language and Social Identity*. Cambridge: Cambridge University Press.

Haynes, Nell. 2016. *Social Media in Northern Chile*. London: UCL Press.

Hervik, Peter. 2019. "Ritualized Opposition in Danish Online Practices of Extremist Language and Thought." *International Journal of Communication* 13:3104–312.

Hochschild, Jennifer. 2003. "Social Class in Public Schools." *Journal of Social Issues* 59 (4): 821–840.

Hooker, Juliet. 2009. *Race and the Politics of Solidarity*. New York: Oxford University Press.

Horst, Henry, and Daniel Miller, eds. 2012. *Digital Anthropology*. London: Bloomsbury.

INDH (Instituto Nacional de Derechos Humanos). 2017. *Informe anual situación de los derechos humanos en Chile* [Annual report on the situation of human rights in Chile]. https://www.indh.cl/bb/wp-content/uploads /2017/12/01_Informe-Anual-2017.pdf.

———. 2018. *Discriminación racial en Chile: Más* blancos *y menos sucios, así nos percibimos* [Racial discrimination in Chile: More white and less dirty, that's how we perceive ourselves]. https://www.indh.cl/discriminacion -racial-chile-mas-blancos-menos-sucios-asi-nos-percibimos/.

Jenkins, Henry, Sam Ford, and Joshua Green. 2013. *Spreadable Media: Creating Value and Meaning in a Networked Culture*. New York: New York University Press.

Juris, Jeffrey. 2012. "Reflections on #Occupy Everywhere: Social Media, Public Space, and Emerging Logics of Aggregation." *American Ethnologist* 39 (2): 259–279.

Kozak, Piotr. 2017. "Peruvian Immigrants in Hospital after Being Set on Fire by Chile Fishermen." *The Guardian*, July 17, 2017. https://www.theguardian.com/world/2017/jul/18/chile-peru-immigrants-burned-fishermen.

Launay, Robert. 2006. "Practical Joking." *Cahiers d'études africaines* 184:795–808.

Levi, Primo. 1989. *The Drowned and the Saved*. London: Abacus.

Lim, Merlyna. 2012. "Clicks, Cabs, and Coffee Houses: Social Media and Oppositional Movements in Egypt, 2004–2011." *Journal of Communication* 62 (2): 231–248.

Madison, D. Soyini. 2012. *Critical Ethnography: Methods, Ethics, and Performance*. Thousand Oaks, CA: Sage.

Meseguer, Covadonga, and Achim Kemmerling. 2016. "What Do You Fear? Anti-immigrant Sentiment in Latin America." *International Migration Review*. https://onlinelibrary.wiley.com/doi/abs/10.1111/imre.12269.

Miller, Daniel, Elisabetta Costa, Nell Haynes, Tom McDonald, Razvan Nicolescu, Jolynna Sinanan, Juliano Spyer, Shriram Venkatraman and Xin Yuan Wang. 2016. *How the World Changed Social Media*. London: UCL Press.

Milner, Ryan. 2013. "Hacking the Social: Internet Memes, Identity Antagonism, and the Logic of Lulz." *Fibreculture* 22:62–92.

Miltner, Kate. 2014. "'There's No Place for Lulz on LOLCats': The Role of Genre, Gender, and Group Identity in the Interpretation and Enjoyment of an Internet Meme. *First Monday* 19 (8).

———. 2018. "Internet Memes." In *The SAGE Handbook of Social Media*, edited by J. Burgess, A. Marwick, and T. Poell, 412–428. Thousand Oaks, CA: Sage.

Morozov, Evgeny. 2009. "From Slacktivism to Activism." *Foreign Policy*, September 5, 2009. https://foreignpolicy.com/2009/09/05/from-slacktivism-to-activism/.

Nayaran, Gyanendra. 2007. "Addressing the Digital Divide: e-Governance and m-Governance in a Hub and Spoke Model." *Electronic Journal of Information Systems in Developing Countries* 31 (1): 1–14.

Norris, Pippa. 2001. *Digital Divide: Civic Engagement, Information Poverty, and the Internet Worldwide*. Cambridge: Cambridge University Press.

Noy, Shiri, and Koen Voorend. 2015. "Social Rights and Migrant Realities: Migration Policy Reform and Migrants' Access to Health Care in Costa Rica, Argentina, and Chile." *Journal of International Migration and Integration* 17 (2): 605–629.

Núcleo de Estudios Metropolitanos. 2015. *Indice de Calidad de Vida Urbana* [Index of quality of urban life]. Santiago, Chile: Pontificia Universidad Católica de Chile y la Cámara Chilena de la Construcción. http://www.estudiosurbanos.uc.cl/images/noticias-actividades/2015/Mayo_2015/PPT_ICVU_2015_Conferencia.pdf.

Omi, Micheal, and Howard Winant. 1994. *Racial Formation in the United States: From the 1960s to 1990s*. New York: Routledge.

Organization for Economic Cooperation and Development. 2015. *OECD Income Distribution and Poverty Database*. http://www.oecd.org/els/social/inequality.

Papacharissi, Zizi. A. 2010. *A Private Sphere: Democracy in a Digital Age*. Cambridge: Polity.

Pertierra, Anna Cristina 2018. *Media Anthropology for the Digital Age*. Malden, MA: Wiley.

Pink, Sarah, Heather Horst, John Postill, Larissa Hjorth, Tania Lewis, and Jo Tacchi. 2016. *Digital Ethnography: Principles and Practices*. Thousand Oaks, CA: Sage.

Postero, Nancy. 2007. *Now We Are Citizens: Indigenous Politics in Postmulticultural Bolivia*. Stanford, CA: Stanford University Press.

Postill, John. 2012. "Digital Politics and Political Engagement." In *Digital Anthropology*, edited by H. Horst and D. Miller, 165–184. London: Bloomsbury.

———. 2016. "Remote Ethnography: Studying Digital Politics in Spain and Indonesia from Afar." In *Routledge Companion to Digital Ethnography*, edited by L. Hjorth, H. Horst, A. Galloway, and G. Bell, 61–69. New York: Routledge.

———. 2018. *The Rise of Nerd Politics: Digital Activism and Political Change*. London: Pluto.

Postill, John, and Pink, Sarah. 2012. "Social Media Ethnography: The Digital Researcher in a Messy Web." *Media International Australia* 145:123–134.

Richards, Patricia. 2013. *Race and the Chilean Miracle: Neoliberalism, Democracy, and Indigenous Rights*. Pittsburgh, PA: University of Pittsburgh Press.

Shifman, Limor. 2013. *Memes in Digital Culture*. Cambridge, MA: MIT Press.

Spivak, Gayatri Chakravorty 1988. *Can the Subaltern Speak?* Basingstoke: Macmillan.

Spradley, James. 1979. *The Ethnographic Interview*. Belmont, CA: Wadsworth.

———. 1980. *Participant Observation*. Long Grove, IL: Waveland.

Taylor, Erin. 2014. "The Curation of the Self in the Age of the Internet." Paper presented at the IUAES/JASCA Conference, Tokyo.

Thurlough, Crispin. 2018. "Digital Discourse: Locating Language in New/Social Media." In *The SAGE Handbook of Social Media*, edited by J. Burgess, A. Marwick, and T. Poell, 135–145. Thousand Oaks, CA: Sage.

Tsing, Anna. 1993. *In the Realm of the Diamond Queen: Marginality in an Out-of-the-Way Place*. Princeton, NJ: Princeton University Press.

Tufekci, Zeynep, and Christopher Wilson. 2012. "Social Media and the Decision to Participate in Political Protest: Observations from Tahrir Square." *Journal of Communication* 62 (2): 363–379.

Udupa, Sahana. 2019. "Nationalism in the Digital Age: Fun as a Metapractice of Extreme Speech." *International Journal of Communication* 13:3143–3163.

Udupa, Sahana, and Matti Pohjonen. 2017. "Extreme Speech Online: An Anthropological Critique of Hate Speech Debates." *International Journal of Communication* 11:1173–1191.

van Dijk, Teun. 1993. "Principles of Discourse Analysis." *Discourse and Society* 4 (2): 249–283.

Vergara, Jorge Iván, and Hans Gundermann. 2012. "Conformación y dinámica interna del campo identitario regional en Tarapacá y Los Lagos, Chile" [Conformation and internal dynamics of the regional identity field in Tarapacá and Los Lagos, Chile]. *Chungara, Revista de Antropología Chilena* 44 (1): 115–134.

Wade, Peter. 1997. *Race and Ethnicity in Latin America*. Chicago: Pluto.

Weiping, Cui. 2009. "I Am a Grass-Mud Horse." *China Digital Times*. https://chinadigitaltimes.net/2009/03/cui-weiping崔卫平-i-am-a-grass-mud-horse/

Weismantel, Mary. 2001. *Cholas and Pistacos: Tales of Race and Sex in the Andes*. Chicago: University of Chicago Press.

World Bank. 2017. "World Development Indicators." World Bank Databank. https://databank.worldbank.org/country/bolivia?view=chart.

Yilmaz, Ferruh. 2012. "Right-Wing Hegemony and Immigration: How the Populist Far-Right Achieved Hegemony through the Immigration Debate in Europe." *Current Sociology* 60 (3): 368–381.

PART 3

ORGANIZATION AND DISORGANIZATION

IN PART 3, THE CONTRIBUTIONS FOCUS ON COMPLEX political contestations in local political contexts and how organized structures and disorganized networks have fueled extreme speech with divergent consequences for established power and emerging dissenting groups. Implicit in all the contributions is the tension between moral values and legal restrictions, which is also part of a global trend in the mediation of populism. Discourses of moral rage and moral claims often go beyond current constitutional law and international conventions, but they draw attention on social media, thereby facilitating attempts to appeal for support.

In chapter 12, Juergen Schaflechner focuses on Pakistan and stories of individual victims of blasphemy accusations. The author explains that accusations of blasphemy are very serious (especially for the accused), and content posted in another person's name has led to angry mobs killing the accused. Digital communication has exacerbated the force and effect of blasphemy accusations. He suggests that protests and other emotional responses to alleged acts of blasphemy might be understood as performative and "citational"—inasmuch as these responses rely on a framework of previous emotional archives.

In chapter 13, Jonas Kaiser turns to far-right groups in Europe, especially those active in Germany, and observes that social media platforms shorten the path between fringe and center, as the "alternative media and conspiracy theory" community serves as a bridge between distinct communities within the far right. He also shows the role assigned to physical spaces in shaping online expression and participation. By comparing maps of far-right Facebook pages with the maps depicting arson attacks on refugee shelters, the author reveals the connections between online hateful expressions and hate crimes that take place off-line.

Indah Pratidina's chapter 14 draws attention to Indonesia. She observes that greater visibility on social media creates greater scrutiny and policing of women's bodies, behaviors, and status, as can be seen from user responses to prominent female political figures. Examining the presidential elections of 2019 in Indonesia as a critical media event, the author shows how social media platforms have become a key conduit for polarizing extreme speech often drawing reference to gendered discourses around "motherhood."

Erkan Saka's concluding chapter turns the focus to Turkey, with interviews and a study of Twitter trolls, including paid political troll armies. Nonconformists are attacked by trolls, including the nonconforming practices of the airing of old Western movies, unisex restrooms, a woman ceasing to wear a headscarf, antirefugee sentiment (the Turkish government is pro-Syrian refugee), campaigns of political opponents, and other debates. The Turkish online trolls bet on and profit from the ambiguity of hate speech versus acceptable speech.

Revealing the connections between online networks and physical spaces, these chapters illustrate new geographies, material arrangements, and new kinds of digital visibility that multiply the force of extreme speech within local and national political fields.

12

BLASPHEMY ACCUSATIONS AS EXTREME SPEECH ACTS IN PAKISTAN

Jürgen Schaflechner

B LASPHEMY ALLEGATIONS ARE A SENSITIVE ISSUE IN TODAY'S Pakistan. After describing the socioreligious history of such accusations, I will show how the increasing digitalization of Pakistan's public spheres has exacerbated a situation in which an accusation of blasphemy has little or no possible response. The moment such accusations enter a public arena (online or offline), their verdictive force often leads to life-threatening consequences for the accused person. To analyze such accusations, I will provide some background on Pakistan's blasphemy laws. To explore accusations of blasphemy theoretically, I will locate them within the conceptual framework of extreme speech and then turn toward speech act theory to understand how such accusations unfold their force—and often with life-threatening effects.

Setting the Scene: Pakistan's Blasphemy Laws

The blasphemy laws continue to divide Pakistan's society. Many religious scholars argue that the laws represent the Quran and the Sunna and, therefore, cannot be abolished or amended without committing blasphemy in the act (Sayālvī 2016; Turābi, n.d.; Qadrī 2012). More liberal interpretations maintain that the ambivalent nature of the laws make them prone to misuse and to being used as an instrument of personal animosity (Siddique and Hayat 2008; Abbas 2013). Studies show that blasphemy cases have steadily increased since the 1980s (Siddique and Hayat 2008, 322–327). Quoting the Center for Social Justice, a 2016 report by the Human Rights Commission of Pakistan states that at least 1,472 people were accused of blasphemy between 1987 and 2016. The biggest portion of this number is made up of Muslims (730) and Ahmadis (501), followed by Christians (205) and Hindus (26).[1] Furthermore, the report points out that in 2015 alone, courts found fifteen of twenty-five acquitted cases to have been fabricated based on personal vendettas. The remaining cases were cleared on the basis of a lack of evidence or the accused person being declared insane (Human Rights Commission of Pakistan 2016, 96). Liberal Pakistanis take such reports as supporting their stance that the blasphemy laws represent a relic of the past and thus should be amended or abolished. A discussion of the blasphemy decrees and their advantages and disadvantages

198 | *Digital Hate*

for Pakistani society, however, has so far been repeatedly thwarted by the united protests of the religious right.

The Islamic Republic's contentious blasphemy laws are modeled on the Indian Penal Code (IPC), which was put in place by the British in 1860 (Ahmad 2009, 178). Chapter 15 of the IPC dealt with possible offenses to religion and was originally intended to curb tensions within South Asia's multireligious social setting. Later, under the government of military dictator Zia ul-Haq (1977–1988), these decrees became the foundation for laws that were mainly intended to protect Islam and the honor of the Prophet Muhammad. Zia's comprehensive constitutional changes touched all corners of Pakistani society, and the Islamization of Pakistan's laws further marginalized women, Shias, and religious minorities.

The roots of this Islamization process were already visible in the Pakistan National Alliance (PNA), a consortium of left, right, and center parties united through their common opposition to the Bhutto government in the mid-1970s. The PNA's religious parties' demand to implement the *niẓām-i muṣṭafī* (the law of the Prophet) and to create a society built on Islamic law was taken up by the new military regime. Pakistan's strategic position in the Afghanistan war, which coincided with Zia's rule, then brought the United States and international money into the country and cemented the military regime's power. Zia's crucial role in the US–Soviet war gave the dictator a free hand to change Pakistan's society without fearing international protest against some of his severe human rights violations. These alterations included the installation of sharia courts, which aimed to ensure that the country's laws were conforming to the Quran and the Sunna; the *ḥudūd* ordinances, which dictated severe punishment for crimes such as stealing or adultery; and changes in the school curriculum and textbooks to spread the ideology of Pakistan (Ispahani 2017, 118–132). The Saudi support for certain *mujāhidīn* groups fighting in Afghanistan further supported the spread of a distinct Wahabi interpretation of Islam and gave additional momentum to the Islamization of the country (Abbas 2013, 67). Zia's amendments to the Pakistani Penal Code's (PPC's) chapter on religious offenses must be understood with consideration of the background of this general Islamization process.

Zia's government added five additional clauses to the PPC over a period of several years. All the new amendments deal, in particular, with punishable offenses against Zia's Sunni version of Islam. Even though PPC 295-A—an addition made previously by the British in the course of the *Rangīlā Rasūl* incident—states that all "malicious acts intended to outrage religious feelings of *any* class" (emphasis added) are punishable, non-Muslims file blasphemy charges only rarely in Pakistan today.[2] The addition of 298-B and -C are particularly designed to criminalize the rituals and practices of the Ahmadi community, which had been declared non-Muslim by the Bhutto government as early as 1974. Zia's amendments also make any maltreatment of the Quran (295-B) and any derogatory remarks about the Prophet Muhammad (295-C) and his family (298-A) punishable by law (Siddique and Hayat 2008, 338). The first amendment to the PPC from 1980, for example, reads, "**298A. Use of derogatory remarks, etc., in respect of holy personages.** Whoever by words, either spoken or written, or by visible representation, or by any imputation, innuendo or insinuation, directly or indirectly, defiles the sacred name of any wife (Ummul-Mumineen), or members of the family (Ahle-bait), of the Holy Prophet (peace be upon him), or any of the righteous Caliphs

(Khulafa-e-Raashideen) or companions (Sahaaba) of the Holy Prophet (peace be upon him) shall be punished with imprisonment of either description for a term which may extend to three years, or with fine, or with both."[3]

Although offenses disrespecting the Prophet's family do not call for capital punishment, pejorative remarks about the Prophet's wives can have serious consequences, as illustrated by the case of Junaid Jamshed in 2014. Jamshed originally rose to fame as a Pakistani pop singer with the band Vital Signs but later turned toward religion and became a television preacher for the Tablighi Jamaat, a proselytizing branch of the Deobandi school. In 2014, Jamshed spoke about the "frail female nature" in one of his TV sermons and used Ayesha, the Prophet's wife, as an example. Following the broadcast, a leader of the Sunni Tehreek, a militarized Barelvi party, registered a First Investigation Report (FIR) under 298-A in response to Jamshed's alleged derogatory remarks about Ayesha. Because an insult to the Prophet's wife is also an insult to the Prophet Muhammad, Jamshed was also charged with blasphemy under 295-C, a clause that, when proven in court, calls for the death penalty. In a subsequent video published on social media, Junaid publicly begged for forgiveness for his remarks. Although his followers were willing to overlook his mistake, the Sunni Tehreek stated that there were no excuses for what Jamshed had done and that the only proper response to an act of blasphemy was the death of the blasphemer. Jamshed did not face any formal charges but died shortly thereafter in a plane crash in 2016. Many Barelvi communities interpreted his death as a stroke of divine justice. Their opinions can be found on social media and often describe the incident as the legitimate price Jamshed had to pay for his sacrilegious words about the Prophet's wife.[4]

Within the scope of this chapter, Zia's last addition to the PPC, 295-C, is of particular interest. This section punishes derogatory remarks about the Prophet and demands the death penalty for blasphemers. The clause is written in an enigmatic style that makes it prone to misuse. As the aforementioned case has shown, the absence of a definition for what counts as a "derogatory remark" makes it possible to attach 295-C to a variety of other accusations: "**295-C. Use of derogatory remarks, etc., in respect of the Holy Prophet.** Whoever by words, either spoken or written, or by visible representation, or by any imputation, innuendo, or insinuation, directly or indirectly, defiles the sacred name of the Holy Prophet Muhammad (peace be upon him) shall be punished with death, *or imprisonment for life, and shall also be liable to fine."[5] In the 1990s, the Federal Sharia Court made the death penalty mandatory for blasphemy cases and removed the possibility of life imprisonment.[6] The amendment followed a petition by an advocate and religious scholar named Muhammad Ismail Qureshy. According to his own statement, Qureshy had had a dream about the Prophet Muhammad that incentivized him to legally struggle for the removal of the imprisonment option (Qureshy 2008, 60). In 2005, the contentious clause was reaffirmed by the Supreme Court of Pakistan (Qureshy 2008, 61). Notwithstanding this harsh punishment, no one has so far been executed by the state of Pakistan for charges under 295-C. These laws illustrate that protection of religious sentiments of the majority population overrides secular systems of public justice and citizenship rights. Nevertheless, the fact that modern nation-states support the religious feelings of majoritarian groups is neither surprising nor limited to Pakistan (Saeed 2015).

This form of rationalizing and legalizing religious violence (Ahmad 2009, 183) is also legally ambivalent given the amendments' vague linguistic style. Besides the crucial question of what actually counts as a derogatory remark, the omission of an intention clause is another contentious point. Although the aforementioned IPC from 1860 stresses intention as a necessary reason to bring blasphemy to court, this clause was left out in the later amendment of the PPC sections 295-B, 295-C, and 298-A (Siddique and Hayat 2008, 342).

The grave outcome of such neglect is seen in the following case. Dr. Younas Shaikh, a professor at a private medical college in Islamabad, was charged with blasphemy in October 2000. During a lecture on the pre-Islamic period, Shaikh had responded to a student's question by saying that Muhammad was a non-Muslim until he turned forty years old and thus that the Prophet had not been circumcised. For such alleged derogatory remarks, a local religious leader, Maulana Abdul Rauf from the Organization of the Finality of Prophethood (Majlis-i Khatm-i Nabuvat), charged Shaikh with blasphemy under PPC 295-C (Abbas 2013, 76–77). Even though Shaikh had not intended to attack the Prophet, his answer was perceived as an affront by some of his students, and he was brought to court as a result. Shaikh could not seek bail and thus remained in jail for three years. Eventually, the college professor was acquitted, but he needed to leave Pakistan shortly thereafter given the danger of being assassinated by religious zealots (Abbas 2013, 78–79). The absence of an intention clause in 295-C rendered a FIR and a subsequent court case possible. The public attention following the case and the likelihood of vigilante justice ended Shaikh's career in Pakistan and forced him to leave the country.

Another consequence following the eradication of the intention clause directly influenced the way evidence for an act of blasphemy is presented in court. The corpus delicti cannot actually be named by the witnesses without perpetrating yet another act of blasphemy. This was evident in the case of *Salamat Masih and Another v. the State* (Feb 23, 1995 PCRLJ 881). Salamat Masih was a 13-year-old Christian boy who, in 1993, was accused with two others—Rehmat Masih and Manzoor Masih—of having written blasphemous words on the wall of a mosque. During the court proceedings, when the witnesses were asked to confirm the crime and to prove that blasphemy had actually been committed, the bystanders could not repeat the words—as this would have recommitted the crime. According to Asma Jahangir, a human rights lawyer from Lahore and cofounder of the Human Rights Commission of Pakistan, the prosecuting side's core witness could not reproduce the blasphemy and thus could not prove that an actual crime had been committed. The court's decision in the case, therefore, was mainly built on the witnesses' personal impressions. The case was acquitted in February 1995. During the trial, however, the three Christian boys repeatedly received threats and, at one point, were attacked by an unknown gunman after leaving a court hearing. The attack left Manzoor dead and Salamat and Rehmat seriously injured. After the court declared their innocence in 1995, Germany granted them asylum (Siddique and Hayat 2008, 327–334).

The opaque formulation of the blasphemy laws, especially of 295-C, together with the absence of the intent requirement, makes the law a malleable means for personal revenge and vendetta. The decrees' enigmatic rhetoric provides a legally ambivalent framework that allows for a variety of accusations to fall under their jurisdiction. Because any remarks may be understood as "derogatory"—particularly when detached from their context—the current blasphemy laws support an atmosphere of paranoia and a culture of denunciation. This does not imply that every allegation immediately leads to an FIR or a criminal conviction in court (Ahmad 2009, 189–197; Siddique and Hayat 2008, 348–350). Blasphemy charges, however, are a serious matter because they invite prosecution, mob violence, and vigilante justice. A blasphemy stigma is often more dangerous than the actual criminal conviction. So far, Pakistan has not executed anyone on the charge of blasphemy. However, many alleged blasphemers have been killed by raging mobs or lone assassins who took it upon themselves to defend the Prophet's honor. How did this situation change with the ubiquitous digitalization of technology and culture in Pakistan in the past few years?

Blasphemy 2.0

In August 2016, the Pakistani government passed the Prevention of Electronic Crime Act (PECA; also Prevention of Electronic Crime Bill), which covered online acts of blasphemy. The PECA marks a watershed moment in Pakistan's engagement with blasphemy, from merely restricting its access to actively prosecuting those engaged in the (intentional and unintentional) distribution of blasphemy on the internet. Beginning in spring 2017, the government started to systematically search for and take down web pages that displayed content that was considered blasphemous. Chaudhary Nisar, the minister of the interior at that time, stated that the government had blocked 152 Facebook pages and had put eight people on an exit control list for the publication of transgressive material.[7] By October 2018, around thirty-five thousand pages had been blocked because of sacrilegious content.[8]

Former blasphemy laws had not covered online content, whereas the PECA targets particular forms of speech on the internet. Section 34, for example, gives the authorities the power to remove anything that is against the "glory of Islam" (PECA 2016).[9] This section helped the Pakistan Telecommunication Authority (PTA) obtain the ability to block any kind of content deemed controversial. After the PECA was passed, arrests for online offenses rose from 49 in 2016 to 209 in 2018.[10] Furthermore, the Pakistani government has requested companies such as Twitter and Facebook to help find blasphemous material shared on their platforms. In a personal interview, Farieha Aziz, a journalist and activist at Bolo Bhi, an organization working for digital security in Pakistan, criticized such measures and argued that a large number of activists were detained on the basis of the PECA. According to Aziz, PECA serves as an instrument of control.

Responding to a court order, the PTA sent out a text message to all mobile phones in Pakistan in May 2017 requesting that citizens report blasphemous content. The PTA told all citizens that "uploading [and] sharing of blasphemous content on [the] internet is a punishable offense under the law. Such content should be reported on info.pta.gov.pk for legal action."[11] The PTA's home page also features a request to report blasphemous content. The text reads, "The public is requested to help the PTA to block blasphemy and other content against Islam present on Social Media and especially Facebook."[12] Such announcements put a spotlight on online communication and give the public the mandate to raise new forms of blasphemy allegations. In an environment where an accusation is often already a conviction, such encouragement exacerbates an already charged atmosphere.

These developments also have a significant influence on the nature of blasphemy accusations. In an interview with the blog *Wired*, Usama Khilji, also from the nonprofit Bolo Bhi, described the emergence of new forms of allegations involving blasphemy online. Accusations surface, for example, in the course of religious minorities and members of sectarian groups arguing about their own religion online. Accusations have also been made possible through fake social media accounts set up to frame (political or personal) opponents. In addition, the simple "liking" of certain online posts that may be considered sacrilegious can lead to accusations of blasphemy.[13] This list is not exhaustive, and as I will show, new kinds of accusations have been made possible through sociotechnological developments. A few examples will help to clarify this point.

In June 2017, Taimur Raza became the first person in Pakistan sentenced to death based on an accusation of committing blasphemy online. Raza, a 31-year-old man from a lower middle-class Shia family, was arrested in 2016 and later charged with blasphemy in an anti-terrorism court in Bahawalpur.[14] Raza had engaged in a sectarian debate on Facebook with, what became later known, an agent of an antiterrorism force aiming to curb online blasphemy. Raza was arrested at a bus stop in Bahawalpur. According to the police, blasphemous material and clips featuring hate speech against the Deobandis, a religious sect in Pakistan, were found on his phone.[15] The verdict in *The State vs Taimur Raza* (2017; Antiterrorism Court, Bahawalpur) states that "this is a purely case of technical and scientific evidence as the accused mobile phone and Face-book [*sic*] for spreading derogatory remarks about the Holy Prophet Hazrat Mohammad (PBUH) . . . and injured the feelings of true Muslims" (under bullet 9). Raza was charged with, among other things, violating 298-A and 295-C of the PPC and awaits execution by hanging.

On April 13, 2017, a 23-year-old a journalism student, Mashal Khan, was killed by an angry mob on a university campus after he had been accused of spreading blasphemous content on social media. The university administration had put an announcement online that three students were under investigation for blasphemy.[16] Even though the accusations were not proven, a mob consisting of students and university staff attacked Khan in his room in the students' dormitory. The men started beating him with fists and wooden planks. One of them drew a gun and shot him in the chest and in the head. After the shots, the group temporarily dispersed but then reassembled to beat Khan's lifeless body. Some reports say that his corpse was thrown off a balcony from the second floor of the university building.[17] Long after his death, students and university staff kept mishandling Khan's body with the police standing by, not intervening.[18] The murder was filmed on a mobile phone, which later led to the arrest of sixty-one people suspected of being involved.[19] In an interview with one of the suspects, the BBC reported that the students initially had no intention of killing Mashal Khan but rather wanted to warn him. The man who shot Khan, however, stated that he had no regrets and believed that Khan deserved to die.[20] A later report by the Joint Investigation Team revealed that the content had been posted in Khan's name by the Pakhtun Students Federation, a secular student group, as a way to get rid of him.[21] Apparently, the murder was semi-orchestrated to silence Khan's popular criticism of corruption at Mardan University.[22] An antiterrorism court in Haripur sentenced the shooter to death and five other people to life in prison. Twenty-five other participants were given jail sentences.[23]

In May 2017, a Hindu man, Prakash Kumar, from the city of Hub, Baluchistan, was accused of blasphemy.[24] Different versions of the events were reported; however, all agree that during the tumultuous riots that followed, a ten-year-old boy was killed.[25] The following version was provided by Kumar, who was understandably reluctant to talk about this issue and only agreed to be interviewed after an influential Hindu nongovernmental organization intervened on my behalf. The following is an excerpt of a phone conversation I had with him in March 2019:

> Somebody sent me the image of the Kaaba to my phone. I knew that the picture was there, but I am not an idiot and would never share this with anyone. Someone framed me. Someone took my phone and said he wanted to make a call. He shared the picture of the Kaaba over WhatsApp. It was shared to all of my contacts, more than a hundred people. After that people started to call and asked me if I am a Muslim. I told them that I am not. So, they asked why I would share such an image if I am not a Muslim. They started to blackmail me. They asked for money and threatened me. I told them that I have no money to pay. Then a group of Muslims came and burned all the things in my shop. Everything I had is destroyed, my work, my shop, my house, everything is destroyed. There were no Mullahs involved in this incident. These were mainly young people. I told them, even if I had shared this picture then it would be OK, this is not a sin. We asked twenty-five or thirty lawyers to help, but they all turned us down.
>
> They put me into jail for my own safety, so that the issue would cool down. Life in jail was good. People really took care of me. They gave me food, and no one harmed me. I was in my cell just as if I would be living at home in my own room. I was not a prisoner. I also got a guy who helped me with washing my clothes, doing the dishes, and with cleaning. They changed him all eight to ten days so that he would not come to know what the problem is. I stayed in jail for fourteen months and now live in a different village. What happened to me happened. I have no complaints with the people who did that. I have only problems with my own community. Because when I came out of jail, nobody wanted to have anything to do with me or gave me any support for my children or for me to start a new life. I have a lot of complaints about my own community.

This case is unique because it circles around the sharing of an image that, in itself, is not considered sacrilegious but, on the contrary, shows one of the holiest sites in Islam. The fact that the image of the Kaaba had been distributed by a non-Muslim was used to accuse Kumar of blasphemy.[26]

Such case studies are only a glimpse into the myriad ramifications of what happens when blasphemy accusations go online. In a June 2019 conversation with Asad Jamal, a Lahore-based lawyer who represents people charged with blasphemy, he pointed out that we currently lack the empirical data to completely understand the link between the digitalization of Pakistan's daily life, the government's attempts to actively persecute online blasphemy, and the rising number of online blasphemy accusations. However, cases such as those described, he states, are indications that stricter regulations of online speech have thus far not curbed incidents of (alleged) blasphemy but rather provide accusers with new planes for polarization.

Extreme Speech Acts

How can we theorize public accusations of blasphemy—both online and offline—on the basis of the significant impact they frequently have on the life of the accused person? What form of speech is a blasphemy accusation in Pakistan when a mere allegation may have life-threatening consequences? In an attempt to answer these questions, I will begin by engaging with the framework of extreme speech (Udupa and Pohjonen 2019). With the help of John L. Austin (1975) and Stanley Cavell (2006), I will argue that the concept of extreme speech may be differentiated by analyzing its performative character. Accusations of blasphemy are a special form of extreme speech acts, set apart by their illocutionary force and their perlocutionary effect.

Pohjonen and Udupa (2019) describe extreme speech as a range of practices marked mainly by three characteristics. First, they emphasize the concept's contextuality, which aims at understanding "the cultural variations of speech acts." In other words, what may count as an extreme utterance in one context may not trigger any kind of reaction in another. Pohjonen and Udupa's second point pertains particularly to processes triggered through "sociotechnological" developments. While not all extreme speech is articulated online (Hervik, chap. 8), new forms of digital communication have encouraged the production of online vitriol. Third, they establish a link between extreme speech and violence. Forms of violence incited by extreme speech may be both exclusionary and emancipatory, depending on the politics involved.

The concept of extreme speech covers many of the things that matter when we speak about blasphemy accusations in this context. First, they are highly contextual and contingent on Pakistan's particular history. Second, as we have seen, digitalization processes have provided new planes for accusations. Finally, they are linked to (often extreme) forms of violence. In short, accusations of blasphemy form an incitement to violence (state and vigilante violence) that is highly specific to Pakistani mass publics and has also moved recently to online spaces.

There is more to be said about what such accusations do when they are uttered in public. Certain accusations are not only a form of judgment but also force the accused person into a new reality. As we have seen, blasphemy is, first and foremost, conceived by the PPC as a severe transgression that is punishable by death. Although the Pakistani state has never executed anyone for blasphemy so far, public accusations often produce conditions with life-threatening consequences. Not every accusation will automatically lead to such extremes, but publicized under the right conditions, these accusatory speech acts have a strong force and uncontrollable effects. To analyze the power of such speech acts and the subjectivities they enunciate, I turn to the work of Austin (1975) and Cavell (2006).

Force and Effect: Illocutionary and Perlocutionary Speech Acts

In *How to Do Things with Words*, Austin (1975) shows how uttering certain sentences in particular environments can also mean *to do* them.[27] Austin separates the locutionary, the illocutionary, and the perlocutionary speech acts. He writes, "We distinguished the locutionary act . . . which has a *meaning*; the illocutionary act which has a certain *force* in saying something; the perlocutionary act which is *the achieving of* certain *effects* by saying something" (Austin 1975, 120, emphasis in the original). While the locutionary act describes any semiotic plane and, thus, does not need to discern any further, the conceptualization of the illocutionary and the perlocutionary speech acts is important. We will look at illocution first.

For Austin (1975), illocutionary speech acts have the force to perform what they describe. One of Austin's most famous examples in this regard is the "I do" when uttered during a marriage ceremony. In this instance, the sentence is not a description of what is happening (this would be the locutionary act) but rather does what it describes. For the performance to be successful, such speech acts need certain conditions. For a marriage ceremony—to stay with the initial example—a proper location, an authority with the power to wed someone, a few witnesses, and so forth are necessary. This also means that not all utterances evoke their performative power. Imagine, for example, the bride or the groom suddenly panicking after hearing their partner's "I do" and leaving the church or registry. In such a situation, the wedding has not been performed and the performative potential of the "I do" is ineffective. Utterances need certain conventions to produce their illocutionary force (Butler 1997).

In contrast, the perlocutionary act produces effects that do not follow from the speech act's illocutionary force. They are marked by the absence of any convention and are "not illocutionary in force and not meant to inform an addressee of something" (Norval 2009, 169). Nevertheless, perlocutionary speech acts have "consequential effects on the feelings, thoughts, and actions of others" (Austin 1975, 101). It is important to note that the distinction between the two speech acts also proceeds on a temporal axis. While the illocutionary produces simultaneously as it utters, the perlocution triggers—often uncontrollable—consequences that follow after the enunciation (Butler 1997, 17).

To differentiate between successful and unsuccessful performative speech acts, Austin (1975) introduces the distinction of "happy" and "unhappy" performatives. For illocutionary speech acts to be "happy" and obtain a certain force, they ought to peruse an "accepted conventional procedure . . . that includes the uttering of certain words by certain persons in certain circumstances" (Austin 1975, 14–15). Because there are no conventions for happy perlocutionaries, their conditions to produce effects are redefined in each and every speech act. Such distinctions invite us to think about the conditions that produce the force and effect of blasphemy accusations in today's Pakistan.

Force and Effect of Blasphemy Accusations

As we have seen, accusations of blasphemy may have significant consequences for the accused person, including stigmatization, social expulsion, loss of wealth, imprisonment, necessary hiding or flight, and—at the most extreme—assassination. In such cases, to speak (to accuse) is to do something. This shows that we are in the realm of performative utterances. Accusations have both illocutionary forces and perlocutionary effects. While the illocutionary describes the fact that accusing someone of blasphemy is simultaneous to constituting the addressee as a blasphemer, often with little chance of redemption, the perlocutionary points at the accusation's uncontrollable effects. Similar to Austin (1975) and Cavell (2006), we can now think of the conditions that need to apply for blasphemy accusations to be "happy" extreme speech acts.

Blasphemy accusations work with and through power structures that help to enact what they signify. Once an accusation is uttered, it is difficult for the accused person to redeem themselves of such an allegation. As we have seen, this illocutionary force builds on Pakistan's Islamization period during and after the time of Zulfikar Ali Bhutto, which produced moral economies circling around the honor of the Prophet Mohammad. Scholars have already pointed toward the history of this valorization and how sectarian conflicts about the ontological status of the Prophet inform this field (Gugler 2015; Blom 2008; Philippon 2014). Certain "hagiohistoric" media also add to a charged atmosphere in which accusations of blasphemy irredeemably stick to the accused person (Schaflechner 2019). Finally, the PTA's text messages transfer the authority to notice and call out blasphemy to its citizens and narrow the space of negation for those accused. Although later court decisions may judge the actual blasphemy—and often declare the defendant innocent—public accusations often do not leave much space for advice. The case of Kumar shows how the mere sharing of an image of the Kaaba by a non-Muslim invited the label of "blasphemer" and unleashed uncontrollable effects, including the accused person's loss of wealth, necessary protective custody, and flight to another village, as well as the death of a ten-year-old child.

The illocutionary force builds on conventions. Although traditional verdictive speech acts are produced in the court of law, the force of the blasphemy accusations emerges from the court of public opinion. A "happy" accusation is, therefore, a public accusation or an accusation that, in the words of William Mazzarella (2013), has crossed over the "open edge of mass publicity." The uncontrollable perlocutionary effects are similarly produced on the basis of the accusation's visibility, mediatization, and successful insertion into the public sphere. The larger the audience, the more uncontrollable the accusations become, often gaining the potential to irretrievably change the accused person's life. This was shown in the interview of one of the perpetrators in Mashal Khan's murder, who stated that initially he intended only to scare Khan. This link between force, effect, and visibility reveals the importance of studying the media practices leading to blasphemy accusations.

Both the illocutionary force and the perlocutionary effects of accusations are supported by a lack of protest against such (mis)uses of the blasphemy laws. In other words, accusations also gain their illocutionary force when accusations are not openly opposed. Imagine someone using a racial slur on a train. The bystanding passengers' silence provides weight to this utterance and the absence of protest sanctions the term (Butler 1997). The assassination of public figures opposing the misuse of the blasphemy laws in Pakistan—such as Salman Taseer, the former governor of Punjab, or Shahbaz Bhatti, Pakistan's former minority minister—silenced opposing voices speaking out against arbitrary accusations and their effects. This dynamic has exacerbated an atmosphere in which accusations of blasphemy flourish.

The accusations' illocutionary force is also linked to an absence of blasphemy's citationality (its ability to be quoted in different contexts). As some of the case studies have demonstrated, blasphemy does not become less blasphemous when it is used as a citation. As we have seen in the case of *Salamat Masih and Another v. the State*, the witnesses were not able to repeat the actual crime without committing blasphemy in the act. Although Butler (1997) emphasizes that a large variety of examples show counterappropriation of derogatory or transgressive speech—for example, terms such as *queer, nigger,* or, more recently, *deplorable,* used by Hillary Clinton for Trump supporters—blasphemy accusations in Pakistan cannot be appropriated. In other words, there is no gap between the original context and the effect of the speech act. This effect is exacerbated by the absence of the intent requirement in section 295-C of the PPC. Because blasphemy does not lose its transgressive impact when it travels through certain contexts, accusations of blasphemy also do not need to be context sensitive. This was revealed in the case of Dr. Younas Shaikh, among others.

Finally, the accuser needs to know about the conventions around blasphemy in Pakistan. In other words, he or she has to understand that blasphemy is a transgression of the norm. We need to assume that an accusation is done with the purpose of pointing out a transgression or even with the intention of putting the allegation's uncontrollable perlocutionary effects into motion. This means that although there are unintentional acts of blasphemy, there are no unintentional accusations of blasphemy.

Conclusion

Social media has helped many marginalized communities in Pakistan make their voices and their demands heard. Digital communication has, however, brought new challenges for engaging with Pakistan's contentious blasphemy laws. The absence of an intention clause, in particular, has disconnected allegedly transgressive speech from its context. The free flow and acceleration of videos, images, and texts with little or no context on the internet renders different forms of denunciation possible and permits new ways of charging people with blasphemy. Rumors were often sufficient for vigilantism before the advent of social media, but the ease with which fake accounts can be set up and used to besmirch people makes accusations of blasphemy especially easy online.

In this chapter, I tried to understand such blasphemy accusations as an extreme speech act with illocutionary forces and perlocutionary effects. In the same way as the sentence "I do" in Austin's (1975) famous example is not used as a description but actually performs something, accusations of blasphemy in Pakistan are not simply descriptions of a certain state of being but rather a performative act producing a new reality for the accused person. Force and effects of such accusations depend on a large variety of conditions, including an environment in which the honor of the Prophet is at the center of religious and political debates, the accusation's visibility, the (increasing) absence of voices protesting arbitrary accusations, the fact that blasphemy is dislocated from its context, and the intention of the accuser. Accusations of blasphemy constitute a special kind of extreme speech act that needs to be separated into illocutionary force and perlocutionary effect. Through the case studies provided, we see that digital communication often exacerbates the force and effect of blasphemy accusations.

Notes

1. This number needs to be brought into context regarding the comparatively small number of non-Muslims in the Islamic Republic. Although it is extremely difficult to rely on such demographic numbers, recent studies claim that only around 3% of Pakistan's population falls into the category of "non-Muslims" (Ispahani 2017, 6).

2. In 2016, five men were charged with blasphemy when they allegedly desecrated the turban of a Sikh man. However, this case is a rare exception to the rule (see https://www.dawn.com/news/1255777).

3. http://pakistancode.gov.pk/english/UY2FqaJwl-apaUY2Fqa-apk%3D-sg-jjjjjjjjjjjjj.

4. See the following anonymous tweet: "A plane crash and the wrath of the God, Junaid Blasphemer, was not being punished by the Government, So now my Allah has killed him in a plane crash" [*sic*] taken from a

presentation given by Bilal Rana (PhD student at the University of Erfurt at the 2. Mitteldeutscher Südasientag, June 2017).

    5. http://pakistancode.gov.pk/english/UY2FqaJw1-apaUY2Fqa-apk%3D-sg-jjjjjjjjjjjjj.

    6. Even though the court's decision is binding, the clause was never changed in the PPC (Siddique and Hayat 2008, 379).

    7. https://newspakistan.tv/152-pages-promoting-blasphemous-content-facebook-blocked-interior-ministry/.

    8. https://www.wired.com/story/what-its-like-to-be-thrown-in-jail-for-posting-on-facebook/.

    9. https://www.theguardian.com/world/2017/jun/11/pakistan-man-sentenced-to-death-for-blasphemy-on -facebook.

    10. https://www.wired.com/story/what-its-like-to-be-thrown-in-jail-for-posting-on-facebook/.

    11. Text message from May 9, 2017. While this particular link (info.pta.gov.pk) was no longer accessible in June 2020, the site for complaints is still available at https://www.pta.gov.pk/en/report-blasphemous-url See also: https://tribune.com.pk/story/1406374/millions-pakistanis-receive-blasphemy-warning-texts/.

    12. https://www.pta.gov.pk/en/report-blasphemous-url.

    13. https://www.wired.com/story/what-its-like-to-be-thrown-in-jail-for-posting-on-facebook/.

    14. Antiterrorism courts were established in 1997 under the Sharif government.

    15. https://www.businessinsider.com/r-pakistan-sentences-man-to-death-for-blasphemy-on-facebook-2017 -6?IR=T.

    16. https://theintercept.com/2017/04/14/students-pakistani-university-lynch-classmate-falsely-accused -blasphemy/.

    17. http://www.spiegel.de/panorama/justiz/pakistan-mob-toetet-studenten-mashal-khan-wegen-angeblicher -gotteslaesterung-a-1143892.html.

    18. https://www.youtube.com/watch?v=ZexWiSO_QUI (11:00–12:30)

    19. https://tribune.com.pk/story/1628444/1-10-months-timeline-brutal-lynching-mashal-khan/; https://www .dawn.com/news/1387707.

    20. https://www.youtube.com/watch?v=ZexWiSO_QUI (14:50-15:20).

    21. http://www.spiegel.de/panorama/justiz/pakistan-todesurteil-im-lynchmord-prozess-gefallen-a-1192248 .html.

    22. https://www.theguardian.com/world/2018/feb/07/mashal-khan-death-sentence-for-pakistan-blasphemy -murder.

    23. https://www.dawn.com/news/1387707.

    24. https://timesofindia.indiatimes.com/blogs/balochistan-insight/strange-case-of-blasphemy-against-baloch -hindu-man-prakash-kumar/.

    25. https://www.samaa.tv/news/2017/05/angry-mob-clashes-with-police-demands-custody-of-blasphemy -accused/ also: https://thewire.in/external-affairs/lynching-arrest-minority-community-members-revive -debate-pakistan-blasphemy-law also: https://www.theguardian.com/world/2017/may/04/10-year-old-boy-killed -attempted-blasphemy-lynching-pakistan.

    26. I am conscious that different versions exist about what actually constituted the transgressive act. Because I was able to interview one of the people involved, I decided to foreground his account instead of the version reported in the news media.

    27. One of his famous examples is the phrase "I do," as uttered during a wedding ceremony. Pronounced in the right environment, the sentence performs the action it describes and thus contracts a marriage (Austin 1975, 6).

References

Author note: All websites accessed in June 2020.

Abbas, Shemeem Burney. 2013. *Pakistan's Blasphemy Laws.* Austin: University of Texas Press.

Abbas, Yawar, and Ali Akbar. 2018. "Mashal Khan Lynching: Shooter Imran Ali Sentenced to Death, 5 Given Life Imprisonment." *Dawn.* https://www.dawn.com/news/1387707.

Afp. 2018. "Mashal Khan: Death Sentence for Pakistan Blasphemy Murder." *The Guardian.* https://www .theguardian.com/world/2018/feb/07/mashal-khan-death-sentence-for-pakistan-blasphemy-murder.

Afp. 2017. "Boy, 10, Killed in Attempted Blasphemy Lynching in Pakistan." *The Guardian*. https://www
.theguardian.com/world/2017/may/04/10-year-old-boy-killed-attempted-blasphemy-lynching-pakistan.

Afp. 2017. "Millions of Pakistanis Receive Blasphemy Warning Texts." *The Express Tribune*. https://tribune.com
.pk/story/1406374/millions-pakistanis-receive-blasphemy-warning-texts/.

Ahmad, Asad Ali. 2009. "Specters of Macaulay." In *Censorship in South Asia*, edited by William Mazzarella and
Raminder Kaur, 172–205. Indianapolis: Indiana University Press.

Austin, John Langshaw. 1975. *How to Do Things with Words*. Oxford University Press.

Blom, Amélie. 2008. "The 2006 Anti-'Danish Cartoons' Riot in Lahore: Outrage and the Emotional Landscape of
Pakistani Politics." *South Asia Multidisciplinary Academic Journal* 2. https://journals.openedition.org
/samaj/1652.

Bukhari, Mubasher. 2017. "Pakistan Has Sentenced Man to Death for 'Blasphemy' on Facebook." *The Business
Insider*. https://www.businessinsider.com/r-pakistan-sentences-man-to-death-for-blasphemy-on-facebook
-2017-6?IR=T.

Butler, Judith. 1997. *Excitable Speech: A Politics of the Performative*. New York: Routledge.

Cavell, Stanley. 2006. *Philosophy the Day after Tomorrow*. Cambridge, MA: Harvard University Press.

Dpa. 2018. "Todesurteil im Fall Mashal Khan" *Der Spiegel*. http://www.spiegel.de/panorama/justiz/pakistan
-todesurteil-im-lynchmord-prozess-gefallen-a-1192248.html.

Gugler, Thomas. 2015. "Barelwis: Developments and Dynamics of Conflict with Deobandis." In *Sufis and Salafis in
the Contemporary Age*, edited by Lloyd Ridgeon, 312. London: Bloomsbury.

Imran, Warda, and Maliha Nasir. 2018. "10 Months On: A Timeline of Brutal Lynching of Mashal Khan." *The
Express Tribune*. https://tribune.com.pk/story/1628444/1-10-months-timeline-brutal-lynching-mashal
-khan/.

Ispahani, Farahnaz. 2017. *Purifying the Land of the Pure*. New York: Oxford University Press.

Kazim, Hasnain. 2017. "Tod durch den Mob." *Der Spiegel*. http://www.spiegel.de/panorama/justiz/pakistan-mob
-toetet-studenten-mashal-khan-wegen-angeblicher-gotteslaesterung-a-1143892.html.

Kohari, Alizeh. 2019. "What It's Like to Be Thrown in Jail for Posting on Facebook." *Wired*. https://www.wired
.com/story/what-its-like-to-be-thrown-in-jail-for-posting-on-facebook/.

Mackey, Robert. 2017. "Students at Pakistani University Lynch Classmate Falsely Accused of Blasphemy." *The
Intercept*. https://theintercept.com/2017/04/14/students-pakistani-university-lynch-classmate-falsely
-accused-blasphemy/.

Mazzarella, William. 2013. *Censorium*. Durham, NC: Duke University Press.

Mustikhan, Ahmar. 2017. "Strange Case of Blasphemy against Baloch Hindu Man Prakash Kumar." *The Times of
India*. https://timesofindia.indiatimes.com/blogs/balochistan-insight/strange-case-of-blasphemy-against
-baloch-hindu-man-prakash-kumar/.

News Desk. 2017. "152 Pages Promoting Blasphemous Content on Facebook Blocked: Interior Ministry." *News
Pakistan*. https://newspakistan.tv/152-pages-promoting-blasphemous-content-facebook-blocked-interior
-ministry/.

Norval, Aletta J. 2009. "Passionate Subjectivity, Contestation and Acknowledgement: Rereading Austin and
Cavell." In *Law and Agonistic Politics*, edited by Andrew Schaap. Farnham, UK: Ashgate: 163–179.

Pakistan Penal Code. http://pakistancode.gov.pk/english/UY2FqaJw1-apaUY2Fqa-apk%3D-sg-jjjjjjjjjjjjj.

Philippon, Alix. 2014. "The Role of Sufism in the Identity Construction, Mobilization and Political Activism of the
Barelwi Movement in Pakistan." *Partecipazione E Conflitto* 7 (1): 152–169.

Prevention of Electronic Crimes Act. 2016. Government of Pakistan. http://www.na.gov.pk/uploads/documents
/1470910659_707.pdf).

Qādrī, Muḥammad Khalīl al-Raḥman. 2012. *Ghāzī Malik Mumtāz Ḥasīn Qādrī kā Iqdām*. Lahore, Pakistan:
Islāmik Meḍyā.

Qureshy, Muhammad Ismail. 2008. *Muhammad. the Messenger of God and the Law of Blasphemy in Islam and the
West*. Lahore, Pakistan: Nuqoosh.

Rasmussen, Sune Engel. 2017. "Pakistan: Man Sentenced to Death for Blasphemy on Facebook." *The Guardian*.
https://www.theguardian.com/world/2017/jun/11/pakistan-man-sentenced-to-death-for-blasphemy-on
-facebook.

Saeed, Sadia. 2015. "Secular Power, Law and the Politics of Religious Sentiments." *Critical Research on Religion*
3 (1): 57–71.

Sayālvī, Śakūr Aḥmad Ẓiya. 2016. *Muḥammad Malik Mumtāz Ḥasīn Qādrī Riẓvī Śahīd*. Lahore, Pakistan: Jāmᶜyah Niẓāmiyah Riẓviyah.

Schaflechner, Jürgen. 2019. "Blasphemy and the Appropriation of Vigilante Justice in 'Hagiohistoric' Writing in Pakistan." In *Blasphemy and Transgression in South Asia*, edited by Kathinka Frøystad, Paul Rollier, and Arild Engelsen Ruud. New York: Routledge.

Siddique, Osama, and Zahra Hayat. 2008. "Unholy Speech and Holy Laws: Blasphemy Laws in Pakistan—Controversial Origins, Design Defects and Free Speech Implications." *Minnesota Journal of International Law* 17 (2): 305–385.

Turābī, Muhammad Śahzād Qādrī. n.d. *Malik Mumtāz Ḥasīn Qādrī. Śakhṣiyat Aur Safar Ākhirat*. Karachi, Pakistan: Self-published.

Udupa, Sahana, and Matti Pohjonen. 2019. "Extreme Speech and Global Digital Cultures." *International Journal of Communication* 13:3049–3067.

Veengas. 2017. "Arrest of Hindu Man, Recent Lynching of Student, Revive Debate on Pakistan's Blasphemy Law." *The Wire*. https://thewire.in/external-affairs/lynching-arrest-minority-community-members-revive-debate-pakistan-blasphemy-law.

Web Desk. 2017. "Boy Killed after Mob Attacks Police Station in Hub." *Samaa*. https://www.samaa.tv/news/2017/05/angry-mob-clashes-with-police-demands-custody-of-blasphemy-accused/.

13

LOCALIZED HATRED

The Importance of Physical Spaces within the German Far-Right Online Counterpublic on Facebook

Jonas Kaiser*

IN 2015, AT THE HEIGHT OF THE SO-CALLED "refugee crisis," around one million refugees arrived in Germany. And while the majority of Germans, including Germany's chancellor Angela Merkel, welcomed the refugees, the country's far right opposed it vehemently. For them, the arrival of Syrian, Afghan, or Iranian refugees signified nothing less than an "attack" on "their" homeland, making the ones who were in favor of welcoming the refugees "traitors." The influx of refugees turned out to be a discursive opportunity (Koopmans and Olzak 2004), that the—until then marginalized—far right harnessed. Most prominently, the civic movement Pegida was formed; protesters—at times, more than twenty thousand people—would meet every Monday in Dresden and rally against the government, refugees, and the *Lügenpresse* (lying press). These protests, however, took place not only in Dresden but also across Germany. Often organized online, these protests highlighted the connection between online communication and off-line action. Against this background, I examine the role physical spaces play in the networked public sphere of the German far right on Facebook.

The refugee crisis not only led to the formation of Pegida but also sparked the success of the far-right political party Alternative für Deutschland (AfD, Alternative for Germany), which, as of late 2018, is represented in all state parliaments and the federal parliament. The rise of the country's far right was accompanied by the rise of far-right violence. In the years 2015, 2016, and 2017, more than four thousand far-right acts of violence were officially documented (Verfassungssschutz.de 2018).[1] Off-line, far-right extremists attacked refugees and even burned down refugee shelters (ninety-two arson attacks in 2015; Diehl 2016). Online, they created websites to document alleged "refugee crimes," filled the comment sections of news outlets with antirefugee comments and extreme speech, and created maps that showed the locations of refugee shelters, including their addresses and telephone numbers (Heimbach 2018). This happened on blogs, websites, and, of course, social media platforms—that is, integral parts of what Benkler (2006) called the "networked public sphere." In short, the networked public sphere is the networked sum of all the spaces that allow for the forma-tion of online publics, connected through users (both through content production and con-sumption), signals (most prominently, hyperlinks), or content (e.g., YouTube videos can both be on YouTube and embedded in a blog).

From a networked public sphere perspective, few online spaces are as interesting as so-cial media platforms. They allow people to connect, communicate, and coalesce with each other regardless of their physical locations. More important, they allow people to express themselves in a way that was not possible in a semipublic or public way before.[2] Conse-quently, social media platforms are especially interesting with regard to their potential for *counterpublics*—that is, oppressed and/or marginalized groups—as platforms like Facebook shorten the path between fringe and center (Batorski and Grzywińska 2017; Puschmann et al. 2016).[3] With its size and societal importance, Facebook, in particular, is relevant for the networked public sphere (Benkler 2006): the platform is being used by more than two bil-lion people worldwide, of which about thirty million are German (Statista 2017). And while Facebook has private and cultural dimensions, the platform is often at the forefront regard-ing political communication and extreme speech—that is, vitriolic speech (Stier et al. 2017).

One aspect that is often ignored in research on the networked public sphere is the role of localities—that is, how off-line spaces affect the formation of online spaces. In this chapter, I am interested in the particular connection between extreme speech and physical spaces. More specifically, I am interested in the role that physical spaces play for the extreme right in Germany on Facebook. This aspect is being analyzed against the backdrop of extreme speech discussions being put forward by Udupa and Pohjonen (2019). The concept is fruitful for this analysis, as it highlights that extreme speech should be understood as a "spectrum of practices" and not a binary distinction. Furthermore, it emphasizes digital affordances as contributors to online communication, particularly in the context of extreme speech. Because the concept is also context dependent, it allows for inquiry into the far right's activi-ties on Facebook and how localities are evoked. The German far right was picked as a case study to understand the connections and potential disconnects between physical spaces—understood here as discrete references to localities (e.g., village, city, region, state, or country names) and off-line incidents like attacks on refugee homes, networks, and situations—and extreme speech.

In recent years, the German far-right party AfD, the far-right civic movement Pegida (English translation: Patriotic Europeans against the Islamization of the Occident), and the far-right extremist identitarian movement (IM; the group refers to itself internationally as Generation Identity, but IM in this context refers to the German faction of the international organization) are making use of the platform to disseminate their messages, to connect with each other, and to recruit new members.

Stier et al. (2017) show, for example, that AfD and Pegida cover distinctly different topics on Facebook in contrast to the established political parties, thus distinguishing themselves starkly. For communication, the German far right is not limiting itself to pages or groups; it also conveys distinct messages through the names of its pages. One page is, for example, named "Für Familie Volk und Heimat Multikulti und Islamisierung stoppen" (For family *volk* [right-wing populist description of the people] and homeland, stop multiculturalism and Islamization). Another is called "Rostock Bürgerinitiative gegen die aktuelle Asylpoli-tik" (Rostock civic movement against the current asylum politics). In doing so, the German far-right counterpublic is not only signaling a clear stance through its Facebook page names but also connecting its online activities with physical spaces.

The latter activity is of particular interest when it comes to the networked public sphere. In the past, publics were usually dependent on physical spaces (e.g., people could only read a certain newspaper in a certain region or town or could discuss a certain issue with the people who were at the same place at the same time). The internet allowed for communica-tion that was uncoupled from physical space and time, forming the networked public sphere (Benkler 2006). But as Friedland argues, "we cannot really separate the types and flows of communication that take place within social networks from the social ecology in which they are embedded" (2015, 25). Similarly, Tufekci (2017) and Chadwick (2016) have highlighted that there is a complicated connection between online communication and off-line political action that goes both ways. In her research, Tufekci (2017) was able to track how impor-tant platforms like Twitter were for Turkish activists during the Tahir Square protests and how online communication and action on the ground were interlinked. Similarly, Chadwick (2016) argues that the online sphere and especially social media platforms contributed to a "hybrid" system in which intermedia agenda setting between old and new media constantly takes place. This strain of research is important in the context of civic movements and the question of where and how they will be able to have an impact (on- and/or off-line)—includ-ing those from the far right such as Pegida.

In this chapter, I am interested in the role that physical spaces (i.e., localities) play for the German far-right counterpublic in its communication on Facebook.

To be able to answer this question, I mapped the structure of the German far-right coun-terpublic on Facebook to then identify the communities within the far right. Based on these results, I analyzed the role that physical spaces play for the German far right. My results show that the far right is disconnected from the political mainstream and has formed a counter-public, including alternative media outlets and different far-right actors (either voluntarily or involuntarily). I am also able to show that the German far right is connected to the interna-tional far right from Italy, France, and Hungary. Physical spaces in the German far right on Facebook usually refer to either local branches of organizations (be it AfD, Pegida, fraterni-ties, or IM) or locality-based opposition to immigration, Islam, and/or asylum politics.

Physical Spaces in the Networked Public Sphere

While scholars often refer to *the* public sphere, Fraser (1990) highlighted that there is not just one public sphere. Instead, the public sphere can be best understood as consisting of numerous publics—some smaller than others and some with more power than others. But Fraser (1990) also pointed out that some publics will face discrimination or marginalization, and thus the so-called subaltern publics or counterpublics have to be considered as the least powerful publics. She also emphasized that this category includes antidemocratic groups. This, too, is true for the internet.

But to make sense of the role that physical spaces might play for networked counter-publics, we have to consider how the public sphere can be traditionally understood. For

Habermas (1992/1996), "The public sphere can best be described as a network for communicating information and points of view (i.e., opinions expressing affirmative or negative attitudes); the streams of communication are, in the process, filtered and synthesized in such a way that they coalesce into bundles of topically specified public opinions" (360).

Particularly in the context of online communication, Habermas's definition seems appropriate because it highlights the networked character of publics as a key trait of the public sphere. Benkler's (2006) concept of the "networked public sphere," which posits that the internet allowed for the connection of numerous publics that would be able to circumvent traditional gatekeepers and thus have a bigger impact on the agenda-setting and public opinion formation process, can also be understood in the tradition of Habermas's definition.

In off-line definitions of the public sphere, the question of physical "spaces" was important because these spaces inherently created in- and out-groups, and online publics seemingly transcended local boundaries. But as Murray highlights in analysis of the Occupy movement, "Discursive interactions, media spectacles, and social media use are all integral to social movement success, but an understanding of their interdependence with the physical spaces of the public sphere is also essential" (2016, 16). Furthermore, Sampson puts forward that "collective action is concentrated ecologically and better explained by the density of community organizations than individual social ties or membership in traditional civic groups" (2012, 181). Indeed, this is in line with research on counterpublics and social movements before the internet and how they used bookstores or similar venues to meet up and organize (for an overview, see Nuernbergk 2013).

This, too, is true for far-right counterpublic movements like Pegida that organized online to meet off-line (e.g., Haller and Holt 2018; Nam 2017). Online references to physical spaces can, in this sense, be understood as an anchor, a direct reference that connects the off-line with the online world and thus enforces in- and out-groups based on locality. This dynamic seems interesting in the context of counterpublics because it allows for the far right to directly relate their online actions to the off-line world and vice versa (think also of the "training grounds" to which Fraser refers that were thought of as both alternative media and physical spaces). In doing so, however, the counterpublics also make themselves vulnerable to counterspeech or other forms of marginalization: in anchoring online speech to a physical space, they open themselves up to counteraction. At the same time, having clear markers that refer to the off-line world might also contribute to a counterpublic's collective identity (Kaiser and Rauchfleisch 2019) because it specifies a clear and less abstract target for counterpublic action (e.g., wanting to enact political change in a local town might be more feasible than wanting to do so for the whole country).

Against this background, it is clear that physical spaces are an important factor in the general public sphere but even more so in the context of counterpublics. This study asks what role physical spaces play for the German far right on the social media platform Facebook.

Method

To answer this study's overarching research question, I searched Facebook for 252 different terms that are connected to the far right (e.g., *patriot*, *afd*, *pegida*, *flüchtlinge*, etc.) using the Graph application programming interface (API). This search resulted in 26,140 unique pages. Because both users and pages can "like" other pages on Facebook, I collected the page likes as a proxy for allegiance between pages, as the "like" feature seems to be frequently used that way (e.g., the pages of political parties will like the other pages of the same political parties and their politicians; media outlets will like other affiliated media outlets of the same publishing house; local politicians will like their local sports clubs). Although this method has been used before to map the network of individual sites (e.g., Krieg, Berning and Hardon 2017), I am not aware of a similar attempt to map a country's Facebook "landscape." I collected the page likes of these 26,140 unique pages and, in a next step, analyzed the pages that these pages liked (liked pages from the liked pages). The method to go from liked pages to the liked pages of said pages is called a "snowball" and aims to unravel a bigger structure in a network (much like a snowball grows the longer it rolls down a hill). Unsurprisingly, what started with about 26,000 pages resulted in 2,536,575 million pages. And while I started with a focus on the German far right, most of those 2.5 million pages are not from the far right. Coca Cola is in the network. And *Vogue*. And Tulsa Zoo. This method, then, unveiled a map of close connections and very different topics and showed how international Facebook truly is. The data were collected in April 2018 with R and the package *Rfacebook* (Barberá 2017) just before Facebook closed down its API access.

To answer the research question more thoroughly, I focused on the German far-right community. I was able to identify the far-right community within the 2.5 million pages through the community detection algorithm modularity (Blondel et al. 2008). The resulting German far-right Facebook "page-like network" consists of 4,054 pages that are connected by 45,263 likes. I then identified the communities within the network through modularity (community detection algorithm; fig. 13.1) and labeled the communities based on their most prominent pages (see Kaiser and Rauchfleisch, forthcoming). And while I had planned on retrieving sample posts from each relevant far-right page, this is, unfortunately, not possible anymore because Facebook has closed the API. Consequently, in this study, I focus on an analysis of the page names.

To understand the role of physical spaces within the far-right counterpublic, I focused on the Pegida community, as it is the most prominent far-right civic movement within the German far right. As was established earlier, physical spaces are especially relevant for civic movements because they reinforce a movement's identity through action both on- and off-line (Murray 2016). In addition, the Pegida community is the one community in the network that has references to physical spaces that go beyond their local affiliation to a party or organization. I then manually coded the 413 page names of the Pegida community based on four categories that were rooted on the earlier definition of physical spaces. "Location (general)" asked whether the page name referred to a general location (ranging from municipalities to countries or country unions like the European Union). "Location (specific)" asked whether the page name referred to a specific location—that is, to a distinct village, town, or city. I further coded whether the page name contained a distinct "message"—that is, whether the name was a message in itself (e.g., "No to the [refugee] shelter in Guben") and not just the name of an organization (e.g., "Pegida Paris"). Furthermore, I coded whether the page names included a "target"—that is, something or someone that the page name was directed at (e.g., Angela Merkel, Islamization, refugee shelters, immigration). In a final step, I mapped

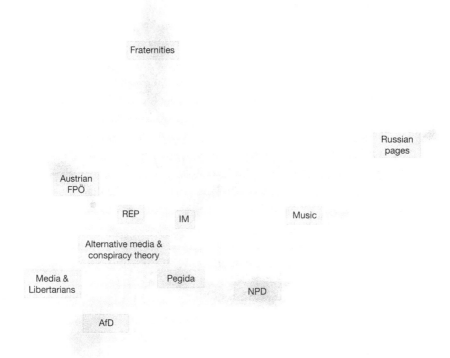

Figure 13.1 The German far-right network on Facebook. Community labels were assigned based on the most prominent pages (i.e., with the most indegree) within the communities (nodes = 4,078, edges = 45,403). Source: Kaiser & Rauchfleisch (forthcoming).

the specific locations on a map of Germany with the R package *ggmap* (Kahle and Wickham 2016) to understand which physical spaces the Facebook pages were referring to and whether there was an underlying pattern.

Results

The network analysis of the Facebook page-like network (fig. 13.1) shows that there are several distinct communities within the German far right. Among them are far-right parties (e.g., AfD, NPD [a far-right extremist political party that can be considered neo-Nazi], Republikaner but also the Austrian FPÖ), the IM, Pegida, German and Austrian fraternities, libertarians, and far-right music, but also alternative media outlets and conspiracy theory sites. The "alternative media and conspiracy theory" community that is represented by pages such as KenFM or RT Deutsch (*Russia Today*'s German branch) especially seem to serve as a bridge between the different communities.

An analysis of the top 100 words of the page names (fig. 13.2) shows two aspects: on one hand, it confirms the prominence of the far-right parties AfD, NPD, and FPÖ as well as Pegida or the IM within the network; on the other hand, it also emphasizes the importance of physical spaces. Among the top 100 words are cities like Berlin, München (Munich), or Dresden. This result is not necessarily surprising. Most political parties will have local Facebook pages to flag events and meetings, to share news articles, or to give their members a virtual space to connect and communicate. The far right is no exception. Indeed, the political party communities that we see in figure 13.1 can be identified so clearly because they mostly consist of local pages that like each other, creating dense clusters. The same is true for the right-wing *Burschenschaften* (i.e., akin to fraternities but usually more conservative and "traditional") that can be found in most German and Austrian university towns and cities (e.g., "Burschenschaft Arminia zu Leipzig in Dresden"). This highlights the role of physical spaces as delineators within a bigger group or organization that might also signify their importance within the overarching structure—for example, there is the general and most important AfD page, but there are also numerous local pages that, although not relevant on the federal stage, have an importance within the local context.

As a next step, I focused on the Pegida community because it can be considered both the most important and the most successful civic movement within the German far right. At its height, the weekly march in Dresden attracted more than twenty-five thousand people in 2014 (Berger, Poppe, and Schuh 2016). Although much smaller in number, Pegida still marches every week through Dresden as of late 2018. A network analysis of the Pegida community highlights that it contains two overarching subcommunities (fig. 13.3): one is Pegida and its local branches; the other one, however, is a dense network of pages that oppose refugee shelters in their villages, towns, cities, or municipalities. The latter is interesting against the background of the overarching research question. These pages are usually called "No to the refugee shelter in XYZ," with slight deviations (e.g., replacing refugee shelter with asylum politics) and are reminiscent in their name of the refugee shelter map that was published by the far-right party NPD. Interestingly, these very local pages form a distinct community in which many pages like other similar pages. Within the overarching far-right network in figure 13.1, the anti–refugee shelter community is located in between the Pegida and the NPD communities.

When looking at the top 100 words of the Facebook page names within the Pegida community (fig. 13.4), three themes become apparent. First is the theme of opposition, which is signaled through words like *no, oppose,* or *stop.* Opposition in this context is mostly directed at the idea of establishing refugee shelters (referred to often as "Heime" or "Asylheim") in a certain place. This general opposition is sometimes framed as opposing the "abuse of asylum" (*Asylmissbrauch*). The idea of abusing asylum is directed at the refugees who came into the country in 2015 (most prominently but also in the following years) and whose claim to asylum are—without evidence—being framed as illegitimate. The second theme is bound to a certain framing of citizenship that is expressed through words like *our, patriotic, patriots, solidarity,* or *citizen's initative* (in the word cloud, the stemmed version "Bürgerin" is prominently visible; however, the word does not stand for the female version of "citizen" but for "Bürgerinitiative"; see fig. 13.4). This theme evokes the idea of the populist "true" people who stand against the elites and who know what is best for the country. The third theme that can be identified within the page names is localities. Unsurprisingly, several cities and towns such as Berlin, Stuttgart, and Heidenau, as well as

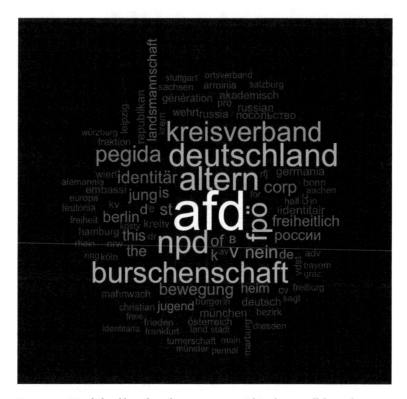

Figure 13.2 Word cloud based on the page names within the overall far-right community (n = 4,078; word size according to frequency).

countries like Hungary, Switzerland, and Austria, are among the top 100 words. As I show below, most of the countries are mentioned in the context of the national Pegida branches (e.g., Pegida France), whereas most of the more specific locations are associated with the anti–refugee shelter pages.

This general analysis poses the question of just how many page names truly express a message, name a specific target to which they are opposed, and/or define a location, (i.e., a physical space). These categories are not exclusive—that is, pages could technically refer to general as well as specific locations and communicate a message as well as a target. To answer these questions, I conducted a content analysis of the 413 Facebook page names within the Pegida community (table 13.1). Based on this analysis, approximately 34 percent of the pages name a general location (e.g., Germany or Saxony), whereas approximately 43 percent refer to a specific location (e.g., Berlin, Stuttgart, Paris, or Munich). Some pages referred to both a specific location and a general one; only ninety-five pages did not refer to any location in their name. Once more, this highlights the importance of locations for the Pegida community. Indeed, it is noteworthy that more pages referred to a specific rather than a general location.

On a content level, the analysis shows that approximately 42 percent of the Facebook page names conveyed some form of message and approximately 23 percent of Facebook page names were even directed at a certain target (table 13.1). This result is in line with

Figure 13.3 Network of the Pegida community with the Pegida subcommunity in the north and the anti–refugee shelter subcommunity in the south (nodes = 413, edges = 3,288; node sizes per indegree; communities identified with modularity).

Figure 13.4 Word cloud of the page names within the Pegida community
(n = 413; word size according to frequency).

the top 100 words that were discussed earlier (fig. 13.4). Although some Facebook pages had names with longer messages, such as "Marburg sagt NEIN zur Überfremdung und zu Asylbetrug" ("Marburg says NO to foreign infiltration and asylum abuse") or "Colditz sagt Nein aus Liebe zur Heimat und zum Schutz unserer Kinder" ("Colditz says no out of love of our homeland and to protect our children"), others were short, such as "Denk ich an Deutschland in der Nacht" ("Should I think about Germany at night," a reference to a famous Heinrich Heine poem that continues, "Then I can no longer sleep, / It's a sleeplessness I could not fight, / And with warm tears I begin to weep"[4]) or "Ein Volk hilft sich selbst" ("A volk helps itself"). In addition, some page names were also directed at a certain target. This was discussed earlier (regarding refugee shelters) but also can be seen in the examples I gave for the page names that functioned as messages. While most of the page names that were directed at a target referred to a refugee shelter, some pages referred to Germany's chancellor Angela Merkel ("Merkel muss weg Mittwoch"; "Merkel has to go Wednesday"), the left wing ("Bündnis gegen Linksextremismus und Inländerfeindlichkeit"; "Alliance against left-wing extremism and hostility against natives"), or Islam ("Für Deutschland ohne Raute Islam und Nestbeschmutzer"; "For Germany without rhombus islam and people who foul their own nest").[5]

Next, I imported the coded information into the Pegida network (done with the app Gephi). This allowed me to visualize the coding information in a more straightforward manner that highlights where general and specific locations were referred to and where in the network messages and targets were communicated (fig. 13.5). A visual inspection of the

Table 13.1 Coding of Facebook page names (of the Pegida community) based on four variables.

Variable	Coding (%)		Total, % (n)
	Yes	No	
Location (general)	34.38	65.62	100 (413)
Location (specific)	43.10	56.90	100 (413)
Message	41.89	58.11	100 (413)
Target	23.49	76.51	100 (413)

four different networks shows how the general locations were usually used in the context of the Pegida pages (the northern community in the network; see also fig. 13.3), whereas the specific locations were mostly used in the community against refugee shelters (the southern community). The network, however, also shows that specific locations are also present within the Pegida community. In contrast, the "message" and "target" networks highlight that barely any page in the Pegida community tried to convey a message and/or identify a target through its page name, whereas the anti–refugee shelter community consists mostly of pages that do both.[6]

By visualizing the coded information, it becomes clear that physical spaces are important both for Pegida and the anti–refugee shelter community. The main difference is that the anti–refugee shelter community is inherently focused on specific locations—that is, the villages, towns, or cities in which refugee homes were planned or located. In that sense, these pages and their reference to specific locations serve a distinct function: to organize the local opposition in one virtual place.

In a final step, I identified all the specific locations that the Facebook page names referred to and located them on a German map (fig. 13.6; created in R with the package *ggmap*). Without duplicates, I was able to locate 139 villages, towns, or cities.[7] Although most were in Germany, some were in Austria, Switzerland, Czech Republic, or France (not all were within the boundaries of the map). In doing so, I located the physical spaces to which the virtual Facebook pages referred. Next, I calculated the density within the map based on the proximity of each dot (i.e., village, town, or city) to another. This analysis shows that although the Facebook page names, in general, refer to almost any area in Germany, three areas show a higher density of Facebook pages: the area around Stuttgart (ranging from Rhineland-Palatia, Baden-Württemberg, Hesse, to Bavaria); the area around Dortmund, Cologne, and Essen in North Rhine–Westphalia; and, most prominently, East Germany. In East Germany, we can even identify two distinct hotspots: one around Berlin and one in the area of Leipzig, Dresden, and Chemnitz. The heat map shows which regions are the most outspoken against refugee shelters on German Facebook. This is interesting because refugee shelters are not only in these regions but, according to the far right's own maps, everywhere in Germany (Sandgathe 2015).

Against the background of counterpublic theory, these findings highlight how Facebook allows the far right to coalesce and, more important, to form a collective identity that is anchored in physical spaces. From this shared identity, the far right might potentially be emboldened to spread their vitriolic speech onto other pages, as they can also use their pages

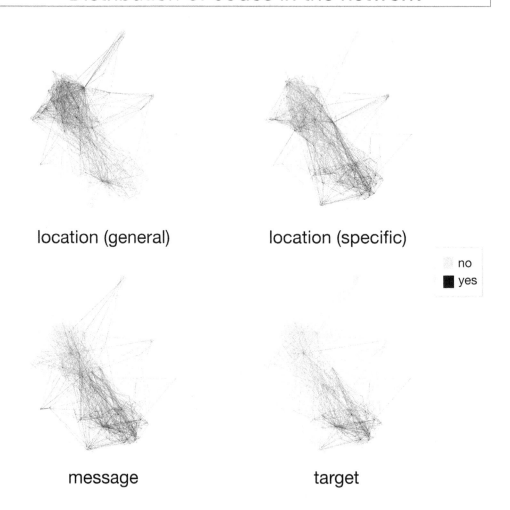

Figure 13.5 Distribution of codes in the Pegida community network (nodes = 413; edges = 3,288) for the variables location (general), location (specific), message, and target.

to call for directed action (e.g., harassment); especially against Islam and refugees, which are core targets for the German far right.

Discussion

In this chapter, I examined how the German far right refers to making use of physical spaces on Facebook. To answer this question, I analyzed a Facebook page-like network based on data from April 2018. In doing so, I was able to show that the German far right uses Facebook not only to connect members with each other and to communicate but also to mobilize; indeed, the community forms its online counterpublic on Facebook. Specifically, by analyzing the Pegida community regarding the variables *location (general)*,

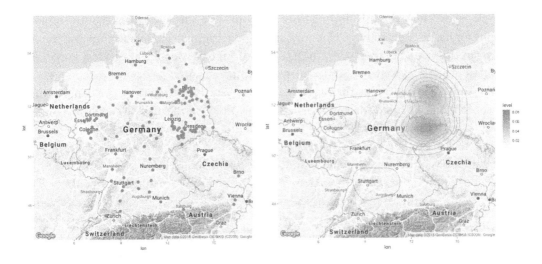

Figure 13.6 Map and heat map of Germany and neighboring countries based on specific locations within the Facebook page names (n = 139; each dot represents a village, town, or city that was referred to by a Facebook page; the heat map shows density estimation of Facebook pages).

location (specific), *message*, and *target*, I was able to contextualize the Facebook network with off-line data.

This analysis shows three important findings. First, three themes are prominent within the Pegida subcommunity: opposition, citizenship, and localities. While the opposition defines the target—that is, the out-group (who are we up against?)—the citizenship defines the in-group's identity (who are we?), and the localities anchor the virtual formation of the far-right counterpublic in the physical space and offer off-line events to get involved.

Second, physical spaces are used in two distinct ways. On one hand, physical spaces (i.e., localities) function as delineators within a bigger group or organization that might also signify their importance within the overarching hierarchical structure. On the other hand, physical spaces function as anchors within collective identity formation because they offer clear in- and out-groups (see the first finding in the previous paragraph) and an immediate way to get involved, making the idea of a counterpublic more direct and meaningful—that is, you know *who* as well as *what* you oppose, but you also know where to directly get involved in the off-line world, making the link between online and off-line more immediate. In addition to these two functions, the localities may also serve a third function: recruitment. As highlighted elsewhere (Kaiser and Rauchfleisch, forthcoming), the far right uses the internet in sophisticated ways to recruit new members. The localized anti–refugee shelter pages may also serve as gateways for local citizens to the greater far-right counterpublic and their messages on Facebook.

Third, the virtual Facebook pages refer to real-life places and, as such, make a pattern visible. Although Pegida and anti–refugee shelter pages refer to almost all German regions, a density analysis highlights three particular areas in Germany where the far right is especially prominent. Most notably, eastern Germany is the region with the highest density of

Facebook pages. However, this finding does not come as a surprise, given that the region is notorious for its far-right activity. Not only did Pegida originate in Dresden but also the AfD is polling as the second biggest party in the states of Saxony, Mecklenburg-West Pomerania, and Saxony-Anhalt, as well as Brandenburg and Thuringia.

This study thus highlights the importance of physical spaces within the concept of extreme speech: on one hand, these spaces allow for direct connection between on- and off-line and thus give access to pages that center around extreme speech; on the other hand, the pages in combination with focused extreme speech might manifest in real-life violence (e.g., arson attacks on refugee shelters). In looking at the intersection of off-line and online on Facebook, extreme speech connections are made visible. For counterpublic theory, this analysis highlights the importance of keeping physical spaces in mind when analyzing a counterpublic's online activity. It is necessary to analyze the functions that physical spaces serve for counterpublics at both smaller and larger scales.

It must be noted that the results account for only a few pages within the broader German far-right spectrum, and no correlation or causality should be drawn from this analysis. Although the identification of the anti–refugee shelter pages is instructive for research into the far right, it is important to acknowledge the limitations of this study. We need more insight into general patterns of user overlap between the far-right pages to understand how successful these pages are in recruiting new members. We also need more qualitative work that outlines the role of physical spaces in the online realm against the backdrop of the public sphere and counterpublic theory.

Notes

* This work on the US and German far right was funded by the German Research Foundation (KA 4618/2-1).

1. There is a notable difference between official numbers and the numbers that observers of the far-right–like foundations or news outlets publish. The official numbers are quoted here because they can be understood as the guaranteed minimum of far-right violence. It is highly likely that the true numbers are higher.

2. This is mostly true for liberal democracies.

3. It has to be noted that neither the public sphere nor counterpublics are understood from a normative but rather a functionalist perspective in this text (see also Kaiser andand Rauchfleisch 2019). Nancy Fraser argues, for example, that "that subaltern counterpublics are [not] always necessarily virtuous; some of them, alas, are explicitly anti-democratic and anti-egalitarian; and even those with democratic and egalitarian intentions are not always above practicing their own modes of informal exclusion and marginalization" (1990, 67).

4. Poem available at http://www.heinrich-heine.net/haupt.htm.

5. "Rhombus" is a reference to the so-called Merkel rhombus, which describes the hand gesture that Merkel does in the shape of a rhombus.

6. Although Pegida is in itself an abbreviation of a targeted message against Islam, the pages were only coded as such if the name was spelled out, as it cannot necessarily be assumed that everyone knows what the abbreviation Pegida stands for.

7. Because some page names referred to towns with names that exist multiple times in Germany or to overly specific places (e.g., one page name referred to a military base), I had to double check which place they were referring to. To do so, I visited the Facebook pages, looked at the Facebook page's information (sometimes it would refer to an associated website that specified the town in its imprint), the pages that the page had liked (e.g., one page liked the village's football club) or the Waybackmachine (sometimes the web archive will have a prior version with more information).

References

Barberá, Pablo. 2017. *Package "Rfacebook."* https://cran.r-project.org/web/packages/Rfacebook/Rfacebook.pdf.

Batorski, Dominik, and Ilona Grzywińska. 2017. "Three Dimensions of the Public Sphere on Facebook." *Information, Communication and Society* 21 (3): 356–374. doi:10.1080/1369118X.2017.1281329.

Benkler, Yochai. 2006. *The Wealth of Networks: How Social Production Transforms Markets and Freedom.* New Haven, CT: Yale University Press.

Berger, Roger, Stephan Poppe, and Mathias Schuh. 2016. Zur Problematik der Zählung von Demonstrationsteilnehmern (Everything counts in large amounts). In *Pegida—Rechtspopulismus zwischen Fremdenangst und »Wende«-Enttäuschung? Analysen im Überblick*, edited by Karl-Siegbert Rehberg, Franziska Kunz, and Tino Schlinzig, 113–132. Bielefeld, Germany: Verlag. doi:10.14361/9783839436585-009.

Blondel, Vincent D., Jean-Loup Guillaume, Renaud Lambiotte, and Etienne Lefebvre. 2008. "Fast Unfolding of Communities in Large Networks." *Journal of Statistical Mechanics: Theory and Experiment* 2008(10): P10008. doi:10.1088/1742-5468/2008/10/P10008.

Chadwick, Andrew. 2016. *The Hybrid Media System: Politics and Power.* New York: Oxford University Press.

Diehl, Jörg. 2016. "Gewaltwelle: BKA zählt mehr als tausend Attacken auf Flüchtlingsheime." *Spiegel Online*, January 28. http://www.spiegel.de/politik/deutschland/fluechtlingsheime-bundeskriminalamt-zaehlt-mehr-als-1000-attacken-a-1074448.html.

Fraser, Nancy. 1990. "Rethinking the Public Sphere: A Contribution to the Critique of Actually Existing Democracy." *Social Text* 25/26:56–80. doi:10.2307/466240.

Friedland, Lew A. 2015. "Networks in Place." *American Behavioral Scientist* 60 (1): 24–42. doi:10.1177/0002764215601710.

Habermas, Jürgen. 1996. *Between Facts and Norms: Contributions to a Discourse Theory of Law and Democracy.* Cambridge, UK: Polity. (Original work published 1992.)

Haller, André, and Kristoffer Holt. 2018. "Paradoxical Populism: How Pegida Relates to Mainstream and Alternative Media." *Information, Communication, and Society* 22 (12): 1665–1680. doi:10.1080/1369118x.2018.1449882.

Heimbach, Tobias. 2018. "NPD veröffentlicht auf Google Maps Karte mit Asylunterkünften." *Welt.de*, February 5, 2018. https://www.welt.de/politik/deutschland/article173227076/NPD-veroeffentlicht-auf-Google-Maps-Karte-mit-Asylunterkuenften.html.

Kahle, David, and Hadley Wickham. 2016. *Package "ggmap."* https://cran.r-project.org/web/packages/ggmap/ggmap.pdf.

Kaiser, Jonas, and Adrian Rauchfleisch. 2019. "Integrating Concepts of Counterpublics into Generalized Public Sphere Frameworks: Contemporary Transformations in Radical Forms." *Javnost—The Public* 26 (3): 241–257. doi:10.1080/13183222.2018.1558676.

———. Forthcoming. *Like, Subscribe, Radicalize: The Internet in the Hands of the Far-Right.* New York, NY: Oxford University Press.

Koopmans, Ruud, and Susan Olzak. 2004. "Discursive Opportunities and the Evolution of Right-Wing Violence in Germany." *American Journal of Sociology* 10 (1): 198–230. doi:10.1086/386271.

Krieg, Lisa, Jenny Moritz Berning, and Anita Hardon. 2017. "Anthropology with Algorithms? An Exploration of Online Drug Knowledge Using Digital Methods." *Medicine Anthropology Theory* 4 (3): 21. doi:10.17157/mat.4.3.458.

Murray, Billie. 2016. "The Sphere, the Screen, and the Square: "Locating" Occupy in the Public Sphere." *Communication Theory* 26 (4): 450–468. doi:10.1111/comt.12101.

Nam, Sang-hui. 2017. "Spontane Mobilisierung und der Wandel kollektiver Formationen im Internet. Eine Fallstudie zur PEGIDA-Bewegung." *Forum: Qualitative Social Research* 18 (1): 1–31.

Nuernbergk, Christian. 2013. *Anschlusskommunikation in der Netzwerköffentlichkeit: Ein inhalts- und netzwerkanalytischer Vergleich der Kommunikation im "Social Web" zum G8-Gipfel von Heiligendamm.* Baden-Baden, Germany: Nomos.

Puschmann, Cornelius, Julian Ausserhofer, Noura Maan, and Markus Hametner. 2016. *Information Laundering and Counter-Publics: The News Sources of Islamophobic Groups on Twitter.* Paper presented at the International AAAI Conference on Web and Social Media, Cologne, Germany. http://www.aaai.org/ocs/index.php/ICWSM/ICWSM16/paper/view/13224.

Sampson, Robert. 2012. *Great American City: Chicago and the Enduring Neighborhood Effect*. Chicago: University of Chicago Press.

Sandgathe, Laura. 2015. "#BrauneKarte: Rassistische Karte zeigt Flüchtlingsheime in Deutschland." *RP Online*, July 17, 2015. https://rp-online.de/panorama/deutschland/braune-karte-google-maps-zeigt -fluechtlingsunterkuenfte-in-deutschland_aid-18710611.

Statista. 2017. "Anzahl der Nutzer von Facebook und Instagram in Deutschland im Jahr 2017 (in Millionen)." *Statista—Das Statistik-Portal*. https://de.statista.com/statistik/daten/studie/503046/umfrage/anzahl-der -nutzer-von-facebook-und-instagram-in-deutschland/.

Stier, Sebastian, Lisa Posch, Arnim Bleier, and Markus Strohmaier. 2017. "When Populists Become Popular: Comparing Facebook Use by the Right-Wing Movement Pegida and German Political Parties." *Information, Communication, and Society, 20*, 1365–1388. doi:10.1080/1369118X.2017.1328519.

Tufekci, Zeynep. 2017. *Twitter and Tear Gas: The Power and Fragility of Networked Protest*. New Haven, CT: Yale University Press.

Udupa, Sahana, and Matti Pohjonen. 2019. "Extreme Speech and Global Digital Media Cultures: Introduction." *International Journal of Communication* 13:3049–3067.

Verfassungsschutz.de. 2018. Rechtsextremistische Straf- und Gewalttaten. https://www.verfassungsschutz.de/de /arbeitsfelder/af-rechtsextremismus/zahlen-und-fakten-rechtsextremismus/rechtsextremistische-straf-und -gewalttaten-2017.

14

"MOTHERHOOD" REVISITED

Pushing Boundaries in Indonesia's Online Political Discourse

Indah S. Pratidina

THE 2014 AND 2019 PRESIDENTIAL ELECTIONS IN INDONESIA set the pace for exponential growth in social media use throughout the country. ASEAN Up (2019) recorded nearly half of Indonesia's 268.2 million population as social media users (150 million), more than half as mobile users (355.5 million), and 130 million as mobile social users. The fact that this growth is fueled by election-related political participation is reflected in Indonesians' timelines on Twitter, Instagram, Facebook, and, to some degree, YouTube, where both the 2014 and the 2019 presidential elections were long-standing trending topics. Users were not only passively following election-related news but also actively expressing political opinions by commenting or posting and engaging in political campaigns to support particular presidential candidates.

Scholars have suggested that the increase in online media use has had a positive impact on Indonesian democracy. New media served as a platform for the movements that dethroned Suharto's New Order and ignited political reformation (the "Reformasi") in 1998 (Abbott 2001; Lim 2003). However, there is another side to online media development that demands attention. Because social media does not have the gatekeeping function of mainstream media outlets, it is difficult to control the accuracy and appropriateness of information distributed on these platforms. *Fake news*, *defamation*, and *hate speech* are among the terms with which Indonesian citizens and authorities are becoming familiar. Indonesia's Ministry of Communication and Informatics (Kominfo) received 203 fake news and hoax-related reports in 2016, a number that alarmingly rose to reach 7,430 reports in 2017 and 14,427 reports in 2018 (Widiastuti 2018). The problem presents a formidable challenge to the nation's legal apparatus, with a flurry of lawsuits involving users who have disseminated fake news and hate speech via social media in violation of the government regulation of electronic information and transaction.

Strong polarization in online discourse surrounding political elections is a well-established phenomenon (Vergeer and Hermans 2013; Yardi and Boyd 2010). This was the case in both Indonesian presidential elections of 2014 and 2019, when only two contestants remained in the final round: Joko Widodo (known as Jokowi) and Prabowo Subianto. The 2014 election saw Jokowi and Jusuf Kalla versus Prabowo and Hatta Rajasa, whereas the 2019 election was between Jokowi and Ma'ruf Amin versus Prabowo and Sandiaga Uno. This study follows Gazali (2018) and Tapsell (2017) in pointing out how polarization during the elections drove supporters from opposing sides to express their opinions in an increasingly violent manner. Extreme speech discrediting the political opponents and mocking their supporters flooded Indonesian social media platforms. This commonly took the form of religion-based identity politics centered on defining what makes "a good Muslim," and a related trend that involved using gendered discourse surrounding women's proper role in the Indonesian public sphere to secure votes (Aldary and Salamah 2018; Candraningrum 2014).

This chapter is focused on the issue of gender-related online extreme speech during the 2019 presidential election. Previous studies show how Indonesian women's status as "mothers," a term long used to connote respect, is increasingly being deployed in the interest of certain political agendas (Amiruddin 2007; Andriasanti 2018; Djajadiningrat-Nieuwenhuis 1987; Ningrum 2018). The sacred institution of "motherhood" and its relation to politics has a long history in Indonesia. During colonial times, Indonesian women played active roles as strong mothers who nurtured the nationalist spirit in the struggle for independence (Djajadiningrat-Nieuwenhuis 1987; Ningrum 2018). Since independence, however, women retreated to an apolitical corner during the Old Order (1945–1965) and adopted the domesticated role of a subordinate (wife) to a leader (husband) during the New Order (1965–1998) (Dzuhayatin 2002). This study aims to investigate whether the period ushered in by the Reformation in 1998 and the rapid uptake of social media brought about another shift in Indonesian women's political role. Gerung (2014) suggests, for example, that winning votes from the country's female population was crucial to Jokowi's success in the 2014 presidential election. Realizing the latent potential of female voters, both 2019 campaign teams were eager to include the notion of "motherhood" in campaign narratives. As a result, the sacred institution of motherhood has become the latest fodder for vitriolic exchange on Indonesian social media—a phenomenon that I argue has ramifications for women's political agency and societal roles.

Feminist studies on gender and social media typically discuss gendered abuse targeting female users (Buni and Chemaly 2014; Citron 2011; Wotanis and McMillan 2014). Wotanis and McMillan (2014) show how female YouTubers receive greater hostile and critical feedback, as well as sexually explicit remarks, compared with male counterparts. Buni and Chemaly (2014) and Citron (2011) use the term *misogynistic* in describing cyber–hate speech against female social media users to argue for the urgency of developing policy in response to the issue. I argue, however, that the lenses of hate speech and misogyny do not fully capture the complex gendered negotiations taking place in campaign-related motherhood narratives on Indonesian social media. Instead, I approach the topic using the concept of "extreme speech," which presents the "production, circulation and consumption of online vitriol" (Udupa and Pohjonen 2019, 3051) as cultural practices and social phenomena that require contextual ethnographic analysis. Understanding the wider implications of the entry of the mother figure into the domain of online extreme speech requires a context-specific apprehension of the boundaries of civility and incivility based on the country's cultural and normative background and historical conditions (Udupa and Pohjonen 2019). As such, this study queries the sociocultural and political parameters that spur users to profane the respectable figure of the mother. It aims to describe the process through which the distinction between acceptable and unacceptable speech is being defined with respect to gender.

This study offers observations from social media to complement the previous studies on gendered social media use and online extreme speech. It forwards three cases in which women have either identified themselves or been identified by social media users as "mothers" on Indonesian social media in the context of election-related debates. While the vitriolic exchanges between competing supporters appear to challenge the sacred status of motherhood and the mother figure, I argue that they demonstrate a more complex reality. First, the image of "good women" no longer rests only on particular symbolic attire (i.e., the hijab) in digital-era Indonesia. The three "mothers" examined here all wore the hijab and were still objects of derision, ridicule, and contempt. Second, the discourse on motherhood has been successfully deployed as a political tool by both parties to such an extent that political success has become defined by which side has earned the support of the true mothers. This demonstrates the consensus that mothers are the defenders of society's welfare and morality. In contributing to this, social media users are not widening women's roles or challenging established gender norms but rather reinforcing them. Third, women actively joining the discussion of what should and what should not be done by these mothers shows that, in this study, women were not merely subjects but also participants in online negotiations of gendered identities and roles.

Methods and Unit Analysis

This study employs an interpretive approach that treats social activity as a text and sees human action as a collection of symbols expressing layers of meaning (Berg 2009). In line with the concept of extreme speech (Udupa and Pohjonen 2019), I maintain the idea that meanings operate within certain contexts and are intertwined tightly with identities and argue that it is crucial to understand Indonesia's sociocultural and political situation in order to assess the ramifications of vitriolic debates on social media.

Observation of online posts tagged with presidential election–related hashtags was carried out between July 2018 and October 2018. The study focused on YouTube and Instagram posts using the pro-Prabowo hashtag #2019gantipresiden (2019 change president) and news related to it. The choice of hashtag was fitting for several reasons. First, it enjoyed immense popularity during the period of the study. The initiator of the hashtag, Mardani Ali , turned to his social media accounts to announce its higher percentage of use if compared with pro-Jokowi ones (Distania 2018). In an Instagram post (August 22, 2018), he quoted data posted on Twitter by a social media observer @nephilaxmus (August 21, 2018) and claimed that between August 11 and 21, 2018, alone, the number of tweets that were using #2019gantipresiden was 346,000 as opposed to pro-Jokowi's 75,000 tweets of #2019TetapJokowi and 33,000 tweets of #Jokowi2Periode. Second, observation revealed that posts tagged with #2019gantipresiden commonly evoked controversial political narratives with religious and ethnic slants, as attested to by the hashtag's involvement in a national media controversy. Finally, the Prabowo campaign in particular gave an ample spotlight to women, making the hashtag especially relevant in understanding the repoliticization of motherhood in the wake of the recent election.

Examining three cases of #2019gantipresiden posts revolving around mother figures and the concept of motherhood at large, in this study, I look at how the supporters of competing candidates positioned female identities and roles at the center of online discussions. The first case centers on an anti-Jokowi YouTube post by a wealthy mother that was refuted by pro-Jokowi mothers who put forward class-based critiques. The second case scrutinizes the "pious woman turned troublemaker" narrative surrounding well-known public figure Neno Warisman. The third case looks at the scandal surrounding Ratna Sarumpaet, a respected female activist turned hoaxer who during the data collection period was facing prosecution. Analysis of compiled data is conducted using directed content analysis, which employs existing concepts, theories, and historical explanations relevant to the research focus.

Indonesian Social Media and Identity Politics

Heightened online political polarization in Indonesia was spurred on during the 2014 presidential campaign between the Jokowi–Jusuf Kalla and Prabowo–Hatta Rajasa teams. The phenomenon was further entrenched during the Jakarta 2017 gubernatorial election when Basuki "Ahok" Tjahya, a Christian with a Chinese background, ran for the position, and hate speech associated with his race and religion flooded social media. Studies argue that the 2014 presidential election and the 2017 gubernatorial election shed light on how capitalization of voter identity, whether religion, ethnicity, or race, is becoming a much-used political tool (Aldary and Salamah 2018; Candraningrum 2014; Gazali 2018; Tapsell 2017).

The instrumentalization of identity politics continued in the run-up to the 2019 presidential election. An extension of the anti-Ahok sentiment from 2017 is observable in the present anti-Jokowi movement, which pushes narratives that show how Jokowi's policies over the past four years have not benefited the *ummah* (Muslim population) (IPAC 2019). These narratives include the alleged "criminalization of ulama," which referred to the controversial imprisonment of Islamist leaders, and the "latent threat of communism" posed by large numbers of Chinese workers brought in to work on Chinese-funded infrastructure projects (IPAC 2019, 3).

Introduced by the Islamic Partai Kesejahteraan Sosial's (PKS; Prosperous Justice Party) leader Mardani Ali Sera in March 2018, the #2019gantipresiden hashtag is part and parcel of this ongoing religious-ethnic conflict. Mardani argued that the hashtag represents a non-partisan and organic social movement of ordinary people who want change in Indonesia (Egeham 2018) and formed Volunteers for Ganti President (Relawan Ganti Presiden) in May 2018 to prove that PKS was not behind the movement (IPAC 2019). Protestors at large demonstrations displaying #2019gantipresiden banners in early May 2018 were joined by thousands of volunteers wearing T-shirts with the same hashtagged slogan in Jakarta, Lampung, Makassar, and other cities in Indonesia. Controversy mounted as media outlets offered long, in-depth discussions on how the #2019gantipresiden hashtag provoked disparities among Indonesians as it played around controversial political narratives based on religious and ethnic identities with a view to unfairly garner support for Prabowo before the official campaign period started.

Motherhood and Political Participation in Indonesia

Earlier studies from various global contexts have discussed the imbrications between politics and gendered identity (Kerber 1976; Lakshmi 1990; Martin 1990). These studies have a bearing on the current Indonesian case, particularly with respect to what motivates women to engage in the political arena. Kerber (1976) discussed the political participation of mothers in the United States in terms of domestic confinement when she described how the model Republican woman was a mother who treated the domestic sphere as a political frontier. The ideal Republican mother should educate her sons to be virtuous citizens and prevent her husband from any violation or lapse from civic virtue (Kerber 1976, 202). In line with this, Lakshmi presented the case of Tamil Nadu in India, where women's involvement in politics was framed by issues that are considered "womanly"—that is, matters that directly affected the home because "home was women's special responsibility" (1990, 82). Martin (1990) noted a similar trend in Latin American women's political roles, with the added insight that economic crises contributed to the formation of many women's political movements in the 1970s and the integration between the domestic and public arenas. Because they viewed children as gifts from God, Latin American women considered motherhood as a societal contribution not available to men (Martin 1990). Martin argued that Latin American women continued to justify their role in politics by presenting themselves as mothers defending their family and community from "economic change, repressive governments, and crises of legitimacy" (474) in order to protect the future of their children and grandchildren.

Women and their roles and identities had long been included in the political discourse in Indonesia (Candraningrum 2014; Gerung 2014). Women in Indonesia are bound by moral and religious identities, similar to the Latin American women featured in Martin's (1990) article. They are wives and, most of all, mothers who are expected to be pious (Wieringa 2015), as is also the case in Tamil Nadu (Lakshmi 1990). In Indonesian popular culture, "good women" are portrayed as weak and obedient and are presented wearing the hijab. In contrast, female antagonists are usually portrayed wearing revealing clothing and thick makeup (Amiruddin 2007; Arivia 2014; Rakhmani 2017). This gendered representation carries over into politics, shaping how the public perceived Iriana Jokowi's (the wife of presidential candidate Jokowi) decision when, nearing the end of the 2014 presidential campaign, she began to wear a hijab consistently (Arivia 2014). Uproar ensued when she removed her hijab after Jokowi's victory, prompting the criticism that she covered up only to help her husband attain the position (Arivia 2014).

The politicization of women's roles both in public and domestic domains has long been discussed, even before Indonesia's independence in 1945. During the first Women's Congress (1928), the proper role for Indonesian women was to act as mothers for their families and the nation (Ningrum 2018). The term "mothers of the nation" was subsequently used in 1935 during the second Women's Congress in Jakarta to refer to the importance of women's involvement in family and society. In this formulation, women are considered capable of shaping economic and social networks and functioning as pillars for the success of family, society, and the nation (Djajadiningrat-Nieuwenhuis 1987). The term later developed to become *ibuism*, derived from the word *ibu*, which means "mother" in the Indonesian language (Andriasanti 2018). She adds that during the 30 years of Suharto's New Order, ibuism narrowed in meaning as Indonesian women gradually came to occupy the apolitical role of homemaker (Andriasanti 2018). Wieringa (2015) suggests that the "prosperous" family model, with its busy but obedient homemakers of the New Order, was replaced by the late-Reformasi Islamist model of the "sakinah" (happy and harmonious) family, with its pious wives and mothers dedicated to their husbands.

This study builds on scholarship tracing the evolution of motherhood in the Indonesian context by picking up the thread that runs from the Reformasi movement that dethroned Suharto in 1998 to the current 2019 presidential election. Today, the concept of motherhood has become a means of attracting female voters, who make up half of Indonesia's relatively young population (Badan Pusat Statistik 2018). This discursive strategy has been particularly effective for the Prabowo–Sandiaga team, whose 1,300 volunteer groups are composed of nearly 70 percent "emak-emak" (mothers) (Tim Kumparan 2019). The Prabowo–Sandiaga team strategically portrayed vice presidential candidate Sandiaga Uno as a charming and down to earth ally of mother voters (IPAC 2019). Pictures and videos of Sandiaga visiting traditional markets and conversing with wives and mothers about food prices were common on social media platforms during the campaign period. He promoted the use of the term *emak-emak* to refer to potential female voters through his personal social media accounts, mentioning and thanking them along with his other supporter groups in an election-day speech that was broadcast by national television networks.

Ibu, *emak-emak*, and *bunda* all mean "mother" in the Indonesian language. While *ibu* has a more neutral tone, *bunda* is deemed as a poetic word of endearment, and *emak-emak* used to have the rather negative image of "simpleton homemaker" from the lower middle class. The female voters of Prabowo–Sandiaga, however, repurposed the name to connote "resilient and strong mother" and adopted it in their volunteer groups' names, for example, Power of Emak-emak (PERMAK), Militant Mothers (Emak-emak Militan), and Mother's Party for Prabowo–Sandi (PEPES; Partai Emak-Emak Pendukung Prabowo-Sandi).

Analysis and Discussion: Online Discourses of Motherhood

Case 1: The Common Mother

In September 2018, video posts of a woman wearing a long black hijab claiming to be a simple, concerned mother were posted on YouTube. The same video was posted by several users with handles such as "Ibu Pemberani Kritik Pedas Jokowi—Viralkan Semoga Jokowi Mendengarnya" (Brave mother gave harsh critiques to Jokowi—make it viral so Jokowi will see it) and "Pesan Cerdas dari Emak-emak Militan Buat Jokowi" (Clever messages from a militant emak-emak for Jokowi). Some users added Islamic themed music and texts in the background, for example, Bela Ulama, 2019 GP News, and Cahaya Islam with the highest number of views, 2.3 million times (in December 2018).

The videos took the form of eight- to ten-minute monologues addressed to Jokowi in which the speaker critiques his policies, particularly those related to the country's economic situation. The video was taken at a selfie angle from the driver's seat of the speaker's car. She begins by mentioning the name of Allah, provides *salam* (Islamic greetings), and introduces herself as Utami. She continues to explain how she understands the difficulties of leadership because she manages her own consulting business and argues that throughout his four years as president, Jokowi did not rise adequately to these challenges. Utami is careful to claim that she is not a politician, not even a party member, but rather a common homemaker who also works on the side to help her husband. Voicing her reluctance to speak out, Utami plays on the established narrative of "mothers" as domestic and apolitical subjects who emerge from the comfort of their homes and enter the political arena due to a state of emergency. She describes how, as a Muslim, she has always managed to find solutions to domestic problems with the help of God, who never sleeps and takes care of those in need. She closes her monologue by casting doubt on Jokowi's faith as a Muslim, given that she feels his policies have not benefited the Muslim population.

Utami's complaints about the rising prices of essential commodities and US dollars that have made it difficult to feed her family and send her only son to school abroad matched opposition campaign narratives claiming that Jokowi has failed to provide for the needs of the ummah by taking away jobs and economic opportunities from the deserving Muslim population. Further, Utami's complaint that Jokowi's weak body gestures are not fit for the leader of a nation reproduces a gendered discourse used by other Prabowo mother-supporters: that Indonesia needs a firm leader to protect the country from threats. In this way, the sort of "feminine rationale" put forward by mother figures falls into line with the opposition's efforts to promote Prabowo's strength and his military background over Jokowi's wavering leadership style and allegedly procommunist tendencies (IPAC 2019).

Utami's video did not go uncriticized online. YouTube users posting in the comments section of the video decry her as an ungrateful rich lady who is only seeking attention, pointing out her car, red lipstick, big shiny brooch, and her big arms and body. With regard to her consultancy work, users note that she is among the lucky ones with a job. They treat her decision to send her son to college in the United States and the car from which she filmed the video as luxuries she could do without. A similar claim emerges with respect to her body, suggesting that she should eat less to lose weight and save money. Finally, they note that if she indeed had managed to solve her own problems with only the help of God, she would not need to post a video blaming others like Jokowi.

In the wake of the Utami video, other YouTube vlogs made by fellow mothers provided counterresponses and critiques through the use of sarcasm. These included videos titled "Balasan Emak-emak Curhat Tajir Berlemak Salahin Jokowi" (Response to concerned fat rich mother who blamed Jokowi) and "Jawaban untuk Emak-emak Tajir yang Nyinyir Jokowi" (A reply to rich mother mocking Jokowi).

These videos were posted and reposted by, among others, InfoForU and RSC video, with the highest number of views 550,000 times (in December 2018). Like the derisive comments section, many counterresponses by other concerned mothers critiqued Utami on the basis of her apparent privilege, claiming that they were in tougher economic situations as low-wage workers or housewives without their own companies. Sending their children to study abroad was never an option for them.

As noted in the previous section, global studies show how good mothers are often portrayed as women who are devoted to taking care of their children, husbands, and the well-being of their communities or nations. In Indonesia, this narrative of devotion is tied to the hijab, which serves as a symbol of piety. Utami cites the notion of a "good mother," with her long black hijab, who is reluctant to speak out but compelled to for the benefit of her son and her country. Framed differently by the opposition, however, her hijab did not shield her from public judgment, derision, and abuse that presented her as a "female antagonist," with bold makeup and not-so-modest accessories, and an ungrateful human being in general. Caught in the crossfire of extreme speech, the Utami video and its counterresponses present a complex, gendered online political landscape in which women are both the object of online bashing (Utami) and also active contributors toward defining what makes a "good mother." In this case, the line between gendered abuse and fair critique is blurred, showing that when motherhood is used to secure political power, the mothers themselves are often complicit and persecuted at the same time.

Case 2: The Public Figure

During the lead-up to the 2019 election, Neno Warisman, a famous singer and actress, emerged as one of the core leaders of the Ganti Presiden movement (Hakim 2018; IPAC 2019) and was appointed by Prabowo himself as vice head for his campaign team in mid-September 2018 (Viva.com 2018). Having become a PKS politician and *ustadzah* (female Islamic cleric), Neno was especially influential in women-dominated Islamic communities and created WhatsApp groups as venues to organize the Ganti Presiden rallies and distribute regular posts that included tips on "how Muslim mothers could be more involved in politics" (IPAC 2019, 5–6). With the help of this celebrity mother figure, the Prabowo campaign was able to successfully exploit gendered narratives regarding a mother's duty "to protect her children from ungodly communism, homosexuality, and other moral threats associated with Jokowi's camp" (IPAC 2019,10).

On July 29, 2018, the controversy that had been building around Neno came to a head when she was blocked from exiting Hang Nadim Airport, Batam, by a protest against the #2019gantipresiden movement. A little over a month later, she ran into a similar problem in Pekanbaru, Sumatra, when the Indonesian police prohibited Ganti Presiden activities for disturbing the peace. By December 2018, there were 6,047 posts tagged with the hashtag #nenowarisman on Instagram. Among these were photographs and a short video of her using the cabin crew's microphone before a Pekanbaru–Jakarta flight to apologetically explain the flight delay because they could not disembark in Pekanbaru (Jordan 2018).

In the comments on these posts, Jokowi supporters were quick to speculate on Neno's true motives for being actively involved in politics. Claiming she was no longer a popular actress, users remarked on the shift in her persona from a beloved heroine in her films and television series to a troublemaker. The posts played on the betrayal trope that forms part of the established motherhood narrative in positioning Neno as a pious woman who was committed to the well-being of her community but now cares only about her own selfish agenda. Comments like these often used abusive language to refer to Neno, calling her a "goblok" (moron), #jandabiangkerok (troublemaking widow), and "a power-hungry woman."

In contrast, Prabowo supporters during the media controversy addressed Neno as "bunda" (a term of endearment meaning mother). Seeing her as a pious mother persecuted by an abusive regime that had violated her right to freedom of speech and compromised Indonesian democracy, supporters created posts with messages of encouragement, such as "We are with you, *Bunda* Neno."

As in the first case, the Neno Warisman controversy showed that women's greater involvement in politics leaves them subject to gendered abuse and, at the same time, acceptance on gendered terms. Whereas pro-Jokowi users framed Neno as a pathetic woman with postfame syndrome who abused her public status, Prabowo's supporters portrayed her as a militant mother who bravely defended democracy and the right to freedom of speech for the good of her home nation. Despite wearing the hijab, Neno—like Utami—was not immune to disrespectful abuse online, suggesting that with greater visibility and agency on social media comes greater scrutiny and policing of women's bodies, behaviors, and status.

Case 3: The Female Activist

On September 21, 2018, Ratna Sarumpaet, a well-known human rights activist, claimed that she had been assaulted in Bandung, West Java. The claim went viral after pictures of her swollen, apparently beaten face were disseminated online. Prabowo himself visited Sarumpaet, who was a vocal supporter of his campaign, and afterward held a press conference during which he expressed his sympathy and demanded an investigation into the "cowardly attack." Numerous other politicians from the Prabowo–Sandiaga coalition turned to Twitter to voice their anger and concern, calling the assault an "attack against our mother, our grandmother" and suggesting that it was a fundamental flaw in the country's democracy that led to the shameful event.

After an investigation by the Indonesian police, however, the news broke that Sarumpaet might be making up the story. On October 3, 2018, she held a press conference admitting the fake story and revealing that her face was swollen due to the plastic surgery she had undergone during the week of the alleged attack. She told the press that she initially told the lies to avoid telling her children the real cause behind her black-and-blue face and became concerned when the story made it outside her home and caused a public uproar. During the press conference, she apologized, calling her fabrication an act of "stupidity" and explaining, "I don't know what came over me . . . it was an imaginary tale given by the devil to me," and "I am just a human being; a woman admired by so many people can also slip up" (CNN Indonesia 2018). She addressed her apologies to Prabowo, "the person whom I fight for and I dreamt to be the leader of this nation in the future," and fellow militant "emak-emak." She added encouragement for emak-emak to go on fighting in the line of struggle: "Ratna could be somebody, could be a nobody. But you are Indonesian emak-emak who will keep on fighting" (CNN Indonesia 2018).

Following the incident, there were 19,800 posts tagged with #ratnasarumpaet on Instagram, many of which also included the hashtag #hoaxterbaik (best hoax). The case was also under close observation by mainstream media through their social media accounts. Solopos.com's Instagram account published a survey captioned "Ratna's Hoax Effect" on October 29, 2018, that argued Ratna's story had created a potential shift of voters away from Prabowo (Solopos.com 2018). Other media such as Liputan 6's (2018) Instagram account published chronological facts of Ratna's case with the title, "Facts behind Ratna Sarumpaet's Fake Report of Assault" on October 3, 2018.

Pictures and memes of Ratna's swollen face continue to remain "viral" after her confession. Her positive personal image as a vocal human rights and feminist activist and mother role model who managed to balance family and politics has been irrevocably tarnished. The support from Prabowo's coalition turned into disowning and distance. Some Jokowi supporters on Instagram took the opportunity to reprimand Prabowo for his lack of wisdom and rational judgment in believing Ratna's hoax. Ratna was sentenced to two years of imprisonment in July 11, 2019, for violating Article 14 of the Criminal Code on hoaxes and for misleading the public. She was given a conditional release on December 26, 2019, after serving 15 months of a 24-month prison sentence.

In this case, the façade of the "good Indonesian mother" was again revealed to be a sham. Given that Ratna was among the brave and pious army of emak-emak, like Utami and Neno, the betrayal was felt most by Prabowo supporters. Interestingly, as in the first case, the narrative that mothers are to be the defenders of society's welfare and morality seems to have been taken over by average Indonesians who take the role of moral police online. When Ratna admitted that she had betrayed this "sacred duty," online users subjected her to public ridicule all the more severely because she knew the rule and led other women to follow it but eventually broke it herself.

Conclusion

In this study, I set out to investigate how Indonesian women's political role may have shifted following the Reformation in 1998 and the rapid uptake of social media. Both 2019 presidential campaign teams acknowledged the potential of large numbers of female voters, although the Prabowo team was more proactive about including "motherhood" in presidential election narratives. Investigating several of these motherhood narratives, this study found that they often sparked contentious debates, drawing in supporters of both campaigns and different genders. Framing these exchanges as extreme speech, this study followed the ways in which the boundaries between acceptable or unacceptable speech were transgressed and redrawn, taking into consideration Indonesia's cultural and normative background and the historical conditions of women's political participation.

The cases presented in this study show women who fit the ideal Indonesian construct of the mother or "good woman," from an average mother devoted to her family, to a pious public figure with a good reputation, to a fighter for human rights and justice. All three women wear the hijab, a symbol of religious and moral appropriateness. Although popular culture continues to celebrate the hijab as a symbol of feminine purity, the cases in this study show that is changing. The images of all three "mothers" examined were subject to irreverent, vulgar, and caustic extreme speech that seemed to shatter the ideal institution of motherhood. Indeed, the cases showed how the platformed environments of social media seemed to accommodate mental distance for users and facilitated the use of the motherhood construct as a political tool. A kind of battle of narratives between the opposing supporter bases of Jokowi–Ma'ruf and Prabowo–Sandiaga split the images of the women between an average sophisticated mother versus an ungrateful fat rich lady, a pious heroine of democracy versus an attention-seeking former actress, and a human rights activist versus a hoaxer granny. Even though these discourses discredit the motherhood institution both claim to respect, both parties seem to be able to detach themselves from the obligation, particularly when the women's agendas are not in line with those of their political patrons.

Revisiting the historically shaped construct of motherhood in contemporary online political discourse, I argue that although social media provides women with the opportunity for greater political engagement and public visibility, the traditional notion of motherhood, and the gender relations that go along with it, are largely preserved. Social media users are ultimately not widening women's roles or challenging established gender norms but rather reinforcing them. Indeed, the only justification for their active role in politics—that the women featured in this study had recourse to—was their status as mothers defending their family and community from economic crisis, unfair governments, and moral threats. As soon as they were discredited and shown not to be true mothers in one way or the other, their public validity was undermined. This sort of restricted participation was especially visible in the Prabowo campaign, which consistently forwarded the notion that a good mother is a believer in God, able to balance the role of homemaker with her thriving career, and first and foremost, devoted to her children and husband. The success of this discourse suggests the rise of a movement of conservative Islamist women in post-Reformasi Indonesia (Kartika 2019; Wieringa 2015).

Nevertheless, the advent of social media has meant that women coming from relatively diverse backgrounds are able to publicly participate in a contemporary political environment where gender is a pressing issue and means of establishing rapport, setting the boundaries of political alignment, and gaining support. While the ideal construct of motherhood is upheld and women are either attacked or lauded on the basis of it, it will become increasingly important to observe how they themselves manage these strictures in maintaining a public presence online. In the cases discussed, women are not merely the objects and victims of this gendered discourse but also participants in the ongoing negotiation of gendered identities and roles in digital-era Indonesia.

References

Abbott, Jason. 2001. "Democracy@ Internet. Asia? The Challenges to the Emancipatory Potential of the Net: Lessons from China and Malaysia." *Third World Quarterly* 22 (1): 99–114.

Aldary, Idham Tamim, and Ummi Salamah. 2018. "Civic Engagement on Social Media: 2018 West Java Gubernatorial Election in Indonesia." *Jurnal Komunikasi Indonesia* 7 (2): 129–139.

Amiruddin, Mariana. 2007. "Dari Identitas Ibu kini Identitas Moral dan Agama" (Refleksi Kampanye Celebrating Women's Diversity). (Indonesian) *Jurnal Perempuan* 54:100–103.

Andriasanti, Lelly. 2018. "Ibuism of Political Islam in the Election of Jakarta Governor in 2017." (Indonesian) *Jurnal Perempuan* 23 (3): 161–171.

Arivia, Gadis. 2014. "Stereotype of State's Mother and the Hidden-Career: A Study of the Roles and Perceptions of Wives of Presidential and Vice Presidential Candidates in the 2014 Election." (Indonesian) *Jurnal Perempuan* 19 (3): 183–189.

ASEAN Up. 2019. "Southeast Asia Digital, Social, and Mobile 2019." https://aseanup.com/southeast-asia-digital-social-mobile/.

Badan Pusat Statistik. 2018. *Proyeksi Penduduk Indonesia 2015–2045 Hasil SUPAS 2015–2045*. Jakarta: Badan Pusat Statistik.

Berg, Bruce Lawrence. 2009. *Qualitative Research Methods for the Social Sciences*. Boston, MA: Pearson.

Buni, Catherine, and Soraya Chemaly. 2014, October 9. "The Unsafety Net: How Social Media Turned against Women." *The Atlantic*. https://www.theatlantic.com/technology/ archive/2014/10/the-unsafety-net-how-social-media-turned-against-women/381261/.

Candraningrum, Dewi. 2014. "Religion, 2014 General Election and Status of Women as Other." (Indonesian) *Jurnal Perempuan* 19 (3): 233–240.

Citron, Danielle Keats. 2011, October 27. "Misogynistic Cyber Hate Speech." *University of Maryland Faculty Scholarship*. 1144. https://digitalcommons.law.umaryland.edu/ fac_pubs/1144.

CNN Indonesia. 2018, October 3. *FULL—Ratna Sarumpaet Akui Bohong Terkait Penganiayaan Dirinya*. (*FULL—Ratna Sarumpaet Admits Lies on Her Assault*) CNN Indonesia. https://www.youtube.com/watch?v=IjgShfGN1Tk.

Distania, Ratu Amanda. 2018, July 22. Mardani: Kontribusi Organik Akun #2019GantiPresiden Sangat Terlihat. (Mardani: #2019GantiPresiden Account's Organic Contribution has Strong Visibility) *Akurat.Co*. https://akurat.co/news/id-259242-read-mardani-kontribusi-organik-akun-2019gantipresiden-sangat-terlihat.

Djajadiningrat-Nieuwenhuis, Madelon. 1987. "Ibuism and Priyayization: Path to Power?" In *Indonesian Women in Focus: Past and Present Notions*, edited by Elsbeth Locher-Scholten and Anke Niehof, 43–51. Dordrecht: Foris.

Dzuhayatin, Siti Ruhaini. 2002. "Role Expectation and the Aspirations of Indonesian Women in Socio-Political and Religious Contexts." In *Women in Indonesian Society: Access, Empowerment, and Opportunity*, edited by M. A. Mudzhar, S. S. Alvi, S. Sadli, and M. Q. Shihab, 154–194. Yogyakarta, Indonesia: Sunan Kalijaga Press.

Egeham, Lizsa. 2018, August 21. Mardani Ali Sera Luncurkan Buku #2019GantiPresiden (Mardani Ali Sera Launches #2019GantiPresiden Book). *Liputan6.com*. https://www.liputan6.com/news/read/3624592/mardani-ali-sera-luncurkan-buku-2019gantipresiden.

Gazali, Effendi. 2018. "Degrading Message and Hate Speech Are Now Obligatory in Elections? A Qualitative Research on Post-truth Populism in Sumatera Utara's Local Election." *Jurnal Komunikasi Indonesia* 7 (2): 110–121.

Gerung, Rocky. 2014. "Feminist Ethics against Stigma of Theocracy-Patriarchy: A Reflection of the 2014 Presidential Election." (Indonesian) *Jurnal Perempuan* 19 (3): 175–182.

Hakim, Rakhmat Nur. 2018, August 28. Alasan Mardani Ali Sera Gunakan #2019GantiPresiden, Bukan #2019PrabowoPresiden (Mardani Ali Sera's Reason for Using #2019GantiPresiden, and not #2019PrabowoPresiden). *KOMPAS.com*. https://nasional.kompas.com/read/2018/08/28/16371641/alasan-mardani-ali-sera-gunakan-2019gantipresiden-bukan-2019prabowopresiden.

IPAC (Institute for Policy Analysis of Conflict). 2019. *Anti-Ahok to Anti-Jokowi: Islamist influence on Indonesia's 2019 election campaign* (IPAC Report No. 55). http://file.understandingconflict.org/file/2019/03/Report_55.pdf.

Jordan, Ray. 2018, August 28. Kemenhub Tegur Lion Air Imbas Aksi Neno Warisman Pakai Mik Pesawat (Ministry of Transportation Reprimands Lion Air Aftermath Neno Warisman Conduct of Usinng Airplane's Mic). *Detik.com*. https://news.detik.com/berita/d-4186414/kemenhub-tegur-lion-air-imbas-aksi-neno-warisman-pakai-mik-pesawat.

Kartika, Dyah Ayu. 2019, April 14. "An Anti-feminist Wave in Indonesia's Election?" *Newmandala.org*. https://www.newmandala.org/an-anti-feminist-wave-in-indonesias-election/.

Kerber, Linda. 1976. "The Republican Mother: Women and the Enlightenment—An American Perspective." *American Quarterly* 28 (2): 187–205.

Kumparan. 2019, February 27. "Tarung Relawan Jokowi-Prabowo." (Jokowi-Prabowo's Supporter Feuds) *Kumparan.com*. https://kumparan.com/kumparannews/ tarung-relawan-jokowi-prabowo-1551235 836900023370.

Lakshmi, C. S. 1990. "Mother, Mother-Community and Mother-Politics in Tamil Nadu." *Economic and Political Weekly* Vol. 25, No. 42/43 (Oct. 20-27, 1990), WS72–WS83.

Lim, Merlyna. 2003. "The Internet, Social Networks, and Reform in Indonesia." In *Contesting Media Power: Alternative Media in a Networked World*, edited by N. Couldry and J. Curan, 273–288. Lanham, MD: Rowman & Littlefield.

Liputan6. "Fakta di Balik Kabar Bohong Penganiayaan Ratna Sarumpaet" (Facts Behind Ratna Sarumpaet's Fake Report of Assault.) Instagram post by @liputan6, posted on October 3, 2018. https://www.instagram.com/p/Bods-9bno2G/?igshid=1wpar5drgp2jx.

Martin, Joann. 1990. "Motherhood and Power: The Production of a Women's Culture of Politics in a Mexican Community." *American Ethnologist* 17 (3): 470–490.

Ningrum, Siti Utami Dewi. 2018. "The Revival of the 'Mothers of the Nation' from the Period of the Anti-Colonial Movement until the Independence of Indonesia." (Indonesian) *Jurnal Perempuan* 23 (3): 129–141.

Rakhmani, Inaya. 2017. *Mainstreaming Islam in Indonesia*. New York: Springer.

Solopos.com. "Ratna's Hoax Effect." Instagram post by @solopos_com, posted on October 29, 2018. https://www.instagram.com/p/BpgtP3IhARL/?igshid=17aslwkyhoyf8.

Tapsell, Ross. 2017. *Media Power in Indonesia: Oligarchs, Citizens and the Digital Revolution*. Lanham, MD: Rowman & Littlefield.

Udupa, Sahana, and Matti Pohjonen. 2019. "Extreme Speech and Global Digital Cultures." *International Journal of Communication* 13:3049–3067.

Vergeer, Maurice, and Liesbeth Hermans. 2013. "Campaigning on Twitter: Microblogging and Online Social Networking as Campaign Tools in the 2010 General Elections in the Netherlands." *Journal of Computer-Mediated Communication* 18 (4): 399–419.

Viva.com. 2018, September 19. "Neno Warisman Jadi Wakil Ketua Timses Prabowo-Sandi" (Neno Warisman Becomes the Vice Chief of Prabowo-Sandi's Success Team). *Viva.com*. https://www.viva.co.id/berita/politik/1076366-neno-warisman-jadi-wakil-ketua-timses-prabowo-sandi.

Widiastuti, Rosarita Niken. 2018. *Menguatkan Eksistensi Lembaga Penyiaran Publik (LPP) di Era Disrupsi Informasi* (Strengthening Public Broadcasting Institutions (LPP) in the Age of Information Disruption). Jakarta, Indonesia: Direktur Jenderal Informasi dan Komunikasi Publik, Kominfo RI.

Wieringa, Saskia E. 2015. "Gender Harmony and the Happy Family: Islam, Gender, and Sexuality in Post-Reformasi Indonesia." *South East Asia Research* 23 (1): 27–44.

Wotanis, Lindsey, and Laurie McMillan. 2014. "Performing Gender on YouTube: How Jenna Marbles Negotiates a Hostile Online Environment." *Feminist Media Studies* 14 (6): 912–928.

Yardi, Sarita, and Danah Boyd. 2010. "Dynamic Debates: An Analysis of Group Polarization over Time on Twitter." *Bulletin of Science, Technology and Society* 30 (5): 316–327.

15

NETWORKS OF POLITICAL TROLLING IN TURKEY AFTER THE CONSOLIDATION OF POWER UNDER THE PRESIDENCY

Erkan Saka

THIS CHAPTER IS FOCUSED ON ONLINE NETWORKS OF support for Turkey's ruling party, the Justice and Development Party (AKP). Founded in 2001, the AKP came to power in 2002, headed by Recep Tayyip Erdoğan, one of the most controversial leaders in contemporary global politics. Although Erdoğan had always acted as the principal leader of the party, his authority increased within the party only gradually. In its first decade, the party acted as a pro–European Union, center-right party with Islamic political origins, operating within Turkey's parliamentary system. However, since the early 2010s, the party has demonstrated strong and increasing signs of authoritarianism (Erensü and Alemdaroğlu 2018), and these signs became more visible with the government's response to nationwide protests at Gezi Park in 2013. One of its responses was to use political trolls against critical voices on social media.

The chapter builds on earlier ethnographic work (Saka 2018) that focused on the evidentiary issues and basic structure of AKTrolls, a group of political trolls who served the ruling party. The earlier study found that there was insufficient evidence for the claim that there was a centralized troll army. The study instead demonstrated that troll networks that surfaced after the antiregime Gezi Park protests in 2013 were decentralized and used various tactics to intimidate and suppress groups that were critical of the regime. This chapter is focused on a period when the ruling party had become politically unchallenged, and its hegemony in the state apparatus was more or less stable. The period starting June 24, 2018, gave more powers to the president (Lowen 2017).

In this chapter, I discuss new roles that trolls have since adopted, including efforts to have a leading role in shaping the government-owned mainstream media agenda. Political trolls have taken on the role of mass media for the government and are engaging in a culture war against government opponents. Political trolls initially played a key role in the surveillance of party outsiders—that is, opposition political figures (Saka 2018). Surveillance lost its centrality in troll functions, but it did not disappear, and extended in the later years to party insiders. The chapter begins with a detailed discussion of AKTrolls in the context of the global phenomenon of online trolls. I will then focus on the distinct features and practices that regime-friendly trolls have adopted in Turkey, comparing them with other significant political trolling practices in different parts of the world. Following a discussion on tactics, I will introduce common themes in online discussions that characterize online support for the regime. Political trolls are not necessarily anonymous or isolated individuals. The nature and effects of trolling depend on the political context. When trolls are aligned with the ruling party led by a president with increased powers, most of them stop being anonymous, and some threaten to sue when called out as trolls. This chapter documents trolling practices in relation to Turkey's experiment with a presidential model that was adopted in 2019. The chapter describes the various tactics used by online trolls, but it also provides examples of their impact to highlight the political consequences.

The chapter concludes by highlighting the implications of social surveillance effected by the human agents behind AKTrolls. It also notes that rivalries that have emerged among AKTrolls, signaling fluctuating loyalties that create enormous uncertainty in terms of how reliable these trolls are for any regime.

AKTrolls

A visible progovernment political trolling scene appeared in 2013 during the Gezi Park protests. A major event in this scene occurred when President Erdoğan forced then–prime minister Ahmet Davutoğlu to resign. Davutoğlu had long been a key figure in Erdoğan's government. A former academic, Davutoğlu was first minister of foreign affairs and is believed to be the ideologue of the AKP's neo-Ottomanist foreign policy plans, which included a particular focus on the Syrian civil war (for more on Davutoğlu's policies, see Aras 2014; Ozkan 2014). When Erdoğan became president in the then-parliamentary democratic system, Davutoğlu became prime minister. The latter's initiatives led to political tensions that ended with Davutoğlu's forced resignation. An anonymous Wordpress blog titled "Pelikan Declaration" appeared before the resignation (https://pelikandosyasi.wordpress .com/). The declaration claimed that Davutoğlu had attempted to bypass Erdoğan's authority and included a list of accusations. The declaration was widely circulated by a section of AKTrolls that would gradually be labeled the "Pelikan group." During the resignation period, some prolific AKTrolls such as Taha Ün were sidelined as being pro-Davutoğlu (Diken 2016).

As opposed to earlier media reports, I found AKTrolls to be much more decentralized and volunteer driven. The "professional" trolls sometimes worked together and sometimes separately. Closest to a business structure was the Pelikan group. This group worked closely with a media conglomerate owned by the Albayrak family, which had increased its wealth during AKP's rule (E. Sözeri 2016). Erdoğan's son-in-law and Turkey's current minister of economy, Berat Albayrak (along with his media conglomerate brother, Serhat Albayrak), were particularly prominent personalities in this relationship. The group quickly received animosity from other AKTroll circles as political alliances evolved.

Methodology

A list of political trolls was monitored for more than two years. A discursive analysis was then used to analyze selected Twitter production. The list of trolls to monitor was based on the findings of previous ethnographic work. Significant impact nodes were found and mapped (Saka 2018), and representative accounts were selected for monitoring. To follow political and personal changes among trolls, the list was continuously updated to demonstrate emerging cliques. The update process was based on both regular contacts from the field and the trolls' own Twitter content and engagements.

The origins of the ethnographic research are based on my active engagement in social media communications with users who took part during and after the Gezi Park protests. Some of those users could be identified as AKTrolls (progovernment party, AKP, trolls). Semistructured interviews were conducted with users who were officially involved in social media political campaigns or who self-identified as AKTrolls. One troll was a digital media producer with close ties to AKP circles whose documentaries have been broadcast on state TV channels. Another troll, according to AKP circles, was a "Gülenist organizer" on Twitter. I also interviewed a relatively high-level bureaucrat who specialized in Turkey's communication sector. In addition, I engaged approximately thirty user-activists in online and offline conversations/interviews to address specific questions. These interviews were conducted between June 2015 and December 2016, and correspondence continued with some of them during the two-year monitoring process for this chapter.

Most engagements occurred online on Twitter and Facebook; however, some offline encounters were critical. Some significant access was obtained by frequenting cafes in the neighborhood of At Pazarı Meydanı in Istanbul's conservative district, Fatih, as Islamists from predominantly pro-AKP circles frequented these cafes. It also became a favorite locale for Gülenists after the December corruption case in 2013. Gülenists were not known to socialize with other Islamists, but at the start of the crackdown, some members seemed to have decided to socialize with other Islamists to propagate their views. A network-mapping tool, Graph Commons (https://graphcommons.com/), was used to create a map of AKTrolls with the initial data obtained during field engagements. The online monitoring of troll activities would later populate the map.

Trolling and its Antecedants

Trolling has existed since the early days of the internet. It was already so common. even on the Usenet, that Tepper (1997/2013) devoted an entire article to trolls' exploits (Phillips 2015), and Shepherd et al. (2015) looked at the late 1980s as they emphasize the historical and networked roots of trolling. Filipovic (2007) and Hardaker (2010) point out the military roots of internet communications in the 1960s and argue that the gendered and vitriolic nature of trolling can be traced back to these years. There is continuity in the gendered consequences of trolling (Suler and Phillips 1998).

A turning point giving trolling a more collective and political sense occurred in 2008 in the course of a showdown between the Anonymous hacking group and Scientology (Coleman 2011). According to Phillips (2015), a theoretical shift occurred in the late 2000s when analyzing trolling. Previously, Dahlberg (2001) and others viewed trolls in terms of "deception," whereas Coleman (2012; 2014), among others, interpreted them as using a "communitarian" approach without ignoring the roots of trolling. Soon the phrase "political trolling," associated with the term "web brigades" (known in English media as "the troll army"), emerged, initially to describe state-sponsored anonymous internet political commentators and trolls explicitly linked to the Russian government (Soldatov et al. 2015). Observations of Russian cases demonstrate that a centralized political trolling structure was made possible with a series of internet laws and the opening of centers, such as the now notorious Internet Research Agency (Funke and Benkelman 2019), to host trolls who intervened in digital agendas (Lokot 2016).

Once accepted as a positive practice, extreme speech movements soon appropriated the "playfulness" of trolling. Hawley's (2017) work on alt-right circles in the United States is a good indicator of this current. Hawley claims that the alt-right is an outgrowth of internet troll culture in many respects. The collective creation of memes and other relevant content go hand-in-hand with spontaneity, but it is fine tuned in an increasingly collective manner (Hawley 2017).

Political trolling may not necessarily be associated with the state, but the latter increasingly monopolizes the practice. Hunt (2014) described both formal and informal mechanisms to control the internet—a familiar process in Turkey (Sözeri 2017). Trolling increased in a context in which other repressive measures were already in force. This negatively affected journalists, with female journalists in Turkey a particularly vulnerable group, as they were increasingly exposed to harassment by trolls.

Nevertheless, anonymity may not be a critical point anymore. Some recent research on trolls corroborates my findings. In the harassment of women in the video-gaming community, known as "Gamergate" (Dewey 2014); in the attacks on the Ghostbusters actress Leslie Jones (Brown 2016); and in the study of comments on online petitions published on a German social media platform between 2010 and 2013, anonymity and public identities are both used (Rost, Stahel, and Frey 2016). Because online aggression is rewarded in their social networks, some trolls prefer not to hide their identities (Coren 2016). Ceren Sözeri (2016), for instance, describes how some progovernment journalists act like political trolls; in fact, they sometimes lead the attacks. A disturbing fact is that political trolling may now be used within more mainstream politics all over the world. A *BuzzFeed* report (Spence 2018) claimed that conservatives in the United Kingdom had formed a Twitter group to use political trolling tactics against the Labour Party leader. At the time of writing, Serbia's governing party admitted to having thousands of "bots" to write positive comments about President Aleksandar Vucic and his party (Piše:Danas Online 2018). It is now common knowledge that in most cases, under political trolls' seeming anonymity, there are often connections to power bases. In another case, the hacked emails of white nationalist troll Milo Yiannopoulos demonstrated that he had connections to some prominent figures inside Silicon Valley but also to explicitly white nationalist circles and families of billionaires (Wagstaff 2017). In some countries, political trolling has already become an industry (Ong and Cabanes 2018), and the Philippines's President Rodrigo Duterte has admitted he paid an army of social media trolls (Ng 2017).

Tactics

An empirical context can be valuable for understanding political trolling. In this section, I will refer to literature that reports different uses of trolling all over the world, and I will compare them with AKTroll practices. As Phillips (2015) noted, even within the same trolling group, there might be considerable behavioral variation. It should also be noted that there are always emerging and overlapping cases.

Microtargeting

Russian trolls seem to have continued to produce divisive content even after discoveries of their roles in the last US presidential election (Graff 2018). These trolls seem to have excelled at targeted advertising, which is vital for social media. They have hijacked hashtags and disguised themselves as average Americans on Twitter (Hsu 2018), and they have mainly used racial themes with their Facebook ads (Penzenstadler, Heath, and Guynn 2018). I could not find a similar algorithm-supported campaign targeting in the Turkish case.

Swarming

Organized trolling attacks work to intimidate targets. In India, Hindu nationalists using the internet followed and intimidated social media users who posted comments that were not aligned with the trolls' own views (Udupa 2015). In the United States, the alt-right's persistent, coordinated trolling would break into the mainstream discussion (Hawley 2017), as both microtargeting and collective content production worked hand-in-hand to produce the expected results for the groups. The sheer volume of threats and insults can discourage targeted citizens; in Turkey, these attacks are usually called "social lynching."

An example involves Pelin Batu, the daughter of a well-known Turkish diplomat and a historian with her own TV show. She used Twitter on July 21, 2016, to state that she was no longer going to tweet because of threats and insults from AKTrolls.

Spreading Disinformation

Trolling can go hand-in-hand with microtargeting but sometimes en masse: the Russian troll farm known as the Internet Research Agency was quick to muddy the news cycle during the Mueller probe in the United States (Glaser 2018). Stray (2017) elaborated on how disinformation is used in swarm attacks along with microtargeting, referring to the modern strategy of disinformation as "the firehose of falsehood" (named by RAND scholars Paul and Matthews 2016). The disinformation is spread through different channels with different levels of content. These channels may range from official sources like Russia Today to curated, hacked, or leaked material with different audiences in mind. The massive volume of disinformation overwhelms alternative voices and creates false sources of credibility. Disinformation is not necessarily explicitly political. BBC News (BBC 2018) claimed that Russian trolls were active in spreading antivaccine stories to create social discord. Many cases exist in Turkey—for example, stories involved women booing the call to prayers (Reuters 2019), people drinking beer in the mosque during the Gezi Park protests (*Hürriyet*

Daily News 2013), and a woman in a headscarf being sexually attacked in Kabataş İstanbul during the Gezi Park protest (Yılmaz 2015).

Spreading Fake News to Discredit Opposition Accounts Later

This is arguably a form of disinformation peculiar to Turkey. A telling case was the circulation of false images related to Silvan, a Kurdish town in southeast Turkey. These images were allegedly disseminated by AKTrolls after a special forces operations in November 2015. When ordinary citizens opposed to it began to use these images, they were accused of disseminating disinformation. Seemingly critical Twitter accounts are sometimes used to seed fake news. When they get wider usage, progovernment "fact-checking" accounts debunk this news and claim how fraudulent the opposition is.

Doxing

Publishing people's personal information is a common occurence among trolls, and *doxing* is already internet slang to define this act. A well-known global case concerned a female Finnish journalist, Jessikka Aro (BBC 2017), who was a victim of doxing. She was framed as a kind of foreign agent by Russian trolls and her contact information was put online. In these cases, what is striking is the collaborative effort put together among online users to find out information about the victims. In contrast, our fieldwork showed that trolls in Turkey mostly gather personal information in collaboration with the authorities.

Phishing for Political Purposes

Phishing goes hand-in-hand with doxing. Phishing differs from mere hacking by masquerading as a trustworthy electronic communication entity but with the intent to steal personal data for malicious reasons. Although it is challenging to develop hard data at this stage, and the situation reflects a general trend, what is verifiable is that nearly all hacked accounts in Turkey begin to produce pro-AKP discourses. A self-proclaimed national hacking team, AyYıldız Team, claims responsibility for Twitter hacking and decorates the hacked account with pro-AKP or pro-Erdoğan images and discourses.

A famous comedian, Atalay Demirci, was a victim of phishing. When private messages on his Twitter account were released, he was arrested based on the allegation that he was a member of the Gülenist movement. To retrieve deleted messages, this hacking group might have received assistance from state institutions, according to one of interviewees. In a previous hack, on June 7, 2016, the account of Akın İpek, a Gülenist businessman who fled to the United Kingdom in 2015, was decorated with Erdoğan's smiling image and a purported apology. In yet another case, the account of Arzu A. Çerkezoğlu, general secretary of Turkey's third biggest trade union confederation with a proleft political orientation, was hacked by the same group. This time the account owner was accused of having links to Kurdish guerillas. I could not find evidence of more sophisticated deception tools in the case. However, a *BuzzFeed* report (Hall 2018) showed that advanced software could have been used in these kinds of attacks.

Cross-Platform Coordination

DFRLab (2018) has shown that many tactics, such as doxing, are deployed through cross-platform coordination. It should be noted that the Turkish case includes not only internet platforms but also close cooperation with legacy media. AHaber news channel is notorious but is not the only example. AHaber either uses the content that is circulated by trolls on Twitter or becomes the source of content that is planned for distribution on Twitter and other digital platforms.

Verbal Abuse

Zimmerman's (2016) study of verbal abuse used by trolls against female journalists in Turkey is a reminder of the gendered nature of the phenomenon. Verbal abuse could be categorized as intimidating insults, humiliating insults, and sexually related insults. However, verbal abuse is not limited to female citizens, although they are the most frequent targets.

Rhetorical Innovation

Trolls' arguments may be limited and repetitive; however, that does not mean there is a lack of rhetorical innovation. Not all rhetoric is verbal abuse. It is essential to create and circulate code words, as Hawley (2017) elaborates in relation to the term *white genocide*. Sometimes these code words are used to bypass filters, but they are not only about the filters. AKTrolls invent new terms to debase their opponents or catchphrases to convey their allegations. They rarely use the pro-Kurdish party name HDP, for instance, but instead use HDPKK to state their relation to PKK, the banned Kurdish armed group. Against Gülenists, CIAMAT, as a pejorative wordplay, was used frequently to denote alleged relations between the group (Cemaat) and US Central Intelligence Agency, abbreviated as CIA.

Appropriating Popular Culture Themes

Divisive content seems to have utilized popular culture themes. Mainstream themes are transformed into polarizing content or devices of disinformation. Ordinary citizens may not always be able to detect transformed content while unsuspectingly consuming it. Russians allegedly referenced pop culture creations such as SpongeBob SquarePants and Pokémon (Penzenstadler, Heath, and Guynn 2018), and the Pokemon Go game was also used in later trolling activities (Kulp 2017). Appropriation of Pepe the Frog, a popular internet meme (Nuzzi 2016), by alt-right groups in the United States may be the ultimate example in this context. Interestingly, some AKTrolls use Western popular culture symbols and nicknames. An prolific troll, @debuffer, uses Dr. House in its Twitter image. Sözeri (2017) narrates how a "sexy girl profile picture" suddenly changed its name and brand to launch a smear campaign using its 42,000 followers against a legitimate election monitoring group, Oy ve Ötesi (Vote and Beyond).

Bot Usage

In the United States, studies have shown that although most Americans are aware of bots and believe bots may have malicious intent, a significant number of citizens may not differentiate bots from humans (Stocking and Sumida 2018). Users with a low level of technical expertise can voluntarily become bot owners. Pirate sites can easily and cheaply offer services or fake followers for Twitter or Facebook. Despite an emphasis on state-level interventions and technical expertise, ordinary people can effectively use bots, as in the case of Micro-Chip, a notorious pro-Trump Twitter ringleader once described by a Republican strategist as the "Trumpbot overlord" (Bernstein 2017). The use of automated bots has been on the rise and does not need sophisticated investment (Agarwal 2017). A group of graduate-student researchers demonstrated that heavy use of automated bots played a crucial role in countering anti-AKP discourse after the Ankara Bombings in Turkey in October 2015. Twitter banished a bot-powered hashtag that praised President Erdoğan (*Hürriyet Daily News* 2016), and Turkish ministers immediately talked of a global conspiracy against Erdoğan; however, it was probably due to Twitter's struggle against spam-creating bots and trolls (Lapowsky 2015). Notable political trolls that have thousands of followers tend to have many accounts. According to an interview with an open-source coder, a troll can have up to one hundred accounts. Use of an automated bot differs from having more accounts in terms of scale. One can sense the use of bots if a message is replicated or retweeted to more than a few hundred other accounts. It should also be noted that as of November 2016, Istanbul and Ankara were the top two cities for bot usage, according to the major internet security company Norton (Paganini 2016).

Luring Power Users

State-sponsored political trolling has the potential to lure influential users with large follower bases on social media. The story of Serkan İnci (Saka 2018), who leads the highly active communities İnciCaps and İnciSözlük, is striking. He was a Gezi Park activist but gradually moved to serve the government agenda and became an active component of AKTroll discourse. Secular columnist Haşmet Babaoğlu (now closely associated with the Pelikan group) and famous cartoonist and producer Hasan Kaçan are also examples of this practice, as their tweets serve the AKTroll discourse.

Mobilizing against International Foes

Mobilizing against international foes has become an essential practice in the posthegemony period. Any critique of Turkish policies is subject to swarm attacks. As a harbinger of cases to come, when Swedish minister of foreign affairs Margot Wallström criticized a Turkish constitutional court decision on the legal age of marriage in a Twitter message, a mass of replies occurred and resulted in the Twitter campaign #DontTravelToSweden, which warned travelers not to go to Sweden because of allegedly high rape rates. In addition, the EU Parliament's Turkey reporter, Kati Piri, is attacked online when a report from any European Union institution is released that criticizes Turkey.

Grabbing Mainstream Media Attention

Hawley (2017) and many others have pointed out that the alt-right aimed to capture mainstream media attention in order to spread its extreme discourse. Turkey's progovernment trolls have rapidly evolved to a new stage. Because Turkey's mainstream media has predominantly progovernment owners, the need is no longer about capturing mainstream media attention. Aligned trolls have the confidence to dictate their rhetoric to media. When a political troll points out an issue, it is now intended to shape the media agenda, and critics of the progovernment agenda are quickly silenced through such means.

Adoption of the "Presidential System"

As noted at the beginning of this chapter, I take the constitutional change as the starting point of Erdoğan's consolidation of power. AKTrolls maintained an ongoing battle mode, but after that point, the overall aim of their content was to justify government policies. It was not a smooth process, and as the intraparty rivalries intensified, it was harder to justify each government policy. Nevertheless, in terms of daily matters, most AKTrolls seemed to have agreed on the government line. When price hikes occurred, for example, a staunch supporter would claim that they were a consequence of an international conspiracy.

In the following sections, I will highlight important themes in Turkey's progovernment political troll discourse from late 2018 to Turkey's local elections in March 2019, when I monitored troll activities on Twitter. Based on previous ethnographic work and continued Twitter monitoring, I argue that these themes have relevance beyond the defined time period.

Troll Infighting

In a relatively decentralized scene, one node, the Pelikan group, became increasingly powerful after Davutoğlu's decline. Well funded and well connected to the party leadership, members of this node have been at the center of troll infighting. Accusing others of being Gülenist has been their favorite line, but some also use this line against members within the group.

Emre Erciş, who rose to prominence with his anti-Gülenist positioning, was accused by another troll who showed that Erciş's old Twitter messages were against state confiscation of Gülenist media. Erciş produced a long Twitter feed to show the evolution of his political identity from his leftist youth. The polemic turned ugly as they swore at each other. My findings showed that Erciş was always against Gülenists in public forums. He had investigated Gülenist prosecutors' accusations against some Islamist circles who were allegedly connected with İran. Erciş's case suggests that the troll scene is a tense place where unsubstantiated accusations are made to gain personal influence. At this specific juncture, being anti-Gülenist was the main currency, and accusations were made accordingly.

Trolls must be careful to note changes in government policies. When the Turkish government's overall sympathy toward jihadists ended, some began to accuse others of being too pro-Salafi. Arguments between projihadists and nationalist, progovernment trolls about Syria would be frequent. In another example, a columnist was accused of pro-US standing because he allegedly did not criticize the United States when he was critical of Turkey's approach to the Venezuela crisis. Not being pro-Erdoğan enough is another common accusation. Even on the Xinjiang issue in China, where China is accused to be commiting genocide against the Uyghur Muslims (BBC 2021), AKTrolls were divided. Some accused others of being pro-China in denying the oppression of Muslims there.

Islamist Others

For outsiders and even for many secularists in Turkey, Islamists may look like a homogeneous bloc. The assumption was that Erdoğan could coordinate and lead most of the Islamists, but after he secured power, a growing number of nonconforming Islamists also became the government's target.

A nonconformist preacher, Alparslan Kuytul, who mostly generated a following in Adana, was rearrested the day after he was released from prison. Trolls were quick to approve his rearrest. Kuytul was found guilty because he did not criticize Fethullah Gülen, even after the coup attempt, and continued to criticize Erdoğan. Ahmet Taşgetiren was known as a wise man for many AKP followers. He is affiliated with an elite Naqshbandi sect and is the founding editor of its monthly magazine *Altınoluk*. Throughout AKP's rise to power, he contributed to progovernment dailies and TV programs. However, the moment he started to voice seemingly well-intentioned criticisms, he became a target. At the time of writing, Taşgetiren lost not only his column and TV programs but also his writing role at *Altınoluk* magazine. Supposedly, conservatives lost interest in Taşgetiren, who had tried to raise suspicions against the accusations that were made against Gülenists, although he was a persistent critic of Gülenists throughout his writing career. Mustafa İslamoğlu is the leader of a political Islamist group who might have some cadres in the current administration. Since the coup attempt in 2016, AKTrolls occasionally target him. Because of his existing cadre, he might be seen as a rival to the powerful Pelikan group. He was accused, for example, of taking money from foreign foundations linked to George Soros, including a human rights award in 1998. İslamoğlu was arrested for an op-ed article that discussed Islamic solutions to the Kurdish question. The award was labeled as a grant from "globalists." A reformist theology scholar, Mustafa Öztürk, was the target of coordinated attacks. He symbolizes those who actively work on non-Sunni theologies. Not all AKTrolls are religious, but the only acceptable religious path seems to be the majority Sunnism. Öztürk publicly stated that he might decide to live abroad after the campaign.

Saadet Party

During local elections in March 2019, the Saadet Party and its voters became a subject of hate for many AKTrolls. This socially conservative pro-İslamist party was founded in 2001 after the Turkish state shut down its previous iteration. Its origins date back to the 1960s, and Erdoğan, along with many others in the AKP leadership, started their political career in this party. The party follows the philosophy of the now-dead legendary leader Necmettin Erbakan. Erdoğan and his friends left the party and founded AKP, with a claim to be on the center-right with more Islamic tones but with a definite break from the Saadet Party tradition. A tense relationship has always existed between these two parties, but it came to a head when Saadet, formally and informally, cooperated with the other opposition parties during the last election. Saadet's critique of AKP resonated with constituencies beyond its traditional voter base. Consequently, AKTrolls increased their focus on Saadet. Any connection with secular opposition would be rebuked in the name of Islamism or for alleged alliance with terrorists (e.g., accusations of cooperation with the pro-Kurdish party HDP).

Weapons of the Culture War

Trolls spend more time on issues that can be classified as part of the "culture wars." I present a few examples in the next sections.

Against Western Movies on Public TV Channels

TRT2 channel was relaunched as an attempt to reclaim the cultural field. It was already a culturally oriented channel but was shut down during the AKP regime. It was been reopened after Erdoğan's statements noting a desire to "win" on the cultural front. However, when the TV channel announced it would broadcast old Western movies, as it had before, some trolls saw this as a tool of cultural imperialism. In addition, Netflix's *Designated Survivor* was cited as a show that whitewashed Gülenists during a particular episode.

Against Gender Equality and Homosexuality

Korean pop cultural themes and a yoga education project by the Ministry of Education led to a moral panic that Turkish children would lose their gender identity. The supposed aim was to destroy the family institution and thus society. Even unisex restrooms were a bad sign. An international project, mostly funded by the British embassy in Turkey, on gender equality became a key target. The accusation was that this project, in the name of gender equality, would create LGBTI youth. This led to domestic partners of the project being targeted.

At the same time, a troll targeted a campaign against a legal amendment that would lower the earliest marriage age from 15 to 12 (Evrensel 2019). The troll complained that those who wanted to marry young (the troll preferred to ignore underage as an issue) were not as free as LGBT citizens. This message served as promotion of a particular conservative worldview colored with homophobia.

Women Who Discard the Veil

Trolls were particularly angry about news of women who stopped wearing headscarves. A particular tactic was to start ad hominem attacks on women. This approach made headlines with the BBC Turkish news (Kasapoğlu 2019), but it had been a talking point in some circles earlier (Çakır 2018) To corroborate this trend, a new survey claimed that the number of pious youth has decreased in Turkey since 2008 (Konda 2019). However, trolls tend to connect this phenomenon to a global conspiracy against the government.

Syrian Refugees

A positive side to AKTrolls is that they are against anti-immigrants given the government's pro-Syrian refugee policy. This is one area on which all AKTrolls agree. Nationalist parties or the center-left Republican People's Party are mostly the source of anti-Syrian agitation. Justifications for the existence of refugees may change, but AKTrolls may be playing the critical fact-checking role. Some have debunked fake news that aimed to agitate against the refugees. Apart from the Syrian civil war, which had a direct connection to Turkey's domestic affairs, political trolls increased content coverage related to Turkey's international relations. From US national security advisor John R. Bolton's visit to Turkey to the crisis in Venezuela, trolls acted like a media force of the Turkish state within the country and abroad on social media.

Engineering Opposition

Trolls were very interested in the candidate chosen by opposition parties during the 2019 local elections. AKTrolls worked laboriously to demonstrate possible links to the Turkish state's currently designated enemies, such as the Kurdish guerilla movement, Gülenists, or radical leftists. The intention was to persuade non-AKP voters to break away from the candidates. Two major opposition parties, AKP and İyi Party, were the main targets. A specific case in point is to observe the rivalries of Abdullah Gül and Ahmet Davutoğlu.

Anti-Davutoğlu, Anti-Gül

As of early 2019, although Gülenism remained a vital enemy, an internal enemy had been constructed. I label this the "Davutoğlu and Gül front." Both played vital roles from the beginning of AKP, and until recently, they were defined as Erdoğan's close allies. However, this relationship changed radically in recent years. During the immediate postcoup attempt, some trolls even talked about detaining them. However, this did not happen, and despite a visible distance from party politics, both Davutoğlu and Gül never took on explicit confrontation. As the Gülenist threat lost its immediate power, AKTrolls criticized both men and their supposed allies daily. Accusations of being Davutoğlu's men or Gül's men were used interchangeably. In the meantime, *Karar Daily* gradually became a pro-Davutoğlu outlet as many dismissed journalists and columnists from more pro-Erdoğan dailies such as *Yeni Şafak* and *Star* began to work there.

All intraparty critics, some of whom were quite influential opinion leaders, were immediately classified as pro-Davutoğlu. Aydın Ünal was the notorious speechwriter for Erdoğan for a long time. Some of his earlier statements were closer to hate speech than mere incivility. According to @Tahaun, he lost the fight against the Pelikan group. Cemile Bayraktar, as a columnist, supported AKP ardently until recently. Both are now accused of being Davutoğlu supporters. İlhami Işık followed a similar career track to Bayraktar. And as far as I recall, Taha Akyol was never an Islamist but a conservative nationalist columnist with a long career that dates back to the pre-AKP period. He had been a liaison between the government and the Doğan Media Group, but his role ended gradually as the latter retreated from the media industry. When he started to write in a pro-Davutoğlu daily, he was labeled as another traitor.

Conclusion

Pohjonen and Udupa's (2017) approach to extreme speech as an anthropological project and how it differs from the hate speech discourse is constructive in understanding political troll networks. "Extreme speech" helps the research to better "contextualize online debate with attention to user practices and particular histories of speech cultures" (Pohjonen and Udupa 2017, 1173) Most of the content produced through political trolling may be in the boundaries of the legal-normative discourse of hate speech, but focus on user practices demonstrates that there may be many assemblages of practice that are hard to classify. Trolling bets increasingly on the ambiguity of hate speech versus acceptable speech, but ethnographic research with a new research agenda, such as in the extreme speech framework, can be more productive.

Unlike Whitney Phillips (2015), whose research was based on self-identifying trolls, not all subjects of my study identify themselves as such. In this study, trolls are understood as progovernment internet users who do not hide their identities and whose productive engagement with the authorities through social media networks can be seen as a form of digital surveillance, which in turn triggers restrictive consequences for citizens located in the ranks of Turkey's opposition. Evgeny Morozov (2012) has highlighted this networked surveillance approach by demonstrating how authoritarian governments use social media to track and crush the opposition. While Morozov emphasized software and platforms, I would like to emphasize social-user–based surveillance. The possibility of being targeted leads to self-censorship. This is strengthened by the fact that not only trolls but all citizens are asked to surveil critical voices. The overall impact is what I would label as the "trollification" of ordinary users. This peculiar kind of vigilance has penetrated every level of user.

Nevertheless, too much emphasis on surveillance may be misleading. As the emerging themes demonstrate, progovernment political trolls in Turkey not only act as moral police but also function as "organic intellectuals" (Gramsci 2005). At the beginning of 2019, Erdoğan complained (*Milli Gazete* 2019) about the lack of success in culture and art scenes and urged his government and supporters to focus on these areas. This political strategy was not easy to implement, and I suggest that the trolls' first move was to replace mainstream media as the agenda setter and shape the public agendas and discourses. After the sale of the Doğan Media Group (*New York Times* 2018), Turkey's mainstream media became progovernment to an unprecedented degree. Along with pressure on senior journalists and mass sackings, the mainstream media establishment was rendered ineffective, and from cultural themes to foreign affairs, political trolls produced a media discourse that shaped the former's output. In the contemporary hypernetworked digital media landscape, trolls may be more digitally savvy natives than ordinary users (Phillips 2015), and progovernment mainstream media mostly follows trolls, not vice versa, in the fast flow of information. This new division of labor in media production leads to a further deterioration in the quality of public debates.

A final finding is that political trolls may not always be reliable, even for an authoritarian government. Troll rivalries occasionally weaken the intended level of discursive inculcations. At the time of writing, I have observed that opposition circles have begun to access the government's many behind-the-doors secrets through these rivalries. Moreover, some trolls become so alienated that they may change sides radically. A typical case is that of @omerturantv72. I have monitored his account since the beginning of this project. After Twitter closed his previous account, when he functioned as a relentless progovernment militant, he returned to Twitter with a new account whose critical messages are frequently shared by opposition users. Reliance on political trolls may thus create vulnerability. Internal rivalries and weakening power of the government can lead to shifting alliances and groups changing political sides.

References

Agarwal, Amit. 2017. "How to Write a Twitter Bot in 5 Minutes." *Digital Inspiration*, July 19, 2017. https://www.labnol.org/internet/write-twitter-bot/27902/.

Aras, Bülent. 2014. "Davutoğlu Era in Turkish Foreign Policy Revisited." *Journal of Balkan and Near Eastern Studies* 16 (4): 404–418.

BBC. 2017. "How Pro-Russian Trolls Tried to Destroy Me." *BBC Trending* (blog), October 6, 2017. https://www.bbc.com/news/blogs-trending-41499789.

———. 2018. "Russia Trolls 'Spreading Vaccine Discord.'" August 24, 2018. https://www.bbc.com/news/world-us-canada-45294192.

———. 2021. "Uyghurs: MPs State Genocide Is Taking Place in China." *BBC News*, April 23, 2021. https://www.bbc.com/news/uk-politics-56843368.

Bernstein, Joseph. 2017. "Never Mind the Russians, Meet the Bot King Who Helps Trump Win Twitter." *BuzzFeed News*, April 5, 2017. https://www.buzzfeednews.com/article/josephbernstein/from-utah-with-love.

Brown, Kristen V. 2016. "How a Racist, Sexist Hate Mob Forced Leslie Jones Off Twitter." *Splinter*, July 19, 2016. https://splinternews.com/how-a-racist-sexist-hate-mob-forced-leslie-jones-off-t-1793860398.

Çakır, Ruşen. 2018. "Başörtüsünü çıkaran kadınlar." Medyascope, September 7, 2018. https://medyascope.tv/2018/09/07/basortusunu-cikaran-kadinlar/.

Coleman, E. Gabriella. 2011. "Anonymous: From the Lulz to Collective Action." *New Everyday*, April 6, 2011. http://mediacommons.org/tne/pieces/anonymous-traveling-pure-lulz-land-political-territories.

———. 2012. "Phreaks, Hackers, and Trolls: The Politics of Transgression and Spectacle." *Social Media Reader* 5:99–119.

Coleman, Gabriella. 2014. *Hacker, Hoaxer, Whistleblower, Spy: The Many Faces of Anonymous*. London: Verso.

Coren, Michael J. 2016. "Internet Trolls Are Even More Hostile When They're Using Their Real Names, a Study Finds." *Quartz*, June 27, 2016. https://qz.com/741933/internet-trolls-are-even-more-hostile-when-theyre-using-their-real-names-a-study-finds/.

Dahlberg, Lincoln. 2001. "The Internet and Democratic Discourse: Exploring the Prospects of Online Deliberative Forums Extending the Public Sphere." *Information, Communication and Society* 4 (4): 615–633.

Dewey, Caitlin. 2014. "The Only Guide to Gamergate You Will Ever Need to Read." *Washington Post*, October 14, 2014. https://www.washingtonpost.com/news/the-intersect/wp/2014/10/14/the-only-guide-to-gamergate-you-will-ever-need-to-read/.

DFRLab. 2018. "#TrollTracker: Journalist Doxxed by American Far Right." *Medium* (blog), June 17, 2018. https://medium.com/dfrlab/trolltracker-journalist-doxxed-by-american-far-right-7881f9c20a16.

Diken. 2016. "'Ak Trol' Taha Ün: Tartışmalar Yatışana Kadar Kenardayım." *Diken* (blog), May 4, 2016. http://www.diken.com.tr/pelikandan-sonra-ulasilamayan-ak-trol-taha-un-tartismalar-yatisana-kadar-kenardayim/.

Erensü, Sinan, and Ayça Alemdaroğlu. 2018. "Dialectics of Reform and Repression: Unpacking Turkey's Authoritarian 'Turn.'" *Review of Middle East Studies* 52 (1): 16–28.

Evrensel. 2019. 'TBMM'de erken yaşta evlilik için af yasası hazırlanıyor.' *Evrensel*, July 25, 2019. https://www.evrensel.net/haber/371042/tbmmde-erken-yasta-evlilik-icin-af-yasasi-hazirlaniyor?a=ee5cd.

Filipovic, Jill. 2007. "Blogging while Female: How Internet Misogyny Parallels Real-World Harassment." *Yale Journal of Law and Feminism* 19:295–303.

Funke, Daniel, and Susan Benkelman. 2019. "How Russia's Disinformation Strategy Is Evolving." Poynter. Accessed May 31, 2019. https://www.poynter.org/fact-checking/2019/how-russias-disinformation-strategy-is-evolving/.

Glaser, April. 2018. "Russian Bots Wasted No Time Trying to Confuse People after the Mueller Indictment and the Parkland Shooting." *Slate*, February 20, 2018. https://slate.com/technology/2018/02/russian-bots-were -active-after-the-florida-shooting-and-the-latest-mueller-indictment.html.

Graff, Garrett M. 2018. "Russian Trolls Are Still Playing Both Sides—Even With the Mueller Probe." *Wired*, October 19, 2018. https://www.wired.com/story/russia-indictment-twitter-facebook-play-both-sides/.

Gramsci, Antonio. 2005. "The Intellectuals." *Contemporary Sociological Thought*, 60–69.

Hall, Ellie. 2018. "Celebrities Say White Supremacists Used A New Video App to Trick Them into Endorsing Anti-Jewish Conspiracy Theories." *BuzzFeed News*, November 30, 2018. https://www.buzzfeednews.com/article /ellievhall/celebrities-white-supremacists-video-app-cameo-anti-semitic.

Hardaker, Claire. 2010. "Trolling in Asynchronous Computer-Mediated Communication: From User Discussions to Academic Definitions." *Journal of Politeness Research* 6:215–224.

Hawley, George. 2017. *Making Sense of the Alt-Right*. New York: Columbia University Press.

Hsu, Stephen. 2018. "Russian Fake Tweets Visualized." *Towards Data Science*, May 1, 2018. https:// towardsdatascience.com/russian-fake-tweets-visualized-6f73f767695.

Hunt, Richard Reid. 2014. "Moving beyond Regulatory Mechanisms: A Typology of Internet Control Regimes." *Dissertations and Theses*. Paper 1801. https://doi.org/10.15760/etd.1801.

Hürriyet Daily News. 2013. "I Did Not See Anyone Consume Alcohol in Mosque during Gezi Protests, Muezzin Says." June 27, 2013. http://www.hurriyetdailynews.com/i-did-not-see-anyone-consume-alcohol-in -mosque-during-gezi-protests-muezzin-says-49573.

———. 2016. "Turkish Ministers Accuse Twitter of Plotting against Erdoğan." March 30, 2016. http://www .hurriyetdailynews.com/turkish-ministers-accuse-twitter-of-plotting-against-erdogan--97106.

Kasapoğlu, Çağıl. 2019. "Başörtüsünü Çıkaranlar: Neden Bu Kararı Alıyorlar, Neler Yaşıyorlar?" BBC, January 4, 2019. https://www.bbc.com/turkce/haberler-turkiye-46758752.

Konda. 2019. "What Has Changed in Youth in 10 Years?" Konda Interactive, https://interaktif.konda.com.tr/tr /Gencler2018.

Kulp, Patrick. 2017. "Election-Meddling Russian Troll Farms Tried to Use *Pokémon Go* to Stir Racial Tensions." *Mashable*, September 12, 2017. https://mashable.com/2017/10/12/pokemon-go-russian-troll-farm/.

Lapowsky, Issie. 2015. "Why Twitter Is Finally Taking a Stand against Trolls." *Wired*. April 21, 2015. https://www .wired.com/2015/04/twitter-abuse/.

Lokot, Tetyana. 2016. "Center for Monitoring Propaganda and Disinformation Online Set to Open in Russia." *Global Voices* (blog). March 26, 2016. https://globalvoices.org/2016/03/26/center-for-monitoring -propaganda-and-disinformation-online-set-to-open-in-russia/.

Lowen, Mark. 2017. "Why Did Turkey Hold a Referendum?" BBC, April 16, 2017. https://www.bbc.com/news /world-europe-38883556.

Milli Gazete. 2019. "Erdoğan: Kültür sanat meselesi terörle mücadele kadar önemli." January 10, 2019. https:// www.milligazete.com.tr/haber/1778425/erdogan-kultur-sanat-meselesi-terorle-mucadele-kadar-onemli.

Morozov, Evgeny. 2012. *The Net Delusion: The Dark Side of Internet Freedom*. New York: PublicAffairs.

New York Times. 2018. "Turkish Media Group Bought by Pro-Government Conglomerate." March 22, 2018. https://www.nytimes.com/2018/03/21/world/europe/turkey-media-erdogan-dogan.html.

Ng, Yi Shu. 2017. "Philippine President Admits He Used an Army of Social Media Trolls while Campaigning." *Mashable*, July 25, 2017. https://mashable.com/2017/07/25/duterte-oxford-paid-trolls/.

Nuzzi, O. 2016. "How Pepe the Frog Became a Nazi Trump Supporter and Alt-Right Symbol." *Daily Beast*, May 26, 2016. https://www.thedailybeast.com/how-pepe-the-frog-became-a-nazi-trump-supporter-and-alt-right -symbol.

Ong, Jonathan Corpus, and Jason Cabanes. 2018. "In the Philippines, Political Trolling Is an Industry—This Is How It Works." OpenDemocracy, February 20, 2018. https://www.opendemocracy.net/digitaliberties /jonathan-corpus-ong-jason-cabanes/in-philippines-political-trolling-is-industry-this.

Ozkan, Behlül. 2014. "Turkey, Davutoglu and the Idea of Pan-Islamism." *Survival* 56 (4): 119–140.

Paganini, Pierluigi. 2016. "Which Are Principal Cities Hostages of Malicious Botnets?" *Security Affairs*, October 6, 2016. https://securityaffairs.co/wordpress/51968/reports/botnets-geography.html.

Paul, Christopher, and Miriam Matthews. 2016. *The Russian "Firehose of Falsehood" Propaganda Model: Why It Might Work and Options to Counter It*. No. PE-198-OSD, Perspectives. Santa Monica, CA: RAND Corp.

Penzenstadler, Nick, Brad Heath, and Jessica Guynn. 2018. "We Read Every One of the 3,517 Facebook Ads Bought by Russians. Here's What We Found." *USA Today*, May 11, 2018. https://www.usatoday.com/story /news/2018/05/11/what-we-found-facebook-ads-russians-accused-election-meddling/602319002/.

Phillips, Whitney. 2015. *This Is Why We Can't Have Nice Things: Mapping the Relationship between Online Trolling and Mainstream Culture*. Cambridge, MA: MIT Press.

Piše:Danas Online. 2018. "SNS botovi napisali 10 miliona komentara." Dnevni list Danas, December 2, 2018. https://www.danas.rs/politika/sns-botovi-napisali-10-miliona-komentara/.

Pohjonen, Matti, and Sahana Udupa. 2017. "Extreme Speech Online: An Anthropological Critique of Hate Speech Debates." *International Journal of Communication* 11:1173–1191.

Reuters. 2019. "Erdogan Accuses Women's March of Disrespecting Islam." March 10, 2019. https://www.reuters .com/article/us-womens-day-turkey-erdogan-idUSKBN1QRoJT.

Rost, Katja, Lea Stahel, and Bruno S. Frey. 2016. "Digital Social Norm Enforcement: Online Firestorms in Social Media." *PLoS One* 11 (6): e0155923. https://doi.org/10.1371/journal.pone.0155923.

Saka, Erkan. 2018. "Social Media in Turkey as a Space for Political Battles: AKTrolls and Other Politically Motivated Trolling." *Middle East Critique* 27 (2): 161–177.

Shepherd, Tamara, Alison Harvey, Tim Jordan, Sam Srauy, and Kate Miltner. 2015. "Histories of Hating." *Social Media + Society* 1 (2): 2056305115603997.

Soldatov, Andrei, Irina Borogan, Maeve Shearlaw, Shaun Walker, Marc Burrows, Luke Harding, and Maeve Shearlaw. 2015. "What Spawned Russia's 'Troll Army'? Experts on the Red Web Share Their Views." *Guardian*, September 8, 2015. https://www.theguardian.com/world/live/2015/sep/08/russia-troll-army-red -web-any-questions.

Sözeri, Ceren. 2016. "Trol gazeteciliği." Evrensel.net. https://www.evrensel.net/yazi/77506/trol-gazeteciligi.

Sözeri, Efe Kerem. 2016. "Pelikan Derneği: Berat Albayrak, Ahmet Davutoğlu'nu Neden Devirdi?" *Medium* (blog). November 3, 2016. https://medium.com/@efekerem/pelikan-derne%C4%9Fi-berat-albayrak-ahmet -davuto%C4%9Flunu-neden-devirdi-5fabad6dc7de#.lfpf8807m.

———. 2017. "Trolls, Bots and Shutdowns: This Is How Turkey Manipulates Public Opinion." *Ahval*, November 14, 2017. https://ahvalnews.com/freedoms/trolls-bots-and-shutdowns-how-turkey-manipulates-public-opinion.

Spence, Alex. 2018. "These Leaked Messages Show How Tory HQ Used A Twitter Army to Attack Jeremy Corbyn. But They Turned on Theresa May Instead." *BuzzFeed*, September 26, 2018. https://www.buzzfeed.com /alexspence/these-leaked-messages-show-how-tory-hq-used-a-twitter-army.

Stocking, Galen, and Nami Sumida. 2018. "Social Media Bots Draw Public's Attention and Concern." October 15, 2018. http://www.journalism.org/2018/10/15/social-media-bots-draw-publics-attention-and-concern/.

Stray, Jonathan. 2017. "Defense Against the Dark Arts: Networked Propaganda and Counter-Propaganda." *Medium* (blog). February 27, 2017. https://medium.com/tow-center/defense-against-the-dark-arts -networked-propaganda-and-counter-propaganda-deb7145aa76a.

Suler, John R., and Wende L. Phillips. 1998. "The Bad Boys of Cyberspace: Deviant Behavior in a Multimedia Chat Community." *Cyberpsychology and Behavior* 1 (3): 275–294.

Tepper, Michele. (1997) 2013. "Usenet Communities and the Cultural Politics of Information." In *Internet Culture*, edited by David Porter, 39–54. London: Routledge.

Udupa, Sahana. 2015. "Archiving as History-Making: Religious Politics of Social Media in India." *Communication, Culture and Critique* 9 (2): 212–230.

Wagstaff, Keith. 2017. "The Dudes Exposed by Alt-Right Troll Milo Yiannopoulos' Gross Emails." *Mashable*, October 5, 2017. https://mashable.com/2017/10/05/tech-bros-milo-yiannopoulos/.

Yılmaz, Mehmet. 2015. "Who Fabricated This Sexual Fantasy?" *Hürriyet Daily News*, March 13, 2015. http://www .hurriyetdailynews.com/opinion/mehmet-y-yilmaz/who-fabricated-this-sexual-fantasy--79599.

Zimmermann, Çağla. 2016. "Feature: Turkey Trolls' Use of Insults Stifling Reporting." *International Press Institute* (blog). October 13, 2016. https://ipi.media/feature-turkey-trolls-use-of-insults-stifling-reporting/.

CONTRIBUTOR BIOGRAPHIES

DAVID BOROMISZA-HABASHI is Associate Professor at the University of Colorado Boulder. He is the author of the book *Speaking Hatefully: Culture, Communication, and Political Action in Hungary*. His research focuses on the cultural foundations of public expression in and across speech communities.

JONATHAN CORPUS ONG is Associate Professor of Global Digital Media at the University of Massachusetts–Amherst. He is co–Editor-in-Chief of the 20-year-old media studies journal *Television & New Media*. His current research as Research Fellow at Harvard University's Shorenstein Center explores voter sentiments and the mediated political practices of diverse Asian American communities.

GABRIELE DE SETA is a postdoctoral researcher at the University of Bergen, where he is part of the Machine Vision in Everyday Life project funded by the European Research Council. His research work, grounded on ethnographic engagement across multiple sites, focuses on digital media practices and vernacular creativity in China.

IGINIO GAGLIARDONE is a media scholar researching the emergence of distinctive models of the information society in the Global South and Associate Professor at the University of the Witwatersrand. He is the author of *The Politics of Technology in Africa*; *China, Africa, and the Future of the Internet*; and *Countering Online Hate Speech*.

SAL HAGEN is a PhD candidate at the University of Amsterdam. He is currently researching online political subcultures through the lens of media studies and data analysis with the Open Intelligence Lab and the Digital Methods Initiative.

NELL HAYNES is an anthropologist who has worked at universities in the United States, the United Kingdom, and Chile. She is author of *Social Media in Northern Chile* (2016), coauthor of *How the World Changed Social Media* (2016), and coeditor of *Professional Wrestling: Politics and Populism* (2020).

PETER HERVIK is an anthropologist and migration scholar affiliated with the Free University of Copenhagen and the Network of Independent Scholars of Education. His publications include *The Annoying Difference: The Emergence of Danish Neonationalism, Neoracism, and Populism in the Post-1989 World*.

JONAS KAISER is Assistant Professor at Suffolk University, Faculty Associate at the Berkman Klein Center for Internet and Society at Harvard University, and Associate Researcher at the Alexander von Humboldt Institute for Internet and Society.

DAVID KATIAMBO is a lecturer at the Technical University of Kenya, Department of Journalism and Media Studies. His current research interests are the discourse theory aspects of extreme speech, agonistic nationalism, new media, and democracy in Africa.

MAX KRAMER is a postdoctoral fellow at the Department of Anthropology, Ludwig-Maximilians-University Munich. He is the author of *Mobilität und Zeugenschaft* (Mobility and Testimony, 2019) on documentary practices and the Kashmir Conflict.

AMY C. MACK is a doctoral candidate at the University of Alberta. She researches European and Canadian ethnonationalist movements.

CAROLE MCGRANAHAN is Professor of Anthropology at the University of Colorado. She is author of *Arrested Histories: Tibet, the CIA, and Memories of a Forgotten War* (2010), coeditor of *Imperial Formations* (with Ann Laura Stoler and Peter Perdue, 2007) and *Ethnographies of US Empire* (with John Collins, 2018), and editor of *Writing Anthropology: Essays on Craft and Commitment* (2020).

INDAH S. PRATIDINA is Secretary of the International Undergraduate Program in Communication and lecturer at the Department of Communication, Faculty of Social and Political Sciences, Universitas Indonesia.

ERKAN SAKA is Associate Professor of Media and Journalism Studies and Chair at the Media Department, Istanbul Bilgi University. He is the author of *Social Media and Politics in Turkey. A Journey through Citizen Journalism, Political Trolling, and Fake News* (Lexington, 2019) and "Big Data and Gender-Biased Algorithms" in *The International Encyclopedia of Gender, Media, and Communication* (Wiley-Blackwell).

JÜRGEN SCHAFLECHNER is a research group leader at the Department for Social and Cultural Anthropology, Freie Universtät Berlin, and has had visiting appointments at Harvard, Princeton, Vienna, and Hebrew universities. His research and teaching include cultural and postcolonial theory, religious and ethnic minorities in Pakistan, and the role of documentary films in anthropological research. He has filmed, edited, and produced six ethnographic documentary films.

MARC TUTERS is Assistant Professor in the University of Amsterdam's Media Studies faculty, where he teaches graduate courses on new media theory. As Director of the Open Intelligence Lab, his current research examines radical visual subcultures at the bottom of the Web and has been published in *Cultural Politics* and *New Media & Society*.

SAHANA UDUPA is Professor of Media Anthropology at LMU Munich, where she leads two multiyear projects on digital politics and artificial intelligence, funded by the European Research Council. She is author of *Making News in Global India* and coeditor (with S. McDowell) of *Media as Politics in South Asia*.

INDEX

Hungary, 24, 25, 26, 27, 29–30, 31, 32, 213, 218; Hungarian Constitution, 28; Hungarian hate speech debates, 27, 30, 32; Hungarian politics, 21, 24, 25, 28, 31; Hungarian public discourse, 24, 27; Hungarian right wing, 28
Huntington, Samuel, 139
Hyderabad, 60, 63, 65, 66

ibuism, 232
identitarianism, 149, *151*, 152, 153; identitarian movement (IM), 152, 154, 159, 212, 216
identity, 6, 13, 16, 38, 39, 40, 77, 95, 110, 139, 157, 187; collective, 76, 90, 147, 152, 214, 221, 223; construction of, 146, 147, 152, 156; ethnic, 8, 167, 231; exclusionary, 109; gendered, 43, 229, 230, 231, 237, 250; group, 67, 69, 75, 189, 223; identity politics, 228, 230; national, 29, 100, 132, 147; political, 31, 79, 164, 248; religious, 63, 68, 163, 228, 230, 231; social, 79, 109; women's, 231
immigrants, 1, 8, 124, 132, 141, 180, 182, 183, 186, 187; anti-immigrant discourse, 11, 76, 127, 132, 140, 146, 154, 155–56, 159, 175–76, 178, 181, 182, 183, 186, 187, 188, 189, 190n2, 250; non-European, 154. *See also* Bolivia, Bolivian immigrants
imperialism, cultural, 14, 250
incivility, 4, 6, 9, 10, 55, 76, 171, 172, 229; and hate speech, 49, 54, 57, 251; in social media, 49–50, 51, 52, 57, 164–65; physical, 65
India, 1, 3, 8, 16, 22, 45, 60, 61, 63, 65, 66, 68, 69, 75, 95, 96, 97, 98, 100, 101, 102, 103, 109, 110n3, 110n7, 114, 231, 244; Akhil Bharatiya Vidyarti Parishad (ABVP, All India Student Association), 95, 98, 104, 110n2, 111n8; All India Majlis-e Ittehadul Muslimeen (All India Council of the Union of Muslims, AIMIM), 60, 63, 65, 66, 67, 68, 70; Bharatiya Janata Party (BJP), 64, 69–70, 71n1, 97, 98, 99, 104, 110n5, 111n10, 111n28; British, 65, 68, 69; and extreme speech, 9, 15; and memes, 104, 106; Indian army, 99, 106; Indian history, 68, 99; Indian National Congress Party, 62, 63, 110n5, 111n28; Indian nation-state, 60, 61, 62, 65, 68; Indian Penal Code (IPC), 62, 69, 198, 200; Indian politics, 60, 68, 69, 70, 101, 102, 103, 104, 107; Indian polity, 62, 63, 64, 67, 70; Indian secularism, 67, 68; Indian society, 63, 70; postcolonial, 99; Rashtriya Swyam Seveka Sangha (RSS, Association of National Volunteers), 110n2, 110n6, 111n10; and right wing, 5, 11. *See also* Delhi; Muslims, Indian; New Delhi
indigeneity, 176, 180, 181; anti-indigenous feelings, 182; indigenous people, 76, 176, 178, 180–81, 182–83, 186, 190n4; indigenous vocabularies, 32
Indonesia, 8, 15, 196, 227, 229, 231, 232, 233, 237; Indonesian citizens, 227, 236; Indonesian democracy, 227, 235; Indonesian police, 234, 235; Indonesian presidential elections, 227, 228, 230; Indonesian social media, 228, 229; New Order, 227, 228, 232; Old Order, 228; Reformasi (Reformation), 227, 228, 232, 236, 237; women's role in, 228, 229, 231–32, 234, 236
in-groups, 82–83, 132, 172, 189, 223. *See also* out-groups
instant messaging, 76, 164, 165, 167, *168*, 169
insults, 48, 49, 50, 51, 69, 83, 103, 118, 121, 165, 199, 244, 246
intention, 35, 207, 224n3; intention clause, 200, 207
interlocks, 53
Internet Research Agency, 243, 244
intersectionality, 15, 181
intertextuality, 83, 177, 178, 187
Iran, 248; Iranian refugees, 211
irony, 8, 24, 30, 80, 82, 83, 88, 89, 106, 150, 154, 157, 167, 171, 172, 189
Islam, 68, 123, 140, 142, 155, 156, 165, 166, 198, 201, 203, 207n1, 213, 220, 232–33, 234, 237, 240, 249; anti-Islam discourse, 146, 157, 158, 159, 222, 224n6; Islamists, 230, 242, 248, 249, 250, 251; Islamization, 152, 170, 198, 205, 212, 213, 215; Islamophobia, 76, 117, 123, 154, 156, 164, 166, 169, 170, 172. *See also* Muslims; Quran; Sunna; Sunni

Jenkins, Henry, 183
jingoism, 106
joking, 14, 50, 110, 184; joking relationships (*utani*), 50–51. *See also* hilarity; humor
Jokowi (Joko Widodo), 228, 229, 230, 232–33, 234, 235, 236
journalism, 41, 64, 65, 81, 109, 111n31, 115, 131; journalists, 38, 40, 41, 45, 61, 65, 69, 77, 91, 102, 103, 114, 119, 122, 169, 243, 246, 251, 252

Kelly, Tobias, 15
Kenya, 1, 8, 9, 15, 21, 55; and extreme speech, 49; Kenyan ethnic groups, 51; Kenyan government, 53, 56; Kenyan politics, 48; Kenyan radio talk shows, 36; and social media, 54, 55; western, 50
Kenyatta, Uhuru, 48
Khan, Tabussum Ruhi, 68
Kumar, Sangeet, 106

Laclau, Ernesto, 49, 84
Larkin, Brian, 7
Latour, Bruno, 52
Leibold, James, 166
liberalism, 65, 79, 90, 117; antiliberalism, 79, 90; neoliberalism, 80. *See also* democracy, liberal; globalism, neoliberal; public sphere, liberal; subjectivity, neoliberal
lies, 13, 76, 115, 116, 117, 120–21, 123, 124, 127, 235
Lipstadt, Deborah, 127
localities, 212, 213, 214, 217, 223
lock-ins, 54, 55
lockouts, 55

Turner, Fred, 117

Twitter, 22, 36, 38, 42, 44, 54, 55, 63, 97, 98, 102, 103, 104, *105*, 115, 119–20, 122, 124, 126, 127, 147, 148, 154, 159, 163, 169–70, 171, 176, 201, 213, 227, 235, 242, 244, 246, 247; accounts, 37, 39, 111n8, 116, 121, 245, 252–53; data, 177, 229; groups, 243; hacking, 245; rules, 117–18, 123; and trolls, 77, 196, 246, 248; users, 111n16, 117, 119, 120, 121, 123, 149. *See also* Trump, Donald J., and Twitter

Udupa, Sahana, 24, 36, 64, 65, 117, 124, 152, 186, 204, 212, 251

Uganda, 36, 50

Unite the Right, 146, 159

United Kingdom, 114, 123, 127, 179, 243, 245

United States, 12, 13, 15, 23, 24, 32, 76, 100, 109, 114, 115, 116, 118, 120, 121, 122, 124, 125, 126, 127, 146, 163, 166, 170, 179, 198, 231, 233, 243, 244, 246–47, 248; US citizens, 114, 126; US Constitution, 116; US elections, 77, 79, 81, 84, 111n16, 114, 244; US history, 118; US military, 119, 121, 125; US politics, 88, 124, 126; US power, 125; US society, 125

universalism, 150, 154, 155, 156, 159n2

Ürümqi, 162, 163

Uyghurs, 162–63, 164, 165–66, 167, 170, 171, 249

van Dijk, Teun, 187

Van Maanen, John, 31

ventriloquism, 5, 49–50, 51, 52–53, 57

Verkaaik, Oskar, 109

vigilantes, 60, 110n2, 204; vigilante justice, 14, 200, 201

violence, 9, 11, 54, 75–76, 85, 99, 114, 115, 122, 126, 131, 146, 162, 163; anti-immigrant, 188; antiminority, 98, 170; anti-Muslim, 1, 65; cultural, 135; culture of, 44; and extreme speech, 6, 7, 49, 135, 204, 228; extremist, 78; far-right, 211, 224n1; group, 63; indirect, 135; mass, 3, 63; mob, 61, 201; physical, 1, 12, 135; political, 6; psychological, 135; religious, 200; and social media, 115, 117; and the state, 3, 61, 204; structural,

22, 61, 65; symbolic, 182; vigilante, 60, 204; violent incidents, 6, 76, 81, 101, 114, 115, 127, 165, 166, 167, 168, 171, 188, 224; violent nationalism, 31, 100, 102; violent regimes, 6; violent speech, 6, 48; xenophobic, 1. *See also* fun, and violence

vitriol, 1, 2, 4, 5, 6, 9, 10, 12, 49, 64, 77, 101, 110, 152, 204, 228, 242; vitriolic cultures, 5, 8; vitriolic speech, 2, 5, 11, 12, 126, 142, 212, 221, 228, 229

Voat, 147, 148, 149

Voice of Ram, 106

volunteers, 41, 60, 75, 96, 97, 98–99, 101, 104, 111n17, 230, 232, 241

Walsh, Catherine E., 11, 16

Walz, Tim, 127

Warisman, Neno, 230, 234, 235

WeChat, 119, 165, 167, 168, 171

WhatsApp, 1, 98, 104, 110n7, 167, 176, 203, 234

white supremacy, 15, 31, 76, 82, 126, 127, 159

Winner, Langdon, 52

Wittgenstein, Ludwig, 80, 81, 86

women, 111n28, 140, 155, 188, 196, 229, 231, 244; attacks on, 104, 196, 234, 237, 243,245, 250; marginalization of, 198; and role in domestic domain, 231–32, 234, 236, 237; and role in politics, 228, 230, 231, 235, 236, 237; transgender, 43; womanhood, 14; women's bodies, 196. *See also* motherhood; mothers; Women's Congress

Women's Congress, 231

World War II, 3, 125, 132; post-World War period, 117, 125; pre-World War II period, 147

xenophobia, 1, 16, 25, 32, 77, 90, 117, 138, 139, 143, 182, 189

Xinjiang, 162–64, 165, *166*, 171, 249

Young, Kevin, 124

YouTube, 9, 104, 148, 155, 212, 227, 228, 229, 230, 232, 233

Zuckerman, Ethan, 79

Printed in the USA
CPSIA information can be obtained
at www.ICGtesting.com
LVHW081523120224
771634LV00007B/793